Masters, unions and men

Work control in building and the rise of labour 1830–1914

RICHARD PRICE

Associate Professor of History
Northern Illinois University

CAMBRIDGE UNIVERSITY PRESS

Cambridge
London   New York   New Rochelle
Melbourne   Sydney

Published by the Press Syndicate of the University of Cambridge
The Pitt Building, Trumpington Street, Cambridge CB2 1RP
32 East 57th Street, New York, NY 10022, USA
296 Beaconsfield Parade, Middle Park, Melbourne 3206, Australia

First published 1980

Printed in Great Britain by The Anchor Press Ltd
and bound by Wm Brendon & Son Ltd
both of Tiptree, Essex

Library of Congress Cataloguing in Publication Data

Price, Richard, 1944–

Masters, unions and men.

Bibliography: p.

Includes index.

1. Trade-unions – Building trades – Great Britain – History.
2. Industrial relations – Great Britain – History.
3. Industrial sociology – Case studies. I. Title.
HD6668.B9P74   331′.042′40941   79–21229
ISBN 0 521 22882 4

Masters, unions and men

*Work control in building and
the rise of labour
1830–1914*

Contents

v

Tables

Acknowledgements

Writing this book has been rendered easier by the invaluable assistance I have received from many persons and institutions, none of whom are responsible for its faults or shortcomings. As I struggled to shape into a coherent whole the ideas that went into the making of this book, my good friend and colleague J. Harvey Smith served at every stage as a supportive and patient commentator and advisor. When the manuscript was finally completed, he generously put aside his own pressing and important work on the French peasantry to read and criticise the book. It is a deep pleasure to record my immense debt to his support and counsel. I would also like to thank J. Carroll Moody whose expertise in American labour history was of continual value as a point of comparison with British developments, who also read and commented on the manuscript and who, as chairman of my department, kindly relieved me of onerous committee duties whilst the book was being written. Geoff Crossick, Thomas Lacqueur and Alfred Young provided intelligent critiques of early position papers, as did the members of the 1975 Popular Culture seminar at the Shelby Cullom Davis Centre, Princeton University. I benefited greatly from all of their comments. Others whose reading of the manuscript, or whose conversations on its subject matter I wish to gratefully acknowledge, include my old friend Peter Keating, John Harrison, C. H. George, James Cronin and Sylvia Grossman. The last two named were also kind enough to furnish me with copies of their important doctoral dissertations upon which I have relied heavily at certain points of the argument. I wish to record special and sincere thanks to my typists Darla Woodward, Elaine Kittleson, and Jean Schiller. Particular mention should be made of Laurel Davies who sustained an unflagging efficiency and good nature throughout the typing and re-typing of the bulk of the manuscript.

The research for this book could never have been accomplished without the generous support of various foundations. The American Philosophical Society awarded me a research grant for the summer of 1972 and the Northern Illinois University Dean's Fund provided assistance which enabled me to spend the summer of 1975 in Britain. I was both fortunate and honoured to hold a Fellowship from the American Council of Learned

ix

Societies for 1973–74 which in conjunction with a sabbatical leave of absence from Northern Illinois University allowed me to spend a year in Britain gathering material for the book. As always, I met with nothing but courtesy and help from the various libraries I used and I would like to record my particular thanks to Richard Storey of the Modern Records Centre, University of Warwick whose magnificent work in collecting trade union and labour movement records has so valuably contributed to research in those areas. I have been a frequent visitor to the Bishopsgate Institute, the British Library's Newspaper Collection at Colindale, the British Library of Political and Economic Science, the British Library at Bloomsbury and the National Library of Scotland whose staffs have been of never-failing assistance. The inter-library loan department at Northern Illinois University doggedly handled requests for obscure books and pamphlets and so eased the way for my work. I would also like to mention the interest and aid I received from the office staff of the Union of Construction and Allied Technicians' Trades at Clapham who allowed me to work among their records in the days before they were transferred to the Modern Records Centre. In particular, I would like to thank Don Speakman who was in charge of their archives and who willingly took time out from matters more pressing than an arcane interest in the builders' history to smooth my way through the archives and to fortify my resolve with cups of tea. Mr Stocks of the Edinburgh District UCATT was also kind enough to grant permission to examine various old records of the Edinburgh carpenters how held by the National Library of Scotland. I always found UCATT to be exemplary in its willingness to allow researchers to rummage through their priceless collection of trade union material. It is also a great pleasure to record the same kind of interest and care that I encountered from the National Federation of Building Trades Employers whose Director-General, Martin Grafton and whose publicity officer, Eric Sadler, kindly searched out old minute books and provided me with working space in a magnificent conference room and sustenance in the shape of the inevitable cup of tea.

Finally, and most important of all, my family have endured with patience and fortitude the demands of writing this book. My son, Marshall, accepted my frequent absences from the play room and home with an understanding that I would have scarcely credited in one so young. This book is dedicated to my wife who, amidst a busy work schedule of her own, has had to live as close to this subject as I and who created the perfect atmosphere in which its work could be done. The debt I owe to her is beyond my power of words to express.

Abbreviations

ASC&J	Amalgamated Society of Carpenters and Joiners
ASE	Amalgamated Society of Engineers
Ass.C&J	Associated Carpenters and Joiners
CAMB	Central Association of Master Builders
GBA	General Builders' Association
GUC&J	General Union of Carpenters and Joiners
LBIF	London Building Industries Federation
LBTF	London Building Trades Federation
LMBA	London Master Builders' Association
NAMB	National Association of Master Builders
NAOP	National Association of Operative Plasterers
NFBTE	National Federation of Building Trades Employers
OBS	Operative Bricklayers' Society
OBU	Operative Builders' Union
OSM	Friendly Society of Operative Stone Masons
RIBA	Royal Institute of British Architects
STA	Shipbuilding Trades' Agreement
TGWU	Transport and General Workers' Union
USB	United Society of Boilermakers and Iron and Steel Shipbuilders

To Barbara

Introduction

It is probably true of most books that they bear little resemblance to the original intent with which the research was begun, and this work is assuredly no exception. But one purpose has remained consistent throughout; for the original impetus to write this book derived from a dissatisfaction with the way in which the problems it addresses were usually approached. By now, of course it is a commonplace – at least amongst a definable group of mainly younger historians – to reject the assumptions and the methods of mainstream, traditional labour history. Conceptually derived from the Webbs – whose political purposes were embarrassingly self-conscious – most labour history has been both enriched and pauperised by the weight of their legacy. Excessively empirical in its method, rigidly institutional in its focus, unadventurous in the questions it asks of its material and eagerly shying away from any interpretation worthy of the name, it seems content to traverse the same ground again and again in the hope, perhaps, of discovering a new fact here or a forgotten organisation there. Inconsistent even in the explanations that it does adduce to explain the rise of labour, traditional labour history is a lode of interesting and important facts crushed together to hagiographically confirm Labour's own mythologies.[1] Perhaps in reaction to this rather depressing landscape, recent years have seen the incursion of the methods of a new social history into the field to cause the general area to become an exciting focus of historiographical change. And, of course, there always were giant exceptions – the subject inevitably attracted some of the best historians of each generation. But it is significant that many of the leads they suggested remain to be built upon or are only recently receiving the attention they deserve.[2]

It is, perhaps, the inadequate level of conceptualisation and theoretical perspectives that has been the most serious omission of mainstream labour historiography. Nor is this just a matter of the repetition of rather stale debates,[3] the near-obsessive concern to trail over the old ground about the emergence of the Labour Party, the continual attention to organisational history and the perpetual interest in the leadership personnel of the Labour Movement. These subjects would be laudable objects of attention if they were treated with a view to casting new perspectives on the social processes

I

of which they were a part. But labour's rise to prominence is seen as a natural, progressive evolution in which conflict was at a minimum and struggle is used as a loose category to emphasise the intrepid nature of the early movement's pioneers. The exact nature of that struggle, the social forces that conditioned and determined its forms and eventual resolution are seldom treated beyond a one-dimensional, over-simplified version of the triumph of class aspiration and organisation. The Labour Movement progressed, it would seem, from struggling roots, through gallant conflicts to establish its legitimacy and strength and by dint of its own efforts forced its claims to attention upon employers, the ruling class and society at large. Marching through history with seven league boots, through 'struggles' for a legal existence, past 'struggles' for reductions of hours, over the many obstacles to an independent political existence, traditional labour history has viewed the dynamics of its subject as lying purely within the movement itself. From this perspective, the sense of motion in labour's history is linear – and uni-linear at that. One outpost is captured and it's on to the gradual siege of the next fortification until Jerusalem is reached.

Labour's victories are generally perceived unambiguously. If trade unions were eventually accepted, it was because they had struggled for acceptance and so grew in strength that employers were forced to acknow‑ ledge their presence. If collective bargaining was eventually instituted, it was because the trade union viewpoint ultimately prevailed over the misguided opposition of its opponents. Yet this is surely inadequate. Labour and its institutions do not exist in a vacuum; their history was not determined solely by their own internal dynamic strength; trade unions were not suddenly accepted because they were more irresistibly powerful in 1870 or 1890 than they had been in 1860. And it is the failure to place the rise of labour within any other perspective than its own heroic boundaries that constitutes perhaps the greatest failing of most accounts of this trade union or that socialist society.

Since the mid-sixties, and particularly since the watershed appearance of E. P. Thompson's *The Making of the English Working Class*, a revisionism of this general view has been underway which is directed not only towards filling the huge gaps that have hitherto been left unattended but also towards making theoretical sense of the development of working-class history. In this respect, we are witnessing a return to the traditions of the old masters who pioneered the subject in the earlier part of this century. At its best, the scholarship of both the old masters (and the Webbs, Hammonds and G. D. H. Cole *were* the best) and that of the recent revisionists combines the virtues of empiricism and historicism to produce a scholarship that is both exciting and enduring. Rather than taking the shape of Labour Movement history for granted, the central questions that have guided this type of research are to ask why the Labour Movement and the working class developed in Britain in the way that they did; what were the internal and extrinsic forces that moulded the character of the movement; and how best may we comprehend the chemistry through which these forces produced the social, cultural and economic forms of working-class behaviour and organisation?[4] It is as a modest contribution to this revisionism that this book has been written.

We are concerned to illuminate only one aspect of the process of the rise of labour, although we venture to believe that it was not an unimportant part. For it is clear that by the end of the nineteenth century, the basis of labour's importance in society rested primarily upon its organisational power in industry and upon the recognition granted to it through the various systems of collective bargaining and industrial relations. This was the springboard from which Labour was able to leap into the political arena and, unlike the late sixties, encounter the Liberal Party from a position of some strength. The story itself is well known; its main outlines are not in doubt. But it is a story that is usually told within the framework of assumptions mentioned earlier as characteristic of Labour Movement historiography. The rank and file, for example, hardly appear at all in the story beyond passive agents upon whom history acts and who may occasionally burst forth – as in the new unionism – into 'revolt against their employers' and become infected with a 'unionist enthusiasm throughout the industrial areas.'[5] And it is an important purpose of this book to restore rank and file actions to their rightfully central role in this particular historical process. Similarly, there is seldom any sense that the process possessed a dimension other than one of changing organisational forms or increasingly sophisticated institutional structures. One can look in vain, for example, for a coherent explanation of the changes in trade union government that occur in the period – let alone any attempt to place them within a dynamic historical context. There is, in other words, no impression of movement from one period to another beyond the perpetual motion of labour's onward march. The historiography is devoid of any sense of a structural dynamic that may provide a better understanding of the process. It seemed worthwhile, therefore, to ask anew: what were the historical and contemporary forces that conditioned and determined the emergence of those institutions that represented labour's power and significance?

In spite of the legitimate and important attention that has recently been devoted to the investigation of other aspects of working-class society, it remains true that it is the working class's industrial experience (I use the term widely) that is of primary significance for any understanding of the mainsprings of labour history. In fact, the separation of these various aspects – the structural and the super-structural – is excusable on the grounds of analytic convenience alone. It is obvious that no total history of the class could ignore the potent social, political and cultural formations that contributed to its development; and the future trend of the discipline should be to explore their inter-relationships.[6] But if we are to understand properly the role played by the industrial experience and how it relates to those other structures, it is clearly necessary that we move beyond the recognition of broad economic trends or general shifts in industrial organisation and direct our attention to the most basic unit of the workplace.

In their treatment of the development of the Labour Movement, both mainstream and revisionist labour historians have tended to neglect the role of work experience.[7] Where its significance has been recognised, however, the results have been of considerable interest and importance.[8] And given the prominence that work and occupation are recognised to play in the formation of class behaviour, organisation and consciousness, it is of pressing concern that historians direct their attention not only to the re-creation of the work experience but to its function as a structural determinant of labour history. For there is little to be gained from a focus upon work structure, work culture and customs and the like that fails to suggest how they may be used to create an added dimension to the familiar features and central problems of labour history. Our examination attempts to do this by showing how the forces, pressures, and changes in the workplace conditioned, shaped and altered the institutional structures upon which labour came to wield its influence and power by the end of the nineteenth century.

But if these links are to be properly drawn, if we are to show how the dynamic of forces at the workplace spawned the methods and systems of collective bargaining and industrial relations, it is necessary to combine a micro- and a macro-faceted approach. A focus upon one industry, therefore, seemed the most appropriate way to gather the kind of source material upon which such an investigation could build. And most of our evidence will be drawn from the largely fortuitous choice of the building industry with additional attention to the very different industry of shipbuilding and some sidelong glances at similar developments in other sectors of the economy.[9] In the light of the fact that the building industry was composed of some half a dozen different and distinct trades – each worthy of study in its own right – the limitations imposed by this method seem to me to be relatively minor. One such limitation, however, is the unevenness with which the different sections of the industry may be treated. Relatively little is said, for example, about plumbers, partly because the evidence is not so readily available as it is for masons or carpenters and partly because that trade did not figure very large in the main developments upon which we focus. And it may be that the specifics of our case would need modification upon further digging in local archives and local newspapers. But, with an eye to the macro-features, the really impressive thing is the similarity between the structures of industrial relations that emerged not just across building but across much of industry. In their essentials, for example, sliding scales in coal mining were the equivalent of the conciliation boards in building; the national systems of collective bargaining in boot and shoe bore strong resemblances to those in building or shipbuilding. Variations in technology, organisation and customs will, of course, dictate important differences between each trade and it should in no way be thought that these structural differences are insignificant or unworthy of study. In fact, from my point of view, just the reverse is the case in order to see whether the kinds of general forces that I believe operated in building were also to be found elsewhere. I suspect that they would, although I recognise that the forms would be different. It is, therefore, a very definite implication that the arguments of this book have a far wider relevance than those parts of the building industry for which the evidence is strongest. They are deliberately suggested as an explanatory interpretation that is broadly pertinent to the rise of labour as a whole (which is why that phrase is in the title) and not just to the rise of those particular manifestations of labour's power in the building industry alone.

The reasons why this claim is made rests largely upon the dialectical evolution of the book itself. What began as a vaguely defined study of the relationship between industrial conflict, strikes and the work process led inevitably to a consideration of the structures of industrial relations. Conflict, it should hardly need to be emphasised, is endemic to industry and far from demonstrating dysfunctioning models of cooperation and consensus, is the very dynamic of progress and change. It was out of conflict that all the major developments of Labour Movement history flowed, but equally it was out of the relationship between workers and employers at the workplace that the mainsprings and shape of conflict were to be found. From this perspective it was critically necessary that we conceptualise the meaning of conflict and its bearing upon the wider developments within the realms of systems and structures of industrial relations.

The central problem was: how are we to make sense of the relationship between industrial conflict and the work process over a broad range of time? It is all very well to point to this or that grievance as the cause of a strike, but how are we to conceptualise the nature of those grievances and are we to see industrial conflict as simply the accretion of collected material issues that eventually bursts forth into a strike? For all sorts of reasons the latter view is an unsatisfactory resting place for the historian, not least because it implies only one, fairly superficial, level of analysis. No one sees the General Strike, for example, as simply the product of miners' grievances but as the result of a far more complex process of historical causation with implications and meaning that extended far beyond mining. Similarly, to take a smaller and less significant example, if we are really to understand the actions of those masons at the Houses of Parliament in 1841 who struck

against the tyranny of their foreman, we cannot simply view it as the product of an oppressive overseer.[10] The pressure of that tyranny may have
been the spark that ignited the strike and may also have been the conscious
motive of the workers involved. But 'tyranny' is not simply a function of
psychopathic personalities; it exists within a material and structural context which may not determine its particular form but which certainly calls
forth and demands its expression.

  Just as it takes no great perception to recognise the poverty of looking at
particular strikes from the sole dimension of articulated demands, so it is
also inadequate to apply a crudely economic framework of interpretation
to the broad span of industrial conflict. It is certainly most useful to relate
strike movements to the fluctuations in the business cycle, but it would be
hard to argue that such linkages contain the whole meaning and nature
of those conflicts. Strikes may cluster around certain moments in the
economic cycle, most strikes may be expressed as demands for more wages
or other economic benefits but no industrial sociologist (and increasingly
few historians) would argue that this was all there was to the question. If
we reduce an economic explanation to its crudest dimensions we may see
the inadequacy of its explanatory force. Even if it is true that, in the words
of an American labour leader, workers go on strike because they want 'more,'
this does not exhaust the implications of their actions. Getting 'more' implies a wider series of changes in the employer–employee relationship than
that of the monetary amount involved; going on strike for more implies
that workers feel they are strong enough to force concessions from the
employer and immediately suggests a changed power relationship. Similarly, depressing wages or conditions is not simply a device to allow extra
benefits to accrue to employers but involves an enhanced domination over
the workers whose facets will extend far beyond the economics of the
matter.

  Yet the dominant tendency of labour history in particular has been to
avoid an explicit conceptualisation of industrial conflict that moves beyond
the focus on individual grievances or a broadly 'economic' explanation of
strike activity.[11] Industrial sociologists in their empirical and theoretical
work have been more adventurous than historians in this respect – although
even here the prevailing school of thought tends to see conflict as an abnormal breakdown of a pluralistic system of checks and balances. In fact, such
models are inadequate not only because they may be internally incongruous with social reality, but also because they fail to illuminate the
historical dynamic that underlies conflict in industry.[12] The search for a
unified theme that would allow us to make sense of the mass of material
derived from a study of strikes and the work process led, therefore, to a
wide, eclectic (and I am sure insufficient) reading of the literature of
industrial sociology.[13] And from the interaction between these two different

approaches to the nature of industrial relations, but also because I found much in contemporary industrial sociology that was familiar from my work on nineteenth-century conflict situations, the conclusion to which I was drawn was that we may best conceptualise the dynamic of industrial relations as a struggle for power and authority.

There is, of course, an obvious distinction to be drawn between the various levels at which the evidence may be read. A framework of inter-pretation which suggests that industrial relations are about power and control does not rest for its validation upon the test that there be a self-conscious articulation of those questions in any particular conflict or bar-gaining situation. It does not demand as proof that when workers talk about higher wages or lower hours, they are really asking for more power without actually saying so. Rather, the test of such an approach as is suggested here, rests upon whether it can provide a coherent and reason-ably consistent fit between the evidence, the events and their implications. In this sense, there is no inconsistency between arguing, for example, that the 'tyranny' of George Allen – the target of the masons' strike of 1841 – was both a concrete cause of the strike and a reflection of the workplace struggle for power; nor that wages demands and power contests are both real aspects of any particular dispute. A level of analysis, however, that took 'tyranny' at its face value as the sole meaning and implication of the strike action would provide an incomplete and superficial historical under-standing. For it would allow only the possibility of explaining events at the superficial level of conscious actions without placing them within the con-text of forces and meaning that call such actions into being. In the same way, an analysis of industrial conflict as a pure and simple struggle for economic benefits would not only fail to encompass those situations where wages were not at issue, but would wrench that struggle out of the wider context of social realities that characterise relations between employers and workers.

Those relationships are complex and multi-faceted; but, at bottom, the relationship is one of authority and power. When workers sell their labour power, they implicitly recognise a certain degree of subordination to the orders and mandates of the employer. Were this not so, then industry could not be organised and run by the employers. But it is precisely from this subordination that many of the problems of industry derive. For employers' authority is never total nor is it ever unambiguously accepted by workers. There is a constant and unremitting resistance and challenge to employers' authority that assumes many different shapes and forms. The complete subservience of their workforce which is the ideal situation for employers has never proved realisable. It is for this reason that industrial discipline has occupied a central place not only in the history of modern industrial organisation but in modern society as a whole. Without a discipline at work that accepted the legitimacy of the industrial hierarchy, discipline in society would remain in question. It is only since the industrial revolution that the junction between industrial and social discipline has become so important because it was only with that transcendental stage of capitalist organisation that employers' authority became critically linked with the necessity to respond to rapidly changing economic trends and competitive pressures.[14]

The extent of employers' authority varies, of course, from place to place and from time to time. What Carter L. Goodrich appropriately called the 'frontier of control' is in constant motion, pushed from one side by workers as a defence against the counter-pressure from the employers.[15] Whilst it is broadly true to recognise the permanent subordination of the workers in this authority relationship and to acknowledge that, in varying degrees, this inferiority is accepted by the working class, it is insufficient to conclude that their part in the struggle for authority is purely defensive and reactive. The struggle for industrial discipline is one in which workers engage as active agents of their own authority and not as passive and obdurate recipients of employers' initiative. Resistance to employers' authority may take many forms – from absenteeism and sabotage to collective bargaining and factory occupations – but its broad effect represents an effort by the workers to carve out a sphere of control over the productive process which is within their autonomous band of authority. This effort to exert a control over the productive process is essentially a product of the nature of the employer–worker relationship; it is implicit in the subordination in which workers are placed and, in a sense, that is the answer to the obvious question of why we may conceptualise worker behaviour in this way. In its broad aspect, then, the struggle for work control by workers is one small part of the natural, eternal search for human freedom, for a mitigation of the domination over men's bodies and lives. The self-consciousness of worker actions, however, is seldom this exalted and neither does it assume a single-minded, constant form but will encompass many different rationales at different times. At one level, it may be expressed in a 'bloody-mindedness' to the employer or his foreman; at another time – as at Fawley in the 1950s – it may represent an effort to stabilise and control earning power; another form is the resistance to changes in technique that may threaten job security or status; and yet a further expression would be the opposition to employer policies that rests upon the dignity and independence associated with the idea of a craftsman. There is, in other words, no single, specific reason why workers act as if to exercise a degree of influence over the productive process, nor is there a constant level of consciousness about the significance of their actions. They do not necessarily conceptualise their behaviour as an explicit effort to stabilise earnings or to exert a formal control over the work. And although this is of some significance for the nature of working-class consciousness, for the purposes of the present argument it is far less important than the fact that the results of their actions are to involve questions of authority and control. Even if the actual motive of their actions, for example, is the protection of various aspects of their economic position, the truly important thing for historical interpretation is that in doing this they will at some point be led to implicitly or explicitly challenge employer authority. It is this that provides the dynamic flashpoint of conflict between the two groups.

Equally, it is less important that this effort to exert control is primarily a defensive measure – to provide a buffer zone through which employers have to travel before they may completely subordinate the workers to their will. By its very presence and in the demands that may be made to expand its sphere of influence it is an offensive challenge to employer prerogatives, a constant reminder of the incompleteness of the employers' area of freedom in dealing with their employees. From the workers' perspective, then, the essence of this struggle for authority must be seen as defensive–offensive, as involving at one and the same time an attempted protection against the unlimited exercise of employer control and as forming an implicit affront to that 'legitimate' industrial authority. By itself, this workers' sphere of control over work cannot usually form a coherently coordinated attack upon the social foundations of the productive system but it is, we believe, an essential ingredient for any such challenge to grow and develop.

The central theme that runs through this book, therefore, rests upon the conception of industrial relations as a struggle for power. Employer–employee relations and conflicts are seen from the perspective of constant clashes, collisions and compromises between two opposed systems of authority which at their most basic level recur at the workplace in the form of a struggle for control over the productive process. When I use the term 'work control' it is just this struggle that I have in mind as expressing the tussle between workers' and employers' discipline. It is important to realise the distinction between my use of this term and the more commonly employed notion of craft control.[16] In many cases, of course, the two might be co-terminous: if masonry was still a 'craft' in the full historical, traditional and technical meaning of the term, then the masons' work control of which we write in this book may be a species of craft control. But that, of course, is precisely the problem with the indiscriminate use of the term 'craft control'; for it rightly connotes a series of special conditions and circumstances whose presence in many cases is at best problematical. Amongst the old 'crafts' whose techniques had been untouched by machinery or factory organisation, there was, by the middle of the nineteenth century, a large variation in the degree of skill, status, and income between the workers in the trades – and, to a certain extent, the same applied to the new crafts whose material basis had been carried by industrialisation. It is, for example, far from clear that we may meaningfully speak of carpentry or bricklaying as crafts – although they doubtless contained many craftsmen within them. The vast expansion of trades like these in the early ninteenth century clearly broke down any effective guild-style craft regulations that may have existed. The changes in technique and in the sub-division of labour that destroyed the 'craft' skill of the handloom weavers was paralleled throughout all of industry. Just how easy it was to pick up carpentry or bricklaying, for example, is not clear but it is apparent that those trades – and, to a lesser extent, masonry – did not rest upon any real skill in the craft sense of the term.

Furthermore, the confusion is compounded by the recognition that for their proper completion many 'unskilled' jobs required the possession of a certain degree of technique and no definition of skill that rests upon a purely technical basis will be adequate to encompass the complexities involved in the actual work process. For it would be a great mistake to assume that only skilled craft workers were subject to the dynamic of authority conflict at the workplace. As contemporary industrial sociology has shown, this is a dynamic that is inherent to industrial organisation and may include those with no craft tradition or recognised skill in their work. Indeed, in our period, the impetus to control over work was manifested by bricklayers' labourers as well as by the bricklayers themselves. Finally, therefore, 'craft control' is too constricting to be of much use to this particular analysis. We cannot understand, for example, the resistance from masons to payment by the hour in terms of a defensive craft control, for the other trades were also generally opposed to that mode of payment.[17]

Great care must be exercised, therefore, with our employment of the idea of craft control, whose usage should be guided by the presence of one or more of the following criteria. First, it may be used where a clearly defined handicraft tradition continues to play a live and operative role in the work process and its culture. Highly skilled workshop trades, such as the flint glass makers, certain types of leather workers, or coopers probably possessed this attribute to a marked extent. Second, either because of their ability to restrict entry, or by virtue of the possession of genuine labour skills that were not easily learnt, craft workers' control could be expressed by the erection of restrictions and limitations that were recognised by employers as having some legitimacy. This may again be due to the force of tradition – as in apprenticeship ratios – or it may be due to the genuine scarcity of skills possessed by certain workers that were in high demand. Certain kinds of workshop trades would fall into this category, as would the new crafts of shipbuilding platers and engineers who maintained traditions of apprenticeship regulation characteristic of their millwright ancestry. And, third, craft control must involve some genuinely distinctive ability to do certain jobs not possessed by other workers and acquired through recognised channels of training. There were, of course, many such jobs in nineteenth-century Britain that still possessed this attribute – plumbers were an example – but they were getting fewer and fewer and by the end of the century most had lost any roots they may have had in an older handicraft tradition.

The term work control, on the other hand, is not subject to these kinds of qualifications and confusions. It may be taken to encompass both craft control (either with or without an historical craft tradition behind it) and the attempts by non-craft workers to exercise some control over their work process. It may include the respectable work control exercised by skilled craftsmen and it may also include the informal attempts at control by workers who possessed no such legitimising sanctions. The difference between work and craft control, then, is a difference between control that was overlain by support systems of tradition or genuine skill and a description of the reality that composed all employer–employee relationships.

Craft control is, thus, a variant of a wider phenomenon whose diverse forms and shape will be found to vary over time and place. The struggle for work control is no static force; it is transformed and altered by an assortment of influences that range from the technology to the method of payment in the trade and it is important that it be analysed within this context of the specific work experience. This book will argue that the struggle for control is a dynamic force which is central to understanding both the movement and the continuities of labour history. It will be seen, for example, that a somewhat different light may be shed upon the important mid-Victorian years by an analysis that focuses upon the nature of industrial conflict. At one level, the notion that these were years overshadowed by the enormous defeats of Chartism is an important part of the historical reality. But it would be a great mistake to see that period solely through the perspective of a docile working class that had been numbed into passivity.[18] Similarly, to concentrate purely upon the political and cultural alliances that were beginning to stir between certain sections of the working class and Liberalism is not to provide a mistaken emphasis so much as an incomplete one. In fact, the mid-Victorian period possessed another side of respectability, one that was just as crucial in determining the future course of the Labour Movement and one that was important precisely because it could not be accommodated within the changing needs and realities of the time. The militancy that we show as characteristic of those years was very different from the militancy that had gone before; but in the enormity of the pressures and challenges that faced the working class it was the earlier period that was abnormal. The forms that militancy took in the age of equipoise were not only more appropriate for the times, they were also productive of equally profound consequences. For we shall argue that it was out of the mid-Victorian struggle for work control that the structural patterns were set for the integration of labour that occurred in the later part of the century.[19]

And that process of the rise of labour – as it was manifested by the recognition that organised labour constituted a legitimate estate in society – is the overriding concern of this book. It will be seen to be a product of the struggle for control over work, of the consequent problems that this posed for industrial discipline, and of the efforts to find solutions to these problems in the creation of various structures of industrial relations.[20] The process is conceived as a dialectical dynamic in which the working class autonomously acts as it was structurally bound to do but whose actions induce reactions which then act upon the workers to move the struggle for control to other levels of experience. In our period, this process culminated in the transcendence of the local focus of work control and rocketed it into the realm of ideology. In this way, we shall attempt to show how understanding the dimensions and the dynamic of the continuing struggle for control over work is a key part of understanding the impelling force of labour history.

But the propulsive role of the work experience may possess an importance that extends beyond the limited focus of this book to illuminate the nature and development of working-class consciousness. And it is important to say a few words about how this might be so. Class consciousness is a dynamic phenomenon whose movement – both progressive and regressive – is moulded not only by the legacy of its particular historical origins but by a wide variety of contingent and transient influences among which the work experience must clearly be included. The great value of the work of Nairn and Anderson has been to explain the general nature of that consciousness as the product of Britain's unique political, social and economic evolution in the modern world.[21] What is generally missing from those kinds of perspectives, however, is the presence of countervailing forces which at most times are contained within the dampening effects of that historical past but whose potential also threatens to transcend its heritage. It is only too true that the particular historical circumstances that created the world's first proletariat also determined that the ideology of change produced by these circumstances would fail to appeal to that working class. Marxism, we all know, came too late; but when it did come, it became the special property of disaffected intellectuals who never found it possible to translate their perceptions into the 'them' and 'us' world of the working class. The fact was, of course, that the British working class was too 'advanced' for the ideologies that it was offered and partly because there was no traditional corpus of dissenting ideology (as opposed to a tradition of dissent), it failed to develop its own indigenous variety. On the other hand, the material of this book may be taken to show that it would be a mistake to see the working class so completely subservient to bourgeois hegemony or so firmly tied to its historical chains, as to lack the substance that would enable it to move beyond the limits of official Labour Movement reformism. Further-more, its firm attachment to constitutionalism and certain other 'bour-geois' liberties is quite compatible with an ideology of revolutionary change: it is, after all, only recently that Marxism has begun to address these issues in terms that promise a decisive rejection of the ugly traditions of Stalinism.

Given the rich sense of history, culture and tradition that characterises the working class and the highly developed general sense of solidarity that the class possesses, its failure to realise its full potential as an agent of social and economic change may lie less within the class itself and more within its relations with other groups and classes. Simply because the British working class developed uniquely, so its ideological needs were unique. The isolation from other social groups has been a source of strength and of weakness – the former because it has allowed a firm sense of class to develop, the latter because it encouraged a resistance to ideas that fitted well into the philistinism characteristic of the general landscape of nineteenth-century Britain. There have been few attempts by intellectuals to transcend the barriers that this created; few attempts, in other words, to relate ideo-logy to the needs and the material experiences of the working class. It is highly significant that only during times of general social upheaval – and especially in the early nineteenth century – has there been any important movement in this respect. The significance of Owenism – multi-faceted though it was – lay in the way in which it spoke directly to needs and expe-riences in terms that working people could understand to permit the crea-tion of a really 'alternative' culture. But the void that has more typically existed encouraged such hybrid forms as the religio-ethical socialism of the late-nineteenth century to serve as a somewhat inadequate substitute. There may be much to be learned, for example, from the success attained by William Cobbett and Robert Blatchford as publicists who could speak to and reach large numbers of working people. Their success lay not so much in the eclecticism of their ideologies (the word is really too strong for neither were ideologues) as in their ability to translate the language of change into the vocabulary of working men and women. But these men were exceptional; even more unusual – indeed, one might argue, virtually non-existent – have been efforts to relate the framework of social and eco-nomic change to the material experiences of the working classes. The failure of the working class to live up to the standards of a desiccated Marxism or the sophistication of working classes elsewhere in Europe, is not only due to the structural constraints of their history. It is due also to the failure to develop an intellectual rationale of change that could speak to the unique experience of the British working class.

To turn to the working-class side of the conundrum, it is important to realise that class consciousness does not develop in a once and for all way, that its progress is modulated and conditioned by the particular and changing circumstances in which the class struggle occurs. It is here, we may suggest, that the work experience becomes relevant to the question because the material of this book suggests that the dynamics of that experience imply a constant challenge to the assumptions upon which capitalist authority in industry rests. The struggle for work control is, therefore, a most basic aspect of the class struggle and it is from the nature of the class struggle that class consciousness emerges. E. P. Thompson has recently reminded us that:

People find themselves in a society structured in determined ways (crucially, but not exclusively, in productive relations), they experience exploitation (or the need to maintain power over those whom they exploit), they identify points of antago-nistic interest, they commence to struggle around these issues and in the process of struggling they discover themselves as classes, they come to know this discovery as class-consciousness. Class and class-consciousness are always the last, not the first stage in the real historical process.[22]

The precise relationship between the struggle for work control and the changing expression of class consciousness lies in the extent to which the struggle for authority at work is appreciated and perceived by workers as a power struggle whose ramifications extend beyond the workplace. Should that struggle be practised and articulated in ways that imply a wider perspective than a mere workplace focus, then the nature of class consciousness as a whole (and the reactions to it from non-working-class groups) will be more penetratingly acute. If, on the other hand, the struggle for work control remains purely within the workplace, if – for whatever reasons – it is unaccompanied by linkages with questions about power and authority in other aspects of societal arrangements or relationships, then the class consciousness that results will reflect those limitations.

Whether the struggle for work control possesses implications that remain purely limited or assume a more expanded form depends upon a complex set of economic, social and political conditions and possibilities. In general, however, we may say that it is not enough that the broad economic and political climate be conducive to the exercise of workplace power. It is additionally necessary that there be an element of uncertainty or crisis in society as a whole that allows the dominant consensus or hegemony to be seriously questioned and widely discussed. This uncertainty is usually generated by economic and social structural changes but the contribution of the struggle for work control to its development lies in the way these changes impact upon the work experience to alter the dimensions and contours in which it takes place. Thus, the relationship between class consciousness and the struggle for work control is not one of unilateral dependence; it is influenced and conditioned by wider forces that serve to encourage the workplace focus to assume a wider or narrower perspective. But the relevance of the struggle for workplace authority to the nature of class consciousness lies in the links that are forged between this particular aspect of the class struggle and the question of authority and power in other social institutions.

The challenge at the workplace to capitalist authority is, therefore, intimately attuned to the realities and potential of the particular period in which it finds itself. Under certain conditions it is a challenge capable of providing the basis for driving beyond the limits of the ideological mish-mash of Labourism. And, in this respect, it seems to me that the syndicalism with which the book ends assumes a considerable significance. For it was most clearly of all at that moment when an intimate fusion occurred between ideology and work experience to show the relevance of each to the other and to permit the dynamics of class consciousness to completely come into their own. This is true especially in contrast to the mid-Victorian period when – according to my perspective – a militancy pervaded that was in no way 'false' but was parochial and isolated. In its ideological dimensions, this militancy was unable to be anything else. Working against it was the unquestioned dominance of British capitalism and an incongruous ideology of respectability whose impact upon working-class history was profoundly important but whose hegemonical fragility was revealed when it confronted the changed circumstances of the late century.

If we are to understand the dynamics of class consciousness, then, it is very important that the role of the work experience be injected into our equations. For that dynamic consists of the interaction between three levels of analysis and experience – the historical baggage that is carried by the working class, the particular constructs of the time within which it must operate (which includes the general level of critiques available to the working class and relationships to other classes), and the relationship these bear to the specific experiences, both historical and contemporary, of the workplace. It may be that the future job of the historian who is interested in such matters will be to explore these relationships within the framework of forces that conditioned the broad evolution of the working class and also within the framework of the internal history of the class at work.

It is, thus, obvious that our terminal date of 1914 is a somewhat arbitrary point at which to end. For it is clear that the themes traced in this book are conceived of as continuous and eternal to modern working-class history and it will become apparent that more than an eye has been cast to the currents that flow through the crisis of contemporary Britain. Both in detail and in broad outline, strong thematic parallels stand out between the evidence of the historical material and that gathered by contemporary investigations of industrial conflict. Present-day problems are, of course, much wider than an intractable lack of labour discipline, but it is undeniable that industrial relations compose a central feature of that crisis. Indeed, the background to this current crisis repeats a pattern that is common to the story of this book of growing worker power at the workplace which challenged and stultified the structures of industrial relations leading to various attempts to reassert the legitimacy and authority of those official structures. Accompanying these developments there has been a distinct raising of the political and ideological temperature which, on the left, has stimulated a renewed debate about the nature of working-class political ideology and which, across the whole political spectrum, has revived discussion about workers' control. In this sense, then, this book may be seen as a contribution to the origins of the present crisis and particularly, perhaps, in the light that it may shed upon the role and function of trade unions as the 'managers of discontent.'

What began as a conceptual prejudice that labour history tended to be written too much around the history of trade unionism – both in the literal sense that it focused exclusively on their organisational history and in the conceptual sense that by equating the development of the working-class movement with that of the trade union movement it failed to investigate the autonomous history of the workers – developed into a more extensive attempt to de-mythologise the historical role performed by organisational trade unionism. In the period with which the book is concerned it remains terribly important to separate the history of workers at work from the history of the trade unions – even if it is true that much of the material to do this must derive from trade union sources. For if we recognise that workers do have an autonomous history outside the boundaries of trade union history, it is no longer analytically adequate to assume a co-terminous relationship between the two. More important than this, however, is to acknowledge that, from the very moment of their acceptance, the historical role that the trade unions have played in the development of the working-class movement has been marked by an ambiguous duality. Managing discontent has been a dominant presence from the very beginnings of the modern labour movement which in no way contradicted the trade union function as associations 'of wage earners for the purpose of maintaining or improving the conditions of their employment.'[23] Indeed, there was an integral relationship between these two functions in that the former was the recognised *quid pro quo* for the legitimate pursuit of the latter.

But to emphasise, as we shall, the work discipline aspect of trade unionism and the profound impact that it had upon the struggle for work control must not be taken to imply either a disregard for the real and positive benefits that trade unionism holds for the working class, or the application of a schematic moralism which would hold official trade unionism guilty of comfortably settling down to impose employer's discipline in return for the right to bargain over economic conditions. The reality was more complicated than that and undoubtedly even more ambiguous than we have managed to portray it. And although we believe that the conflict relationship between official unionism and its rank and file which is analysed in the last part of the book was historically the most significant aspect of industrial relations from the 1890s, it was neither the only ingredient nor was it a relationship to be understood within such simplistic categories as reactionary officials or spontaneous, disgruntled rank and file. Both groups were prisoners of their structural circumstances and, even if it is true that we tend to oversimplify the categorical distinction between 'officialdom' and 'rank and file,' it remains clear that the dominant tendency of the period was the tension within a system whose impulse was to provide respectability at the expense of discipline without actually removing the root causes of militancy. What we shall be concerned to argue is that the tension between discipline and militancy was a *structural* not a behavioural tension, inherent to the negotiated compromise between labour and society that emanated from the acceptance of organised labour's role as an agent with bargaining rights over industrial conditions. To this extent workplace militancy was bound to clash (in varying degrees which remain to be charted by historians) with union policies and official leaderships for both were at different points of contact with the system of industrial relations. Nor was this merely reflective of the difficulties of meshing the various levels of the industrial relations experience. The problem of rank and file militancy is not (as the pluralistic conceptions of most industrial sociologists tend to imply) simply the problem of devising agencies to increase the representational input of constituent groups. It is rather a reflection of the inherent contradiction within systems that are devised to maintain industrial peace without removing the basic impediments to that peace. Ultimately, industrial relations are about power and industrial conflict is about class struggle, but even though collective bargaining systems are called into being by these imperatives they may not generally approach these issues at their most fundamental level and it is, therefore, hopeless to believe that they will fundamentally resolve conflicts that implicitly or explicitly address matters of power and authority. But it is only at certain moments in history under complex and special conditions that this dilemma is clearly revealed and consciously perceived. This book endeavours to sort out the entangled historical and contemporary themes that went into the growing tension between the rank and file and the official Labour Movement at the end of our period. It tries to do this without resorting to a simplistic economic or moralistic analysis of militancy that would be as bad as those traditional perspectives that view the evolution of labour history through a vision of progress that is Whiggish and linear.

Like any other kind of history, the history of labour is impregnated with contradiction and ambiguity; indeed, the aim of this book is to show that it is precisely within those qualities that the very dynamic of labour history may be found.

I

Freedom, authority and control: the imperatives of general contracting

CONTINUITY AND CHANGE

Any study of the nature of industrial conflict and industrial relations in the building industry must begin by a recognition that it will be confronted with a simple but central paradox. It was, and has remained, an industry where the enduring importance of 'tradition' has been a preeminent feature of its structures. Among the important trades of the nineteenth century it would, perhaps, be hard to find an equivalent to the festivals of the guild of plumbers that were held at Preston every twenty years, 'celebrated by great rejoicings' with regalia processions and other 'events of importance' to mark the occasion.[1] Yet it was an industry that was a part of the 'modern' world in a way different from others like the chainmakers, for example, whose industrial structures remained unchanged – if not un-affected – by that vast series of economic changes we know as the industrial revolution. Building was, after all, an industry which employed the fourth largest number of workers in 1851, and one which played a critical – if somewhat complicated and mysterious – role in the cycles of economic growth and depression. And perhaps it is for this reason that building has received a more detailed attention than most industries from economic historians seeking to understand the secrets of its motors and their relation-ship to the wider economy.[2] The industry cannot, then, be simply dis-missed as a 'pre-industrial' remnant whose 'industrialisation' was merely delayed by two centuries. Indeed, the paradox is heightened by the presence of features and characteristics that were to be found with equal prominence in those sectors of the economy that were 'revolutionised' by early industrialisation and which provided the main body of Britain's economic might and her proletarian workforce.

Those elements that composed the continuity to be found in the building industry are well known. In its ownership structure, for example, it con-tinued to be quantitatively dominated by the small firm. Indeed, this characteristic was accentuated in the nineteenth century and although this was by no means a unique consequence of the industrial revolution, it is interesting to note how little modern building differs in this respect from that of the mid nineteenth century. The figures for unit of employment in the 1960s are directly comparable with those gathered for the census of 1851. In fact, at the bottom of the scale the percentage of small employers was precisely the same: in both periods it stood at 80%.[3] In comparison to coal, cotton, or the metal trades, building was an industry where until the late nineteenth century at the earliest large-scale capital formation was rare. In fact, because of the rise of sub-contracting it is probable that for the majority of firms capital requirements declined in the nineteenth century as a whole.

Similarly, and again until the later part of the century it was an industry that remained generally untouched by that hoary, catch-all category of technological change. Postgate – ignoring, incidentally, the slower but more important spread of machinery in carpentry and joinery – noted that only in sawmilling and brickmaking could technology be claimed to have had a sharp and important impact.[4] Of course, the general significance of technology as a replacement to hand labour power in this period has recently been subject to an acute and perceptive questioning and it is only too true that historians have been overly eager to ignore the continuing importance of hand labour in those trades 'revolutionised' by machinery.[5] But there is a legitimate distinction to be drawn between those industries where hand labour became ancilliary to the machine and those where it remained unilaterally dominant; and building was clearly an industry heavily permeated with a high degree of 'craft' stability in terms of the way in which the work was actually done. This distinction is, perhaps, of more interest to economic and business historians than to those concerned with the history of labour. For too much effort has been adduced to singling out the ramifications of the forces of technology and too little to seeking those less tangible but equally important shifts that can occur within the structure of work without conditional changes in the working technique.[6] Building will be shown to provide an interesting example of just this phenomenon.

It was, of course, an important consequence of the lack of technological change that the structure of the labour force in building remained unamenable to concentration within the walls of a factory. For this, among other reasons, labour remained largely impermanent and mobile – another 'traditional' characteristic that is accentuated in the nineteenth century. In some sections of the industry, for example, tramping either within a town or between towns survived longest as a necessary counter-weight to cyclical fluctuations of employment opportunity. Unlike the northern factory towns, there was not the same permanence of place of employment that can illuminate our understanding of the structures of working-class life and organisation.[7] But, as we shall demonstrate, this lack of employment stability was evidently no bar to a highly developed industrial militancy which building workers were to reveal more than once during our period.

These elements of 'traditional' continuity cannot be allowed to mask, as they too often have, the other side of the paradox which we find if we turn our attention to the actions of the labour force itself. The industry was, for example, rife with industrial conflict – much of it of a nature as probably to be missed by the official statistics – and so remains to the present day.[8] Nor did this militancy lack class consciousness. It was, after all, amongst the building trades that Owenism first exposed its potent challenge to industrial capitalism in the early 1830s; and, in the years before the First World War building workers provided one of the centres of the syndicalist challenge. The trades were critical focal points of unionist strength: by common consent, the Operative Society of Stonemasons remained the most powerful of unions until the crippling strike at the New Law Courts in 1877–78. Building unions' mid-century leaders were at the forefront in the battles for political and social respectability; it was their doings and differences that dominated the labour politics of the period and have, similarly, dominated the historiography. And, finally, in spite of the 'traditional' character of the industry, it did not lag behind the textile, metal or mining industries in the development of industrial relations systems and structures. Indeed, just as building had led the way in the local conciliation 'craze' of the 1860s and 1870s, it was also one of the first to be blessed with a national conciliation system. In all these ways, then, the industry was anything but 'traditional' and revealed that in spite of the persistence of continuity it was fully a part of the world of modern labour.

Too often, it seems to me, this paradox has been ignored; no attempt has been made to come to terms with its implications. Thus, in his useful survey of industrial relations in building, Keith Burgess concludes – in direct contradiction to the mass of his evidence – that 'the persistence of a large number of small firms, and the extent of mobility between employers and employed, masked the social relations of capitalist production' and that 'the aspects of continuity are all pervasive' so that industrial relations in building lacked 'the well-defined phases that distinguished one period from another in the engineering industry.'[9] In a similar manner, Postgate – in what is clearly one of the very best trade union histories ever written – was content to see no real difference between the gigantic conflicts that punctuated the history of the industry in 1833, 1859, 1872, and 1914. Continuity was dominant and if the 'document' was used in 1859 and again in 1914 that merely showed how little had changed.[10] But this is all too easy: if capitalist social relations were masked why did industrial – and, therefore, class – conflict pervade the industry, and why was it that syndicalism could find considerable support in the trades? If there were no phases to industrial relations how are we to comprehend the sophisticated structures designed to regulate industrial relations that were constructed in the 1890s? And *was* the 'document' of 1914 simply a reflection of the inbred conservatism that governed employers' relations with their men to make it indistinguishable from the 'document' of 1859? In fact, of course, it was the relationship between the two sides of the paradox that contain the answer to these and to other questions. For it was in the reaction between the elements of continuity and those of change that we must seek an understanding of industrial relations and industrial conflict in building. And, in particular, it is on that one aspect of 'continuity' which has been systematically ignored that we must focus if any resolution of the paradox is to be sought. It is a simple but important fact that just like those industries which were more obviously changed by the industrial revolution, the demands of industrial discipline were as great in building as elsewhere. This was the central, integrative element of continuity whose dimensions and features, once understood, enable everything else to fall into place.

Industrial discipline is, of course, a wide-ranging phrase whose meaning can only be discussed upon a specific and concrete empirical basis and we trust that its content will become clear throughout the course of this study. For if the 'problem' of industrial discipline was one that was common to all industries by the early nineteenth century it was, at one level, because all workers were subject to the logic of capitalist social relations.[11] But to pursue our analysis no further than that would be to leave it quite meaningless, devoid of content and understanding. We have to ask what it was about the precise nature of those social relations, of the way they were manifested and worked, that made building workers act the way they did and how it was out of these relations that industrial conflict and industrial relations structures assumed the form and functions that they did. And to do this we have to understand the logic that lay within the structure of the industry; for the forms that industrial conflict and relations assume and the nature of the problem of industrial discipline are determined by the forces that dominate the topography of any particular industry. That topography in building was dominated and determined by the appearance in the early nineteenth century of the new organisational form of general contracting. It was the imperatives derived from the structure of general contracting that were to set in motion pressures and conflicts whose implications were eventually to go beyond the narrow limits implied in the phrase 'industrial relations'.

THE LOGIC OF GENERAL CONTRACTING

The origins of general contracting remain obscure. It does seem clear that it was, indeed, a *new* organisation of the industry for, even though large-scale projects had been known to building at least since the time of Herod the Great, in the seventeenth century they were removed from the monopoly of church and monarch into the hands of the small and independent master craftsmen.[12] Even then, it may be too early to speak of the building capitalist. It is significant that the one historian who has undertaken a detailed investigation into the eighteenth-century building process nowhere mentions the system of general contracting. The industry was dominated by the small-masters who only infrequently initiated building projects and even where they did there is no evidence of a gathering together of all the crafts under one enterprise which is the distinguishing mark of the general contractor.[13] It was not unusual for those small investors who undertook the majority of building operations to contract with the individual crafts for specific parts of the job or to contract with a partnership of craftsmen, or to appoint one craftsman to a supervisory capacity – and for this role carpenters and joiners were usually chosen.[14] But these expediencies were in no way comparable to general contracting, for 'it was customary for craftsmen to employ men in their own skill alone' and to sub-contract the other parts of the work to other skilled men. Thus, in Nottingham in the 1790s one John Carter, a carpenter, who frequently entered into contracts to build or repair would engage David Bradwell to ' "perform that part of the contract which was to be done by persons in his business of a bricklayer at a given sum" ' and similarly with William Coe to do the smith's work and Jonah Favell to do the painting.[15]

It was natural that general contracting should first emerge in those parts of the country – the northwest and London – where urbanisation and industrialisation created the most rapid demand for mass produced housing. And it was the second decade of the century that saw the first real beginnings of the system. Why it should have emerged at this precise moment is unclear; the building boom of the 1770s and 1780s had not occasioned any organisational change in the industry and it might be that the influence of changing credit policies in the early nineteenth century was a decisive factor.[16] However that may be, it was Thomas Cubitt who is generally credited with being one of the first to introduce the new system when, in 1815, he expanded out of his luxury wallpaper trade into an enterprise that was to build Cubitt's Town in the East End and, by 1876, employ three thousand men. Cubitt: 'introduced an innovation regarded at the time as very daring . . . Instead of arranging with craftsmen to carry out particular jobs, he started to employ them under craft foremen . . . to work on whatever job he had for them.' It is interesting to note that an immediate consequence of this system was that Cubitt 'started in the field of speculative building' to keep this body of workmen constantly employed.[17] By the middle twenties – 1825 is a date that appears in the sources[18] – the system was becoming common in the northwest, coincident with the beginnings of a steep fall in wages which did not endear the workmen to the new methods. And an additional stimulus to employing large

numbers of direct labour on building projects was provided, it would
seem, by the railway boom of the 1830s.

There was a distinction between general contracting in London where
the true contracting capitalists like Trollope, Dove and Cubitt towered
over everybody else and that of the northwest where, as far as one can
judge, the firms were of a more middling size. It was in the north, for
example, that the association between the master-joiner as the contractor
was strongest – an association not found in London – and one well illustrated
by the rise of Robert Neill, a unionist joiner in the 1840s, to Mayor of
Manchester in the mid-sixties and a prominent building employer until
his death in the 1890s.[19] In the northwest, also, there is some evidence
that the practice of sub-contracting with master craftsmen continued and
it may be that it was for this reason that that area was to remain, in distinction to London, the cockpit of work control struggles.[20] But whatever the
local variations the general effects and features were the same. Ownership
became polarised between the very big and the very small. Even though
the latter continued to dominate the industry in numerical terms, their
influence in deciding the main conditions of work, the wage rates and the
hours of work was decisively overshadowed by the general contractors.

And it is necessary to insist upon this assertion because although the
structure of the industry was very complex and generalisation is fraught
with danger, those complexities cannot be allowed to cloud the very real
dominance of the general contractors. The pattern of industrial conflict
will be shown to reveal time and again that it was the general contractors
whom the men had to battle on all the decisive issues of the period.[21] By
virtue of their superior power, they were the 'leaders' of the trade – challenged only momentarily by the master craftsmen in the struggles of 1833 –
whose conditions of working set the standards for the rest of the industry to
follow.[22] The small builders, the jobbers, were in no position to challenge
the men on critical issues; of course they would behave as Tressell's
Rushton & Co. when they were given the chance and the Webbs were
quite right to remark that it was such men who most frequently contra-
vened the working rules, for by the 1890s it was in the large employers'
interests to negotiate such rules to regulate the trade. But when necessary,
and when the conditions allowed, enforcement action by the men against
the small builders was both easy and inconsequential. If the general contractors could be brought to adhere to certain standards of hours, wages
and conditions then the smaller masters would fall, or be pulled, into line.
Furthermore, the small men were almost totally dependent, both directly
and indirectly, upon the general contractors. Although they could eke out
a living doing the smaller kinds of jobs that the contractors were not
interested in, their main function was to provide the larger builders with
the host of sub-contracting services that they required. The subject is well

worthy of study, but it is neither possible nor necessary to do justice here to the complexities of the ownership structure of building and of the relationships between the various kinds of employers. Our main concern is not so much with the contractors as individuals as with the system which they personified and represented. The importance of the emergence of general contracting lay not so much in the creation of a relatively small class of dominant owners but more in the profound series of changes it stimulated in the structure of the industry.

Although we should beware of exaggerating the extent to which general contracting created a totally new set of characteristics, it does seem clear that its broad effect was to replace the stability which had previously been a distinctive feature of the industry with a restless and competitive anarchy. The system did, for example, alter the social patterns of the industry, destroying or modifying the traditional hierarchy of the trades and denuding of meaning – and eventually destroying the usage – of the term 'master craftsman.' Just how much and what kind of social mobility there had been before the early nineteenth century is unclear and would be well worth investigation but it is not unreasonable to assume that the progression from journeyman to independent master craftsman was a valid expectation for many who entered the industry. General contracting did not destroy the possibilities of social mobility which, paradoxically, was enhanced by the system's insatiable demand for sub-contractors. But this was mobility of a different and, we may safely assume, less secure kind. For while it was true that sub-contracting allowed any man to call himself a 'master' and even graduate to a jerry-builder, the vagaries of existence at this level in the system were deeply uncertain and the likelihood was that downward mobility back into the ranks of the workmen was just around the corner. The sense that the traditional hierarchy of the industry was being transmuted into a new kind of chaos informs much of the rhetoric that accompanied the struggles of the early 1830s. From the masons and the bricklayers come two such examples addressed, let it be noted, not to their specific economic grievances but to the wider question of the transformation they saw their trades undergoing:

When we take a retrospective view of the times past, what a particular change we perceive in the situation of our once respected Branch, in those days masters had confidence in each other, they contracted for their own, they spurned the idea of being led by those who thirsted for rights not their own . . . We have not only seen but felt the bad effects of the change, we have had sufficient proof that the viper has been admitted, basked in the warmth of that you ought to have enjoyed, and wallowed in the fruits of our labours.

The masons' eloquence was not matched by the bricklayers but the point was the same: 'Those groups of hungry monopolisers, who not only reaped the profits of our industry, but even degraded us more so, by assuming a proud aspect by taking the first place in the building, not only in their own department, but even over that trade which we and our fathers have been justly proud.'[23] The threat general contracting posed to the traditional hierarchy of the trades was not limited, of course, to the workmen; indeed, it was directed primarily against the master craftsmen themselves. It was this that explains the alliance that lasted throughout 1832 until the spring of 1833 between the men and the lesser employers.[24] Many of these craftsmen looked with approval upon attempts to regulate the industry, as a way to combat the unsettling competition that accompanied the contract system and they actively encouraged the unions' efforts.[25] In Manchester they claimed to be neutral in the contest but kept their works open, to the fury of the large contractors who were busy enforcing a lockout. And one hundred and fifty of the master craftsmen, announcing that '*They* were the trade of Manchester' met and passed a resolution vaguely hostile to the contractors.[26]

In addition, general contracting destroyed traditional stability by accentuating fluctuations in employment. It was an obvious consequence of the system that labour costs now became the largest single item of cost to the employer and with increased competitiveness and speculation it became much more important that there be a pool of reserve labour which could be hired and fired at a moment's notice. It was this sense of increased instability that informed much of the men's complaints in 1833 of the 'tyranny' and 'oppression' under which they were suffering. Again, it is difficult to know the precise dimensions of the changes that were involved here but there is little doubt that the imperatives of general contracting were such as to demand that employers have a maximum freedom in this regard. It was asserted in 1857 that there was a greater constancy of employment before the industry became dominated by speculative building and general contracting and Dearle, in his 1908 study of the London building trade, pointed to the inherent fluctuations in employment depending upon the amount and type of work that a firm had on hand.[27] It was an expression of this imperative to secure and discharge men at will that the masters in 1833 began to develop the theme of individual bargaining in their attacks upon the unions. And the necessity for the employers to possess this freedom of manoeuvre was to be a very important determinant of the future course of industrial relations in the industry.

General contracting was a more dynamic mode of organising the industry – the direct equivalent of the factory system in other trades – but it threw into question the relative stability and security that traditionally came from small-scale units of production who built to a real rather than to a potential demand. Stability was replaced with chaotic competition in which speculation became, for the very first time, a dominant characteristic of building activity, an integral part of the process. Large employers were forced to supplement their contract work with speculative enterprise not only to supply the burgeoning demand for construction but also to utilise more efficiently their capital and resources. This was, we may be certain, a real difference with the past. Whilst speculative activity had not been unknown before – the rebuilding of central London after the Great Fire and other periods of peak activity had provided ample opportunity for such enterprise[28] – it had not played the central, integral role to the building process that it was now to assume. Eighteenth-century building crafts-men, who were the most likely group involved in the industry to build on speculation, had never been able to make this a full-time occupation because of the limited size of their capital or available credit and this was true even in the boom years of the seventies and eighties.[29] The dominant pattern of investment, especially by those outside the industry who at this period were the major source of capital, was for long-term returns rather than for a quick turn-around: 'House ownership and its natural extension in the rapidly-growing towns, house construction, was usually aimed at providing a sound rather than a rapidly growing income-yielding invest-ment and an asset which could be realised for a reasonable price when the capital was needed.'[30] But general contracting was to change all this; the industry now became dominated by speculative activity – ninety per cent of houses in Camberwell in the 1870s were built on speculation – and by the sharp competition that was its natural partner.[31] Speculative activity was part of the inescapable logic of general contracting, it was the only way to secure an efficient utilisation of resources, a main chance of securing a reasonable profit; it avoided the equally uncertain business of tendering for contracts and, once entered into, the constant influx of fresh credit or sale funds on the basis of buildings already completed became a major source of maintaining liquidity.

The pressures to undertake speculation were unavoidable but the result, as Parry Lewis has demonstrated, was to enhance the instability of the industry by tying its fortunes firmly to credit supply and to fluctuations in the availability of credit. In addition to changing demographic and migra-tion patterns, the rate of interest had always been an important deter-minant of the building cycle. In the eighteenth century fluctuations in building activity followed the movements of yield on Consols. But it is likely that the Usury Laws worked to restrain the supply of capital for building and this was probably a factor which helped to maintain the small-scale nature of the industry. With the increased predominance of speculative building, however, the importance of credit supply was heightened because this kind of building needed credit 'for the whole of the construction period – or even longer – rather than for part of it.'[32] These developments were undoubtedly encouraged and stimulated by the freely floating interest rates that resulted from the Bank Acts of 1819 and

1844 but their cumulative effects were to create that insecurity of boom or bust for which building now became notorious. Edward Capps, a surveyor and builder, described the relationship between credit and speculation before the *Select Committee on the Bank Acts* in 1857: 'Forty years ago, what houses were built on speculation were built out of the savings and profits of builders upon their ordinary jobbing business.' But, due to the fluctuations in the value of money and the competitiveness of the trade, not enough profit could now be made from a purely jobbing trade; large-scale speculation, therefore, became the only means of making money. A man:

Must go and take a large plot of ground, and he must perhaps engage to lay out twenty to fifty times the amount of his own capital upon it; and if he can get through his undertaking before any crash comes . . . he may make a good slice of money, but he is liable to be pulled up very suddenly by a failure in the finances.[33]

But in addition to the inevitable instability that was injected into the industry by the rise of speculation, the practice of tendering for contracts resulted in an anarchic competition which encouraged employers to underbid and operate on the smallest of profit margins with obvious consequences for the 'sweating' of the men. The desperate recklessness with which tenders were formulated is well-known; the important thing was to get the work and worry about the payment and profit afterwards. In his study of Camberwell, Dyos calculated that one of the most successful of the local speculative builders operated on a margin of around one half of one per cent – and this was at a time of very high activity in the industry. Edward Capps claimed that he had seen his tenders, which allowed for a 5% profit margin, underbid by some 20% of his prices.[34] It was in recognition of the consequences that would follow from this system of tendering for jobs that made it one of the central objections of the men in the 1830s to the introduction of this new organisation of the industry.[35]

The opposition of the men was, of course, well-founded and based not upon a 'conservative' attachment to 'tradition' but upon an attachment to relative security and stability. If they were to cope with the vicissitudes that now lurked in every corner of the industry, the employers needed to secure a maximum freedom to arrange and rearrange the conditions and means of working. Nothing was certain. Even once a contract was successfully taken up with a due allowance being made for unforeseen eventualities (and even Capps' moderate five per cent was a small enough margin to work with), the price of materials might suddenly rise, there might be unanticipated problems with any part of the construction, the weather might turn bad, or, worst of all, there might be difficulties with the men. And because these and other hidden dangers were all distinctly possible, the efficient exploitation of the labour force now assumed a far greater importance. Labour was the one segment of the industry which lay directly under the control of the employer. It was, in addition, the most visible – because the biggest – cost burden and the most volatile of the impediments to successful completion of a project. Labour was, thus, in a very immediate and direct way the source of success or of failure, of profits or potential bankruptcy; even 'scamping' of the work (a potential source of profits) was inseparable from 'sweating' of the labour force. Consequently, it was necessary that ways of working be devised to both minimise the threat that labour implicitly posed to the success of a project and to maximise the work that could be prised from its exertions. From the very beginning, therefore, and in a more critical way than in factory industry where there were other means available to counter such problems, productivity was of central concern to building employers. We shall have occasion to examine in more detail some of the methods created to unravel this difficult conundrum; for the moment let us focus upon sub-contracting as an example of the new imperatives that general contracting forced upon the industry.

Sub-contracting was a perpetual source of friction between the masters and the men but its precise extent and dimensions in nineteenth-century building are difficult to assess. Although it would be useful to know more about the exact mechanics of its operation, of its relationship to the piece-work with which it was in some trades frequently associated and of its impact upon the ownership structure in the industry, its integral relationship to general contracting is of prime importance and interest for our purposes. In the first place, there was a distinction to be drawn between what the men regarded as genuine sub-contracting – that which included finding the materials in addition to the labour – and that of sub-contracting for the labour alone. Although the former, too, was subject to the same kind of competitive, cost-cutting pressures as the latter, it was not opposed by the men because it preserved the small-master principle of each trade being responsible for its own part of the work and it retained the craft element in the process. But the second kind of sub-contracting for labour only was unknown before the emergence of general contractors who in London by the early 1830s had already established the practice of buying their own materials from the docks.[36] Its advantages to the masters were obvious and considerable; as in other industries it was a way of avoiding the problems of management; it answered the need to have at hand a ready supply of impermanent labour; and it thus ensured a maximum efficiency in labour utilisation.[37] But sub-contracting was not without its advantages to the men. As we suggested earlier, it was a new avenue of social mobility: sub-contractors were most frequently of the working, not the master, class. There was even a high proportion of union or ex-union men amongst the group and, indeed, in the 1830s some lodges of the Operative Stone Masons' Society were prepared to advocate the system: 'We believe the question of sub-contracting to be a question of right, and think it would be

unjust to prevent the members of the Society from the enjoyment of that
right whilst any masters unconnected with the society sub-contract . . . for
the stonework of any mansion they may have contracted to erect.'[38] It was,
of course, true that sub-contracting was a very uncertain way to social
betterment and the extent to which it made 'men that ought to be mere
journeymen into a sort of master' we cannot know, but our main concern
is with the clear and obvious disadvantages that sub-contracting involved.[39]

The ineluctable effect of sub-contracting was to subvert and to continually depress reasonable standards of working conditions. It inevitably
implied speed-ups, 'sweating,' 'chasing,' 'scamping,' an increased division
of labour and the general depression of wage levels. The competitiveness
charactcristic of general contracting was mirrored amongst the sub-
contractors who were subject to precisely the same pressures as the large
employers. Indeed, the pressures at this level of the industry were probably
even more intense because of the lesser resources of the sub-contractors
and, if the work was taken by the piece, the necessity to 'sweat' the men
even greater. In the bricklaying trade, for example, the system worked in
the following way:

A certain man takes a quantity of bricklaying work; he takes it from the master
builder [who] . . . has given in an estimate for it; the master builder lets it to
another . . . And he, expecting to realise a profit, would drive those men to do a
certain amount of work which [they] . . . would not be able to do properly, and
they would therefore scamp the work.[40]

The men hardly needed a parliamentary committee to reveal for them the
'evil' logic of the relationship between general contracting and the myriad
of sub-contractors that the system spawned; it was a part of their argument
in 1833, at which time it was explained that 'The whole management of
this [building] is placed in the hands of some great personage who employs
inferior masters at a profit to himself . . . These masters frequently contract
for an amount which will scarcely allow them to pay their men [and to
make a profit they have to ensure that] . . . the men perform more work for
less wages.'[41]

Sub-contracting was, thus, one of the new forms of work organisation
created by general contracting. In spite of the appearance of continuity in
the industry, therefore, general contracting had revolutionary effects upon
the nature and the structure of the work. It had replaced the small-master
craftsmen who contracted for a specific part of the work with the large
entrepreneur who contracted for the whole job and either employed his
own craftsmen or sub-contracted a portion of the work out. Jobbing work,
small speculations all continued to be important but were now subordinated to the imperatives of general contracting which included a sharp
competitiveness and a dependence upon speculation and credit fluctuations – all of which made the industry a mainstay of the bankruptcy

courts.[42] Unlike most other industries, building really was an industry where laissez-faire was an accurate description of reality. There never was the same kind of basis for the regulation and manipulation of competition in building that one could find elsewhere. Even though the large general contractors in London, for example, numbered only around fifty at mid-century, they had far less in common than did the similar sized group of families who dominated, say, Oldham's textile industry. They were in a different sort of immediate and direct face-to-face competition. When they banded together in 1859 to confront the men, they would allow no collective negotiation and insisted on preserving the individualism of meeting only with their own men.[43] Not until the early years of the twentieth century did such men begin to talk of rationalising the inherent instability of the industry by controlling competition.[44] A structural anarchy, thus, settled on the industry whose consequences for its labour relations were extremely profound.

Sub-contracting was one aspect of that anarchy but it was merely symptomatic of a deeper, more important, aspect of the question in which lies the key to understanding the history of industrial conflict and relations in the industry. It was clear that the ultimate imperative of the structural forces engendered by general contracting was that employers possess a total freedom to order and organise the work and the labour force as they pleased. In most other major industries of the industrial revolution there was, in the short to medium term between cyclical fluctuations, a certain interest for employers that stable conditions of work and wages should prevail. This was why employers in textiles, for example, 'learned' to deal with unions earlier than they did in building. But this interest was never the case in building where even on long-term, large-scale jobs, it might be necessary to alter the organisation of work to secure completion by the contracted date and thus attain profitability. Survival and profits depended not upon stability but upon the employers' complete authority to rearrange the work, to hire and fire at a moment's notice, to demand overtime working suddenly, to sub-contract; in other words, to order the conditions of working according to the particular and immediate needs of the moment. It was because employers needed this kind of total flexibility that the question of labour discipline was, ironically, of central significance in this most anarchic of industries. Built into the very structure of the industry was the imperative of an untrammelled employers' authority. This need was explained by the firm of Grissell and Peto during the 1841 Parliament strike when they pointed out:

What is called contract work . . . [is] undertaken for specific sums, and for which our calculations have . . . been made on the presumption that a good workman will execute a certain quantity of work . . . The position, therefore, in which we . . . must be placed by having the necessary authority of an employer wrested from

[us] . . . by a combination of workmen upon whose honesty and performance we calculate for the due performance of our engagements, may easily be imagined.[45]

It was this imperative that underlay the development of new methods of working such as sub-contracting or the extension of old ones such as piece-work in carpentry, this that demanded the opposition to the standard rate which continued longer in building than elsewhere, and this imperative that gave the opposition to unionism an extra special kind of force.[46] It was no coincidence, therefore, that building employers were the first to raise the cry of 'free labour,' nor that they were the first to try to organise a Free Labour Society twenty years before the shipping magnates, nor that they were, perhaps, among the first to use the telephone as a means of monitoring progress at the worksite from the head office.[47] Within this imperative for the freedom of the masters to exercise their total authority there lay, of course, the irresolvable conundrum that what was being demanded was a complete subordination of the men to the whim of the employers. But only thus could enterprise in the industry attain the maximum degree of certainty possible. This was how a Liverpool employer in 1846 expressed the imperative as an explanation of his opposition to unions:

So long as these combinations are permitted to interfere with the freedom which is the inalienable right of every man . . . so long as they promote discord, and cause uncertainty to rest upon every transaction, there is no security for any man in taking a Contract; nor is there the . . . hope for a return to a better state of things, unless the Unions . . . are completely broken up.[48]

But if the imperatives of general contracting demanded an unshackled exercise of masters' authority the dialectical response of the men could not be merely to resist 'oppression,' but also required that they protect themselves by attempting to control the anarchic conditions that were implicit in the new structure of the industry. And it was in this concrete dialectic of class struggle – a dialectic that revolved around the poles of 'freedom' and 'control' – that the pattern of modern industrial relations in the industry was forged and determined. It was from this basic equation that the course of labour history in the industry flowed. From this was to follow the constant and unremitting struggle for control over the conditions of work between the demands of the employers for 'freedom' and the restraints the men desired to protect themselves from freedom's deleterious consequences. In comparison to factory industry, the nature of building with its impermanent labour force gave this struggle a more pointed character for it made the efforts of both employers and men that much harder to achieve. There was little opportunity for the 'loyalty' to develop between masters and men that characterised certain factory districts. The problem of industrial discipline was more intractable than elsewhere, its solution more problematical. And it was, in part, simply because of this that building did not lag behind other, more 'advanced,' industries in the construction of sophisticated systems of industrial relations to address the problem. It was also because of the nature of the industry that this struggle for control was largely a local matter and not until the systems devised to deal with it were made national did it become 'nationalised.' In this, building may not be so different from other industries – one thinks of engineering – that were widely spread across the country. But it was in the intensity of that localness that the difference lay, so that the struggle in building fluctuated widely over time and space and has led historians to puzzle over the absence of distinct phases in the development of industrial relations, or to wonder at the 'meaning' of the irregular pattern of strike propensity in the industry.[49]

It was a further consequence of the context in which this struggle occurred that much of its character could be mistakenly seen as purely a defensive resistance to encroachments; as conducive, therefore, merely to a 'labour' rather than a 'revolutionary' or 'class' consciousness. This distinction derives, of course, from Lenin's famous diatribe against economism in *What is to be done?* but it is a distinction which allows no room for the struggle to control the productive process.[50] Yet it is just this struggle for control which provides the link between a 'labour' and a 'revolutionary' consciousness. It is true that it can only do so at particular times – and here the conditions external to 'spontaneity' become relevant – when that struggle can move beyond the workplace to link into the surrounding culture. The conditions under which this link can be forged are complex and special but they generally occur at a time when the whole society is undergoing some kind of social and industrial transformation. The 1830s and 1840s were obviously such a time which, from the perspective of control over the work process, saw the critical triumph of industrial capital's general authority. But this did not mean that the struggle for control was then to disappear and be subordinated to a purely 'economic' wages struggle. As we shall see, that former struggle continued but within a different, more localised, context. For the struggle over 'the appropriation of nature' is a continuing phenomenon which takes different forms at different times but which always contains within it the seeds of both a labour and a revolutionary consciousness.[51] Whether it becomes the one or the other will depend partly upon the pressures to which it is subjected by external forces but at all times it poses a continuing challenge to the basis of the capitalists' industrial authority. Both kinds of consciousness are integrally related. Revolutionary class consciousness which moves beyond a resistance to 'encroachments' to challenge the social basis of society cannot be understood apart from the more limited labour consciousness; for, as James Hinton has shown, it grows out of that continuing struggle for control. Consciousness is a dynamic phenomenon; the 'defensive' challenge of the building workers in the 1830s assumed an 'offensive' form once it was translated into the demand to control and monitor the productive process by the inspection of contracts. But, although this was its root, the seriousness of its challenge came not only from this but also from the fact that it was a part of the wider series of challenges that were being made to the whole spectrum of industrial society's structures.[52] A similar process will be seen to be in operation at the end of our period in the years before the First World War where the total situation was far more complex but where the challenge that was mounted contained implications far beyond a narrow industrial perspective. Yet, as we shall show, that challenge rested firmly upon the continuities of a 'defensive' struggle for control within industry without which the wider menace would not have been possible.

THE STRUGGLES OF THE 1830s AND 1840s

The main outline of the struggle against general contracting in the northwest has been adequately told before and there is no compelling reason to repeat it here.[53] What interests us is the duality between the defensive and the offensive aspects of the struggle. On the one hand, the men were fighting against the encroachments that were being made into the working conditions and, on the other, they clearly recognised these encroachments as a consequence of general contracting which they were seeking to challenge and to control. There had been, for example, a disastrous decline in wages since the mid-1820s which the men attributed, no doubt with good reason, to the: 'Illegal monopoly of other tradesmen [i.e., general contractors] which reduces our employers to that extremity that they are not able to pay workmen their just wages, or realise themselves any reasonable profits, which causes some unprincipled masters to take into their employ men for a few years servitude, etc., at a lower rate of wages.'[54] Between 1825 and 1832 masons' wages in Manchester had declined from 24/- to 18/- per week, and those of the bricklayers from 24/- to 17/- per week. Indeed, the general offensive which was led by the masons in June 1833 had been preceded by a bricklayers' strike in May for a standard rate.[55] In addition to the wages question, however, there were a whole series of other 'encroachments' that were now to be commonplace features of the building industry. From the joiners, for example, came the demand for an end to the hiring of boys and the sub-division of work by machinery;[56] from the plasterers, in May, came the admonition that 'you have not treated our rules *with that deference you ought to have done*' and a whole series of demands that would regulate the conditions of the work;[57] from the masons came the demand for an end to piecework.[58] A year later, the same battle was replayed in London where the hostility to general contracting manifested itself most sharply in the attempts of the men 'to control the discretion of the masters in the selection of their foremen.'[59]

As a group, this collection of demands – which also included the standard rate, daywork only and no overtime – were a sufficient attempt to restrict the freedom of the employers to occasion a fierce conflict. But they were only part of the story, for the actual aim of the men was to control the whole process of general contracting. In alliance with the small master craftsmen, they had achieved some success in this direction in 1832. A prohibition was declared against one man taking a whole contract and for a while it would seem that this was enforced. Possibly because there were fears that this restriction was being evaded, it was the attempt to go further and to demand that all contracts be submitted to the union for their approval that signified the extent to which the men were aiming to 'control' the trade and provided the occasion for the lockout and document.[60] It was at this point, we may note, that Owenism really became a relevant and meaningful ideology for the men. For Owenism, with its vision of 'a new moral world' of small, independent, craftsmen–producers where labour was the only index of value, spoke directly to the industrial transformation which the building workers could see happening with their own eyes. On the basis of their work experience, Owenism gave a legitimacy to their efforts to protect their living and 'craft' standards by controlling the conditions under which the work was organised. Conversely, for Owen, the effort of these men to halt the onward rush of competitive building and the 'evils' that followed in its wake, provided a practical manifestation of how the new moral world might arise out of the old. The movement to control general contracting was, thus, both 'progressive' and 'backward looking' as all revolutionary movements must be. The rhetoric that accompanied the movement was dominated by images of the real or imagined past; it was the language of men who were 'oppressed' and 'tyrannised,' who felt the 'degraded' state into which their 'once highly distinguished and respectable trade' had fallen, who would begin their addresses with the reflective and proud statement that 'when we take a retrospective view of the times past, what a particular change we perceive in the situation of our once respected Branch.'[61] But the demands that accompanied this appeal to the past were those which laid down an explicit challenge to a system based upon the need for a total authority of the employers. The challenge was one that threatened that authority; it was the challenge of class warfare. And if it did not overtly question the principle of capitalist ownership of the means of production, it was no less revolutionary for that because had the men been successful in achieving their aims the 'freedom' of the general contractors would have been so restricted and controlled that ownership in itself would have meant little. It was, therefore, with considerable justification that the masters responded to the challenge with an assertion of their authority and a determination to break the unity of the men. The language of masters' authority, which we shall meet again, now appears for the first time. The men's demands, they argued, amounted to the establishment of 'a system of dictation which would have the effect of making the masters humble dependents on the will of the journeymen.'[62] Once the struggle clearly began to assume these dimensions, the smaller masters broke off their alliance with the men – realising that 'the present dispute is not about wages; but . . . a sort of struggle in order to ascertain whether the employers or the operatives are to be masters.' However reluctantly, the smaller employers knew where their ultimate loyalties had to lie.[63]

This was, indeed, the issue of the conflicts in the northwest and in London in 1834; they were the first time that the dialectic of freedom and control was to clearly manifest itself; and from this point onwards it is only within the context of that dialectic that we can make any sense of the course and pattern of industrial relations in the trades of the industry. It was the totality of the efforts to challenge general contracting that made the conflicts of the early 1830s unique but the dialectic that called them into being may also be clearly seen in the celebrated Parliament strike of 1841. On 13 September 1841, the 230 masons, together with an unknown number of labourers, who were working at the site of the new Houses of Parliament went on strike. The issue was the 'tyranny' of the foreman, George Allen, whose reputation had earned him the nickname of the 'Black Prince.'[64] The strike lasted until May 1842, it received the support of masons from all over the country, attracted the attention of the Chartists and some Radical Members of Parliament and caused Feargus O'Connor to make one of his infrequent forays into the capital.[65] The strike's impact upon the Operative Society of Stone Masons, whose resources were crippled for a while, went deep; there were cases of blacklegs from the strike still being pursued in the 1860s. Although the focus of this strike was narrower than those of 1833–34, the *Narrative* written at the time by the general secretary illustrated how it continually threatened to break out into the wider perspective of those earlier struggles.[66]

What was it about this strike that could make it into such an important event for the masons? Allen's tyranny was, indeed, reprehensible. A whole series of accusations, never effectively refuted and some independently confirmed, testified to its oppressive force. Until stopped by the contractor, he had compelled men to buy beer from a pub owned by a relative; he had locked up a water pump used by the labourers; he had discharged men for lending or borrowing tools; he had refused to allow rest breaks ('which they have heretofore been accustomed to have'); he had abused a man who took leave to bury his wife, another was fined because he was off work sick, and another was refused permission to visit his sick mother in Manchester (and only got it when the men threatened to strike); and he had continually harassed and abused a man crippled from an accident on the job.[67] These were the 'tyrannies' that were indignantly paraded before the public meetings as the causes of the strike, as the reasons for the demand that Allen be dismissed. And it was clearly true that they were abuses strongly resented by the men: there had been at least one deputation to the contracting firm of Grissell and Peto to complain of Allen's treatment of the man who wished to visit his mother.[68] But they were 'issues' that bear a close resemblance to the pattern noted by industrial sociologists in contemporary strikes of accumulated grievances later being brought forward to justify a strike that has deeper roots. And in this case – unusual in the historical reconstruction of strike episodes – we have some evidence as to what those roots were. For it was not until six days after the strike began that this catalogue of charges was developed to justify the strike; what is more, the resolution that the work group originally passed demanding Allen's dismissal gave as its reason that he required them to do more than a fair day's work.[69]

The meaning of Allen's tyranny was twofold. In the first place, he was well-known as a 'chasing' foreman. Indeed, there had been a similar strike against him for his attempts to introduce piecework on the London–Birmingham railway construction in 1837. His predilection for piecework was notorious; by some he was even credited with inventing the system.[70] And several weeks before the 1841 strike began, there was an attempt by the men to restrict the amount of work done per day as a response to Allen's chasing. On 4 August, a meeting of masons had fined William Geggie – who was presumably Allen's bell-horse – and a strike for his dismissal was just barely avoided.[71] At some of the public meetings this other form of 'tyranny' received some attention amidst the litany of personal oppression. Thus, at a meeting in the Woolwich Town Hall in October:

He hoped the day would never come when Englishmen would have to be driven with the whip . . . What man of feeling or of principle would force men to attempt a certain quantum of work which would at once destroy the physical energies and bring on a premature old age? . . . A fair day's work for a fair day's wages ought to be the principle of every man.[72]

And, at another meeting with the representatives of other trades, it was 'Thought unfair to get a man of great physical strength [presumably Geggie] and urge him to do a certain quantity of work, and then go around to all the men, many of whom had worked for years for the firm, and to tell them "if you do not come up to this standard you will be discharged." '[73] But, in the second place, Allen's tyranny was only in part a reflection of his horrible personality; it was more a reflection of the logic of general contracting. Allen was a good foreman for the contractors; that was the major reason why they refused to dismiss him. His 'tyranny' consisted of attempting to impose an 'industrial' discipline on the men – the locking of the water pump and the refusal to allow rest periods were particularly good examples of that – but all of the charges against him may be seen in the light of the need to establish a regularity of work at the maximum speed. From the employer's point of view, 'chasing' and 'tyranny' were the attributes of a good foreman; they were a natural expression of the discipline necessary to general contracting: the faster the work was done, the more punctuality and regularity was attained, the greater the profit that could be gained. Grissell admitted all this in an interview with the men a few days after the strike had occurred:

> To complain of his foreman's conduct to him was perfectly useless . . . On a works so extensive as he [Allen] superintended, it was necessary that a discipline similar to that maintained in the army or navy should be enforced, and the masons, in not quietly submitting to it, must be bent on ruining the firm . . . the competency of the foreman to superintend such work would consist in his being such a man as he was . . . a harsh and severe individual would only answer his purpose.[74]

It was for these reasons that the employers could hardly afford to let the issue pass unchallenged. The strike could easily have been resolved by dismissing Allen but had they done so the underlying problem would have remained unattended and the role of the foreman as the employer's agent of authority would have been delivered a serious blow. And this authority was axiomatic for the employers' freedom to impose working arrangements best suited to their needs. The issue had, after all, been festering in London at least since 1834 and Grissell and Peto had themselves been bested once before on this very question. Although the men do not seem to have been claiming the right to choose the foreman, the employers clearly realised that the implications of a masons' victory would have made that question ambiguous: 'They might be called upon to dismiss other foremen, and thus the combination might turn out to be a curse . . . as employers of every description . . . would be laid prostrate at the feet of the workmen.'[75] But, in the main, the authority dimensions of the struggle were rather more complex and attenuated than that. It was a 'matter of principle,' an attempt to 'control the price of labour and regulate the quantity of work to be performed,' whether 'we are to be treated like beasts of burdens, or . . . as moral and intellectual beings.' The ultimate question was who was to decide the working arrangements and what constituted a 'reasonable amount of labour.'[76] To sacrifice Allen would be to surrender to the men's right to circumscribe and limit the freedom demanded by the conditions under which general contractors were obliged to exist.

In addition, therefore, to revealing the implicit struggle between the master's authority and the workmen's control, this strike is interesting as presenting in a stark light an early illustration of the 'marginal' situation foremen occupied between employers and men. The dilemma of the foreman's role as an agent of employers' authority who needed to ensure the viability of that authority by maintaining good relations with the men was now to be a constant theme of modern industrial relations – a theme which has received its due attention from industrial sociologists but which has been generally ignored by historians.[77] Indeed, this dilemma was realised at the time. There is a very interesting account of a meeting of foremen in November 1841 where the issue caused a protracted discussion on the attitude they should take to the strike and the role they should play. There were those who believed that a foreman's prime duty was 'to carry out the works with a profit to their masters' and those who wished to preserve their links with the men. For the first group, it was claimed that 'foremen in a large works are almost compelled to be irritable. If I had been in Allen's place, it is likely I might have acted in a similar manner.' The foremen it was pointed out:

Had a duty to perform; and they were at times obliged to adopt stringent measures . . . Foremen were placed in an awkward position; they . . . were compelled to be strict; but if conduct like that of the men to Allen were to be submitted to . . . what would be the consequences . . . many of Allen's men were now working under a foreman in their establishments, and he had already felt their insolence. He was almost afraid to speak to them.

On the other hand, there were those who, with a mixture of realism for their situation and sympathy for the men, felt that 'the name of Allen would be no credit to them. If the men were treated as men they would do a fair day's work . . . Our situation cannot last forever; we may ourselves be placed in a similar position, and be compelled to act as they [the men] have done.' The meeting had been called to discuss the formation of a foreman's society but it was felt necessary to delay any decision on this because 'public sympathy was so in favour with the masons that many foremen who might be favourable to it, would not attend this evening as it looked suspicious whether the object was not to oppose the men on strike.'[78] It would be too much to claim that this strike resolved the tension caused by the foreman's marginality. Strikes against their 'tyrannies' continued, but foremen continued to be eligible for union membership and attempts to deprive them of this right or to prohibit their appearance at lodge meetings failed in recognition of the value they could be to the employment of union men or as upholders of union standards.[79] It is not without significance, however, that never again was the union to support a strike against a foreman and that their role as agents of the employers' authority was, in the final analysis, unambiguously recognised.[80]

THE NINE HOURS ISSUE

It would be a mistake to exaggerate the shift that occurred from the dramatic challenges of 1833 and 1841 to the more prosaic demands for a reduction

of hours that formed the core of the conflicts of 1846 and 1859. If the
challenge to the very system of work organisation that marked 1833 was
not maintained this, in itself, was quite unremarkable.[81] Once the working-
class movement had been decisively defeated as it was in the 1840s and
once the ideological perspectives of Owenism and Chartism had been
replaced and absorbed into a variant of the dominant culture, then we
could hardly expect strike movements to reflect anything more than a
purely industrial perspective, with an occasional and obfuscating genuflect
in the direction of the values of liberal hegemony. But, paradoxically, this
makes those later conflicts of even greater interest. For if, from one perspective, they were marked by a narrowing of focus to the work situation
alone they also represented the development of specific techniques and
efforts to control the imperatives of the work structures. And this was
hardly regressive for it was in this arena that the ultimate course of labour
history was to be decided. These conflicts represented, in a sense, the
industrial perspective of the driving in upon itself that marked the mid-
Victorian working class; a coming to terms with the realities within which
men now had to operate given the undisputable triumph of industrial
capitalism by the early fifties, and the development of strategies and tactics
to control and to tame that reality. Nor should the importance and significance of this be allowed to escape us. Indeed, much of the rest of this
book will be concerned with the profound consequences that resulted from
these often undramatic but cumulatively very impressive efforts. And if the
context within which this occurred was different to that of the earlier
struggles, this should not be allowed to disguise the continuity provided
by the on-going imperatives of general contracting and the dialectic of
'freedom' and 'control' that composes the central features of our story.

To understand the conflicts that erupted over the demand for the nine
hours day in 1846 and 1859 – the first in the northwest and the other in
London – it is best to start with the rhetoric the masters used to characterise and to condemn the demands and actions of the men.[82] And if we
do this there are three themes which immediately gain our attention. First,
there seems to have been little distinction drawn between the conflicts of
1846 and 1859 with those of the past. Indeed, in 1846 the experience of the
thirties was a constantly recurring point of reference to which there were
frequent allusions. At a meeting of the masters of Liverpool and Manchester (the focal points of the struggles) Samuel Holme – a leading opponent of the men in 1833 who reprinted a pamphlet he had written on that
earlier occasion – pointed out that if the 'union' had been properly dealt
with in the 1830s they would not be facing the 'dictation' of the men now.[83]
In the second place, this was not an unimportant indication of the be-
leaguerement the masters felt; for the same themes of authority pervade
their castigation of the men. The codewords they used were those of

power: 'control,' 'interference' with the 'internal management of the various employers.'[84] These were from 1846, but there had been no discernible modification by 1859. The Address of the Master Builders to their Workmen in August 1859, for example, virtually ignored the ostensible issue of the nine hours day (except to claim that it threatened bankruptcy), launched into a torrent of denunciation against the 'dictation' of the Conference, and painted a lurid picture of secret meetings, intimidations by 'piquets,' spies and terrorism.[85] At a meeting of employers with the Home Secretary – who was very puzzled because he believed the main issue to be the nine hours – one builder:

Said that the real question . . . was whether the masters were to be allowed to conduct their own establishments, or they were [sic] to continue to live under the thralldom of the trade societies. Things had now come to such a pass that really the matter of the nine hours . . . was not of so much importance as securing the right of the master to employ who he pleased.[86]

But, in the third place, these blanket denunciations of the threats posed by the men were not mere empty shells of class hostility; they were accompanied by the sense that these struggles were climacterics to several years of growing tension and guerrilla warfare. As one Liverpool newspaper editorialised in 1846, the lockout was an attempt to put an end to the 'petty annoyances in their workshops . . . and [to attain] a security against "strikes" for a fixed period.'[87] The uncertainty that prevailed over what the men would next be demanding bore an obvious relevance to the cry for 'security' as an essential condition of successful contracting:

If the men at Birkenhead had gained their demands . . . before the summer had passed a further demand would have been made . . . and this evil would have gone on until there would have been no possibility of calculating what the cost of an edifice would be until the completion, and those who had contracts on hand . . . would have risked ruin, if not be ruined.[88]

Precisely the same pattern was present in 1859: 'We were not only embarrassed by the nine hours question but by a host of smaller but most important questions which were hampering us to an extent that it rendered it impossible for us to conduct our business.'[89] The *Report* of the temporarily created Central Association of Master Builders agreed:

Your committee were fully of the opinion that the time had arrived when it was imperatively necessary to grapple with the rights of the master builders in the legitimate control of the businesses, and that the demand [for the nine hours] . . . was only . . . a further development, of the arbitrary and extravagant demands which the building operatives of London had been forcing on their employers during recent years.[90]

The petty annoyances to which the master referred were not just part of an incidental background to conflict; they provide, in fact, the key to understanding the meaning and significance of the strikes of these years. But in order to grasp just where their importance lay, it is necessary to move away from the generality of rhetoric into the specific and concrete reality of the events of 1846 and 1859 themselves.

For several years before 1846 there had been a growing tension in the northwest which revolved around the familiar theme of the larger employers' 'encroachments' upon working conditions. Amongst carpenters a prominent issue was that of craft training, the masters' attempts to enforce shorter terms of apprenticeship met with the men's response of an insistence upon a restriction of numbers.[91] In addition, there was the question of candlelight working, an issue that first emerged concurrent with general contracting and which had reached what would seem to be its climactic struggle in a large and violent strike directed at the Manchester contractors of Pauling and Henfrey in 1844 and 1845.[92] From all other branches of the industry the same kind of tension was visible. Like the carpenters, the slaters and plumbers were both involved in efforts at apprenticeship regulation. In early 1845, the bricklayers – in probable alliance with the militant brickmakers – had struck against the use of 'illegal' bricks; and over the past year bricklayers, masons and carpenters had all gained shortened hours on Mondays and Saturdays as well as an increase in wages. Indeed, it was reported that the sum total of these economic advances had increased the wages bill by 22% over the pre-1845 cost.[93] If this was true, then the restriction of production that the bricklayers and their labourers were engaged in enforcing must have pressed very heavily upon the employers. In 1845, for example, the labourers had reduced the number of bricks to be carried in a hod from fourteen to twelve and refused to move materials in wheelbarrows.[94]

Probably because their efforts to control 'encroachments' had been the most successful, it was the masons who seem to have initiated the movement – although they were certainly matched in militancy by the carpenters. In September 1845, the masons delivered a circular to the Liverpool masters which give notice that they would no longer work with boys who were not legally bound, nor could apprentices be older than 16 years and no master was to be allowed to take an apprentice until he had been in business and employed two masons for at least one year.[95] Four months later a similar notice was sent to the Manchester employers. In addition to these efforts to regulate more completely the labour supply, there were constant local actions against pieceworking and overtime. The Manchester men had abolished overtime in 1841 but were forced to re-address the problem in 1843; similarly, Birkenhead took action against the reappearance of piecework in 1844. The Central Committee of the Society devoted a great deal of attention in 1845 to exhortations against piecework and approved a large number of grants to strike for its abolition.[96]

It should be clear that the pattern suggested here is the dichotomy we noted earlier as implicit in general contracting between the masters' efforts to 'encroach' upon the conditions of work in order to maintain a maximum flexibility and freedom in the organisation of the workplace and the efforts of the men to control that freedom by regulating the conditions under which the work was to be done. But if this speaks to the nature of the pattern, it says nothing of the score in the petty contests at the frontier of control. Certainly, the impression we gain from the generally uninformative local newspapers and the more revealing *Fortnightly Returns* of the Operative Stone Masons' Society is not only that the men were aggressively pushing their claims but that they were meeting with some considerable success. Fortunately, it is unnecessary to rely solely upon our impressions to form a clearer picture of what was happening at the workplace during these years. We have to hand a set of masons' strike statistics, to which we shall refer again, which enable us more surely to assess the impressions that we gain from the other evidence.[97]

The picture that emerges from the forty-four recorded masons' strikes that occurred in the northwest between 1840 and 1846 is as shown in Table 1.

Table 1. *Strike issues in the northwest 1840–46 as percentage of total*

	No.		(1836–96)
Wages	23	52.3	(31.1)
Hours	2	4.5	(7.3)
Organisation of work	8	18.2	(9.9)
Conditions of work	6	13.6	(11.4)
Control over labour	5	11.4	(19.8)
Craft enforcement	0	0.0	(14.2)
Working rules	0	0.0	(5.5)
Other	0	0.0	(0.9)

Wages, as might be expected, formed the largest single category and of the total strikes in the area 31.8% were against a reduction and 20.3% were to secure an advance. The small percentage of hours strikes should not surprise us, they always formed a small cluster of the total population and for reasons that we shall discuss at a later point, tended to occur in the form of large general strike movements rather than small, work group job actions. Strikes over the organisation of work were evidently more important in this period than they were over the period as a whole; furthermore, the issues in this category of strikes – piecework, sub-contracting and overtime – were just those where general contracting most demanded employer's freedom. All of the strikes in this category between 1840 and 1846 were over piecework which had the second largest single number of strikes (8) after those against reductions of wages (12). Finally, the remaining categories of 'conditions of work' and 'control over the labour force' are of interest because the issues within these categories – the demand for sheds, disputes over meal hours and lodgings money, the enforcement of union membership and strikes against the dismissal of union men – were all issues that reflected a confident militancy amongst the men. They were, in some ways, peripheral to the encroachments of general contracting and they represented not so much a defensive reaction to these encroachments as one which was engaged in expanding the men's sphere of control. Strikes on these issues seldom occurred during depression years nor when, for some other reason, the men were in a weakened or disunited position. The erection of sheds for the men to work in made working conditions more comfortable but they were essentially a 'luxury' item to be secured when other, more central issues were not pressing. It is curious that strikes over craft enforcement issues and specifically on apprenticeship do not show up in the statistics but this may merely signify that the masons, at least, had already secured tight control over the question or that they were biding their time on an issue which in a period of booming activity did not assume a major importance. In any case, the absence of this issue did not imply that the men were incapable of enforcing their demands, as we can see if we compare the results of these strikes with those for the whole period 1836–96 – whose figures are placed in parentheses.

Table 2. *Results of strikes in the northwest 1840–46*

	Victory %	Failure %	Compromise %
Wages	75.0 (69.0)	18.7 (22.3)	6.3 (8.7)
Hours	100 (70.3)	0.0 (23.2)	0.0 (6.5)
Organisation of work	80.0 (75.7)	20.0 (19.8)	0.0 (4.5)
Conditions of work	100 (81.7)	0.0 (14.6)	0.0 (3.8)
Control over labour	66.7 (77.7)	33.3 (21.6)	0.0 (0.7)
All strikes	79.3 (74.8)	17.2 (19.9)	3.4 (5.3)

With the exception of 'control over labour' strikes, each category is marked by a high level of success. And this confirms what the qualitative evidence would lead us to expect, that the men were not only capable of defending themselves against 'encroachments' (they achieved an 85% success rate in resisting reductions of wages) but were also capable of expanding their control over the work to secure the provision of sheds and other 'privileges.' That the men were capable of such success was due, in part, to the building boom of these years which peaked in the early part of 1846 and whose collapse came just at the moment that the men presented their demands for the nine hours.[98] But it is clear that 1846 was the climax to a growing offensive by the men. The 'petty annoyances' to which the masters were subjected thus assume a central importance; they were the manifestation of the men's success in expanding their control over the productive process. It is, therefore, easy to understand why the masters felt that the time had come to take a stand; their 'freedom' to manipulate the arrangement of the work was increasingly circumscribed by the 'control' that could be exerted by the men.[99]

In the pantheon of labour's 'great events' the massive struggle of the London building operatives against their employers in the lockout of 1859 has always been assured of an honoured place. It was sustained for eight months, eventually petering out in March 1860 when it was soon succeeded by the strike against hourly payment which lasted into 1861. In its early stages, 24,000 men out of the total of 40,000 building workers in the city were involved. It has been regarded as 'distinctly the starting point of a new phase of the labour question,' as the beginnings of the serious discussion of trade unionism and its role in society, as stimulating the habit of cooperation between the various parts of the labour movement (signified by the creation of the London Trades Council), as the event which forged that potent mid-Victorian alliance between labour and the positivists, and as marking the arrival of new model unionism in the building trades.[100] It is certainly not our wish to quarrel with the exalted level to which these assessments have raised the conflict; they are, in the main, true. Nor is it our intention to retrace the furrows so ably ploughed by those who have preceded us in their accounts of this dispute. And whilst none would wish to deny the 'heroic' quality of the battle, nor the importance of its impact upon such sensitively attuned social observers as Frederic Harrison, it remains true that most previous accounts have located the struggle as a way station in the political progress and evolution of the organised Labour Movement. So completely has this view predominated that we have tended to lose sight of the fact that the dispute was essentially an industrial struggle which then attained the status of a political myth. It was, we should remember, the first large-scale attempt by the London building workers to control their working conditions by the 'modern' device of an hours reduction. As such, it also established a legacy of industrial mass action in London which was to revive again in 1872, 1891 and, most importantly, in 1914. The industrial dimensions of the contest, therefore, deserve an attention they have not yet received.

The origins of the movement were to be found in the small carpenters' and joiners' clubs of the metropolis. It was George Potter's Progressive Society which on 25 February 1858, initiated the first meeting of delegates to discuss the question of a reduction of hours.[101] Over the next nine months a constantly growing agitation developed; first by means of local trade meetings which often included bricklayers, masons and painters and at which the leadership of the future Conference of Building Trades emerged, then by mass meetings at the Exeter Hall, and finally in November 1858 by the presentation of a memorial from the major sections of the trade in joint conference.[102] By April 1859 a conflict was clearly imminent. In that month the masters called together the moribund Builders' Society to refuse and condemn the nine hours demand; on 21 July, a strike erupted at the shop of Messrs Trollopes and was immediately followed by a general lockout and the presentation of the notorious 'document.'[103]

In order to understand the 1859 movement, it is necessary to begin with the evolution of arguments that were used to justify the nine hours day, for although they were to culminate in the 'respectable' paradigms of social and moral 'improvement' it was not from this point that they began. The movement had originated with the large number of carpenters (about one third of the total) who worked in the ten per cent of workshops where machinery was used. It was their fears about the effects of the machine which dominated the early justifications of the nine hours demand. Undoubtedly, the commercial crisis of 1857 and the hard winter of 1857–58 (which made that year worse than 1879 or 1886 for unemployment)[104] drew the attention of the men to the 'rapid and enormous increase in machinery' which has 'supplanted manual labour . . . and caused unemployment.'[105] The 1850s had seen machine joinery make its first widespread forays into the trade and in 1854 the carpenters of Bolton and Nottingham had conducted significant, if futile, strikes to halt its use.[106] But the aim of the London men was somewhat different. Learning, perhaps, from the failures of their northern brethren, they recognised that 'machinery was not in itself a curse, but a blessing . . . so long as those who had to do with it would make it a blessing and not a curse.' Thus, they sought to control the machine: 'In time they must take advantage of machinery, and not let it take advantage of them, as it did at the present time . . . The employer had derived advantage from the employment of machinery, but what had the working man derived from it?'[107]

But the machine was only one amongst many agents and symbols of exploitation and as the other trades began to join with the carpenters, the issues began to broaden. Thus, the masons had attempted to ban systematic overtime in 1853, the bricklayers – who as soon as they entered the movement brought the issue to the fore – did the same in April 1859, and the memorial presented in June 1859 included a demand for the prohibition of overtime.[108] Piecework, too, was an issue that during the previous decade had constantly harried the bricklayers, plasterers and masons. T. Nelson March, an architect who made a study of the roots of the dispute, claimed that the masters continually tried to force piecework on the bricklayers and plasterers; and this is confirmed by the evidence of the men who claimed that 'the system of piece and task work that the masters endeavour to force them into is oppressive and productive of bad work,' and by that of the masters who complained of the restrictions placed upon this method of working.[109] In 1856 there had been a strike at Kelk's yard when it looked as if that firm was to be the stalking horse for a general introduction of the piece system and resolutions had been passed by the Builders' Society piously supporting the system as improving the condition of the industrious man and condemning restrictions upon it as 'subversive of the whole principle of contracts and the rights of labour.'[110]

These were the kinds of arguments, and especially that of the machine, that dominated the discussions in the early days of the movement. It was totally appropriate, however, that the justification of the nine hours on the grounds of its moral and social benefits should make its entrance on 11 June 1858 when the first mass meeting was held at Exeter Hall. This meeting marked the emergence of the movement out of the secret world of the club houses into the open world of 'respectable' society. It is not to be thought that the argument had been absent before but until that moment it had not figured as the primary justification that it now became. It was George Potter who, contrary to the floor speeches at this meeting, first thrust the 'improvement' argument to the fore in preparation for the memorial to be presented in July. In this memorial the claim for the working classes to reap 'some benefit from . . . [the] extensive introduction' of machinery still held its primacy but it was now linked with the need for increased leisure time. And in the final memorial of the spring of 1859, the machinery argument occupied a very subordinate role to that of 'improvement.'[111] It was as the movement attracted growing public attention and especially with the publication of Evan Daniel's prize essay on the question – which served as a public manifesto for the movement – that the resolutions at the mass meetings began to change their character from statements of the baneful effects of machinery to the health and moral advantages of a shorter work day.[112] If one looked at the floor speeches, however, it was the old issues of machinery, overtime and piecework which continued to provide the heart of the men's case. In part, this shift in the presentation of the men's arguments had to do with the general trade character that the movement had assumed by early 1859. But, more importantly, it reflected the need to present a public face upon which middle-class opinion could gaze with approval and in this public relations exercise the men were enormously successful, for the amount of support they received from 'respectable' society was quite unprecedented.

This development in the nature of the argument of the movement was important because it disguised, and has continued to disguise, a proper appreciation of the 'deeper issues involved than appear on the surface.'[113] We have already noted the questions of machinery, overtime and piecework, but there were also others which it is appropriate to mention here. Conflicts over the authority of foremen, for example, were still very much alive. To quote the architect Nelson Marsh again:

Many masters, it is said, take strangers as foremen, instead of raising their own men by rotation if their workmen belong to clubs or trade societies . . . The workmen have no respect for the foremen so placed over them, the masters, to insure obedience, invest their foremen with extreme powers, even to the discharging or engaging men without consulting the masters . . . The foremen also . . . subject the workmen to small reductions in their daily pay for occasional stoppages [like] showers . . . and the workmen . . . lose half an hour in pay. This was not formerly the case, and the men used cheerfully to 'fetch up' their lost time . . . The masters insist on retaining their foremen however obnoxious they may be to the men.

Similar complaints were echoed by the plasterers who asserted that 'the masters were in the habit of taking low contracts, and then placed some tyrannical foremen over the working classes in order to make them work like slaves against each other.'[114]

In the light of the above, it is interesting to pay some attention to the event that actually precipitated the conflict. According to both the Webbs and Postgate – in what is a nice vignette of the 'heroic' view of labour struggles – the strike was sparked by the dismissal of a member of the deputation which presented the memorial at Trollope's workshop. Enraged at this, the men struck spontaneously without consulting the Conference which was forced to ratify their action and call the rest of Trollope's men out; the document and lockout followed in the course of the succeeding week.[115] But twenty years later, another account was given by George Trollope's brother who claimed that the mason had been dismissed by Trollope himself because he was not producing a sufficient quantity of work. And, in fact, there were suggestions at the time that this was more than a simple case of victimisation, it being reported that the man was dismissed because he was 'working badly.'[116] Now, none of this would really matter except for the fact that it conforms to the case which the masters were to continually present of the conflict as one of authority; and, in particular, it jibes with the catalogue of 'union' restrictions that figured in the master's meetings and their letters to the press in the weeks preceding the strike.[117] But in order to place all this in its proper context let us turn again to our set of masons strike statistics to see what they reveal about the course of industrial conflict in London in the 1850s.

In the first place the issues of the twenty recorded strikes for the decade show a distribution at marked variance with the national pattern for the whole period.

Table 3. *Strike issues in London 1850–60 as percentage of total*

	No.		(1836–96)
Wages	4	20	(31.1)
Hours	7	35	(7.3)
Organisation of work	5	25	(9.9)
Conditions of work	1	5	(11.4)
Control over labour	3	15	(19.8)

But the importance of this lies not so much in the differences themselves as in the character of the strikes in each category which, in the main, are revealed to be primarily defensive. Thus, three quarters of the wages strikes were against reductions; 25% of all strikes were against an extension of working hours, only 10% for a reduction; the relative absence of 'conditions of work' strikes reinforces the defensive character of conflict during these years. And, as in 1846, the relative prominence of the organisation of work category (in the main, strikes against piecework) confirms what we suspected from other evidence about the importance of these issues.

Our second point confirms this general picture, for the results of these strikes all showed a markedly high level of failure rates in comparison to 1846 and to the total period surveyed whose figures are again in parentheses. What this suggests, of course, is that at every significant level the men were losing their battle against the encroachments of the employers.

Table 4. *Results of strikes in London 1850–60*

	No.	Victory %	Failure %	Compromise %
Wages	3	33.3 (69.0)	66.7 (22.3)	0.0 (8.7)
Hours	7	42.9 (70.3)	42.9 (23.2)	14.2 (6.5)
Organisation of work	5	40.0 (75.7)	40.0 (19.8)	20.0 (4.5)
Conditions of work	1	100 (81.7)	0.0 (14.6)	0.0 (3.8)
Control over labour	1	100 (77.7)	0.0 (21.6)	0.0 (0.7)
All strikes	17	47.1 (74.8)	41.2 (19.9)	11.8 (5.3)

But there is a further twist to all this. For, if it is clear that, unlike 1846, the employers were pushing their 'frontier of control' forward and were enjoying a considerable degree of success, it is not so clear that they were equally successful in weakening the resistance of the men who remained militantly willing to strike for above-average periods of time. This can be seen if we look at the distribution of strikes by length in London and especially if we compare those figures with the average lengths for the country as a whole over the decade and for the total period.

Table 5. *Length of strikes in London 1850–60*

	No.	London %	(Country) %	(1836–96) %
1 day or less	3	18.7	(37.4)	(32.3)
2–7 days	3	18.7	(30.4)	(31.2)
8–14 days	4	25.0	(18.7)	(16.3)
15+ days	6	37.5	(13.4)	(20.0)

Neither are these figures merely a statistical freak caused by the over-weighting presence of 1859 – eight of the ten strikes which lasted more than one week are recorded before 1859. London can be seen to be at marked variance both with the national figures for the decade and with those for the whole period.

What this paradox of low success rates but lengthy resistance appears to suggest is that the balance of power at the workplace was in a state of considerable disequilibrium. The masters' encroachments were unsuccessfully, yet stubbornly, resisted by the men in such a way as to deny either side a general advantage. In this respect, it should be remembered that the previous ten years had seen some success for the men even (and in spite of the statistics) in the area of hours reductions.[118] The short Saturday had been won by the carpenters, bricklayers and labourers in 1851; and the masons had secured the same 'privilege' in 1855.[119] Indeed, it was the success of the masons of the northwest in securing the half-day Saturday in 1856 which induced the London masons to try to gain the same advantage for themselves in 1858. Only when this attempt failed did they join the Conference to agitate for the straight nine hours.[120]

1859, then, was a climax to the tensions we have discussed but it was also a function of the basic stalemate that had developed. It is this that explains why the strike took several months to erupt, both sides knowing that a conflict was inevitable but neither side quite sure how it was to be brought about. The men, for example, did not employ the rolling strike tactic they had tried in 1846 and even the July ballot on the tactics to be followed revealed a sizable minority opposed to a strike.[121] Likewise, although the masters consistently refused either to grant the demand or to negotiate and could see the movement gaining momentum, they did not launch a pre-emptive lockout as they had done in 1846. For both sides it was critical that these stalemated tensions be resolved but both quailed at the uncertain nature of the battle itself in which neither had a decided advantage. But if both 1846 and 1859 represent climacterics to the growing tension between the logic of general contracting and the attempts of the men to control that logic, we still have to explain the relevance of the demand for the nine hours day to this equation.

In the first place, it is not irrelevant to note the tactical benefits that derived for the men from a focus around this issue. It was a question upon which all the trades of the industry could unite without fear of the complications of sectionalism. This was especially important in a large and diverse city like London where even within trades uniformity was hard to achieve;[122] and the masons had received a recent lesson in the limitations of the sectional approach when they had failed to gain the Saturday half-day. It is easy and dangerous to overestimate the importance of sectionalism in the industry. In the past emphasis has been placed upon the centrifugal tendencies of the different vested interests to explain, for example, the continuing persistence of craft unionism as an organisational form.[123] But, of course, there was nothing very surprising about different trades with different customs and needs acting separately. Furthermore, there was nothing necessarily pejorative attached to a sectionalist activity which was, in fact, frequently relevant to the interests of all the trades. The pattern of wage demands in the industry illustrated this: one section's demand for a wages increase served to operate like a 'strike in detail' which, if successful, immediately legitimised demands from the other sections to maintain the traditional differential.[124] In general, it was neither possible nor desirable for the men to unite on a wages demand when the differentials and status distinctions between the trades were still so important and this pattern did not break down until after the First World War when technological and organisational changes had begun to obliterate those distinctions. Neither was it appropriate to unite over matters of restrictive rules or practices where the interest and policies of the trades were also very different. But an appeal for a reduction of hours left all these sectional differences undisturbed, it benefited and affected all the trades to the same extent and in the same way and was, therefore, an appropriate issue for united action. And this was especially true because of the respectable gloss that could be imparted to an issue which had for some time been a shared value between the working class and the 'advanced' sections of the bourgeoisie.[125] The leisure argument itself has to be viewed almost totally in this light; the incentive for reducing hours of labour does not derive now, nor should we assume that it did then, from the desire for increased time for 'rational recreation.'[126]

Where, then, did the demand derive its force and potency? The usual answer to that question is that it was a reflection of the desire of the men to combat unemployment.[127] And, indeed, there is a certain amount of truth to this: certainly, the 1859 movement was conducted under the shadow of that problem. But, coming at the tail end of a three-year boom, 1846 does not fit this model nor does it explain why the employers should respond on both occasions with the rhetoric of 'authority' and their 'rights.' In fact, this argument is not so much wrong as incomplete. Reducing unemployment was only one amongst a number of ways in which the hours issue was calculated to reduce the rate of exploitation and enhance the control of the men.

When the men claimed that the nine hours would prove 'a check to the unnatural and ruinous system of competition,' it was clear that the beneficial effects of the new day were intended to extend beyond the mere redistribution of labour.[128] The purpose of hours reductions whether in building, cotton spinning, or mining was to bring the fluctuations of production under control, to provide the industry with a new kind of stability which would spread the work and employment evenly amongst the men and over the year. In 1846 the masons had believed that the nine hours would end that monotonous pattern of summer wage advances and winter reductions, thus diminishing the causes of friction between masters and men.[129] The problem was, as the men equally realised, that this stabilisation struck at the heart-springs of the contracting system whose imperatives lay in the need for flexibility on such questions as hours and wages. As the Oldham cotton spinners had quickly learnt, to talk about hours reductions led inevitably to talk about *power*.[130] And if in 1859 the hours issue did not lead to the same kind of revolutionary consciousness that it had earlier done in Oldham, this was merely a reflection of the different contexts in which both movements occurred. The one appearing out of a continuing struggle for political as well as economic power at a time when all those issues were open to debate; the other coming out of a more muted but on-going struggle which occurred in isolation from any wider struggles and without being surrounded by a questioning of the fundamental basis of authority in society.

By its stabilisation of the trade and by its constriction of the labour supply, an eight or nine hours day would put an end to cheap labour, provide the basis for the men to secure wage advances (or at least attain wage stability),[131] enable the men to more effectively enforce restrictions on the organisation of work and allow advances to be made in the general conditions of working. Ultimately, it was those kinds of issues that made the nine hours demand such a sensitive issue. What Tom Mann said about the power implications of the eight-hour day applied with equal force to the nine: 'When the unemployed will be absorbed . . . the workers will be able in their turn to dictate terms to the employers.'[132] And we can find a more complete echo of this from an unknown workman in 1846 who, in reply to the masters' 'freedom of labour' manifesto, went to the heart of the matter in admitting that the question was one of power:

According to the present system, everything is in favour of the employer. He engages and dismisses: he arbitrarily directs, controls and exacts, and appropriates to himself a most unfair proportion of the profits. Here, then, is the cause of dissension – an unequal and unfair distribution of profits and labour and while it exists the working class will resist every species of wrong inflicted upon them.[133]

It was this, too, that informed the men's rhetoric in 1859: 'The true reason why the employers refuse to concede the nine hours was that they might continue to oppress, tyrannize, and trample the workpeople.' What this meant was that until the nine hours stabilised the industry in the men's favour, employers would persist in their encroachments of piecework, overtime and the rest. On a less rhetorical, more sophisticated level it was this that formed the core of Potter's impressive pamphlet *The Labour Question* whose message was that the rate of exploitation of labour had been increased by machinery and other devices and that the hours reduction was designed to reverse that particular 'progress' of the working class.[134] And it was this need to bring working conditions under control, to restrict the freedom of the masters to do as they willed with machinery, piecework and the like that not only explains the 'petty annoyances' that lay just below the surface of the nine hours demands in 1846 and 1859, but which also explains why the employers had no choice but to resist its implementation. Thus, the masters' association explained in 1859:

The time had arrived when it was imperatively necessary to grapple with the whole question of the rights of the master builders in the legitimate control of their business . . . the demand [for the nine hours] . . . was only another illustration and further development of the arbitrary and extravagant demands which the building operatives of London had been forcing on their employers during recent years.[135]

Had the issue been simply a matter of wages, explained one builder, 'I will be one of the first to yield' but the issue was 'the republican notion of controlling the labour market' whose wide-ranging implications were well-expressed by T. L. Donaldson:

The real question is not one of the mere nine hours movement. The ultimate pretensions of the Unionists . . . is eight hours a day [and, indeed, this demand had been made at some carpenters' meetings in 1858], six shillings a day, and the half-holiday on Saturday; the liberty to banish from labour all who will not join the unions; compulsion on foremen to be unionists – foremen whom they will control, and who shall not dare to do justice to the employer, nor urge the mechanic to do more work than he likes.[136]

It was further reflection of these implications that led the masters to respond to an informal approach at conciliation by the London MP Thomas Ayrton with the demand that before the document could be withdrawn those rules and practices that were 'contrary to the spirit of the law of the land' must be removed from the union rule books.[137] Similarly, when Richard Harnott – who had never really approved of the conflict – entered into some informal talks with Henry Pomeroy of Myers and Co., he was urged to revise the masons' rules on overtime, piecework, the standard rate and 'all rules and practices . . . which interfere with the freedom of the workman in preventing members of trades unions from working with other workmen' as a condition for the withdrawal of the document.[138] These 'negotiations' came to nothing, but they illustrated where the real concerns of the masters lay. And it was fitting that following the defeat of the men in 1860 when they were in no position to effectively resist, that the employers should take this opportunity to replace the system of daily payment with that of payment by the hour. This method of wage payment, which we shall examine in greater detail at a later point, was designed to enhance the freedom and flexibility of the masters in the conduct of their businesses and it was, thus, an appropriate form with which the employers could cap and maintain their victory.

The duality of the rhetoric that we noted earlier between the imperatives of employers' authority and the complaints about 'petty annoyances' reflected, therefore, the dialectic implicit in the structure of the trade between 'freedom' and 'control.' The employer's profits depended upon his ability to work within cost lines already determined before the work was begun; it necessitated, therefore, that he be free to introduce piecework, overtime, sub-contracting, 'chasing,' 'tyrannical' foremen and wages reductions. Any attempt to restrict his freedom in these areas was a threat that could pose a serious danger to his survival and any general attempt to swing the balance of power in favour of control by the men had to be met and crushed. This is just what the demand for the nine hours threatened to do; it represented a climacteric to that dialectic struggle between 'freedom' and 'control.' In 1846 it was a bold attempt – which failed in its main objective – to complete the success which the men had already achieved in extending their control over the work; in 1859, it represented a somewhat desperate attempt – which also failed – to resolve the undecided contest between employer 'encroachments' and the men's resistance.

2

The dynamic of autonomous regulation

THE SYSTEM OF UNFORMALISED INDUSTRIAL RELATIONS

The 'heroic' conflicts of the thirties, forties, and fifties have tended to dominate our vision of early and mid-Victorian industrial relations. They were dramatic reflections of the clash between the disciplinary imperatives of general contracting and efforts to control the productive process by the workers. But they represented not so much turning points in the social relations of the industry as local climacterics to the tensions between authority and control that were heightened and accentuated from the early 1830s. These tensions were now to be permanent and this book is very largely the story of attempts to resolve the dilemmas and problems that they created. As solutions to the problem of discipline, however, the big battles of the first half of the century were dismal failures. At most they provided a momentary advantage for the masters who won all four contests. And even when the advantage of victory was used to change the structure of the work so as to enhance the master's power, as it was in the imposition of hourly payment in London in 1861, the disciplinary advantage would seem to have been mitigated by the failure to apply the system universally, by the building boom of the sixties and by the increased militancy of the men. Changing the way in which the work was done was to be an important part of the solution to this mid-Victorian phase of the problem of discipline; but, as we shall see, it could be effective only if it was coupled with changes in the way in which industrial relations were actually conducted, governed and mediated.[1]

If the strikes and lockouts of 1833, 1841, 1846, and 1859 were ample testimony to the intractability of discipline and authority, they also revealed the absence of any other means of resolving these problems. Nor was this simply an accidental matter of oversight. Parliament had placed conciliation and arbitration legislation on the statute books, it had investigated the question of industrial relations several times during this period; but the universal failure to act upon this permissive legislation was a reflection of its essential irrelevancy at this particular time.[2] Indeed, this is of some significance. Until the late 1860s, the central characteristic of industrial relations – and not in building alone – was the absence of any formal, institutional structures to systematise worker–employer relations, to

provide rule-making procedures and to mediate issues of contention. And
if occasionally and in some industries, local attempts were made to create
such a system (one thinks of the Wear shipwrights' Court of Arbitration in
1853–54 as an example) such efforts were distinct oddities that in most
instances collapsed after a short and varied life.[3] Worker–master conflict
and contact were governed, then, by totally different kinds of rules and
values than those associated with a modern problem-solving industrial
relations system.

As W. L. Burn has shown, authority systems in the period until the
1870s were informal and voluntary. Their power rested upon the sanctions
of convention and acceptance rather than upon a body of formal, statutory
rules.[4] For the industrial worker, of course, the law stood ominously in the
background ready to be used if other means should prove inadequate but
the sense prevailed that it was up to the various parties involved in the
relationship to sort out their modus vivendi in a direct, face-to-face way.[5]
This was the reality that underlay those anguished wails which from the
fifties were increasingly heard – even in building – about the loss of personal contact between employer and employed. The employers' objections
to trade unions, or to men from 'outside' the shop coming to interpret what
'his' men wanted was not simply a matter of one-dimensional anti-
unionism. Nor, in the days when formal unions were so ludicrously weak
could it have been a recognition of the eventual power that unions could
exercise. It was more a reflection of the undesirability of external systems
of authority intruding into the large sphere of freedom that governed one's
relationships with others. This conception of freedom lay at the very heart
of employers' attitudes to their men. When Sir Morton Peto addressed the
men of Lucas' works at Lowestoft he claimed that ' "the reason they had
got on so well with their masters . . . was that they had no strangers in
Lowestoft stirring up mischief between them." '[6] And 'strangers' could be
masters as well as men. Mr Mclymont, a large London builder, sounded
distinctly old fashioned when he declared in 1872 that 'he did not recognise the Masters' Association or the committee of the men. He should carry
on his business as he pleased . . . and work the men as many hours as it
suited him.'[7] But he was expressing the values of 'freedom,' 'independence,'
and 'manliness' that lay behind the unformalised system of industrial relations. These conceptions carried over to the men: the Manchester branch
of the ASC&J expressed their opposition to the idea of a membership-
checking Walking Delegate as 'an interference with that freedom of choice
allowed to candidates or members leaving the Amalgamated Society of
Carpenters and Joiners.' It was 'degrading and debasing for the society to
pay a man to go about dragging people into it against their will.'[8]

But if industrial relations were unformalised in the sense that there were
no external structures of authority to mediate the opposing claims of the

masters or the men, this most certainly did not imply that all was anarchic chaos. There was a coherence and a unity to unformalised industrial relations that it is critically important to understand but it was a logic markedly different from the more clearly definable system that governs a formalised system of industrial relations. Under any circumstances, for example, rule-making must take place, but within a formalised system there lie regular and permanent procedures embodied in institutional forms to fulfil this function. Our task, or one of them, is to discover the 'system' that prevailed in an environment where such structures were, if not unknown, generally unimportant or a-typical. And it is important to do this for two reasons.

The first, a general and obvious point, is that the transition from an unformalised to a formalised system of industrial relations was the critical event in modern labour history whose significance can hardly be underestimated. And although in various guises this matter has been treated by many others there has been little attention paid to the process by which this transition was achieved. At this point it is unnecessary to enter into a lengthy and diversionary treatment of the previous historiography – our differences with that scholarship will become apparent enough throughout the remainder of this book. It will suffice to point out that in spite of a wide agreement that the Webbs failed to adequately address the historical roots of how labour moved from the method of mutual insurance to the method of collective bargaining, neither has anybody else specifically improved on their account. The general assumption is aptly summed up by Allan Flanders who wrote that 'collective bargaining was the offspring of trade union organisation and industrial conflict,' and that 'the history of collective bargaining during the nineteenth century is largely the history of trade unionism.' And Hugh Clegg (like most industrial sociologists very conscious of the need for a historical approach to his subject) sees 'custom' as the determinant of the conditions of work in the nineteenth century until it 'was gradually taken over by collective bargaining.'[9]

The second reason why it is important to address the system of unformalised industrial relations is more immediate. Indeed, it is central to this particular chapter. For it will be argued that it was out of the internal dynamic of this unformalised system and out of its failure to resolve the disciplinary imperatives of the employer–worker relationship that an eventual crisis point was reached which demanded a total change in the structures of industrial relations. Furthermore, this change involved the demise of mid-Victorian conceptions of authority and the beginnings of their replacement by a formalised system to govern and mediate relations between masters and men.[10] In short, the paradox of this unformalised system as it operated in building was that, contrary to our popular conceptions about the relative balance of forces during this period, it allowed, facilitated and encouraged a worker challenge to managerial authority that was so critical that it could *only* be resolved by shifting the bases upon which industrial relations were conducted. But in order to show this we have to address three broad questions: first, it is necessary to identify the character of collective organisation within this unformalised system; second, we must then explore how rule-making and collective bargaining actually worked; and finally, we must explain how it was that the dynamic of the system created a crisis of power that culminated in the late sixties.

THE WORK GROUP

Beginning with the Webbs, labour historiography has consistently failed to explore the collective basis upon which workmen generally acted before the institution of collective bargaining. The implication to be drawn from the Webbs' schema is that there was a choice only between individual bargaining or mutual insurance.[11] In fact, to anyone who has examined mid-Victorian industrial relations, the idea that individual bargaining was the major, or sole, determinant of working conditions must be patently absurd. If individual bargaining had predominated in reality there would have been no necessity for the lockouts of 1846 or 1859. But, as we have shown, the whole point of those lockouts was the inability of the masters to enforce their singular authority. Indeed, in many places until the 1890s it was the employers who faced their men alone and made their individual bargains. In building, the ironic paradox is that the Webbs' conception of the individual bargain was a more accurate reflection of the employers' predicament than it was of the men. Neither is the Webbian category of 'mutual insurance' an adequate analytical tool with which to understand the collectivity that did exist. Other historians have pointed to the false polarity the Webbs set up between mutual insurance and collective bargaining. On their own admission, mutual insurance was of very limited extent and as 'an effective weapon . . . of aggression' was to be found only amongst the small, highly skilled crafts like the Spanish and Morocco Leather Finishers' Society or the Flint Glass Makers.[12] But from the evidence of the shop memorials, the deputations and the like that criss-cross the length and breadth of mid-Victorian industrial relations, it is clear that there were other forms of collective organisation and bargaining and it is, therefore, important that this whole question be re-considered and re-conceptualised.

Ever since the famous Hawthorne study in the late 1930s, industrial sociologists have recognised the presence of informal associations of workers at the workplace. These associations – the work groups – are the basic unit of worker organisation; they function as the collective agency of the men towards the methods and conditions of their jobs: their activities may range from the trivial to the obviously important and the major role they play in industrial relations is well-recognised.[13] Work groups are most readily formed and effective amongst skilled workers but they are to be found across the whole spectrum of the industrial experience and it is important to realise that craft skill is not an essential precondition for viable work group organisation.[14] The printers' chapel may be the most highly developed form of work group association (and unusual in that it coincides with the basic unit of union organisation) but, as the Devlin Report showed, the ganger was as powerful a representative of the dock labourers as the father of the chapel was of the printers.[15] In addition, our evidence from the building trades will suggest that building labourers were just as capable of work group formation and activity as were the more highly skilled masons or bricklayers.

If much remains that is uncertain about the formation and operation of work groups, their autonomy from union organisation is not in doubt and, as an American study from the 1930s revealed, their effective power is in no way confined to unionised establishments.[16] Indeed, historically a highly developed experience of work group organisation was an essential prerequisite for the emergence of strong unions. The Webbs, for example, puzzled over the 'ephemeral' nature of early cotton spinning unions without perceiving their role as a temporary formalisation of work group forms of collective action that had been brought into open life by the momentary need for a more complete organisation.[17] The relationship between the union and the work group is of great importance and interest and it is a matter to which we shall return.[18] But for the labour historian the central significance of work group action lies in its purposeful assertion of worker authority over the activities of the workplace. Modern industry provides ample testimony to the fact that work group control over work cannot be dismissed simply as negative impediments to rational managerial control. In the engineering workshops of Tom Lupton's experience, those men who observed official time, violated the standards of good workmanship, dodged work, endangered the standard rate by 'tear-arsing' were all the object of sanction, condemnation and ridicule because they threatened the standards of earnings and conditions established as 'fair' by the men.[19] Similarly, the control of overtime exercised by the Fawley oil refinery workers in the 1950s represented a work group authority over the distribution of work which the famous productivity deal aimed precisely to buy out. In the context of pre-1960 Fawley, systematic overtime threatened managerial authority rather than the exploitation of the men because it lay firmly under the control of the representatives of the men who charged the company for work which the men decided should be done.[20]

The Fawley experience provided a particularly good illustration of the bifurcated system of industrial relations that had grown out of the full employment affluence of post-1945 Britain. The official world of national agreements, grievance and conciliation procedures bore little relationship to the subterranean, unofficial world which at Fawley had allowed work groups to implant job demarcation boundaries of their own making and to impede attempts to increase productivity by the control of overtime. Indeed, the Fawley productivity agreement was one of the first to reveal the necessity of negotiating directly with the representatives of the work groups outside of official union channels. Only when the work groups had been brought into the discussions could progress be made in the removal of those informal rules that restricted managerial authority over the work.[21] Furthermore, the whole course of the negotiations were an object lesson in the work groups' clear recognition of the importance work structure bore to their ability to influence the productive process. The unskilled machine cleaners, for example, who saw themselves as the 'aristocrats of the non-craft world' and who had built up a strong group structure that distinguished them from the other labourers, resisted the decline in status involved in the proposal to re-deploy them into a new category of cleaner–labourers who could be shifted around as needed to do any cleaning work. Here was an expression of work group control and status that had little to do with the union in which they were enrolled (the TGWU) and which revealingly illuminated the job consciousness of even unskilled labourers.[22]

The unofficial system of industrial relations is a reflection of the growth of work group power and influence and it has been found to be particularly powerful in those areas of industry where the formal structure of bargaining presses but lightly upon the workplace. Engineering provides the classic example of this situation: the industry is characterised by a loose national system which allows considerable power to accrue to the unformalised local structures. Indeed, it is reckoned that about 50% of the restrictions imposed at the workplace emanate from informal work group decisions rather than from steward or union policies.[23] Contemporary experience suggests, therefore, that an important condition for the growth of workplace power is the absence of formalised procedures and institutions at the work site level. Within a modern system of industrial relations the result of this work group power is to create a complex set of cross currents in which the 'informal organisation of the group is . . . often in conflict with the formal organisation of the undertaking' and the union to which bargaining is entrusted.[24] It was the challenge that this work group power presented to the ability of the official structures to effectively maintain industrial peace and order that lay at the heart of the industrial relations crisis of the late 1960s and early 1970s and which led state policy to search for some way of integrating the unofficial world into the formal system of industrial relations. But the situation will be somewhat different in the absence of any formal structures to govern industrial relations and to complicate or mask the operation of work group activity. It is precisely in this respect that the work group becomes an important part of our conceptualisation of Victorian industrial relations.

Unless we regard the work group as a purely modern creation – an idea we can surely discount – the logic of an unformalised industrial relations system demanded that the work group be the central agent of the men's side of industrial relations. And we have devoted some attention to our contemporary knowledge of the work group because it is only by transposing that knowledge on to the historical evidence that we can make any sense out of the system of unformalised industrial relations. Although we are aware that the work group is a transient phenomenon whose power and presence vary widely over time and industry we are also aware that building is not one of those industries where its existence is problematical. The Cameron Commission, for example, provided ample evidence of the presence and power aspirations of such groups in the industry. Indeed, in some places – as when it recounts the autonomous and independent action of the men – that document could be a study of industrial conflict in the Manchester of the 1860s.[25] What we are now concerned to argue, with specific reference to building but with a recognition both of its wider application and limitation, is that the dynamic of the system of industrial relations that prevailed in mid-Victorian Britain was determined by the relationships of work groups to employers. But if the work group could be as important to mid-Victorian labour history as we have suggested how does that affect our conception of the union which in the previous historiography has been accorded a primacy it may not deserve?

In order to consider both these questions, it is instructive to examine the evidence presented before the *Royal Commission on Trade Unions, 1867–1869* and parroted in the pamphlet literature of the period that catalogued 'trade union tyrannies.'[26] So damning was the evidence against the building unions provided by Alfred Mault (secretary to the General Builders' Association) that Frederic Harrison was moved to remark that Mault was ' "an exceedingly clever fellow who has got up his case perfectly." '[27] It was, indeed, fortunate that the masters were called before the Commission after the union officials who otherwise would have been hard put to present such a successfully respectable case for their organisations. Mault detailed the kinds of 'union' restrictions that the employers had to face: control over the labour supply exercised by the plasterers, painters and masons;[28] the rules of the bricklayers and their labourers that restricted output; the masons' refusal to allow worked stone into many districts;[29] the rules against overtime; the opposition to machinery; the rules over walking time from home to an out-of-town job; the enforcement of the standard rates; and the regulation of apprenticeship.[30] As we shall later see, these complaints cannot be dismissed simply as anti-union rhetoric, nor as unreliable expressions of class antagonism to union organisation. There is little doubt that what Mault and others saw as unconscionable interference in the business of the masters was precisely that. The problem was that these tyrannies were commonly associated with trade union organisation and it was this that allowed Harrison and Hughes, after momentary panic, to attack the credibility of the evidence and reduce Mault to something approaching a gruff absurdity.

The weakness of the employers' case lay in the logical discrepancy – which Mault failed to allow for – between the numbers of unionists and their supposed power and influence. It was impossible to explain how it was that a minority – and a small minority, at that – of men could 'dictate' not only to the employers but to their workmates as well. In 1871, for example, of the 95,000 masons in Britain only about 14,000 were in the OSM. Of the 205,000 carpenters and joiners, about 10,000 were in the ASC&J, some 9000 in the General Union with another three and a half thousand in the Scottish society. The OBS in 1870 had all of 1400 members out of a total population of some 100,000; and the plasterers had just 2400 in their National Association out of 27,000 plasterers in the whole country.[31] It was ironic that Mault's own estimate that between 10–20% of building workers were unionised was quite accurate.[32] But when confronted with the disjunction of power relations that these figures implied, Mault was reduced to arguing that in a shop of fifty men, the five unionists were able to impose their will on the forty-five non-unionists by the 'unfair' influence of 'moral and physical' pressure. Or, when questioned about the oddity that few of the rules he had referred to actually appeared in union rule books, he was forced to reply that the unions always supported the men in their 'illegal' strikes.[33] In fact, Mault's testimony, and that of the other building employers rested, as did the rebuttals of Harrison and Hughes, upon the important distinction between the work group and the union. There was only one item of 'union tyranny' that actually appeared in the union rule books – the masons' chasing rule and that only for three years between 1865–68. When the masters spoke as they frequently did from the 1830s through the 1860s (and, indeed, even earlier going back to the seventeenth century) of 'conspiracies' they were speaking not of trade unionism but of work group activity. The restrictions that they recounted in outraged detail were restrictions that were – and are – typically those of the work group and bore little relationship to union existence or function.

Thus, on the grounds alone of the obvious illogic between numerical strength and power, the evidence before the Royal Commission suggests the historical inadequacy of regarding such restrictions as a function of institutional unionism. But this does not mean that such a terminology was inappropriate for Mault and his peers. For it is important to recognise that 'union' as a codeword was not necessarily coterminous with a permanent institutional presence but referred also, and perhaps more frequently, to any attempt by the men to act 'in union' to interfere with the free market model of employment conditions. In 1859, for example, the employers used the unions as a rhetorical target rather than an accurate description of how the nine hours movement was organised or where the power within it lay. Their image of the 'rules' of the trade unions bore no relationship to the reality as they found when they asked Edwin James, QC, if he could find anything illegal in the rule books. Although for public consumption the employers' association asserted that by 'their formidable combinations' unions 'succeeded in dictating to both masters and men', on other occasions it was merely 'the men' who 'were in the habit of dictating to the masters.'[34] In fact, as the masters well-realised, the 'unions' were in no position to 'dictate' to anyone, but the 'men' might be; and the employers' general refusal to collectively negotiate was as much an assertion of the legitimacy of autonomous regulation as it was of an anti-unionism.

We can apply the same kinds of perceptions to the significance of the documents that were presented to the men in 1846 and 1859. The purpose of the document was to legitimise the autonomous authority that the masters were trying to assert over the men. Each time it was presented – and we can include both the Birmingham discharge note strike of 1865 and the London conflict of 1914 in this – was on the occasion of a critical struggle for control in the industry. Its purpose was not so much to break 'union' power as that of the collective work groups in the trades. Indeed, it was highly significant that in both 1859 and 1914 union and non-union men were united in their opposition to the document. As one workman in 1859 put it: 'I belong to no society. I would never belong to those existing . . . but I will remain out . . . rather than swallow that document.'[35] Although the document of 1859 pledged the signer to neither join nor support any society which interfered with the working arrangements in an establishment, it may be argued that the key part of the declaration was that which, if achieved, would have given the employers a total authority over working conditions by establishing individual bargaining: 'I recognise the right of Employers and Employed individually to make any trade engagements on which they may choose to agree.'[36] The document would obviously have discouraged unionisation but it is hard to believe that the size of union membership was the major problem facing the masters. Indeed, the examples of union 'dictation' with which the London employers justified the document were mostly of a kind that could only be the result of work group activity.[37] The document was a part of the employers' concerted attack upon the assertion of work group power: the main demands of the masters in 1846, 1859, and 1914 were that various kinds of restrictive practices be ended. But the document was only one device and, at that, an ultimately counter-productive one which in both 1859 and

1914 was soon withdrawn once it was seen to increase rather than fragment solidarity. It did, however, provide a useful diversionary tactic,
turning demands for improved conditions into fights against the 'tyranny'
of the document. But the ultimate significance of the weapon lay in its
expression of the employers' claim for a freedom from worker control over
working arrangements and a legitimisation of their own authority and
discipline.

If the document served to reinforce union and non-union solidarity, the
existence of this solidarity was not at all unusual. The whole question of
relations between union and non-union men is one that is rent with ambiguity and complexity which makes any generalisation at best uncertain.
In part, attitudes towards non-unionists were moulded by the relative
numerical strength of the two sections and by the extent to which control
over entrance into the trade could be exercised. Thus, H. A. Turner's
account of the textile industry's open unions showed them to be far more
tolerant of non-unionists than the closed spinning unions; and in weaving,
cooperation continued well into the twentieth century.[38] But the question
was also a reflection of the changing nature of the work and the changing
structures of industrial relations. As we shall later see, opposition to non-
unionism in London building only emerged once the structure of the work
changed to require a more solid basis of worker organisation and when,
concurrent with this, the imperatives of the industrial relations system
required a viable union presence. What is clear is that it was not until the
later part of the century that the distinction between the two sections
began to assume a real importance. Where the union was locally strong or,
in a given shop, constituted a majority, there were likely to be informal rules
that pressured newcomers in joining. Where the union men were in a
minority – as, for example among the masons and joiners of Glasgow in the
1850s – the men worked and cooperated together peacefully. And, among
the joiners of Greenock in the 1860s, about two thirds of whom were non-
unionists:

The compact between both classes is so reciprocal and so solid that they work
together in a unity and make common cause with them, to be a unionist is seemingly to be little else than a member of a particular friendly society and . . . is
regarded [by some] as merely involving the payment of so much a week into a
fund.[39]

In the same period, a similar kind of amity seems to have characterised the
carpenters of Hastings where regular cricket matches between the two
groups were a symbol of their cooperation.[40]

Indeed, the distinction that is frequently suggested by the evidence is
that between 'blacklegs' and 'rats' and those who worked together to maintain and protect standards. This distinction was one that could cut right
across organisational boundaries. Thus, on separate occasions both Potter

and Howell pointed out the irrelevancy of the union–non-union distinction. The former argued that only rarely was there any antagonism between the two and the latter – pre-figuring the Webbs' argument on the standard rate – pointed out that 'it makes little difference whether a man belongs to the union or not; a man not belonging to the union obtains the same rate of wages as is obtained by union men, although it is obtained for him.'[41] Similarly, Edward Beesly, an informed observer of labour relations in the 1860s, suggested that union membership was essentially a reflection of friendly society benefits:

If a man does not join a Union it is almost invariably for reasons connected with his private circumstances and convenience. He is perhaps a member of some other benefit society, such as the Odd Fellows, and does not feel inclined, or cannot afford to contribute to two . . . There is no ill-feeling on the subject. The Non-Unionist looks to the Union to protect the trade just as much as if he was a member. When a strike occurs he generally contributes during its continuance. In the builders' strike [1861] the large majority of skilled non-unionists have cooperated heartily with the Unionists.[42]

The distinction between the real non-unionists whom unionists 'never put down' and 'those called "rats" . . . [who] they strongly objected to' was one that was maintained well into the 1890s.[43] It was a distinction that had more to do with behaviour during a strike or a willingness to contravene recognised working conditions than with formal membership in a union. As such, it could just as easily take in union members who might find it necessary to 'blackleg.' There was nothing particularly unusual about union men taking other union men's work: the Markeley dispute of 1869 was just such a case where members of the London based OBS were quite willing to work under conditions that the Manchester Unity men found objectionable. The great Manchester strike of masons in 1869–70 was broken, it was later claimed, by blacklegs 'who . . . transferred their allegiance from our society and became the pliant tools of capital.' But twelve months later a majority of those deserters had rejoined the union.[44] Regional loyalties may also have played a role in blacklegging. In coal mining and shipbuilding, for example, men who would not have black-legged in their home locality were quite prepared to travel from Staffordshire to Lancashire, or from Sheffield to Newcastle to take the work of those on strike: 'Down there we don't consider that we are blacklegging except when the masters want to reduce the wages, and here we go to work for wages which their men refused to accept.'[45] Even within a given town there were times when unionists could be tempted to break with union rule. Thus, in 1868 the Sunderland masons reported on the necessity for a rule to prohibit sub-contracting for 'there has been a new church here sub-contracted for by our members and there are two or three new jobs to start which parties are trying to sub-contract from the contractors; and if it is not stopped immediately it will be the ruin of the trade in this town.'[46]

Both in the origins of demands and in the conduct of trade movements, the dominant tone of the evidence is that of a close and classless cooperation between the union and non-union sectors. Indeed, it was not at all unusual for non-unionists to initiate – rather than follow – a movement for improved conditions. There are many examples of this during our period. Of the widespread carpenters and joiners movement in London in 1865, for example, it was noted: 'It is a peculiar but pleasing feature that this movement spontaneously emanated from non-society men.'[47] And three years later the Greenock joiners were led into a strike by the non-union majority in the trade.[48] In 1873, the non-union carpenters of Kidderminster called a trade meeting to discuss an increase in wages after which it was reported that 'the Society men it is expected will concur in their [i.e. non-union] views.'[49] Nor was this feature of non-union initiation of strike movements confined to building. Indeed, the major examples are to be found in shipbuilding and engineering where the most celebrated strike movements of these years took precisely this form. Thus, the Clyde conflict of 1866 had its origins amongst the semi-skilled holders-up, caulkers, hammermen, helpers and rivet boys who between January and April had struck ten times in one company alone to force wage increases. Ultimately, the skilled workers were dragged into a dispute after a nine hours demand had emanated in a 'revivalist' manner from the non-union men.[50] The same pattern marked the nine hours movements on the Tyne in 1866 and 1871.[51] Amongst the engineers of the northeast, union organisation was weak and both movements probably originated in obscure, small meetings like that organised by Andrew Gourlay at Sunderland in 1870. In addition, there was the example of the building trades in the area who during the later sixties had proved very successful in reducing their hours. The first group to secure the nine hours had been the 'unorganised' quarrymen who had successfully fought a twenty-two week strike on the issue.[52] All the evidence suggests that the impetus came from the rank and file irrespective of union affiliation. The strike was run in the traditional way by delegates from all the shops; it is well-known with what suspicion the ASE regarded the whole thing; and Burnett himself did not emerge as a prominent leader until some time after the strike had been going on.

But even where the question of how these movements were initiated is unclear, as it usually is, their organisational form emphasised that they were movements of the 'trade' in which the sense of collective trade or craft unity transcended the distinctions of other organisational affiliations. We have only to remember the character of the large movements of 1859 and 1872 (with which we shall deal more fully later on) to realise this. Neither was this cooperation necessarily limited to particular moments of mass militancy. At York in 1845, for example, a meeting of union and non-union masons resolved to abolish piecework and secure an advance and a trade committee was formed to communicate their demands to the masters. In the same year at Newcastle, over 200 masons were on strike for an advance of whom only 13 were unionist. At Huddersfield, in 1858, 20 union and 117 non-union men were on strike against hourly pay where it remarked that there were 'many non-members who are decidedly against it, and intend to act upon principle.' At Hereford, in 1864, eight members and twenty-two non-members were on strike to resist an infringement of meal hours.[53] Nor was this cooperation unique to the masons. The movement of Leeds' carpenters in 1864 to reduce hours and regulate overtime was initiated by a trade meeting which appointed a committee of ten non-union and six union men to oversee the movement; the same was true at Scarborough, Birmingham and Bradford and in the last place this unity 'greatly contributed to the success of the movement.' In the big Midlands strikes of 1865, non-union men usually constituted a majority of the strikers.[54]

Nor was militancy solely the preserve of unionists. When union men complained, as they often did, that non-unionists were reckless and hot-headed and were frequently 'the ringleaders in disputes between the masters and the workmen,' it reflected the greater determination of the non-unionists to maintain the advantages of autonomous regulation over conciliatory mutual negotiations.[55] There is an interesting episode in George Howell's autobiography where a group of labourers (presumably non-unionised) working for Messrs Dove suddenly demanded a wage increase: 'It was quite unexpected . . . and the demand was so unreasonable in manner as it was sudden in point of time. It was made about 7 o'clock in the morning with the threat there and then to leave work.'[56] Howell, who was the foreman, was told by Dove that he could grant the raise to those who were worth it and sack the ring leaders, which he did. Thus, here we have the example of a group of labourers acting in a tactically suitable way – the early morning was an appropriate time to seek an increase because if labour conditions were right and the work important the employer would be obliged to grant it – and Howell, the union man, only two years off the blacklist for his role in the 1859 and 1861 strikes, enforcing the discipline of the employers.

But the interest of this vignette is not simply to illustrate the depths of Howell's desire for respectability. It is significant, too, in that it must have been typical of the way in which industrial relations operated at the worksite. Unlike the present day where the work group is at best an adjunct or, at worst, an irritant to official unionism, this episode reveals the work group as the unhindered and autonomous agent of industrial relations. Industrial sociologists generally agree that the scope of workplace bargaining depends upon the nature of the collective procedures that govern a particular industry. A system which limits the issues available for workplace negotiation will naturally mean that the union role in the workplace will be greater than a system, such as that in engineering, which allows for bargaining over and above national minima. In contemporary footwear and hosiery, where successful cooperation between union and management stretches back to their nineteenth-century conciliation agreements, the all-encompassing modern system is deliberately worked to inhibit independent workplace organisation. But where the industrial relations structures allow workplace organisation to thrive, the union's function is essentially that of a secondary source of support to the control and power autonomously exercised by the work group.[57] This kind of situation is obviously analogous to the atmosphere within which mid-Victorian industrial relations were conducted, where the system operated with a looseness unknown in modern industry to allow a high degree of work group autonomy. The means and devices of work group action varied. Petitioning of employers, as recounted in this case of a carpentry workshop, was obviously very common: 'In my old workshop the men twice won reductions of hours by agreeing together and petitioning the employer.'[58] But it is clear that strike activity, also, was within the capacity of all kinds of work groups; in fact, some of the best examples of the primacy of work group action are to be found amongst the unskilled labourers in the building trades. Thus, we can instance a very interesting strike that occurred at the new Manchester Assize Court in 1864.

The strike began when the informal rules of the bricklayers' labourers were violated by a foreman who, complaining that they were working too slowly, appointed a man of his own choosing (and a stranger to the town) as their gang leader. The gang leader – whose job it was to 'see that the supply of material [to the bricklayers] be properly regulated' and who, therefore, determined the pace of the work – was by general 'trade usage' the longest serving labourer of the group. This violation of work group custom caused the men to strike, taking the bricklayers and joiners with them. The authority implications of the issue were quite obvious, for it involved the right of the employer or his agent to appoint whom he wished to responsible positions. A gang leader who was the longest serving labourer not only involved principles of seniority, it also implied a closeness to the gang as a whole which ensured that his loyalties would not lie totally with the employer or his foreman.[59] The significance of the issue could be seen by the way in which the strike sparked a full-scale battle into which other contentious questions obtruded and whose repercussions were still being felt several years later.[60] That the Manchester bricklayers' labourers had a powerful union was incidental to this kind of industrial action which was not so much a function of unionisation as it was of the ability of the work group to act in a cohesive and decisive manner. The case of the Bradford stone getters and dressers in the 1870s is even clearer, for here no union existed at all: 'But [they] have as short hours as, and are better paid than, the workmen employed in the building trades who have trades' unions. They seldom have much difficulty in obtaining an advance of wages or other requests, as they are guided by the state of the trade.' And when they saw a good demand for stone 'each set of workmen asks their employer or master for an advance of wages, shorter hours . . . or other advantages.'[61] Contrary to the traditional assumption of labour history that 'the ability of workers to engage in industrial action depended largely upon the condition of their union organisation,' the potential for achieving advantageous conditions of work would seem to have been far more a function of work group solidarity.[62]

The predominantly local autonomy in union government was an organisational reflection of the supremacy of local groups of men, whether in the branch or in the work group. Even within the new model unions this was true. Not until the 1870s did they expand their central authority beyond control of union funds to acquire a bureaucratic responsibility over a wider sphere of affairs; and not until the 1890s did this centralisation really mature. The Operative Society of Stone Masons provides an interesting illustration of the relationship between the centre and the locality. They had a procedure whereby permission to strike for improvements in working conditions was vested in a vote of the whole society. The significance of this system lay in the support that it secured to the local branch from the whole body of the union. If permission was refused there were no sanctions that could be applied against the branch, which could then decide whether to go it alone. Indeed, by the middle sixties the high point of local autonomy had been reached when a new procedure appeared in the *Fortnightly Returns* whereby the union delivered an ex-post facto approval to improvements that had been independently gained by the men. In the event of a masters' offensive, union support for the locality was automatically secured in defence of privileges won without prior approval.

This procedure expressed in an extreme form the subordinate and supportive relationship of the union to the branch. But the same pattern of authority was to be found at the most elementary level of the organised structures. The branch coordinated, supported and at times attempted to restrain work group activity. Thus, the secretary of the Edinburgh branch of the Associated Society of Carpenters and Joiners in May 1872 wrote to a Mr Brodie:

I have been requested to correspond with you, as it is rumoured that you and your men [are in dispute over?] Rule [?] of the bye laws. I beg to state that it all lies with the man, if the majority wishes to be paid weekly, then you are obliged [?]

to pay them weekly, but if the majority are in favour of fortnightly pays then you must pay them accordingly.[63]

Or, again the Ashton branch of the General Union which in October 1859 discussed the grievance of the low wages paid to men in Mr George's shop and resolved that 'If Shaw has more wages he gets it by his own exertion. [And that] Barraclough . . . remain at his present rate of wage at Present [*sic*], but his [*sic*] requested to make an effort for an advance at the first opportunity.' And in probable response to a request for support, a few months later it was decided that men in various shops were to have the standard rate 'or else they shall strike.'[64]

The lodge was not, of course, simply a passive bystander in the local conduct of industrial relations: the Manchester 1st. Branch of the Amalgamated Society of Carpenters, for example, condemned the men working for Edward Johnson for their hasty strike action in 1863.[65] But their authority did not possess the independence that it was to achieve once branches were subordinated to central control. It expressed the collective will of its members whose sphere of autonomous action remained large. Thus, in the example quoted above, Barraclough is assured of the support of the branch but when he asked for the advance was left to his own discretion. Similarly, when, in 1862, the same lodge asserted that it shall 'always have the opportunity of judging what are cases of emergency' to justify overtime, it was not to appropriate that authority from the men (because it did not preclude them from taking independent action) but to ensure that uniform standards were applied throughout the shops. Or, when the lodge resolved that: 'The members from Sigley's shop see Mr. Sigley in the course of this week and if he does not comply with their wishes they act up to the general laws,'[66] it was clearly an expression of support to the basically autonomous decision making of that particular group of men.

Within an unformalised system of industrial relations, no legitimately prescribed function exists for the union to occupy a central role in the determination of industrial relations. There were, of course, particular exceptions as, for example, at Greenock where an informal understanding between the shipwrights' lodge and the employers in the sixties assured the union of an established role.[67] But these relationships were usually fragile and temporary: the 1866 strike destroyed the accord at Greenock and it was to be another eleven years before a new *modus vivendi* was reached – this time on the basis of a formalised system of arbitration.[68] It is also true that we know too little of the precise process through which demands were formulated to be sure of the typical source of their origins. How far the twenty or thirty lodge members in a given town acted as initiators of demands that were then accepted by the trade is uncertain. To judge from the account given by a 'Rolling Stonemason' of the early twentieth century of the activities of those carriers of the union message who tramped from place to place, this was quite a common pattern. But his account, quoted below, also suggests how in the days before the union acquired a corporate and bureaucratic character, its meaning and focus were oriented primarily towards the work group.

These roadsters were always good union men . . . They could tell us of outside jobs how wages and conditions were. If trade justified going in for a rise in wages, or a shortening of the . . . hours . . . If it came to a strike, they would clear out so as not to deplete the [local] union's funds . . . They were the unpaid organisers of the union. If they struck [i.e. came across] a mansion being erected in an out of the way place, and there was no lodge . . . they were not working there long before they would call a dinner hour meeting out of which a lodge would be formed and a schedule of wages and hours drawn up.[69]

In the absence of formalised structures and procedures of industrial relations, the nature and meaning of union membership will be different from that of a system which provides the union with a legitimate place and role. To be 'in union' in mid-Victorian times did not necessarily imply an exclusive organisational affiliation. When the Edinburgh joiners lost their bid for the nine hours in 1862, it was ambiguously remarked that 'there was no union worthy of the name existing amongst them . . . It is themselves that is to blame for the want of union.'[70] This implied not that they needed a union but that they had failed to act in unison. Indeed, in testimony before the Royal Commission in 1867 J. C. Proudfoot (a long-time union man) explained how before the formation of the Associated Society the only organisation amongst Edinburgh carpenters was a small tool insurance society which provided the organisational nucleus of men who acted together – 'whether they paid into a trade union or not' – to bring about various increases in wages. He then went on to explain the springs of collective action in these terms: 'So long as you find two or three working men come together, you will always find that whether ostensibly or not in a trade union, virtually they are, as all are anxious to get the best wages possible.'[71] And to be 'in union' in this sense was undoubtedly a more common – perhaps a more meaningful – experience than to be 'in the union.'

As far as the men's conduct of industrial relations was concerned, the union and union membership served as both a symbolic and practical expression of the collective cohesion of the work group on a given issue of dispute and not something that expressed an ideological commitment to certain values and principles. Outside of industrial relations there were two factors that explain the presence of a substantial minority of permanent union men throughout the period: the friendly society benefits they offered and their representative role as an institution of respectability for the skilled working class. Thus, it was one of the characteristics of union membership to fluctuate wildly from year to year and from place to place, fluctuations that accorded with the expansion and contraction of the particular frontier of control exercised by the men. The OSM, for example, increased its membership by 100% during the 1860s, reflecting their successful achievements of the decade in controlling the work. But by 1870 following their important defeats in the northwest, they had lost 24% of their 1868 numbers. Membership revived again in the early seventies to reach an all-time peak of 22,619 in 1874 but by 1886 the society was more or less back where it had started in 1860.[72] The boilermakers' union provides another example of the same pattern. Between 1865 and 1869 they lost 27% of their membership and on the Clyde alone, where in 1863–64 they had recruited 864 new members, they lost 600 of these following the defeat of 1866.[73] For all but a significant minority, membership in unions was a casual matter which reflected both changing personal and work circumstances. The habits of the Box quarry masons reveal a pattern which must have been replicated many times over. Within the context of their work at the quarries, they were non-unionists and, indeed, were strongly opposed to the union whose rules against worked stone they saw as depriving them of work. But because they frequently went on the tramp to find work 'They generally join the branch in the town they stop at, but they invariably leave the society again on returning to the quarry district to work . . . in fact the Box branch has not found one new member for many years.'[74] The Webbs' informant only stayed in the union because after a membership of twenty-six years he was due for some benefits.

A high degree of membership turnover and the association of union membership with current or impending industrial struggle is, of course, not peculiar to mid-Victorian unionism. Nor has there been any diminution in the significance of work group needs as constituting 'a major reference group for the formation of attachment and the formulation of [union] membership needs.'[75] But it is the context within which these forces operate that provides the critical distinction between the modern trade union function and that of the mid-Victorian period. Until the post 1890s creation of a modern industrial relations system which demanded unionisation if it was to function properly, membership fluctuations bespoke the symbolic role of union attachment as an expression of work group solidarity and power. Without a legitimising system to encourage union membership, fluctuations in membership served not only to induce financial insecurity – which was not overcome until unionism was stabilised by formal structures of industrial relations – but also served to confirm the generally secondary role that the union could play in master–men relations. The loss of membership after the general strike of 1926, for example, did not seriously affect the standing and role of the unions within society, but the leakage from the OSM in 1869 and 1870 perfectly expressed the lessened power that masons could exercise over their work.

AUTONOMOUS REGULATION: RULE-MAKING IN AN UNFORMALISED SYSTEM OF INDUSTRIAL RELATIONS

The presence of collective work group organisation provided the basis for such rudimentary methods of collective bargaining as the memorial, petition and deputation. But these methods existed without any legitimisation from external sources of authority; they were utilised as the occasion required but had no permanent status or standing within recognised procedures to govern relations between masters and men. They were patently 'informal' and transient methods; any 'agreement' they might facilitate rested solely upon goodwill or naked force if it was to endure. Rule making, therefore, occurred without any acknowledged procedures to ease its passage, interpret its clauses or enforce its conditions. It focused solely around the precise and concrete issues that were in dispute. Unlike the system of modern collective bargaining where the procedural elements are the most important, the emphasis within the unformalised system lay purely on the substantive issues that were in contention between masters and men.

Neither is this a matter of small importance. Systems dominated by procedural rule making create different kinds of relationships and tensions to those where there are no procedures to define the status of the parties or to provide the machinery for making and interpreting the bargain.[76] And the differences between the two systems need to be emphasised because although it is the procedural system which is taken to represent the tradition of British industrial relations, this has been to ignore that older practice of autonomous regulation that lay at the heart of the unformalised system and which lives on today in the nether-land of unofficial systems and 'informal' rules.[77] The importance of the distinction between procedural and substantive rule-making systems lies in the diverse way each will work and in the differing constraints on behaviour each impose.

Within a procedurally dominated system the ' "emphasis is on institutions such as joint industrial councils, and the like, on the machinery, its constitution, above all its procedure. The substantive rules . . . appear as occasional decisions emanating from permanent boards on which both sides are represented and sometimes they are informal understandings." '[78] The overriding and explicit function of such a system lies in the preservation of industrial peace. It is, after all, the purpose of procedural rules to regulate the way in which relations must be conducted, to lay down the proper procedures to be followed, to legitimise the role of each party within the system, and to provide the means by which they are to be brought together to resolve problems. Substantive issues within this system are abstracted 'occasional decisions,' secondary to the purpose of ensuring that they do not erupt into conflict.[79] The most important clauses of such systems are those that provide the machinery for complete and full consultation in place of a strike. On the other hand, a system without these procedures will, of necessity, be more conflict prone. Conflict will lie nearer the surface, its avoidance will not have the same kind of imperative priority. Under a system that emphasises and provides for procedures, conflict will be the last resort; but under a substantive system it is the first or second resort. And it is inevitable that this should be so; for it is the role of procedural rules to resolve disputes that arise from substantive issues such as wages or hours. A system without those procedures will only avoid conflict if one side accepts the 'bargain' offered by the other.

It follows naturally from this that an unformalised system is less likely to be characterised by mutual negotiation between employers and employed. A context of rules and procedures which define and legitimise the authority of the various parties demands of necessity mutual negotiation, but it is neither mandated nor required within an unformalised system whose focus is purely the resolution of substantive issues by informal means. This does not imply that mutual negotiation can never take place but it does suggest that it will tend to be sporadic and transient and will occur only when strikes or lockouts have failed to achieve their objective.

Autonomous regulation of the productive process was, thus, inherent in the system of unformalised industrial relations. Far from being the preserve of limited groups of highly skilled craftsmen who practised mutual insurance, it was the basic characteristic of the system itself – the way in which the system actually worked.[80] The success with which either side was able to practise autonomous regulation was the main determinant of working conditions in industry. With the exception of a few union leaders and assorted members of the professional classes, permanent systems of mutual negotiation were opposed by both sides because they were a denial of autonomous regulation in which both masters and men believed. Employer opposition to negotiation with organised bodies of men was a reflection of the coherence of autonomous regulation with their conceptions and assertions of a singular authority.[81] Equally, for the men, the system of unformalised industrial relations legitimised and encouraged work group independence and autonomy. The process of rule making, then, was a product of these conditions. Autonomous regulation was central to the function of rule making, but the same could not be said of mutual negotiation and peaceful bargaining to resolve disputes.

Mutual negotiation entered into the structure of unformalised industrial relations only when the tactics of confrontation had been stalemated by the inability of either side to force an undisputed victory. This basic pattern could be seen amongst the carpenters and joiners of Manchester in 1857 and Leeds in 1864, the masons of Bristol in 1860, the bricklayers of Barrow in 1865 and of Liverpool in 1868.[82] Rules were drawn up by the men and communicated to the masters who then met and responded either by a refusal or with their own set of rules; a strike occurred and only when the strike was failing or clearly irresolvable would some form of meeting or negotiation emerge. Although there might be meetings between individual employers and their men, communication between the two sides usually took the form of letters, announcements to the newspapers or, in the case of the men, resolutions passed at public gatherings.[83] When mutual negotiation occurred it was usually initiated by the intervention of a third party such as the local architects, mayor or chamber of commerce who took it upon themselves to bring the two sides together.[84] And if the habit of mutual negotiation was then carried over for a number of years, it remained purely a habit liable to be broken when either side felt itself strong enough to revert to unilateral imposition. Thus, the procedural rule-making institutions to be found amongst the masons of Manchester and Glasgow in the fifties and sixties failed to sustain a prolonged existence.[85] The boasts of the Manchester men against those who 'failed to [consult] their employer . . . as to how far they would agree' to proposed rules looked rather foolish by 1868 when both masters and men were each trying to unilaterally impose their rules upon the other. And in Glasgow, too, the mutual negotiation characteristic of the fifties was nowhere to be found by the early eighties when a permanent formalisation of industrial relations grew out of a defeated strike.[86]

As long as mutual negotiation remained incidental to the system of industrial relations and while there were no procedures to provide regular channels of mediation between the parties, rule making was a process of the enforcement of rules that had been autonomously formulated. Attempts to predetermine the negotiation position of one's opponent were rare, as the following exhortations against unilateral imposition from Richard Harnott (Corresponding Secretary of OSM) illustrate:

The question of lodges forming local codes or rules is one of very grave consideration; inasmuch as it involves sweeping demands upon employers without having any consultations with them on such important matters . . . had there not been such, enormous demands in time, money, and other privileges, probably arrangements might have been amicably settled without striking. It is the safest plan for members . . . to gain privileges separately, and give their employers timely notice of what they wish, treat them with courtesy, as men whose interests are identical with their own.

That was in 1857 when several lodges had announced their intention to secure improvements in their 'privileges' and in similar circumstances Harnott returned to the same theme in 1862:

The Society has of late been frequently called on to ratify local codes of rules, which have been represented as working rules amiably agreed to by employers and employed. Now, however, lodges who never had any local rules at all . . . apply for ratification of a series of rules which employers and themselves have never consulted upon . . . Why not, before putting the new rules to the society, invite the employers to meet some half a dozen members and discuss the objects of the new rules?[87]

Negotiation by imposition was not, of course, the sole preserve of the men.[88] But the greater degree of collective unity that characterised the men's activities made it more likely to emanate from their deliberations;[89] and in the 1850s and 1860s it was clear that the tempo of industrial relations was set by the men. This pattern of the unilateral determination of working conditions and their imposition by strike action was particularly common amongst the masons. In 1844, for example, the Huddersfield masons circularised each master with the demand for a wage increase of 4d per day; when the request was ignored a general meeting set a strike date. On the appointed day the men refused to work and the advance was given. Precisely the same pattern was followed in 1852.[90] At Newport in 1851, placards were issued giving notice that a reduction of hours was expected on a certain day, there was no attempt at negotiation and the demand was achieved. In 1852, a code of rules was published in Sheffield which was then 'offered' to the employers and accepted. Similar examples may be found in the late fifties at Liverpool, Manchester and Birkenhead, and in the same period the men of Ashton-under-Lyne struck when the employers failed to send notice of their assent to changes in working conditions demanded by the men.[91] In the heart of the disorganised southwest, the mainly non-union masons of Plymouth in 1865 went on strike for a code of rules ' "to be imposed upon us by the workmen" ' and were victorious.[92] And it is worth noting that the crisis of 1869 began by the presentation of unilateral rules by the masters and counter-notices by the men. Nor were the aggressive, craft-conscious and independent masons alone in utilising this method of rule making: the Newcastle painters, the carpenters of Bradford, Derby, Chesterfield and Shrewsbury and the bricklayers of Hull provide confirmation of the typicality of this pattern.[93]

Inherent to the rule-making process under unformalised industrial relations, therefore, was an explicit and constant challenge to employer authority. Much of the time, the implications of this challenge remained largely abstract. Wages and hours demands, for example, did not necessarily confront managerial prerogative and employers could hardly deny the men a right to put a price on their own labour. But rule making could not be confined to these matters and inevitably reached into the more sensitive areas of the conditions and methods of working. Rules determined by the men to govern these aspects of the productive process were direct and immediate affronts to the employer's authority over his own business. And there were basically two kinds of substantive rules to be found in this period which presented this kind of challenge. There were formal codes of working rules which by the 1860s were a common feature of the industry and to which we shall return; and there were the 'informal' rules, imposed as circumstances allowed, which sprang from the collective activity of work groups. A constant feature of any industrial relations system, these kinds of rules became important not (as they are today) as evidence of disaffection from the system of industrial relations but as a direct and central product of the system itself. Their 'informality' extends only to the manner of their formulation and not, as under a modern collective bargaining system, to their 'illegitimate' status as determined by external, procedural sources of authority. It is, therefore, important to stress both their centrality to the system and to gain some brief idea of their nature and dimensions because they were to play a major role in the challenge to employer authority that climaxed in the sixties. Furthermore, it is important to stress that the 'restrictive practices' these rules embodied were a positive and dynamic force whose meaning lay beyond a simplistic reduction to devices whose purpose it was to uphold the standard rate. Because they are a manifestation of the 'autonomous enforcement by work groups of their own rules – a refusal to accept the managerial definition of their roles . . . a collective assertion of their own power and individuality,' they must be seen as the results of a struggle for power over the work itself.[94] Their nature and extent were a sensitive register of the location of the frontier of control between the employers and men.

Indeed, there is a distinctly modern ring to the constant complaints that were made about rules designed to restrict output. When we read of electrical engineering workers fitting the pace of work to provide what they consider to be a fair rate of pay, we can better understand the complaints of a joinery shop owner in the 1870s that the productivity promised by machine joinery had not materialised because of the deliberate adjustment of output to the speed of the machine.[95] The Bradford plasterers in the 1860s refused to enter the shop more than ten minutes before starting time, insisted that all jobs have three coats of plaster, and required that no employer be allowed to fire a man without explanation.[96] Throughout the whole century one of the most commonly cited devices to restrict output was the limitation imposed by the bricklayers on the number of bricks to be laid a day. Union officials could truthfully claim that there were no rules on the subject, Howell and Thornton regarded the question as representative of a primitive and dying form of unionism, the Webbs chose to see it as an old-fashioned device to maintain the standard rate, but its persistence suggests that it was more than just an aberration to pass away under the influence of changing organisational forms.[97] In the 1830s the standard of 800 bricks per day that was generally observed in the north-west compared unfavourably to the 2000 that the masters would have liked to have seen lain. This figure was constant it would seem until the later part of the century when the limit was reduced to between six and four hundred. Indeed, during the thirties it was reported that the bricklayers even determined the amount of work to be done each day.[98]

Occasionally, as at Darlington in 1874, one comes across examples of a deliberate go-slow action when one group of men took over four days to complete a job that should have taken only one and a half days. This case is particularly interesting because it was a clear example of work group activity. The job in question involved ready-worked stone which was being re-worked in spite of the fact that in 1872 the Darlington masons had surrendered their rule against worked stone in return for a wage increase.[99] More usually, the references are less precise but no less convincing. It is clear, for example, that informal rules against 'chasing' were widely enforced. The Bradford labourers' union had a rule, it was claimed, which warned the men 'not to outstrip good rules by doing double the work you are required.'[100] In similar manner, the Manchester bricklayers fined men who walked or ran over a certain speed.[101] And a joinery employer claimed to have frequently 'observed with anxiety and regret how the men were playing with their work, or carefully trying how not to do it, and thus acquiring a slow habit of working.'[102] It is certain that chasing was widely resisted by work groups: the Parliament Strike of 1841 is an example of just this kind of resistance – as was a similar strike of shipwrights at Jarrow in 1879.[103] Generally, however, chasing was a matter that could be dealt with more quietly. On entering his first joinery shop James Hopkinson was warned by his fellow apprentices 'on no account [to] do a job quicker than they had been in the habit of doing.' And W. T. Thornton quoted George Trollope who told of admonishing his men about the amount of work they were producing and who received the frank reply that they were 'not allowed to best my mates.'[104]

But this kind of informal activity was not limited to the skilled workers. In the 1830s and 1840s, the building labourers so consistently restricted production that attempts were made to introduce mechanical hoists. In 1845 the labourers of Liverpool and Birkenhead imposed a restriction of 12 bricks per hod (they had previously carried 14) which was still the accepted number in the 1860s – although in Leeds the labourers carried only eight.[105] At Liverpool, in the 1860s, a breach of contract court action revealed that the labourers demanded the employers honour a type of St Monday regulation which preserved the job of any man until Monday dinner hour, only then could new men replace those who had not come to work in the morning.[106] And in Manchester it is apparent that the labourers had established an extensive network of informal rules because the employers' counter-offensive of 1869 specifically addressed the restrictions they had imposed. It was, thus, demanded that the prohibition on the use of machinery be lifted, that wheelbarrows be used to move bricks, that the employers have the right to determine the ratio of labourers to bricklayer, and – significantly – that they obtain the right to appoint the gang leader 'and it is not necessary that he shall be the oldest in the shop.'[107]

In a similar manner to these restrictive rules, the enforcement of the standard rate was frequently a matter of informal work group rule. London builders in the early 1830s testified to the difficulties they faced in circumventing this unity: 'I have now ordered twenty men to be taken on next week, and we are endeavouring to get them at £1.8s, and I find I cannot; my foremen have told me that none of the men we discharged a month ago will return to work under £1.10s. a week.'[108] In the same period it was remarked of the carpenters and joiners that 'it would be a very dangerous thing for anybody, however extensive their concerns may be to attempt to interfere with that which is a sort of standard rate among the joiners; they would have a strike.'[109] In times of labour scarcity, of course, these kinds of 'rules' could be expected to thrive. But we find precisely the same patterns suggested by the evidence of a man in the early part of the twentieth century who recounted his experience of working above the standard rate: 'The men did not openly protest, but I could see that first one and then another would not speak to me, and all that sort of thing. Then you get this kind of thing: "Oh, he is the bell-horse. He does this, that and the other." I do not know what they did not say.'[110] Should sickness or ill-health make one of their members a candidate for a lower wage, bricklayers were known to informally agree to lay an extra number of bricks in order to protect the standard rate.[111] In some places, the masons went even further and successfully gained a voice in judging the rate that each man should get. Thus, in Sheffield there was a 'rule' (it did not appear in the working rules) that: 'Neither . . . an employer or foreman be allowed to judge a man as to his qualifications. But a meeting shall be called of all the members on the job, who together with the employer or the foreman shall decide the question.'[112] And at Bristol in 1860 it was reported that there 'were many men whose wages had been fixed by their shopmates at from 2/- to 3/- below the regular rate.'[113] As these episodes showed, if control over wage determination lay in the hands of the men there was no need for the standard rate.

THE GROWTH OF WORKER POWER

For rule making of the kind outlined above to be successful, work groups had to be able effectively to assert the potential power that lay in their hands. Both the extent of their power and the degree to which it could be fulfilled depended upon forces that were largely external to their experience and beyond the immediate control of their influence. These exogenous forces are many and complex; they play a critical role in determining the fluctuations in the frontier of control and because their impact is seldom universal the particularity of their influence across and within industries is responsible for the different location of that frontier in the different sectors of the workforce. Industrial relations crises occur when a conjuncture of these structural conditions overrides local differences to allow worker power to push the frontier of control back along a wide front. At some point this process has to be stopped, 'legitimate' authority re-asserted and worker power reduced or reformed to manageable proportions.

Since the First World War such confrontations have been central to social relations in capitalist society because it is only since that time (beginning in the 1890s) that the truly national integration of economy and society has lifted the problem of industrial discipline out of its parochial focus. Thus, it is easy for us to identify the years 1911–14, those of the War itself, and those of the 1950s to the late sixties as periods marked by impressive advances of work group power.[114] But although their form will change, such crises are not peculiar to modern times. The decisive struggles of the 1830s and 1840s revolved, in part, around the question of industrial discipline and authority. And whilst its dimensions and seriousness were of another scale, there was a similar – if more localised – crisis in the 1860s which grew out of the expansion of work control power during the decade to force a change in the structures and styles of industrial relations in building.[115] But to establish this argument, it is clearly important that we pay some attention to the conditions that allow such developments to take place.

Industrial sociologists have not fully explored this question but the presence of two basic groups of conditions would seem to be necessary for work group power to be effectively wielded. In the first place, there are those factors that depend upon the structure of the work, how it is organised, the methods of payment and its technology. And, secondly, there is the surrounding environment within which the work is conducted – such influences as company size and employment opportunities. In many cases these various elements work together. Thus, in both the factories that Tom Lupton studied, opportunities for work group activity existed but only amongst the electrical engineering workers was it a highly developed feature of the sociology of the workshop. Virtually no attempts were made by either male or female garment workers to influence the production process. Ultimately, this reflected the nature of the industry and the structure of the work, both of which served to discourage any 'will to control,' inhibited work group activity and, in its place, emphasised the individualism of 'looking after number one.'[116] But the absence of a 'will to control' was not the result of a poorly developed sense of consciousness: it was based upon a rational assessment of the workers' own position in the industry. Acutely aware of the insecure nature of the industry, possessing no transferability of skills (like much unskilled work the jobs were highly specialised) the garment workers were led to an individualistic maximisation of earnings as a buffer against hard times and as a substitute for their inability to influence the course of events in any other way.

This consciousness, however, could change if the structure of the work began to change. It is clear that changes in the technology and in the way in which the work is carried on are bound to affect the activities and power of the work group. Leonard Sayles tells, for example, of grinder operators in a steel plant who wielded a considerable power both in the plant and in their union. When a series of technological changes undermined the importance of this work, their power began to crumble, the cohesion of the group shattered and their position in plant and union was destroyed. What happened to these grinder operators was directly paralleled over a longer period of time by the Manchester brickmakers in the 1860s and 1870s. But technological change does not always lead to the destruction of work group power; nor, of course, even where it does is that destruction necessarily permanent and it can revive on the basis of new kinds of techniques. Thus, Sayles also tells of a group of upholstery trimmers whose power was not destroyed when electric stapling and new materials rendered their upholstery skills redundant because there remained plenty of job opportunities for their kind of work.[117]

In addition to these conditions, work groups develop most readily in large units of employment. Although the experience of the masons would suggest that this is not exclusively true, it is clear that the focus of conflict and the determination of broad working conditions in building occurred within the larger-scale general contracting sector of the industry. And finally, as contemporary experience has shown, it is certain that low rates of unemployment are an absolute condition for the successful exercise of work group power. This is especially true for less skilled workers who, deriving some strength from specialisation, cannot hope to maximise their potential power without the presence of a sellers' labour market.

Overlying these broad and general conditions that are a reflection of predominant macroeconomic trends, however, are the specific circumstances in which the work is conducted. In this respect the method of payment is of a significance that reaches 'far beyond the immediate bargain for wages.'[118] Work group cohesion is threatened if one group, or one member of the same group, doing identical work is paid differently. As Leonard Sayles somewhat clinically explains: 'The fewer the differences there are in work group status [and pay] . . . the more likely is the internal structure of the group to stabilize itself and the more likely are its members to accept internal leadership.'[119] It was for this reason, for example, that 'bell-horses' were resented; it was not simply the standard rate that was questioned by their presence but also any other improvements that might demand united action.[120]

The particular method of payment most suited to the enhancement of work group unity varied from trade to trade – the Webbs' famous distinction between those unions who insisted on piecework and those who preferred timework suggests the complexity of the question. But the importance of the issue was well-expressed by the Weymouth engineering workers in their 1918 statement against pieceworking:

The outstanding characteristic of the day rate is this feature of its being a collective concern of all workers . . . [The day rate] is a sacred minimum below which no worker . . . shall be paid. It has been established by collective action, increases are sought by collective action, and a reduction would be resisted by collective action. . . . The old collective spirit, which characterised the day-work system has broken down under the modern development of the piece-work system. In its place there has grown up individual interest, individual anomaly, individual discontent, and the gradual break up of that spirit of harmony and good fellowship.[121]

Except to make two general points, it is unnecessary to enter into the difficult question of the relationship between the method of payment and the exercise of work group power. But it is important to realise that changes in the system of payment may lead to new forms of work group control over the work. In engineering, the emergence of the stewards as group bargaining agents may be seen as a response to the spread of piecework which demanded a more formal work group organisation if cohesion was to be preserved.[122] And, secondly, in work where other means were present to stimulate work group power, changes in the method of payment did not pose a serious threat. The boilermakers provide an example of this. Until the 1860s they had resisted pieceworking but with the rapid expansion of iron shipbuilding and the consequent growth in demand for their skills this method of payment allowed them a greater freedom from managerial authority than timeworking would have done.[123] In addition, the division of labour in boilermakers' work was minimal; they did all the work necessary to the cutting and fitting of the plates. And this control over the total job was important. It explains, for example, the willingness of the London workshop carpenters and joiners to work by the hour when all the other trades insisted on straight day work.[124] The metropolitan joiners carried a job through from beginning to end; the division of labour to be found in Lancashire joinery, for example, was absent. To the London men, therefore, who 'could produce in wood anything properly represented in a drawing,' who had a relatively stable occupational group, and who had a total control over the job, hourly or piece payment posed relatively little threat. To men already divided – as were those in Lancashire or those on the building sites – such methods of payment threatened to accentuate fragmentation.[125] The method of payment, therefore, assumes a central importance for the ability of the work group to maintain the cohesion necessary for it to exert power and control. It is a question to which we shall return; for the moment we need only note that until the 1870s, the usual method of payment in the industry was by the day and one of the necessary conditions for work group power was, thus, fulfilled.[126]

But in the 1850s and 1860s these specific conditions were fused with those of a general, macroeconomic nature to provide the basis for a successful assertion of work group power and influence. A high level of building activity marked the period. It was, we may recall, the time when the large urban centres were being modernised and the demand for skilled labour (especially masons) placed those workers in a particularly advantageous position.[127] In spite of certain bad years like 1857, unemployment remained at a relatively low level throughout the period and the golden nature of these years for the Victorian artisan could be seen in particular by the progressive reduction of working hours and in the frequently spectacular gains that were made in wage levels.

Although there were some important defeats in the effort to reduce hours of work – most notably that of 1859 – the general picture was one of a steady advance throughout the fifties with a quickening of pace into the sixties. After first being secured by the carpenters of the northwest in 1848 the 4 p.m. Saturday became increasingly common and by 1851 it had been established in London. In 1861 the Saturday half-holiday was granted in London in return for payment by the hour and by 1871 four hours had been knocked off the 1861 day. Elsewhere the nine hours movement found more success. It was achieved first by the masons of Todmorden in 1859 and this was followed in 1860 or 1861 by victories in Rochdale, Heywood, Bacup, Huddersfield and Halifax.[128] In 1861, also, the Leeds' masons secured a shortening of hours on Monday and regular winter hours; those of Edinburgh won the nine hours; the Manchester bricklayers reduced their hours and the masons of genteel Bath obtained an advance of 4d per day and the early Saturday leaving.[129] By the mid-sixties towns which had previously been devoid of any aggressive activity were able to make similar kinds of gains. Dewsbury and Plymouth masons, for example, obtained the nine hours day in 1864 in which year the Poole, Leicester, Grimsby, and Burslem bricklayers, the Swansea, Wick, Penzance, Hull and Middlesbrough carpenters, and the Coventry labourers also won reductions in hours and advances in wages.[130]

Wage levels saw a general increase of something of the order of 50% between 1850 and 1874. Bowley's and Postgate's raw and specific figures tell the same story with the really large advances in wages coming in the

1860s. Thus, the following crude increases for the carpenters, bricklayers and masons can be seen from Postgate's table:[131]

1861–65 over 1853–61	16%
1865–66 over 1861–65	21%
1866–72 over 1865–66	6.6%
1872–73 over 1866–72	6.2%
1873–78 over 1872–73	6.0%

For London, figures collected by Thomas Brassey in 1878 revealed that the wages of skilled men had increased by about 23% between 1861 and 1875 and those of general labourers by about 35%. In particular towns or trades impressive gains were made. Using Bowley's series of wage statistics we can calculate that, for the years 1864–69, Birmingham carpenters achieved a 15% increase in their pay, those of Derby 13%, of Oldham 11.5% and of Sheffield 12.5%.[132] Even allowing for the fact that these make no provision for unemployment or the rise in the cost of living (both of which were fairly low) there is little doubt that the decade of the sixties was marked by a general forward movement on the wages front. These economic gains were a manifestation of the favourable external conditions for the exercise of work group power and they were complemented by the presence of appropriate internal conditions. Uniformity in the methods of payment, the focus of the system on substantive rule making alone, the practice of autonomous regulation and negotiation by imposition all provided the necessary basis for a successful interaction with the external conditions to allow an expansion of worker power that had not been experienced at any time before.

As a reflection of the crisis that had been reached in industrial relations by the late 1860s a Royal Commission was called to investigate associations of workmen and employers.[133] The Commission was generally welcomed by the union leaderships as a gamble that it could be used to counteract the slough of bad publicity that currently engulfed trade unions and that a new, and necessary, body of statutes would result to firmly define their legal position. That gamble ultimately paid off, but it would be a mistake to view the Royal Commission solely as the inspiration and creature of the unions and their friends amongst the intelligenstia. The essential background to its inception was the growing criticism of trade union activity. The *Hornby v. Close* decision, the tone of the public debate about unions, the predominantly anti-union pamphlet literature of the period and the obvious thoroughness with which Mault had prepared his brief were evidence that a counter-attack upon unionism was pending. As we have seen, Mault's case focussed primarily upon the restrictive practices of the 'unions' and, but for some fast and fancy footwork by Harrison and Hughes and the obvious 'respectability' of men like Applegarth, it might very well have turned out to be more influential than it was. But the case itself had been mounting for several years and its credibility is unquestionable; there was nothing extraordinary about Mault's evidence of the 'dictation' and 'restrictions' of the men. Of course, 'dictation' like 'unionism' was an inevitably common codeword in an industrial environment so deeply penetrated by autonomous regulation and it was not a charge peculiar or unique to the 1860s, having appeared in the contracting struggles of the thirties and the hours and conditions struggles of 1846 and 1859. What made the sixties different was that no big issues were involved. When the masters complained of 'dictation' and then illustrated it with examples like 'chasing' or walking time rules, it was hard, as the Junta and their allies in the intelligentsia so skilfully exploited, to associate this kind of 'dictation' with the picture of unionism that was painted by the most prominent union witnesses.[134] And the special investigations of Sheffield cutlery and Manchester brickmaking only served to reinforce the impression that these kinds of problems were limited to primitive local unions and would go away with the growth of the large amalgamated societies.

But, in fact, neither kinds of evidence were mutually exclusive and the reality of the building employers' evidence cannot be dismissed as a faulty perception or as the product of a blind hostility to unionism. In sharp contrast to earlier years, the trade journals of the 1860s are full of details of the 'dictation' that constituted the growth of worker power during the decade.[135] But it is unnecessary to take this kind of evidence at its face value; there are several other ways to determine and gauge the nature and dimensions of this expansion of the men's frontier of control. Indeed, it is possible for us to move beyond the particular incident and the general assertion and focus specifically upon the experience of the masons, whose records are the most complete. Although their achievements represented the outermost limits of work control power reached by the men, their case was extreme only in its degree and not in its quality.

There are some interesting insights to be gained into this question if we return to our series of strike statistics and examine the pattern of strike activity during the fifties and sixties. In particular, we are concerned with the category labelled 'control over labour' which were strikes that revolved around the respective authority of the masters or the men over the labour force and within which the largest issue was that to enforce union membership.[136] From the middle fifties this category became particularly important and by the 1860s it was the largest single strike issue. The following tables explain the distribution of strike issue by decade and show the clustering of these strikes in the mid-Victorian years. Out of a total number of 540 control over labour strikes, 390 occur in the years between 1850 and 1875.

Table 6. *Strike issues as a percentage of total strikes by decade*

	1836 to 1840	1841 to 1850	1851 to 1860	1861 to 1870	1871 to 1880	1881 to 1890	1891 to 1896
Wages	60.9	51.3	41.9	21.0	24.9	33.6	11.4
Hours	1.7	5.9	12.7	7.4	7.2	3.9	2.9
Organisation of work	20.7	18.2	8.9	7.8	6.8	13.6	9.0
Conditions of work	6.7	11.2	10.1	14.0	10.4	13.6	11.8
Control over labour	7.8	7.1	19.3	27.5	21.9	9.7	20.8
Craft enforcement[137]	2.2	6.3	5.0	15.5	18.2	17.5	33.1
Working rules	0.0	0.0	1.4	4.3	10.4	8.7	11.0
Other	0.0	0.0	1.2	4.9	0.5	0.0	1.7

Table 7. *Percentage distribution of control over labour strikes by period*

1836–50	1851–75	1876–96
6.1	72.0	21.8

The following tables illustrate the most pertinent structural features of control over labour strikes.[138] They reveal that such strikes were essentially conducted by small groups of men, that they were much shorter than the 'average' strike and that they possessed a somewhat higher rate of success than other strike issues. Control over labour strikes were short sharp job actions emanating from the workplace groups whose demands were fairly easily enforced.

Table 8. *Size of control over labour strikes 1850–75*

	(No.)	1–20 men %	21–50 men %	51–100 men %	101+ men %
Control Strikes	(83)	61.4	28.9	3.6	6.0
All Strikes	(551)	52.6	28.1	11.4	7.8

Table 9. *Length of control over labour strikes 1850–75*

	(No.)	1 day or less %	2–7 days %	8–14 days %	15+ days %
Control Strikes	(276)	67.7	21.4	6.9	4.0
All Strikes	(1121)	37.3	29.9	16.3	16.5

Table 10. *Results of control over labour strikes 1850–75*

	(No.)	Victory %	Failure %	Compromise %
Control Strikes	(344)	78.5	20.9	0.6
All Strikes	(1312)	75.2	20.3	4.5

If we tabulate their results with their length, however, an interesting picture begins to emerge. Whilst most control strikes were short and most of the victories attained immediately, the same also held true of those that failed. This pattern contrasts very markedly with that of wages strikes – which are included for purposes of comparison – and that of the strike population as a whole. As would be expected, the normal pattern was for there to be a close concordance between duration and failure. Nearly half of all strikes that failed were those which had lasted over a fortnight; but with the control strikes almost exactly the same proportion of failures were those of one day or less.

Table 11. *Results of control over labour strikes as a percentage of length 1850–75*

	Victories				Failures				
	(No.)	1 day or less	2–7 days	8–14 days	15+ days	(No.)	1 day or less	2–7 days	8–14 days	15+ days
Control strikes	(244)	71.3	22.1	4.9	1.6	(24)	45.8	12.5	25.0	16.7
Wages strikes	(228)	33.3	33.3	21.1	12.3	(41)	2.4	17.1	22.0	58.4
All strikes	(902)	43.1	33.3	14.3	9.3	(132)	12.1	15.2	24.2	48.5

What these figures suggest is that control over labour strikes were prosecuted with far less determination than other issues. In this period, masons were capable of winning over 23% of all strikes that lasted more than one week but only 6% of victorious control strikes lasted this long. It would seem to follow that this particular issue was one that was not felt deeply enough to inspire the men to fight to the bitter end.

In the light of the fact that most of these strikes were fought to enforce union membership, their structural features paradoxically confirm the relative insignificance of institutional unionism as an agent of industrial relations and its symbolic role as an expression of work group solidarity. The importance of such strikes during the period under consideration was only loosely connected to the expansion of union membership; their uncertain and weak nature reflected the 'softness' of a union membership that fluctuated wildly from year to year. In the main, however, the significance of control over labour strikes lay in their assertion of a work group discipline that could also be found in other guises. Their character was of a similar nature to the autonomous discipline revealed in this account of a court of justice that James Hopkinson encountered:

> There was one custom which prevailed in the shop . . . which enabled the men to live much more peacefully with each other . . . And that was by holding a court of justice . . . It originated in the desire for drink, yet at the same time it afforded protection to the weak. If any workman struck another or any one had a grievance, they would call the court together in the following manner . . . By simply striking a holdfast with a hammer . . . Upon hearing the sound all the men from the various rooms would come together . . . to try the case by jury concisting [*sic*] of all the men on the premises . . . The men worked piece work . . . so that the master did not mind so much about it. And they were such an independant [*sic*] lot of men that they would not have cared much if he had . . . One of the men was chosen to act as judge by a show of hand . . . Which ever side was found to blame had to pay a fine of not less than one shilling but if it was a very hot day and they were very thirsty sometimes as much as four or five shillings had to be spent.[139]

Resting on the basis of an already expanded realm of control over working conditions, control over labour strikes were a frequently successful attempt to push that control to the even greater limits of the labour force itself. They lay, therefore, at the most distant point of the men's frontier of control and it was just this that explained their short duration and weak prosecution. Failing to meet with an immediate success, the issue was too tenuous to pursue any further. At the same time, the importance of the issue transcended any of these considerations. Their concentration during this period is a clear statement both of the extent to which the men were emboldened to assert their control and of the intensity of the myriad of small-scale authority struggles that marked the mid-Victorian years.

In addition to the assertiveness of the men over who was and who was not to be employed, it is also clear that the period experienced an expansion of 'unofficial' and 'official' restrictive rules. The informal work group rules that we discussed earlier were gathering in strength and vigour as the sixties wore on. It was, for example, in 1865 that the habit of informal action against chasing was formalised by the masons into a union rule which legalised the imposition of fines upon chasers. This may have been an attempt to transmute a 'custom' into an established practice because it was claimed that the problem itself had been virtually eliminated by this date.[140] It was during the sixties, too, that the evidence of a worker role in fixing individual wages is at its strongest; during this time, also, that walking time was so strictly enforced that the Darlington masons would walk past their job site to reach the recognised starting place and then walk to work from there. And even where there were no formal rules, as in London, it was reported the combined hostility of union and non-union men had 'pretty well done away with' piecework.[141]

But perhaps the most powerful testimony to the growth of worker power during this period is the emergence of formal rules to govern the conditions and methods of work in the trades. Working rules first appear in building in the early fifties. They spread as the power of the men grew so that by the sixties they were a common feature throughout the whole industry – although it is for the masons that we possess the most complete information on their evolution and character. Their origins are usually taken to lie in the growing power of trade unionism to force employers into mutually negotiated collective bargains.[142] But, in fact, this view is almost totally false. Whilst they were to become the means of mutual rule making in the industry, their origins are firmly situated within the system of unformalised autonomous regulation. Before the late sixties and early seventies, for example, very few of the working rules contained any specifications for procedural rule making: their clauses were addressed solely to substantive issues. In the 1860s such rules represented a formalisation of autonomous regulation by the men. They were a manifestation of the power of the men and their character and nature were functions of the successful fusion of informal restrictive rules with negotiation by imposition.[143] It is true that the successful achievement of working rules drawn up by the men encouraged and stimulated 'habits of association' that could then lead to unionisation. It is also clear that they contained the seeds (or some of the seeds) of modern collective bargaining which their very presence was to make easier to achieve. But in the context of the 1860s neither trade unionism nor mutual negotiation were pre-requisites for the implementation of a code of rules. Indeed it is likely that in most cases their emergence owed nothing to either of these agents.[144] Working rules in this period, therefore, represented the ultimate achievement of the opportunities for autonomous regulation that were presented by the unformalised system of industrial relations. That they were to become the prime means of mutual regulation of the industry was more because they stood to hand than it was implicit in the way in which they emerged.

The letter a master builder wrote to carpenters in his employ during the Plymouth strike of 1865 illustrates the context in which these rules were achieved:

I received your notice this day, in which you ask me to establish your rules in my shop; but . . . I pay the rent of my shop, and when you pay the rent you can rule if you like; but as long as I pay the rent I shall rule. We live in a land of liberty, but the way you are going to work is to do away with my liberty, and establish a liberty of your own to have power to oppress.[145]

The dilemma this man faced was typical and was repeated time and again across the whole spectrum of trades in the industry during this period.[146]

But it reached its apogee amongst the masons who, at Birmingham for example, consistently declined to 'accede to any rules save those which they themselves have drawn up.' Similarly, in 1849, the Bradford masons' strike against piecework and sub-contracting was ended by the imposition of 'written agreements for the future conduct of the trade.' At Ashton, four years later, the men submitted a code of rules (the main one was to prohibit piecework) and required a meeting to discuss them. The masters refused to accept the men's rules, tried to bring in non-union labour and were defeated in a strike which resulted in the adoption of the restrictive rules of the men. In the same year a successful strike at Sheffield saw the men 'actively engaged in bringing about a code of regulation.' The Retford masons in 1855 secured the agreement of two major employers before imposing their rules upon the rest.[147] The Leeds masons who 'for a series of years have been guided by the most despotic rules and regulations [of the masters]' struck in 1860 for a code which abolished piecework and insisted upon a conciliation committee.[148] In 1865, the Doncaster masons – union and non-union – held a meeting for the purpose of drawing up a code of rules which was then presented to the masters who refused to accede. The men 'conceded a few things which we considered did not interfere with us . . . we then gave notice for the rules to come into operation on Monday, May 29th. when we were informed that we might stand out as long as we liked.'[149] The strike was successful and the rules were secured.

More important, perhaps, than the way in which the working rules were achieved and equally instructive of their role as formalising the power of the men, was their transformation from relatively simple statements of hours and wages to complex and detailed exegeses which minutely regulated the conditions under which the work was to be done. The changes in the working rules reported in the masons' *Fortnightly Returns* throughout the sixties establish beyond any doubt that the rules were becoming more restrictive than ever before and, unlike the earlier pattern of fluctuating gains and losses, the restrictions were in danger of becoming permanent. Sheds began to be demanded, overtime effectively controlled and piecework largely prohibited, walking time rigorously enforced, apprenticeship ratios established and the importation of worked stone prevented. The formula of increasingly restrictive working rules plus an imposition style of negotiation gave content and point to the masters' complaints about the 'dictation' and 'tyranny' of the men. Manchester was one of the earliest towns to have a code; its rules were always more extensive than most other towns and those of 1839 were doubly unusual in that they included restrictions on piecework and overtime in addition to their main concern with hours, wages and boundaries. But these restrictions were milder than they were later to become: overtime could be worked 'when necessary,' sheds were to be erected 'where reasonable.' By the late sixties, the limits had been more tightly drawn: overtime was banned, sheds were required, piecework forbidden, worked stone and polishing machinery prohibited and apprenticeship controlled.[150] The same was true elsewhere. In Wolverhampton, for example, the first working rules of 1853 were solely concerned with wages and hours. In 1861 walking-time restrictions were added and in 1864 the provision of sheds for outdoor working was required. The Sheffield and Bolton codes of 1853 were notable for their lack of specificity on hours, piecework and overtime; by the early sixties successful attempts were made to prohibit piecework and worked stone. And in Bolton the 1868 rules prohibited overtime unless it could be shown to be necessary from causes such as breakdown.[151] Similarly, the Pentach lodge of the Liverpool masons in 1863 demanded and received rules which provided for sheds, walking time and prohibited piecework or overtime.[152]

Of all the restrictive rules that symbolised the power of the men the prohibition on the importation of worked stone into a town or district was, perhaps, the most notorious. As might be expected, the Webbs regarded it as merely another device to uphold the standard rate but the masters of the sixties saw beyond that to its real significance as one of the most arrogant manifestations of the men's power.[153] To restrict worked stone not only kept more work within a given town but, in combination with the general labour shortage, it also served to enhance the power of the men over a whole range of bargaining issues. The rule was even featured in a speech Gladstone made at Oldham in December 1867 which was devoted to a condemnation of the restrictive practices of trade unions and in which this particular rule was stigmatised as 'worthy of savages.'[154] The worked stone rule had occasionally appeared before the 1860s, an attempt was made to introduce it at Stockport as early as 1836 and there was a strike against worked stone being brought into Preston in 1853. It is not clear whether its emergence in the 1860s reflected a structural change in the industry which made quarry stone more available, or whether the problem had always been present without the men being strong enough to do anything about it. The evidence is conflicting and probably reflects local differences. Thus, the Preston masons in 1853 claimed that there was 'an acknowledged law between the old established masters . . . and the men, that no worked stone be introduced' and that some small masters were trying to infringe this custom.[155] At Glasgow, on the other hand, stone had always been dressed at the quarry until 1855 when the masons managed to assert a worked stone rule that proved to be 'peculiarly vexatious to the masters.' In any case, it was only with the early sixties that the rule began consistently to appear in the codes and not least amongst its vexations to the masters was the 25% it added to the cost of labour.[156] By 1867, it was reported that the rule applied everywhere outside London but it is clear that it was concentrated in the northern and midlands counties' heartland of work control power.[157]

The first appearance of the rule in the sixties was at Sheffield in 1862, after which it spread rapidly to Altrincham and Manchester and by the mid-sixties virtually all towns of any size had a prohibition of worked stone in their working rules. Warrington provides a typical example. It was explained that the men intended to restrict the use of worked stone because: 'Our old rules do not stop worked stone from coming into the town, and one of our master builders having done one large job with worked stone from Wales, we think the time has arrived when we should no longer remain in the background, for if not stopped now the same will be carried on by all.'[158] Nor did the worked stone rule stand alone, but was part of a package of restrictions which included the prohibition of sub-contracting, the necessity for sheds, and apprenticeship regulation. And the same pattern may also be found elsewhere. By the late sixties so completely had the men asserted their control over the issue that it was not unknown for them to insist on re-working any stone that had been even partially worked on a rough planing machine within their own workshop.[159] As we have shown, the worked stone rule was merely one of a number of restrictive rules that were successfully imposed by the men in the 1860s; its interest is not simply that of a specimen, however, but as a practical illustration of the extent to which the growth in worker power severely constrained the freedom of the employers to operate their businesses as they pleased. If the men could determine what kind of material was used, how many bricks were to be carried in a hod, when overtime was to be worked, who was to be employed; in other words, if they would decide how and in what style the work was to be done, then the cry that was heard from Liverpool in 1861 that ' "the natural order of things is reversed; they [the men] are the real masters" ' was one that was to aptly characterise the whole decade.[160]

The struggle for control over work is, of course, a constant theme of industrial relations but its particular phases are moulded and shaped by the contextual limits of the industrial relations system within which it occurs. It was the distinctive feature of autonomous regulation that it allowed a total freedom for either side to reap the full harvest of the power equation in which they were placed to their opponents. This meant, of course, that it was as possible for employers to establish their supremacy as it was for the men to establish theirs. That, after all, had been the objective of the great authority struggles of the thirties, forties and fifties and that, too, was why the position of the frontier of control varied from place to place. Most of what we have detailed above, for example, applied particularly to the Midlands and the North of England. In rural Wales, small-town Southern England and other places, it is doubtful whether the same case could be so strongly argued.[161] But although the limits of the system were theoretically infinite and allowed for the total supremacy of either side, it was in reality a balance of power that determined whether the advantage lay with the masters or the men. During the two decades of the fifties and sixties that balance turned decisively in favour of the men who used it, as they were bound to do, to extend the frontier of their control. They could not have accomplished this had it not been for the structural conditions under which they worked nor without the advantageous economic circumstances of the period. But neither could it have been achieved without the freedom allowed by the unformalised structure of industrial relations. With no procedural rules to hamper them, with no union authority to restrain them, the men were able to gather in the rewards of the laissez-faire system of industrial relations. But for the employer, it was precisely this that created the imperative to change the very system itself.

3

'No hours: no arbitration.' The crisis of the late sixties and the formalisation of industrial relations

ANXIETY AND AUTHORITY

One of the most perceptive historians of the mid-Victorian era has written that by the end of the 1860s there were distinct 'signs of national anxiety.'[1] The qualified implications in the word 'anxiety' make it appropriately well-chosen; for there was no sense of crisis but rather a recognition that in some disturbing way values were changing under the pressure of deeper, structural tensions that could not be fully comprehended. A central theme to the end of the 'age of equipoise' was the need for new sources of authority: British society stood at the edge of a divide between a conception of freedom and authority which firmly linked behaviour to standards derived from informal, individualist association and one where standards were to be defined by more collectivist relationships and institutions.

In spite of the generally comforting conclusions that Bagehot could draw from his study of the constitution, it was the Matthew Arnold of *Culture and Anarchy* who most accurately appreciated what was happening at the tail end of the 1860s. Arnold, in whom it is possible to see one of the first commentators on the problems of a 'mass society,' was very much a man of his times intimately involved in the machinery of government and society.[2] And unlike Carlyle, who also feared the Niagara of unthinking change, Arnold cannot be dismissed as a cranky old man whom time had overtaken. Arnold was concerned about the need for an authority that would set and judge certain standards of value. Or, to put it more precisely, he was worried about the serious void that was created by the absence of any such authority at a time when both the populace and the philistines were insisting upon the need for change. In this sense, Arnold reflected in an intimate way the process of change that British society was about to undergo. The 'old' ways of doing things – the dependence, for example, on voluntary and informal effort in education – were no longer adequate. The standards, the authority structures that reflected and rested upon these old methods would, therefore, need to be replaced. Arnold's fears may or may not have been mistaken, his identification of the State as a source for qualitative authority may have been prescient and naive. Into those questions we hardly need to enter because, for us, his importance lies in the identification of authority – its standards, legitimacy and values – as the critical question of the period.

The grounds for 'anxiety' lay primarily in the confluence of commercial uncertainty (it was no stronger than that) and the growing recognition of the necessity for social and political change. There may have been little collective understanding of the forces that were in motion and, indeed, the economic shifts of the period are still inadequately understood but it is clear that their central feature was a movement away from a supremacy that rested upon industrial might to one which would depend upon the export of capital. The uncertainty – reflected by Goschen's famous article about capital being on strike – was a function of this shift combined with the first blush of an awareness that a world of multi-lateral economic power was beginning to dawn. The social and economic structural changes – the growth of a commercial, white-collar sector of employment, the emergence of the large-scale company, and the break in productivity rates that seems to characterise the period – were all a reflection of this changing economic emphasis.[3] And the 'reforms' of the period reflected it too because they pointed towards a formalisation of relationships that had previously been left informal. In politics, for example, the effect of the franchise extension, the ballot box and the new caucus machinery was to redefine in a more discrete way political roles and relationships between the classes.[4] In the House of Commons, party discipline and leadership authority now assumed a far greater importance than they had previously possessed: the fluid political alliances of 1831–32 or the cross-voting of 1867 were (as the Liberal split, paradoxically, revealed) inconceivable by 1884. In education, especially at the elementary level, responsibility and authority began to devolve away from the individual effort of the churches and philanthropists and onto the formal sanction and power of the state in its broadest sense. And, in an ironical reversal of the main direction of redefinition, Bagehot's discovery that deference did not need the overt presence of 'influence' to survive but would continue to flourish through informal obeisance was also a reflection of these changing structures and relationships. Class organisation now began to assume a greater role in the functioning of society than heretofore: it is the difference between the mass movement of Chartism and the permanent implantation of trade unions with a clearly defined place and status within the framework of society. Formal and permanent associations of businessmen to represent their interests now begin to emerge for the first time. They were merely one illustration of the way in which the definition of relationships moved away from a personal individualist framework and into a context of collective association and organisation.

This is neither the time nor the place to examine the connections between these superstructural changes and those within the base of

Britain's world economy. But the links are not too hard to find. The emergent economic order of multi-lateral competition demanded a 'populace' that received, at the very least, a lower-class education for lower-class employment; it demanded, furthermore, that labour be productivity oriented and that it be integrated into the body politic; it demanded that 'business' move out of its parochial control of local affairs and decisively take charge of national politics. And as an example of this latter development, the career of Joseph Chamberlain – a representative figure of the haute bourgeoisie – illustrates to great advantage the relationships between the economic, political and social features of the period.[5] Whatever the imperatives that may have been operating (and they were many and wider than purely mechanistic economic forces) the real meaning to the end of 'equipoise' lies in the emergence of new kinds of authority relationships between the groups and classes of society. Participants now meet within formal structures of association and organisation which serve to assign them discrete and determinate roles and to provide a common ground over which they may sort out their common interests. To this general phenomenon industrial relations were no exception – indeed, they provide an interesting case study of this wider movement. For the period saw a formalisation of industrial relations; it saw the creation of new sources of authority in industrial affairs that was to move them beyond the individualism of master and men into the collectivity of employers and unions and in that process an end was declared to the wide conception of freedom that was autonomous regulation.

In common with the other developments that have been mentioned, however, industrial relations were only formalised. They were not corporatised into a modern 'system.' And it is important to realise and understand the distinction that is being drawn. The 1870s to the 1890s were a period of transition. In the economic sphere, for example, these years are the bridge between the unchallengeable supremacy of the first industrial nation and the necessarily shared economic world of the later nineteenth century. It is the period when society and economy are – to over-schematise the process – shaking down in preparation for the challenges of 1890–1914. The problems inherent, for example, in the check to productivity that occurred in this period begin to be hesitantly addressed in the 1870s but were not to be fully appreciated until the 1890s. Although the export of capital and its consequent financial imperialism begin to play a more important role in the British economy, it is not until the 1890s that they attain a parity of importance with the industrial sector. Tunnelling its way under the surface of moral consensus from the 1870s, the challenge to mid-Victorian convention does not explode into decisive confrontation until the last decade of the century.

And so it is with the changes in the structure of industrial relations – they become formalised not thoroughly systematised. That is to say, autonomous regulation does not suddenly disappear but it increasingly becomes illegitimate, outmoded and is steadily replaced by mutual negotiation and the beginnings of a procedural system. Even if its authority is not yet fully safe-guarded by a modern network of collective bargaining structures, the habit of mutual negotiation is irrevocably established. In building, for example, conciliation schemes now become a permanent part of the industrial relations world and although it was not until the 1890s that a fully secure local, regional and national matrix was created, the period from the seventies to the nineties saw the basis laid for this later development. It was the time when industrial relations were being rearranged and the foundations established for a completely modern system. Thus, until the nineties, across industry and the nation, industrial relations presented an amalgam of the old and new. Procedural rule making was now a permanent element in the national picture but it co-existed uneasily with the remnants of substantive bargaining reminiscent of the unformalised system. It is the new elements that are the most significant; they betokened a spirit of formalisation that was wider than the limits of their immediate influence. The growing consensus was now to perceive industrial relationships in terms of formally defined roles and procedures. Transitional though it was, therefore, the period does mark a decisive change of direction and it is critical that we understand the process by which this substitution of one set of structures for another took place. And to do this we have to return to the themes of anxiety and authority which opened the period. On a national level, the end of equipoise was unaccompanied by any sense of crisis; difficulties were recognised but they provoked neither despair nor any real uncertainty as to what should be done about them. But it is appropriate to speak of a crisis of industrial relations in building and, perhaps, elsewhere. It was a 'crisis,' however, which aptly illustrates Burn's comment on the spirit in which the 'difficulties' were approached, for it was with 'a vigorous effort towards their solution' that the large building employers faced the climax to their problems with labour at the end of the 1860s.[6]

THE STRUCTURE OF CRISIS

As we have already shown, by the late sixties building employers were confronted with a serious assault upon their authority over work that could not be ignored. The expansion of worker power posed a serious challenge to that sphere of freedom which masters regarded as rightfully theirs. It was the paradox and contradiction of unformalised industrial relations to allow the growth of a balance of power relations that stood at odds with the legitimate ranking of the social hierarchy. Only a few 'advanced' souls dared even to argue the legitimacy of a recognised trade union role; none were prepared to condone what amounted to a sharing of power at the point of production. The language of authority was, therefore, appropriate: it was in tune with – if not in direct contact – the similar but wider concerns of men like Arnold. Beneath its rhetorical surface, however, that language spoke not just to the philosophical illegitimacy of an imbalanced power relationship, it was grounded in a reality that had to do with baser concerns. If the 'natural' order of things was, for a while, reversed the problem was not simply a matter of power in the abstract but of practical survival and of profits.

For the challenge presented by the growth of worker power also possessed an economic dimension which had to do with the pressure that it placed upon the masters' ability to cope adequately with the nature of general contracting. More than in most industries, perhaps, the role of labour costs is critical in determining the extent to which building employers can competitively flourish.[7] Builders stayed in business only so long as they could viably tender without under-pricing themselves into bankruptcy. In fact, this kind of collapse was relatively unusual for the large contractors, although it was probably a fact of life for the many small men who constituted the tail of the industry. But the small men were of virtually no importance in defining the structure of industrial relations and it is, therefore, interesting to note the suggestion that in London, at least, competitive tendering 'by the sixties had . . . reached a fierce intensity.' The company of Henry Myers & Son, for example, tendered for forty-four contracts in 1865 and won only five; the firm of F. L. Dove tendered for twenty-four and won three.[8] Furthermore, the collapse of Peto and Betts – who were reported to have driven up labour costs by ten per cent because of their huge demand for men on the London, Chatham and Dover railway – not only touched off the commercial crisis of 1866 but served to remind all large contractors of the dangers of allowing labour costs to move out of control.[9] It was ironic that Peto's own battle with the masons in 1841 had become a classic example of the need for a tight discipline to avert the dangers of bankruptcy:

The successful execution of any contract depends on the talent and vigilance of the foreman; it is the labour department in which the risk is mainly concerned . . . In a large work . . . unless the cost of labour can be controlled, it is impossible to undertake the work by contract . . . We believe that half of the bankrupt builders become so by the labour and not by the materials.[10]

Just how far this was so, it is impossible to determine: no readily available bankruptcy statistics exist which would allow us to determine whether builders were particularly notable in the general increase of bankruptcies that occurred during the late sixties.[11] But from Cairncross' careful examination of the Glasgow building industry, we do know that labour costs play a central role in the pressures of total costs and the collapse of building booms. Indeed, at one point it was even suggested that the 'final *coup de grâce* to building booms came from the side of cost rather than demand.'[12] Not all economic historians would agree with Cairncross and, in addition to a focus on cost, it is obviously important to recognise – as Cairncross did in a subsequent work – the irrational character of speculative building, the ultimate importance of empties, credit and population migration.[13]

But what struck Cairncross about Glasgow and where his work is of interest to us was the close correlation that could be drawn between the rise in costs and the downturn from booms: 'In 1877, 1899, and 1903 there are clear maxima in building costs and the bursting of a speculative bubble; in 1883 there is another maxima that may have checked an incipient revival.' Since materials costs were stable or declining during these years, 'we are left with wages as the element in construction which rose in the closing stages of the boom.' Indeed, on the basis of his Glasgow figures, Cairncross estimated that every penny on masons' wages translated into a £10 increase in the cost per room.[14] Most suggestive of all, however, is the relationship that may be posited between these forces and the formalisation of industrial relations in the Glasgow masons' trade which occurred in 1884. Throughout the sixties, and for most of the seventies, the masons had steadily improved their position – wages doubled between 1863 and 1877. Then came the Glasgow bank crash of 1878 which crippled their union, destroyed the building boom and caused wages to tumble from 10d per hour to 6d per hour. Two strikes in 1881 and 1883 successfully forced wages back up to 7½d but they also precipitated an eventual jump of £15 in the cost per room. Not only was this one of the sharpest cost increases in the period 1873–83 but it was the only one clearly associated with a wage demand. In 1876–77, for example, costs had increased by £19 per room but wages had remained stable; in 1881–82 costs had actually fallen whilst wages had risen. It is, therefore, hardly fanciful to see the masters' determination in 1884 to reduce wages as a direct response to the confluence of sharply increased costs and wages. A strike was called, the men defeated and on the masters' initiative a permanent conciliation board created which, we are assured from testimony before the *Royal Commission on Labour*, met annually to settle disputes and determine conditions.[15]

The pattern to be noted from Glasgow suggests an unsurprising – if somewhat tenuous – link between pressure from labour costs and a particular local turning point in the structures of industrial relations. We have already shown how large wage gains were made in the north in the 1860s, but there is more to this matter than a simple correlation between those advances and the crisis of the late sixties. Wage increases alone would not explain the frantic obsession with 'authority' that marked that decade and the pressure from wages is only part of the story. The content of the rhetoric of authority derived from the contribution of restrictive practices to total labour costs. Since the effect of restrictive practices is to constrain and prevent any compensatory improvements in productivity, they may be more critical to total costs than a monetary wage increase. It is within this context that we must view the disagreements amongst those historians who have examined the course of labour costs in the building cycle.

G. T. Jones, who was the first to address the problem of productivity in building, suggested that labour costs increased more sharply and to a greater extent during the sixties than at any other period to reach a plateau at the end of the decade before rising again to 1875.[16] The presence of certain insensitivities in Jones' index led Maiwald to attempt a more accurate assessment of cost fluctuations which he believed followed a smoother pattern than Jones had suggested. Maiwald established that labour costs did rise during the sixties but not as steeply as Jones had claimed, while material costs tended to fall or fluctuate around the same level. It was in the mid-seventies that Maiwald claimed the sharpest rise in costs came and in which the increase in material costs was operative.[17] But in spite of the greater sensitivity that is claimed for this index, there are several qualifications that need to be entered which suggest that Jones' analysis might after all be the more insightful. In the first place, one of the things that led economic historians to question the Jones index was its apparent lack of conformity to the curve of unemployment: out of fourteen turning points in the rate of unemployment between 1860–1915, there were only three or four comparative turns in the cost curve. Thus, 'Jones' index continued to increase for two years after 1865 though the curve for employment went down.'[18] In fact, there may be nothing very surprising about this if we take account of the influence of restrictive practices whose precise economic effects we cannot measure but which will be insensitive and resistant to immediate fluctuations in unemployment. Unlike most economic historians, Jones was alert to the importance of restrictive practices and for the period 1890–1910 he was able to show how they served to reduce 'efficiency' by some 14%.[19] Part of the problem with the earlier period is that it is less susceptible to the same kind of measurements but, in the light of the overwhelming evidence that does exist for the presence of widespread restrictions, Jones' belief in substantial labour cost increases does not seem so outrageous. And this is suggested even on the basis of Maiwald's own figures where it is necessary to bear in mind the changing mix in the labour–materials components of the cost burden. The cost jump in the early seventies reflected that of materials rather than of labour which represented a far smaller proportion of the total increase than it had in the 1860s. At Maiwald's peak of costs, between 1870–73, his materials cost index had risen by 39%, that of labour by a mere 4.7%; and if we take the percentage increase or decrease in each of his categories for the fifties through the eighties, the impression that it was the sixties which saw wages as the most pressing burden on costs is reinforced.[20]

Table 12. *Cost index for building 1850–89*

	% Rise/fall wage cost index	% Rise/fall material cost index	% Rise/fall total cost index
1850–59	+6.7	+2.2	+3.4
1860–69	+22.6	+4.1	+3.9
1870–79	+12.3	−10.0	+2.0
1880–89	+1.7	−10.4	−6.4

Finally, the movement of the building cycle itself suggests that there were some grounds for concern at the end of the 1860s. Because of the multiplicity of national and local influences that are known to condition the course of the cycle, any generalisation about specific fluctuations is dangerous. Except in London where capital movements were possibly an important factor, much depended upon the state of the dominant industry.[21] In South Wales, for example, whose pattern stood in an inverse relationship to Manchester, the state of the coal industry was the predominating influence whilst in Manchester the textile industry played a similar role. But over the north as a whole there is a general dip and faltering of the cycle in 1869 which is reminiscent of Cairncross' suggestion about incipient booms being halted by wages costs. Then, subsequent to the defeat of the men in 1869–70, a sharp jump follows to a peak of activity during the middle seventies.[22] This would suggest that the 'anxiety' expressed by the Manchester contractor, Edward Johnson, before the carpenters' and joiners' arbitration board of 1869 was not misplaced. Johnson complained that many jobs were lost by the local employers because the wage costs were higher in Manchester than the surrounding towns and that this had led to a low level of investment in the trade.[23]

As we have pointed out, the employers' freedom to vary the conditions of working was more critical to the prosperity of building companies than in most other industries. Competitive tendering and the high ratio of labour to fixed costs (there was little machinery, virtually no plant) made it a business for hard men: 'The big builders' business was conducted with a ruthless efficiency . . . If he was to survive he had to face his men, command them and, if necessary, endure their hatred.'[24] Even under the most propitious circumstances this ideal was difficult to attain. And in the 1860s it is evident that circumstances were anything but favourable to the employers' necessary freedom of action. Not only were the inherently heavy labour costs accentuated by the sharp rise in wages, they were additionally burdened both by a general shortening of hours of labour and by extensive restrictive practices. Labour was not only becoming more expensive, it was also becoming less intensive and, therefore, less productive. Herein lay the critical elements of a crisis, for it was directly analogous to that situation Marx had in mind (although his point was meant to apply to crises of capitalism as a whole) when he wrote:

Crises are always prepared by precisely a period in which wages rise generally and the working-class gets a larger share of that part of the annual product which is intended for consumption ... Capitalist production comprises conditions ... which permit the working class to enjoy that relative prosperity only momentarily, and at that always only as the harbinger of a coming crisis. [25]

Indeed, one of the interesting things about the building industry in the 1860s is that it manifests a phenomenon that Marx doubted could ever really happen. That is, a declining rate of exploitation (through less intensity of labour) remained unbalanced by any changes in the composition of capital to overcome that decline by increasing productivity. [26] With regard to the shortening of the workday, for example, Marx argued that its economic benefits would not in reality accrue to the men, for it never occurred under conditions where labour productivity remained stable: 'A change in the productiveness and intensity of labour either precedes or immediately follows, a shortening of the working day.' Because a shortened day reduced surplus labour and surplus value, only by lowering the price of labour in some way could 'the capitalist save himself harmless.'[27] But even if we admit the local variations in the extent to which the hours of labour were shortened in the sixties – the big push coming in 1867, significantly just before the crisis – and even if we recognise the important exception of London, we are still left with an overwhelming picture of declining intensity of labour through restrictive practices combined with a stable or declining number of working hours.

This combination of circumstances held ominous implications for the rate of surplus value. As Marx pointed out, changes in the magnitude (i.e. intensity) of labour could not leave unaffected the amount of surplus value derived from the labourer and, if other factors remained constant, a decline in the productivity of labour must cause a rise in the value of labour power and a fall in surplus value. [28] Thus, the 'rate of surplus value is ... an exact expression of the degree of exploitation of labour power by capital, or of the labourer by the capitalist.'[29] It follows, therefore, that there can be no change in the rate of exploitation (in the length of the working day, in the productivity and in the intensity of work) if other factors remain constant without a consequent change in profits. But it is important to realise that declining rates of exploitation or surplus value do not necessarily lead to a crisis of profits. Indeed, Marx argued that it would not do so because capitalists could not be expected to sit still while they saw their profits whittled away by increased labour power. On the contrary they could quite easily sustain a falling rate of surplus value provided they maintained or increased their freedom to expand their rate of profit, which comprised the true test of capitalist profitability and depended upon the relative mix between that 'part of capital exchanged for living labour and the part existing in the form of raw materials and means of production.'[30] Changes in the relationship between variable (i.e. labour) and constant (i.e. materials etc.) capital could differently affect the rates of surplus value and profit. An increase, for example, in the rate of surplus value did not necessarily imply an increase in the rate of profit: for if less labour power was employed on more machinery the rate of surplus value would rise but the rate of profit would fall because the proportion of variable capital to constant capital would have fallen.[31] In such a case, the rate of exploitation would increase (through, for example, faster working), but the actual rate of profit would decline with the declining mass (i.e. number of labourers) of surplus value: 'the rate of profit does not sink because labour is exploited any less, but because generally less labour is employed in proportion to the employed capital.'[32]

Marx seems to have conceived of the dynamic relationship between surplus value, the rate of profit and the rate of exploitation, mainly in terms of changes in the organic composition of capital which increased the ratio of constant to variable capital by the adoption of a new technology or the concentration into larger units of production. Indeed, something like this seems to have happened in engineering during the 1870s where the fall in the rate of exploitation consequent upon the success of the nine hours' movement stimulated the search for better organisation and techniques to increase productivity.[33] It is also possible that carpentry underwent a similar kind of structural change: there being a close correlation between successful hours' reductions in the early seventies and the decisive appearance of machine joinery.[34] But within the building trades carpentry was a clear exception for the ready application of machine technology to its craft and Marx paid far less attention to what would happen if the rate of exploitation declined without responsive changes in the composition of capital or in the nature of worker productivity. He did admit, however, that a falling rate of profit could express a falling rate of surplus value if the organic composition of capital remained unchanged or if 'the amount of labour power increases in relation to the value of constant capital.'[35] But this was precisely what was happening in building in the 1860s where material costs remained relatively stable and during the first half of the decade actually fell, but where the total labour costs – through wages, shortened hours and restrictive practices – rose sharply.

Thus, a decline in the rate of exploitation occurred which found an expression in a decline both in the mass of surplus value and in the rate of profit and the central problem for building employers was to find ways of increasing the rate of exploitation to claw back the surplus value and maximise their profits. In theory there were two, not necessarily separate, ways in which this could be done. Either the organic composition of capital could be changed to increase labour productivity and so increase the mass of profit; or, the rate of exploitation could be increased by changing the conditions of work. In practice neither of these alternatives was open to the building masters during the 1860s. Although we cannot absolutely discount a change in the organic composition of capital through an increase in large-scale companies, there is no evidence that this was a major theme of the period. Nor were there important changes in the reverse direction: sub-contracting, which was the way the rate of exploitation was to be increased in the 1890s, was successfully resisted by the men in this earlier period.[36] Until the later part of the century and outside carpentry, there were no new technologies to be applied in an industry notoriously resistant to innovation. Where machine technology was applied the results were astounding, but over the broad range of trades no such development occurred.[37] Neither were employers able to increase the rate of exploitation by the classic techniques of extending the working day and reducing wages.[38] In this they were constrained both by the power of the men and by the booming condition of the trade. Even if the rates of surplus value and profit were falling, the competitive nature of the industry meant that employers had to continue to take advantage of the generally good conditions. To do otherwise by increasing hours, reducing wages or attacking the conditions of work in other ways would be to risk a stoppage and the loss of tenders and workmen. Yet these were just the techniques to increase the rate of exploitation that building employers had traditionally used and needed to use now. In the 1860s their freedom of action to drive the men hard, to scamp (difficult with rules against chasing), to work by the piece or to sub-contract and to enforce overtime were all unnaturally restricted. At the same time, it was difficult to attain a united front against the men on the basis of these classic techniques of exploitation – one employer's battle with his men over wages was another employer's opportunity to increase his business. Thus, the indictment of the men had to rest upon the question of authority. The condemnation of restrictive practices was certain to secure a favourable response from the bar of public opinion and the assertion of the employers' right to be master in his own works was more likely to achieve a unity amongst the employers themselves that could not be secured by simple economic issues.

When the employers' counter-offensive was launched in the late sixties, therefore, it focussed particularly upon those trades – the masons, bricklayers, plasterers – and in those towns of the north where restrictive practices and 'tyranny' were most widely successful. The issues around which the struggle was fought – the substitution of hourly for daily payment, an end to restrictive practices and to autonomous regulation – were precisely those means that would allow employers the freedom to conduct their businesses as they pleased so as to increase the rate of exploitation and destroy the power of the men over the productive process. It was an apt expression of this struggle that, following the defeat of the men, there appeared in the working rules a new clause entitled 'Authority of Employer' which spelt out the prerogative of the master to arrange working conditions in his firm as he alone wished.

THE MASTERS' OFFENSIVE AND HOURLY PAYMENT

The imperative of an offensive to grab power back from the men had been recognised since the late fifties when an attempt was made to create a regional masters' association in the Midlands.[39] Nearly two hundred firms attended the quarterly meeting of this National Association of Master Builders in December 1857, but their attempt to introduce hourly payment floundered under the weight of their own disunity.[40] Unity could be secured only once the loss of control had attained serious proportions and it was an indication that this situation had arrived when the first successful and permanent masters' organisation was formed in the mid-sixties. The General Builders' Association – whose secretary by 1866 was the eloquent Alfred Mault – originated with the large builders of Wolverhampton and Birmingham who in May 1864 'unanimously acknowledged that the constantly growing demands of the workmen rendered it absolutely necessary that some steps be taken' to counteract the 'power of the operatives.'[41] By December about 120 delegates out of 370 members attended the first meeting of the Association at Birmingham to observe and coordinate the opening salvo in the masters' counter-offensive – the presentation of the demand for a discharge note.[42] The strike that resulted from this demand is of some interest. Limited essentially to Birmingham and focussing especially upon the carpenters and joiners (although by its end the bricklayers were also included), its form was a mixture of old and new techniques of authority. The discharge note (an idea borrowed from the Clyde Shipbuilders) was a permanent form of the document which would provide employers with a record of employment and form the basis for a blacklist.[43] In this sense, the tactics of the masters were 'traditional,' for the note represented the assertion of a paternalist, unilateral masters' authority which 'would deprive them [the men] of the power of striking but the masters would have the power of locking them out.'[44] The central issue was the question of authority: there was the soon to become familiar list of restrictive practices and the assertion that 'with the exception of making the arrangements for the various works, and finding the needful, the men on all large jobs and in the larger towns, are completely the masters.'[45] As the President of the GBA put it: ' "We meet here today to decide if capital shall have any voice, or whether labour shall in future first dictate its own terms as to price, and then control operations of capital in the building trades" '[46] But, unlike the earlier documents, the counterfoil of the discharge note was coupled with the employers' intention to bring a new structure of industrial relations to the town similar to that recently instituted in Wolverhampton. Settlement of the strike was reached when withdrawal of the note was linked to acceptance of hourly pay, a conciliation and arbitration structure and a code of rules which expressly legitimised the masters' authority. It was in this way that mutual negotiation was established for the Birmingham carpenters and bricklayers, to be followed by those of Coventry and Kidderminster where the note had also been presented.[47] But the example of Birmingham was not copied elsewhere: even in the trade journals the masters' presentation of the note had incurred some odium and the successful pleas of the men about the 'tyrannical' purposes to which the note could be put discouraged other towns from following the trail blazed by the Birmingham General Builders' Association.[48] Even more daunting, however, were the difficulties that would be encountered if they had tried to repeat their success against their prime enemies – the masons. And, for the next few years, the GBA turned its attention to the more prosaic, though hardly less important, matter of the law of contract between builders and proprietor.[49] The discharge note strike was important, however, as marking the first incursion of the hourly system outside London and the first victory of the new style of industrial relations.

In 1867–68 Birmingham was once again the scene of an important trial-run for the general offensive of 1869. For reasons that are totally obscure, the masons – who had refused to enter into the new system in 1865 – accepted a code of rules that were a masters' dream. There was to be no standard rate, no restrictive rules, hourly pay, overtime at request, an 'authority of masters' clause and a court of conciliation with a no-strike provision.[50] Other lodges, aware of the precedent that was being set, reacted with horror and amazement: 'It was with the utmost astonishment we read the rules in question . . . it would be impossible . . . to find anything to equal the degradation which the masons of Birmingham have tamely submitted to.'[51] An attempt in 1868 to reassert rules more favourable to the men was seen as 'the rallying point of the future destiny of the society' against the GBA which had made known its hope to establish similar rules elsewhere.[52] A strike of sixteen months followed which was eventually closed in August 1869 and whose failure set the stage for the wider offensive of that year:

The success [in Birmingham] . . . in great measure, decided the questions of the worked stone rule and hour system throughout the country, and swept away the only restrictions . . . that remained upon the trade of Birmingham . . . The cause of trade emancipation so well inaugurated in Birmingham is extending far and wide.[53]

An arbitration clause was added to the rules and thus was mutual negotiation and collective bargaining introduced to the Birmingham masons – whose conciliation and arbitration board remained in continuous operation until 1892.

By the end of 1868 the masters of the GBA felt sufficiently confident to 'make a simultaneous effort to rid the trade of some of the trammels and restrictions imposed upon it by the trade rules and customs' and they determined to broaden their offensive into a full-scale assault upon autonomous regulation and its restrictive practices. In thirty northern towns notices were delivered that, as of 1 May 1869, 'Birmingham rules' would come into force – the most important of which were hourly pay and a court of conciliation and arbitration.[54] As a London masons' lodge put it, it was clear that a 'giant struggle was coming upon the society' for, as a Liverpool employer explained, ' "if they once mastered them [i.e. masons] there was nothing that they could not master afterwards." '[55] But masons were not the only trade whose 'tyranny' was at stake. It was the employers' purpose to change the basis of work in the industry by standardising the method of payment and removing restrictive practices wherever they existed. Furthermore, it was also their intention to alter the nature of industrial relationships by a wholesale creation of conciliation and arbitration systems. The masons were the most unified in their opposition to these new structures but all over the north carpenters, bricklayers and plasterers were to be involved in the struggle to different degrees in different places.[56] Opposition from these other trades was more fragmented, however, and by October 1869 their resistance had either slipped away or been appeased.[57] It was the masons who, thus, bore the brunt of the attack from the large contractors who had initiated the struggle; and in Manchester work on all the large contracts was completely halted.[58] The critical nature of the contest was illustrated by the masters' refusal to accept any of the compromise offers suggested by the men and to hold rigidly to their insistence of hourly payment and arbitration.[59] And for the men, a letter eloquently reminiscent in tone to those of the early thirties, summarises their correct perception of what was at stake:

They tell us we should submit tamely to every innovation that greed, avarice, and a desire for self-aggrandisement [demand] on the part of our employers . . . We should not attempt to strike even for the preservation of our dearest interests . . . We must remain passive while our rights are invaded, our privileges rudely torn from us, and ourselves enslaved . . . [It is only] through the instrumentality of strikes that we have been enabled to emerge from the bondage and serfdom of bygone years to the possession of the privileges we now enjoy.[60]

By the end of the summer the struggle had been reduced to the cities of Liverpool and Manchester. The masters of York, for example, had withdrawn their demands at the end of July and in August it was reported that only in two of the seven towns where the strike continued did it still assume serious proportions.[61] But as the importance of the contest transcended its limitation to the masons' trade, so the significance of Liverpool and Manchester dwarfed its geographical limitation. Just as Birmingham in 1867–68 had been a prelude to the contest of a year later, so the focus on the metropoli of the northwest was to be the crucial test for the generalisation of the new system of industrial relations. These towns had been the cockpit of the industry since the 1830s. It had been in Manchester and Liverpool that the general contracting struggles had been decided and there that the pace was set for the subsequent expansion of worker power. Amongst all sections of the industry, the men's sphere of control had found its fullest expression in these towns and they set the standards and example to which the rest of northern England could aspire. Once hourly pay and arbitration were established in these cities they were sure to ripple out – as soon they did – to the surrounding towns and regions. It was for this reason that Manchester was described as 'in the most important position in the struggle.' Victory there would be an object lesson to building workers elsewhere, it would set a powerful precedent for a more peaceful adoption of the masters' system: 'If these towns suffer defeat, all the other places which this year have been victorious must also succumb.'[62] Thus, the final defeat of the strikes in Manchester and Liverpool in the spring of 1870 was a critical event. It was the first time that the bricklayers of Manchester had been defeated in twenty-five years. The finances of the masons' union were crippled and it experienced a huge drop in membership; the local masons' work group power to impose restrictive rules was broken and the towns were reported as 'swarming with blacks.' 1869, crowed the masters' journal, 'will be remembered as the year in which the great blow was struck for the freedom of the building trade.'[63] In Liverpool there were to be no rules until 1873, in Manchester the masters' rules were imposed in December 1870 and they included hourly pay and a court of arbitration.[64] The change in the character of the working rules was decisive: when Liverpool regained a set of rules in 1873 they were virtually identical to those that Birmingham had accepted – and never lost – in 1867.

We shall have occasion to return to the changes in the character of working rules; what it is important to realise at this point is that although there were few places which escaped some of the effects of the defeat, the employers' victories did not immediately transform working rules everywhere. Furthermore, as we shall see, by the early seventies there were additional influences coming into play conducive to furthering the masters' intention of weakening the restrictive nature of working conditions. It is in the character of the resolution of crises that there should be this kind of ambiguity and the significance of these defeats lay beyond their immediate and material effect to the basis they laid for a new structure of work and industrial relations. The masters' victories legitimised their programme for a new system which replaced the day with the hour as the unit of pay and which replaced autonomous regulation with formalised conciliation and arbitration structures within which mutual negotiation was to be conducted.

The large contractors had long sought to institute payment by the hour (this had been the purpose of the abortive 1858 offensive) but not until 1861, when it was established in London, could hourly payment register any significant successes. The system spread slowly throughout the 1860s, frequently being achieved in the wake of local defeats of the men: it was imposed upon the Leeds bricklayers by a lockout in 1862 and upon the carpenters of the same town after a defeated strike in 1864.[65] One of the first acts of the Wolverhampton arbitration board in 1864 was to introduce the system; and, of course, the Birmingham area saw its inception following the discharge note strike of 1865. By 1867 the prevailing opinion amongst employers was that it was 'very desirable that this system of payment should become universal,'[66] but it remained confined to specific localities until the crisis of 1869–70 provided the real impetus to its expansion. And by the time the *Royal Commission on Labour* met in 1892, out of 127 towns surveyed, in only seven were men still paid by the day. Table 13 illustrates the spread of the system amongst the carpenters:[67]

Table 13. *Spread of hourly payment amongst carpenters*

	Branches on	
	Day system	Hour system
1864	51	9
1865	75	19
1871	87	95
1875	52	212
1879	32	283

Hourly payment promised many advantages for the masters, but its general effect and purpose was to restore that 'freedom' and flexibility to conduct their business as they pleased which had been so noticeably absent in the 1860s. It simplified and standardised cost accounting which in the 1860s had been complicated by the differences in pay periods that resulted from the variations in each trade's definition of a working day. Justifying its offensive in a letter to architects, the GBA explained that: 'The day has no longer been [*sic*] the definite time it used to be . . . Now there are in summer time three different lengths of working days . . . The hour is now the largest unit of time left to us. It means the same all the week and all the year through.'[68]

But, more important than this, hourly pay was a device to increase the rate of exploitation, to return to the masters the productivity that was lost through restrictive practices and shortened hours. By tying wages firmly to the number of hours worked it acted as a kind of pieceworking system and promised to secure a more efficient utilisation of labour. It was a way to combat those successful efforts by the men that had shortened the hours of work without any consequent reduction in the wage levels or increases in productivity. The GBA put this aspect of the question in the following way:

There is another consideration . . . that has had great weight with us . . . [it] will remove the most fruitful source of discord between us and our workmen. At present disputes are continually occurring in consequence with the periodical variation of time and rates of wages. One year our workmen give us notice for increased wages. Another year the notice is for shortening the time of work . . . and sometimes both . . . come together. In all these cases both the element of time and that of wages are equally involved; but the workmen seem to have lost sight of this fact, and consequently matters get complicated . . . But under the hour system the intimate relation of time and money are apparent and disputes are confined to the proper issue. So long as men can get as much for an eight hour day as for the ten hours day so long will the present agitation for unduly shortening the hours of labour continue. If the workmen are brought to see that each hour is represented by a corresponding amount of wages, the question of limiting the number of hours may be left to take care of itself.[69]

Such reasoning seldom appeared in public statements of the masters' case, which more frequently stressed the advantages for the men to work a day of their own choosing. Rupert Kettle was naively surprised when, at the Manchester carpenters' and joiners' arbitration of 1869, Edward Johnson blurted out that, working the way suggested above, the hourly system would lower costs.[70] But if it promised to allow employers to pay a more appropriate wage by linking wages to hours actually worked, it also allowed them greater flexibility to demand that any or all hours be worked. As Godfrey Lushington remarked at the time of the 1861 strike: 'To the contractor, that his men should be ready to work at his beck, all day and all night . . . is a frequent necessity.' And, as Marx pointed out, the consequence of this was that under the pretence of paying ' "the normal price of labour," [he can] abnormally lengthen the working day without any corresponding compensation to the labourer.'[71]

Hourly payment was not simply, then, a more efficient distribution of the wages bill in the industry. Both in the context in which it was introduced and in its structural implications for the nature of the work, the system possessed a clearly definable series of power imperatives. The general opposition from the men which greeted the system was based upon this fact: that hourly pay would make more difficult the exercise of the work control that had been achieved since the fifties.[72] From the Manchester masons it was 'held that the hour system was the stepping stone to the overthrow of all the rules which now regulated affairs between masters and men . . . In fact, it would remove the necessity for any trade rules at all.' The Sheffield bricklayers believed that 'if the hour system was adopted they would be placed entirely at the mercy of their employers, and the privileges which had cost them thousands of pounds to obtain would be abridged or wholly taken from them.' From the Manchester carpenters: 'the workmen of Manchester had a great many privileges, and they were chary of losing any of them'; and from London, ten years earlier, came the telling fear that 'if the hour system was established it would reduce them to the position of the casual labour at the docks.'[73] The strength of feeling and suspicion of the men were obvious in the long and bitter strikes that were fought against the system – the six-month contest in London in 1861 and the twelve-month struggle in Manchester and Liverpool in 1869–70. A giant demonstration of the building trades of Manchester in August 1869 featured the stonemason's contingent carrying banners on which were inscribed 'No Hours. No Arbitration.'[74] To most outsiders, the hourly method of payment seemed eminently reasonable. Fair to both masters and men, it secured for the former an honest day's work and for the latter an independence to work the number of hours that they pleased.[75] The strong resistance of the men was, therefore, puzzling – explicable only by their 'communistic' (the word is Kettle's) desire to maintain an artificially high price of labour, or by their inherently conservative resistance to innovation.[76] In fact the men had sound reasons for their sometimes inadequately expressed fears. Hourly pay promised to enhance the power of the masters and weaken that of the men in four specific ways.

In the first place, as was clearly recognised at the time, it destroyed any notion of a 'normal day.' The workers, a Leeds carpenter pointed out in a neat reversal of a favourite middle-class argument, might want 'time to attend Mechanics' Institutes . . . They would not be able to do so if they agreed to work by the hour, for they would be at the masters call at any hour of the day.' The system, Marx argued, would destroy 'all regularity of employment, and according to his own conventions, caprice, and the interest of the moment, make the most enormous overwork alternate with relative or absolute cessation of work.' And this was echoed by the positivist Lushington who explained that the nature of the large contractors' business was to 'undertake great works at short notice under heavy penalty; whose whole trade is a series of races against time, to win or lose a heavy stake.'[77] But, in particular, the threatened destruction of the normal day would remove from the worker the security of settled summer and winter hours. It would, a mason explained, 'be the means of shortening of the number of hours in winter and lengthening them in summer,' and the consequence of this bore directly upon such questions as regularity of earnings, and an accentuated rate of unemployment in winter.[78] The summer was the time when the men were most favourably placed vis-à-vis the masters: to destroy the accepted day meant that the employer could work them long hours during the fine weather, minimise work sharing over the year, weaken their labour scarcity potential and, therefore, their ability to restrict or control the productive process. Nor were these fears of the men misplaced. In what was believed to be a kite flown for the other large builders, the London firm of Lucas declared in the January of 1865 its intention to reduce winter working hours. The *Bee-Hive* explained why 150 non-union men struck to resist this alteration:

It will be recollected that the main reason why the men . . . so obstinately resisted the introduction of the hour system . . . was, that it would place the power in the hands of the master builders to destroy the recognised day of ten hours' labour all year round and shorten the day's labour to any extent they pleased in winter, and lengthen it . . . in the summer, without having to pay extra for overtime.

Although this 'first attempt on a large scale' to reduce winter hours was unsuccessful, a year later the men had to fight off another effort aimed at the same reduction.[79]

One further consequence of the destruction of a normal day was that it became more difficult to restrict overtime. The Bolton masons summarised this aspect of the question: 'Once let the system be fairly introduced, and there is an end to the recognised day . . . it will be impossible to claim time and half for overtime, a boon that so many of our brothers have struggled hard to obtain . . . the importance of keeping a legitimate check to work overtime cannot be too highly estimated.'[80] When the Birmingham master painters introduced hourly pay in 1866, it was their announced intention to do away with overtime and the 4 p.m. Saturday. And it was claimed by an authoritative witness that the London masters had the same inclination in 1861.[81] It is not clear whether they were able to carry through with this threat but it was certainly not until 1872 that any definite agreement was reached as to recognised hours or overtime pay and it seems probable that overtime flourished in London during the sixties. But even where an extra rate was specified for overtime working it was not unknown for that rate to only come into effect several hours after the day had finished. Furthermore, in those places where the masters won decisive victories in the late sixties it was standard procedure for all restrictions on overtime to be removed and for it to be worked at the employers' request.[82] But restraint upon overtime working was not the only 'privilege' to be threatened by the possible disappearance of the normal day.

All the 'customs' of the trade rested upon a fixed period of work and the regularity of a day's labour and the destruction of the normal day would threaten walking time – which masters claimed had been so twisted to the men's advantage – carpenters' grinding money, lodgings money (attacked in London in 1866) and the other 'privileges' that contributed nothing to output and productivity.[83] Such customs were more than just a supplement to wages, they were an expression of the autonomy of the workmen and of the limits to employers' authority and it is significant that only where the masters specifically promised to maintain such privileges could hourly pay be accepted with some equanimity.

Apart from the ramifications of the threat to the normal day, a second way in which hourly pay enhanced the masters' authority lay in the challenge it posed to the standard rate. Following the introduction of hourly pay into the Birmingham carpentry trade and the defeats of the late sixties, the employers inserted 'efficiency' clauses into the working rules which, in the case of Birmingham, laid down an average wage of 6¼d for the skilled men but which provided for 'superior and inferior workmen to be paid at such rate of wages as may be decided by the foreman or employer.'[84] Hourly pay thus opened the way for an individual bargaining which masters had always desired but had never been able to achieve. It is possible, but unlikely, that individual bargaining did increase as a consequence of the system. More significant, however, was the enhanced importance that now attaches to a formal expression of the standard rate – and, incidentally, to the 'normal day.' In building, at least, the central role that the Webbs assigned to the standard rate in employer–employee relationships was essentially a product of this new system. Only if the rate was expressly and 'legally' agreed upon could a protection be offered against individual bargaining.

The threat to the standard rate illustrated (and this is our third point) how hourly pay accentuated the insecurity of work and conditions that was already inherent in the industry. It made the kinds of protections erected in the fifties and sixties harder to achieve and maintain and it is very probable that the proportion of casual labour increased as a consequence of the system. Hourly pay meant hourly dismissal and although there were exceptions to this rule (such as the Northampton carpenters and joiners who were allowed a 4½ hour period of grace) they were fairly unusual. In 1875, the Liverpool bricklayers' attempt to re-assert the old standard notice of one quarter day was appropriately linked with a futile effort to re-establish payment by the day. Under the hourly system, wrote Postgate, 'the operative paid for bad weather: if it rained he could be stood off for an hour, put on again, taken off again, and the master suffered no loss.' It meant, also, shades of dockwork; hanging around a site all day in the hope of getting work and maybe getting one or two hours.[85] By 1875, even Rupert Kettle, who had done so much to legitimise the system, was to be found admitting that hourly pay accentuated irregularity of employment:

From the way in which the building trade has been carried on of late years under the hour system, men are frequently taken on for the job . . . and discharged when the job is finished . . . It is this system of taking on occasional hands for a short time when work presses, and suddenly discharging them, which causes the number of men to be walking the streets in idleness.[86]

And, finally, the hourly system threatened to fragment the cohesion of the work group. Similarity of conditions amongst the members of a group is an essential requirement for effective action and if men were to be paid different rates, to work different hours under different conditions, then there would be no basis for collective action. The possibilities that hourly pay held for this kind of fragmentation were borne clearly in mind. The GBA, for example, felt that: 'It would be most desirable to endeavour to check the movement [for a reduction in hours] until proper steps could be taken to allow each workman to exercise his own judgement as to his time of work by introducing the hour system.'[87] The plasterers of Manchester were equally aware of the threat to solidarity: their opposition to the system was based upon their belief that its object was 'to break up their union.' In the carpentry trade, hourly pay accentuated the division between the outdoor and indoor men and (perhaps what amounted to the same thing) between the more and less skilled – a fact which helps explain their divided attitude to the system.[88] Thus, the Leeds carpenters' resistance was partly based upon the way it would widen the differential between the top and bottom of the wage scale. As Table 14 illustrates, those at the lower end would receive less whilst those at the top would receive a 3% raise.[89]

Table 14. *Effects of hourly payment on wages*

	Wages under day system for 56 hour week		Wages under hour system for 56 hour week
Men receiving	19/-	would get	18/18d
	20/-		19/11d
	21/-		21/-
	22/-		22/2d
	23/-		23/4d
	24/-		24/6d
	25/-		25/8d

The promise of the changes that would be wrought by the hourly system explain and illuminate the enthusiasm with which the masters pressed its case. But the working reality of the system was somewhat modified by the ambiguities that existed both in the power relations of master and men and in the divided attitudes of many of the trades. In actuality the masters were not usually able to impose the system in its extreme form – and this was true even in Manchester. Furthermore, there was less need for confrontation with the carpenters and some bricklayers where conflicting attitudes to the system made compromise more possible. Even amongst the masons there was a clear division of opinion between London – who thought the fears of their northern brethren exaggerated – and the rest of England. Thus, although it is important not to minimise the significance of the defeats in the northwest, there were countervailing forces that kept those conflicts localised and which served to complement their effects in easing the spread of the system.[90]

One of the keys to a more ready acceptance of hourly payment and the major reason why some places and trades accepted it more easily than others lay in the guarantees that might be offered to mitigate its threats to the conditions of work. As George Cornish – a Sheffield mason – pointed out, the masters clearly 'wished to re-introduce all the evils [such as piece-work] which for the last thirty years the operatives had been trying to surmount,' but 'for himself, he could not see any great evil in the hour system if the operatives could have the "handling" of it.'[91] Similarly, the Manchester carpenters and joiners overcame their suspicions of the system once Kettle had secured from the masters a commitment that it would not be used to reduce winter wages of the outdoor men. The Bolton carpenters were induced to accept hourly pay once the masters had agreed to an unbroken day; and its passage had been sweetened in Wolverhampton by the maintenance of a day's notice for dismissal.[92] Even those rules that were imposed upon the Manchester masons in December 1870 retained certain 'privileges' such as walking time and an 'average' day of ten hours which must have served to smooth the passage of hourly pay and arbitration. In other cases, as amongst the Wolverhampton bricklayers in 1866 (the year they entered into the conciliation structure of that town) substantial wage increases were used to secure a more willing acceptance.[93] In addition, it was found that the insecurity threatened by the system did not materialise to the extent that had been feared – especially because of the boom of the early seventies – but even in the sixties the London masons had found that starting and finishing times remained intact and that men had not been stood on and off at the employer's whim.[94]

Industrial warfare seldom results in unambiguous victories; and if the men could retain certain 'privileges' which preserved a modicum of protection against over-exploitation, then some restraints remained upon the employers' freedom of action. But these restraints were far weaker than they previously had been and, as we shall see, begin to be dismantled even before the economic climate changed in the late seventies. Furthermore, the rapid decline after 1870 of the language of authority and the frequency of the 'authority of employer' clauses testified to the greater flexibility and freedom that the employers had gained since the sixties.

FORMALISATION: THE END OF AUTONOMOUS REGULATION

If it was in the nature of things that the implications of the hourly system could not be as complete as its proponents might wish, standing alone, it remained, therefore, an insufficient device to establish the supremacy of the employers' industrial discipline. In addition, it was inadequate precisely because it established new structures of work which threw into question the matrix of 'privileges' and customs that had previously formed the substance of master–men relationships. At the heart of hourly payment there lay the paradox that its simplification of industrial affairs was a chimera; in reality, the system could only complicate and confuse master–men relationships. If it made collective work group action more difficult, for example, it remained unlikely that the substitute of individual bargaining would suddenly or completely emerge to take its place. Indeed, it is very probable that hourly payment stimulated unionisation as a more necessary imperative in the face of the work group fragmentation promised by the system. Unionism now becomes a more important way of expressing solidarity than it had been all the time it served merely to complement work group activity. Similarly, even if hourly pay threatened to make working arrangements and wage levels even more chaotically diverse, questions were bound to arise about overtime, when the day should end, walking time and other contentious issues that would need to be settled and, in itself, the hourly system had no answers to these matters. It might ensure the employers a greater authority over the workforce but there was no guarantee that this authority would prevail to ensure a smoothly functioning industrial discipline. Hourly payment, therefore, created the imperative for a procedural rule-making system whose structures of mutual negotiation would encourage discipline by the orderly resolution of contentious issues through formal and regularised channels. It was for these reasons that the masters' offensive was not limited to hourly payment alone but included the tandem demand that boards of conciliation and arbitration be created to bring a new structure of industrial relationships to the industry.

Wherever the masters were victorious, or where the men accepted their demands without a struggle, conciliation boards with an arbitration clause were established. These institutions marked a real and decisive break which it is important not to underestimate. Apart from a few enthusiasts whose legislative and propaganda efforts generally came to nought, neither masters nor men had previously revealed any inclination to allow strangers

to make judgements on matters of which they had little real understanding. Where such methods were to be found before the mid-sixties, it
was usually as a manifestation of imbalanced power relations rather than
indicative of any structural shift towards a new system of industrial relations.
Had it not been the link now forged by the masters between conciliation
and arbitration, it is unlikely that the mid to late sixties would have deviated
from this pattern.[95] But this link was to effect a permanent change in industrial relations: it admitted an external authority into affairs that previously
had been a matter for autonomous regulation and it institutionalised a permanent form of mutual negotiation as the only way of avoiding arbitration.

In spite of the public support given to arbitration by the union leaderships, the injection of his method into industrial relations was usually
achieved in the face of rank and file hostility.[96] Masons, the most determined in their opposition, had 'an unenviable reputation for obstinacy
[and] until recently they have not made any attempts to establish boards
of conciliation and arbitration.' Only under the stress of depression in the
late seventies did this resistance begin to crumble.[97] Neither was the situation very different in the other trades. The London carpenters condemned
its acceptance by the Birmingham area because it would 'be giving the
employers great dominion over us, to do in a manner as they might think
well.'[98] Just three months after the Manchester carpenters' reluctant
arbitration of 1869 (which, incidentally, was the first since 1857), they
gave notice to strike the clause from their rules because of 'the manner in
which the proceedings of the late Court . . . were conducted'; and eighteen
months later the Leeds carpenters began a similar campaign to drop the
rule.[99] The bricklayers, likewise, were generally only persuaded to accept
arbitration under the pressure of defeat; and the Birmingham painters
pointed to the rules arbitration had secured for the carpenters as the reason
for resisting it in their trade: 'Producing a large poster containing the rules
for regulating the carpenters and joiners . . . Mr. Call went on to say that
those were the rules adopted before [i.e. by] an arbitration and the trade
had never seen such rules as those before. It was the general opinion
amongst his fellows that they were better off without them.'[100]

The Birmingham area furnished pertinent lessons in the disadvantages
of arbitration, even when it was linked with the less objectionable conciliation board. It had been under the auspices of Rupert Kettle, the
arbitrator for Wolverhampton, that hourly pay and the notorious 'authority of masters' clause had made their first appearance; and in Birmingham
the newly formed conciliation board had sanctioned the masters' rules
that closed the discharge note strike. Thus, when the TUC debated the
issue in 1869 the arguments of those opposed to arbitration – and they were
a distinct minority of the trade union leadership – drew heavily upon the
experience of the Midlands. In a speech hardly calculated to appeal to the

likes of Howell and Odger, Thomas Connolly of the OSM gruffly asserted that arbitration would 'degrade working men to the lowest possible level.' A delegate from the Birmingham building trades in a reasoned and impressive speech which also failed to move the majority, explained the role that arbitration played in limiting the power of the men:

> [He] urged the delegates that in adopting arbitration they must be careful not to arbitrate away the fundamental principles and privileges of trades unionism. That was the rock upon which the Birmingham building trade . . . had split. If the masters, under arbitration, were given the power to employ as many apprentices as they liked, to alter the hours of work, or to employ free labour, then their fundamental rights and privileges were bartered away . . . Arbitration had led to disturbance in the building trade. It had weakened their forces, and he wanted the Congress to profit by *their* [i.e. Birmingham] experience, not by their own.[101]

The conciliation 'craze' of the late sixties was a signal that a new structure of industrial relations was coming into being. At first limited to a few isolated towns and trades, by the mid-seventies there was 'barely a town where trade unions existed which did not have either a standing joint committee of employers and workmen to settle disputes, with provision for arbitration, or the experience of settling disputes through arbitration on an *ad hoc* basis.'[102] And building was one of three major industries, which included coal and iron, where this was particularly true. Testifying to the sudden fashionability of these schemes was the stream of pamphlets and books, the attention devoted to the question by the Royal Commission, and the revival of attempts to provide them with a legislative framework. But the re-discovery of conciliation and arbitration merely reflected the growing recognition of the potential they contained for resolving the labour crisis. It was 'the masters [who] introduced arbitration, not the men' Edward Johnson told the Labour Law Commissioners, and their purpose was to bring the power of the workmen under a permanent control. Even the celebrated board at Wolverhampton emerged not of a peaceful, evolutionary progress towards mutual negotiation but from the continual warfare that had occasioned a seventeen week strike in 1863. The Birmingham masters put it succinctly enough in their battle with the masons in 1868: if they failed to obtain their conciliation and arbitration rule they 'would find themselves in precisely the same difficulty as that in which they were now placed; and then all the work which they have gone through on account of the present strike, would have to be repeated.'[103]

As permanent additions to industrial relations in building, arbitration and conciliation emerged out of a crisis that had ended in the defeat of the men; they were instruments in the employers' new armoury of authority, designed to bring a discipline and order that autonomous regulation could not provide. In this there was nothing unique about building and, as evidence of the evolutionary 'progress' of labour and of trade unions in particular, these industrial relations structures have a far more ambiguous history than has generally been realised.[104] Aside from the support of trade union leaders, the movement for conciliation boards did not spring from the world of labour but from those outside the working classes who perceived the threats posed by the 'labour-problem.' Nor is it at all clear that the boards reflected an accommodation to trade union strength that was too powerful to be defeated.[105] Institutionally, trade unionism was probably no stronger in 1869 than it had been in 1860 but it was in the later part of the decade that the conciliation movement was to be found. Indeed, the experience of building suggests if not the exact reverse, then something more complex. Placing aside all considerations of trade unionism, these boards were established precisely where the great power that the men wielded over the productive process had been compromised or defeated.

Thus, to adopt the conventional view and see conciliation as both a victory for trade unions and as an agent of their disarming we must oversimplify to the point of tautology.[106] As an institutional force, trade unionism had never been anything other than an incipient agent of collective bargaining and at this historical moment, having yet to find a role let alone an armoury, it hardly needed to be disarmed. It was the men who had to be disarmed, tamed and disciplined and it was this problem that conciliation and arbitration boards were designed to meet. They did this in several ways – some of which we shall have occasion to mention again. They secured a constancy of working conditions for the fixed period of a year which helped to stabilise costs and competition. A formal regularity now entered into bargaining; the possibility of demands arising outside the negotiating period was reduced. This changed the yearly strike distribution to a more regular and predictable pattern and it induced a greater sense of 'responsibility' amongst the leaders with whom the masters had to deal.[107] Thus, Alfred Mault on this advantage to the boards: 'If you could get some general reference to arbitration adopted both by masters and men when they were on friendly terms, and before any dispute had arisen, the fact of the establishment and the existence of such a court of arbitration would operate very much in the way of inducing men after a dispute had arisen to accept arbitration.'[108] More important than this, however, conciliation and arbitration legitimised masters' authority and their definition of negotiable issues. Far from signifying a surrender of managerial prerogatives to mutual negotiation, they were a means of re-asserting and redefining those prerogatives to enable employers to secure a better discipline. It was no coincidence that in the period 1869–75 restrictive rules amongst the masons were harder to maintain where there were conciliation and arbitration boards. Once conciliation and arbitration – along with hourly pay – were established in Birmingham and Manchester, for example, the character of their working rules changed. The Birmingham masons' rules of 1867 which allowed no standard rate, overtime at request, hourly pay, conciliation and arbitration with a no-strike clause, and the authority of masters to conduct their businesses as they saw fit, remained intact throughout the seventies.[109] The same was true of Manchester where, if anything, the rules of 1873 were worse than those of 1870: no restrictions were to be placed on worked stone, nor on sub-contracting; piecework was allowed on certain jobs; overtime was worked when necessary; employers were free to vary the standard rate by right of an efficiency clause; a no-strike clause was linked to the conciliation and arbitration board; and no mention was made of walking or lodgings money. Perhaps in the face of Bolton's taunt that 'from one end to the other the only thought that seems to pervade them is to cringe before their rampant capitalism,' the Manchester masons apologetically explained:

> Let us state that we are not blind or insensible to the defects of these rules. There are three which we especially condemn – the overtime, arbitration, and nine months notice . . . They are not what we would like, but what we could get under the circumstances . . . Remember that we are only emerging from a three years' thralldom unexampled perhaps in any other town in the country.[110]

But things were not much improved by 1875 – at which time, it was reported, the union claimed eight hundred members in Manchester with available work for another two hundred. Proposals to increase restrictions on overtime, piecework, apprenticeship, the provision of sheds, and a renewed attempt to change the nine months notice rule were all (with the exception of a higher rate of pay for overtime) unsuccessful.[111] The presence of conciliation and arbitration structures was not, of course, the sole influence on these developments; as we shall see, there were other factors that worked to cause a decline in restrictive rules in the prosperous seventies. But the lesson of Manchester, Birmingham and Liverpool, previously centres of the most extensively restrictive rules, was that the new structures of industrial relations were, for a variety of reasons, not conducive to the exercise of the kind of control over work that had flourished in the sixties.

But conciliation and arbitration were symptomatic of a deeper, more profound change within the structures of industrial relations than the creation of a new institutional form. Implicit in the creation of the boards was the replacement of autonomous regulation with mutual negotiation as the governing mode of employer–employee relationships. In the Nottingham hosiery trade, the previous practice had been for piece rates to be fixed by printed lists 'and the battles formerly fought were as to whether the masters or men should make these statements,' but latterly no wages statement was legitimate unless the Board had signed it.[112] But it is important to appreciate that boards of conciliation and arbitration were not always a necessary prescription for the investiture of mutual negotiation. If the principle of negotiation with responsible bodies was established this might suffice without representation within formal institutions. Thus, conciliation boards were not created in London until the 1890s but, as elsewhere in the country, industrial relations in the city's building trades were formalised by the early seventies.

The experience of London was always different from the north of England. It was possible to establish hourly pay earlier in London partly because trade customs were different:

They [masons] were found artificial light and the hours of working were the same in winter as in summer, but the masons of the north are very differently situated. Their time of working was from light to dark in the winter, subject to a reduction of wages, consequently . . . the masons on whom this new system was about to be thrust, were the best judges as to how it would affect them.[113]

Furthermore, the early imposition of hourly pay and the less stable workforce consequent upon London's magnet effect on migration meant that restrictive rules of the kind to be found in the north were virtually unknown in London. There were no known instances, for example, of attempts to prohibit worked stone. Throughout the sixties, the increased power of the men was less concentrated, more difficult to realise and more cautiously exercised.[114] Nevertheless, the carpenters' 1872 wages and hours movement represented the climax to a militancy which had affected even the lowly painters.[115] In 1864, 1865, 1866, and 1870 there had been carpenters' and masons' demands for increased wages, reductions of hours, overtime and piecework restrictions and (in 1870) for a code of rules. When the conflict of 1872 erupted these demands formed the core of the 9d and 9 hours demand and the London masters were, therefore, presented with a similar challenge to that faced by the northern employers in the 1860s. They responded in similar ways. Like the Birmingham masters of 1865, they insisted upon establishing the principle of delegations with full authority to settle but, unlike the Birmingham employers, they did not require that a conciliation board be the means of ensuring this collective responsibility. In fact, at this moment in time such a board would have been impractical: the masters had only just organised into the Central Association of Master Builders which, unlike the GBA, had been formed in response to a discrete set of demands; nor were the city-wide standards of wages and work yet a formal code. But the formulation of standards, centrally negotiated and officially recognised by masters and men henceforth made mutual negotiation a necessity and demanded a certain degree of formal habits and procedures. This, indeed, was the *raison d'être* of the CAMB, and when problems with the 1872 agreement arose – as, for example, with the grinding money question – the precedent of mutual negotiation set by 1872 was naturally followed.[116]

In the years immediately following the defeat of 1870, the pages of the masons' *Fortnightly Returns* bore compelling witness to the displacement of autonomous regulation by mutual negotiation. Those rules submitted for Ratification no longer possessed the character of autonomously determined codes to be imposed upon the masters, but were quite clearly the product of consultation and mutual agreement. Striking a tone that was increasingly out-moded, the Stockport masons in 1872 required permission to strike 'for the purpose of compelling our employers to grant us the nine hours movement.'[117] More typical were the Nottingham masons who promptly absorbed the implications of the closure of the Manchester strike by reaching agreement with their employers on hourly pay and threatened to leave the society should it fail to ratify their rules: 'We can say [they wrote] that the Nottingham men never were working in more harmony with their employers.'[118] The Sheffield masons prepared their 1872 rules to meet in a conciliation committee for their negotiation, and in Leicester, where the employers were 'trying to break up our local code of rules,' continual meetings were held until 'a friendly understanding [was] . . . arrived at' which negotiated away daily pay and the restrictions on worked stone.[119] By using various techniques of mutual negotiation, the Newcastle men announced that they had obtained 'not only our original demand, but also a slight reduction in our working hours.' In Birmingham the habit of mutual negotiation was long-established by 1874 when they reported that 'we have had several meetings with [our employers] . . . in conference, and after a deal of discussion . . . we have succeeded in obtaining a code of rules which meets the approbation of all the members connected with our lodge.'[120] Two years later, the Leeds masons in conference with their employers reached an agreement on the hourly system which guaranteed a minimum winter wage and the use of artificial light. Finally, we may note the example of the Bristol masons in 1876 who, in contrast to their behaviour in 1860–61, proudly proclaimed: 'The first local code of rules we have had . . . that has been mutually drawn up and agreed upon both by employers and employed and likewise signed by both parties. The employers in the past, although submitting to the rules would never consent to sign them.'[121] Elsewhere, and in other trades, the same pattern repeated itself: notice would fall due for new rules, meetings be smoothly arranged, and agreements reached and signed.[122]

There were, of course, the exceptions to this new style that one would expect in a period of transition from autonomous regulation to a fully developed industrial relations system. Masons in York, Oxford, Huddersfield, Rochdale, and other places revealed a continuing attachment to the old method of negotiation by imposition and the masters in those towns reciprocated, sometimes even refusing to acknowledge receipt of the rules. But the trend of events was moving inexorably and irreversibly in favour of mutual negotiation. And it was this that explained the contrasting tone of the employers' evidence before the Royal Commission of 1867 and that given to the Labour Law Commission of 1874–75. To the latter body, for example, James Wilson of Leeds spoke of the new reasonableness that had come to characterise the men in that town: 'What we had to complain about before was that we had notices given to us [for changes in wages, conditions etc.] of perhaps only a fortnight or three weeks. [But] . . . they have recently given a very fair length of notice . . . in the Leeds trades of late the men have been very considerate indeed.'[123] As one moved into the 1870s there are far fewer complaints to be heard about 'tyranny'; even the GBA took grudging note of the fact that although the working rules still contained restrictive clauses 'this used to be so to a much greater extent formerly than it is now.'[124]

Unlike autonomous regulation, mutual negotiation legitimised and formalised a role for the unions within the structure of industrial relations. If mutual negotiation was to be effective organised representation of masters and men was essential; unionisation and the institutionalisation of masters' associations followed naturally from the demise of autonomous regulation. This had been true in other trades such as hosiery, and in the iron industry the union was kept alive only by its role in the arbitration board. Even Rupert Kettle was reluctantly brought to agree that 'there must be some means of bringing them together and if the union is the best means . . . by all means have the union.'[125] Mutual negotiation automatically transformed the status of the unions; for the first time they began to be treated as representative agents of the workmen. Appreciating that their 'struggle' for acceptance was inextricably bound up with the masters' efforts to implement their authority through procedural rule making, the union leaderships respond enthusiastically to conciliation and arbitration and avidly join forces with those working to de-legitimise autonomous regulation.[126] An examination of the 1871 OSM rules revisions will illustrate the contribution the unions could make in the establishment of the new structures of industrial relations.

Seizing upon the defeats of 1870, the full weight of Harnott's authority was thrown against traditional rules at precisely those points where they conflicted with the imperatives of formalised mutual negotiation. It was proposed that autonomous regulation be outlawed, local autonomy diluted and certain restrictive rules (together with the means by which they were maintained) be made illegal. Even before the defeat was final, Harnott had urged that representatives from each of the union's thirteen districts be chosen and endowed with powers never before accorded a deputation to negotiate the elimination 'from the various local rules such matters as . . . are found to be the most prolific sources of contention and expense.' Everything except the 48½ hour week would be open for negotiation; and although this suggestion was favourably received in some quarters, it was

rejected by the Society as a whole.[127] Not that this rejection seemed to
matter very much, for it was this spirit that dominated the rules revision
committee of 1871. A new rule appeared which *mandated* consultation with
employers before any new code could be submitted to the Society for its
approval. Consultation, the last recourse of unformalised industrial relations, now became by union mandate the court of first resort. Restraints
were also placed upon the freedom of the men to strike against employers'
infringements of working conditions. Previous rules had obligated the men
merely to inform the central committee of the reasons for a strike and then
to secure a majority vote of the members for it to be made legal. But the
rules now required a two thirds favourable vote of either the lodge or the
men on the job before a strike against an infringement could be called. In
itself, such a condition might seem unobjectionable; but it added another
layer to the decision-making process and began the trend (to be followed
in subsequent revisions) of constraints upon strike action in a trade where
lightning stoppages were always the most effective. Together with the
insistence upon mutual consultation, this new rule was a complementary
partner to the no-strike clauses that employers were busy inserting into the
working rules. In addition to these changes, a blow was struck against
work group organisation. Shop or job meetings were prohibited as 'a
fruitful source of annoyance to employers and our members' and an
unsuccessful attempt was made to forbid the ratification of rules which
contained 'provision against the introduction of worked stone into their
locality.'[128] In this new illegality of the workshop meeting we are granted
the unusual privilege of witnessing the transformation of a 'custom' into a
truly modern 'informal' practice outside of the legitimate structures of
industrial relations authority. In the contribution thus rendered to the
ordination of the formalised structures, the OSM was by no means unique.
The unions were about to embark upon their 'magnificent journey' and it
was natural that they should acquire the necessary travelling equipment.
Indeed, it was at precisely this moment that the whole balance of union
government began to shift towards a tighter central and bureaucratic control of policy. But aside from the similar changes that could be found in
other unions, the prestige of a much bigger 'official' body was also engaged
in discreetly promoting the viability of the new structures and the destruction of the old.[129] We are referring, of course, to the State.

The complex of legislative changes that marked the late sixties and early
seventies may best be viewed as another instalment in that process of
'liberalisation' which John Foster has so brilliantly analysed for the late
1840s. Undertaken in very different conditions, the central core of this
later phase was to begin the institutional integration of the upper level of
the working class (or, more properly, its representatives) into the bodies
politic and economic. Of course, its mechanics and its implication extended

far beyond a simple institutional focus. The absorption and redefinition of the shared values of 'respectability,' the easy abandonment of the wages fund theory as an unwarrantable obstacle to a proper accommodation were both essential adjuncts of the same process.[130] But the law also had a liberalising role to play and it is from this perspective that we must view the various changes in the law as it affected labour.

The law came to impinge more directly upon working-class life during these years. Its trend towards closer regulation served to provide a sound framework within which working-class institutions could flourish and grow.[131] But the law's effects were selective and discriminating. The acts of 1875 and 1876 relating to Friendly and Building Societies, for example, placed them upon a secure legal footing within which they continue to function. But this legislation was also critical in the demise of that local and genuinely working-class tradition of self-help from which these institutions had sprung; it allowed the affiliated orders to expand by absorbing the small provincial societies and it encouraged a centralised control over the local branches.[132] Actuarially sound and bureaucratised, these institutions were now purely in the *business* of providing insurance and other services to the working class. Similarly with the changes in the law on trade unions where a duality of purpose may be detected which, on the one hand, strengthened and legitimised the institutional basis of unionism and, on the other, maintained legal restraints upon rank and file activity.[133]

It would be a mistake, however, to assume that the labour legislation of these years was the clever result of scheming lawyers and positivists: its tendencies rested upon a far wider consensus. The Birmingham branch of the GBA sent the *Royal Commission on Trade Unions* a remarkable proposal which showed precisely what employers had in mind when they formalised industrial relations and which illustrated the distance they were prepared to travel in their search for discipline. There were three parts to the document. First, it urged the registration of trade unions to ensure the legality of their rules; if they registered they would become corporate bodies liable to sue and be sued. Second, it recommended that district courts of masters and men be established whose jurisdiction would include civil actions involving breach of contract. And, third, these courts would also possess the power to decide all trade rules, rates of wages and hours which, once registered, would have force of law in the district.[134] What the masters were proposing, therefore, was to bring the men fully into the rule-making process which they planned to endow with the force of law. So much, then, for their complaints about *trade union* 'tyranny': they were quite prepared to share rule making with unions provided there were adequate safeguards against the kind of rank and file power that had marked the past decade.

It is not clear whether this memorandum had any influence upon the majority of Commissioners, but it certainly matched the spirit of their recommendations. For the majority report urged that the protection of trade union funds should be contingent upon the absence of 'restrictive' rules such as those on apprenticeship or those which prohibited piecework. In view of the large number of control over labour strikes, it is also interesting to note that it was planned to hold combinations liable to prosecution for restraint of trade if 'they refused to work with any particular person.' And whilst no trade union would be formed specifically to ' "to do acts which involved breach of contract" ' and few outside the building unions specified restrictive rules in their rule books, it is clear that these sanctions would fall very heavily upon work group combination.[135] In the event, of course, the Trade Union Act of 1871 was more ambiguous, more truly 'liberalising' but no less purposeful in dealing with the question of discipline. Thanks to the influence of the minority report – whose whole point was the stabilising role that trade unions played in the labour force and the necessity to formalise that tendency – the taint of illegality was removed and stability encouraged by the legal protection afforded to funds through the fact of registration.[136] On the other hand, it was the function of the notorious Criminal Law Amendment Act to address the problem of discipline. By its 'molestation' clause, it effectively re-enacted and codified all the judicial restrictions placed upon strike activity since the Combination Laws.[137] It is interesting that this Amendment received such an ambiguous reception from the labour leadership who had to be virtually bulldozed into campaigning for its eventual repeal. Some, like Howell and MacDonald, were quite prepared to accept its essentials with only minor amendments.[138] The point was that the Criminal Law Amendment revealed the dual purposes of the labour legislation: on the one hand, to buttress the institutions of stability and, on the other, to legitimise employers' discipline. The Amendment did not challenge the stability of trade unionism – thus the leadership's ambiguous attitude – but it bore directly against the methods of autonomous regulation which work groups (whether union members or not) had used to realise their power. The virtual prohibition on picketing threatened the power of work groups, not the survival of unionism. Picketing was defined as the activity of individual or small groups: persistently following a person; hiding, depriving or hindering the use of tools or clothes; watching or besetting a person's house, place of work or the approaches thereto; following a person with two or more persons in a disorderly manner. All were subject to a fine or three months in prison.[139]

The Amendment thus widened the area of possible prosecution and even managed to encompass some wives who said 'Bah, Bah' to blacklegs. As Henry Crompton pointed out at the Leeds TUC in 1873: ' "men have been convicted for simply standing still in the street . . . The cases show . . . that if there is a strike, the magistrates will infer coercion from any facts, or even from the strike." '[140] James Davis noted that the Act was being so interpreted that men were liable for criminal prosecution under conspiracy law for acts which repeal of the Master and Servant Act had removed from the penal code. In a case similar to that of the celebrated London gas stokers, a jury at Leeds in 1874 was directed that an uncoercive refusal to work with a person or employer could still constitute a common law conspiracy against the employer. And two years previous, a Bolton magistrate had sentenced a shop steward to one month's imprisonment for 'besetting' a workman when he demanded a union fine which went unpaid and so caused the other masons to leave the shop.[141] Indeed, the employers were virtually unanimous in their praise for the beneficial effects of the Act: 'To its effect they attributed the if not entire cessation of . . . picketing yet the alteration in its character which had rendered the relations existing between master and men much more satisfactory, and the adjustment of trade disputes much more easy.'[142] Following the Amendment, strikes in Liverpool had been 'characterised by comparative quietness and order'; in Leeds, picketing was reported to have ceased entirely; and in London a mere threat of prosecution under the Act was enough to get the 'pickets slackened and ultimately retired.' By making strikes more difficult, the Act 'has brought the men and the employers nearer to each other' and thus strengthened conciliation and arbitration.[143] Of the builders who testified before the *Labour Laws Commission*, only Edward Johnson – still struggling to subdue the Manchester brickmakers – was less than wholehearted in his assessment of the Act's good work and even he had to admit that: 'All through the great crisis that there has been on the labour question throughout the country for the last two or three years the building trade has never been so quiet . . . the men are receiving higher wages . . . the masters have proper control over their business . . . and altogether a much happier state of things exists.'[144]

The Criminal Law Amendment Act was fully appropriate to the times in which it was passed and operated. By the restrictions it placed upon trade union 'methods' it was an additional weapon employers could use to push back the men's expanded frontier of control. The Act, therefore, played a critical role (how critical only detailed, local research could answer) in the shift towards mutual negotiation and the destruction of autonomous regulation. It was an important ancilliary to employer efforts to create a new kind of industrial discipline and in the future it might be worthwhile to pay special attention to its role as an agent in the formalisation of British industrial relations. But the Criminal Law Amendment Act lasted only until 1875 when it was replaced by the Conspiracy and Protection of Property Act. By this time, we may suggest, the Amendment had done its work. Mutual negotiation was firmly established, formal structures of industrial relations were to be found emergent in virtually every major industry; trade unions were working well within the system and already beginning to exercise their disciplinary role; and the boom was providing the basis for large wage increases to take the place of restrictive practices. In any event, it was clear that there was an arguable case – which even *The Times* recognised – that the Amendment was bad law, allowed magistrates too wide a discretion and created many injustices. It was absurd to argue that the meaning of 'coercion' could be twisted (as it was in the Jackson and Graham case) to encompass *no* overt acts of molestation or intimidation. In the long run, such use of the law threatened to undo all the good that had been achieved by legalising the unions in the first place. But in spite of this it is interesting to note that both the recommendation of the *Labour Laws Commission* and the original intention of the government was to leave the 1871 Amendment substantially unaltered.[145] And, indeed, it may be wondered just how substantive the changes eventually accepted really were. The major difference was to purge the definitions of 'coercion' and replace them with a simple statement that any attempt to compel another person to do what he had a legal right to do was punishable. But the 1871 definition of picketing was retained basically unchanged and the conditions that encompassed 'molestation' remained as evidence of conspiracy and illegal behaviour.[146] As some Erith engineers discovered in 1876 when they 'dogged the footsteps' of some blacklegs, there was still a wide discretion for proof of conspiracy and molestation.[147] In 1875 *Capital and Labour* (whose main constituents were building employers) opposed these alterations but by 1878 they had discovered how little had changed: 'Whilst in language it has been made more acceptable [to the men] . . . it has preserved to the independent workman full liberty to undertake work which other workmen combining have refused, and that any threat or intimidation in restraint of that full liberty, or any combination to exercise tyranny over others . . . is still an indictable offense.'[148]

In fact, the main effect of the 1875 Acts was not to reduce the possibilities for legal harassment of the 'methods' of collective action, but to remove the final barrier to labour's legal integration by separating breach of contract from penal suits of conspiracy and placing them into the civil law. Paternal masters and servile servants were, thus, transformed into manly employers and workmen whose contract squabbles the law would impartially referee. Autonomous regulation had been brought to a close; mutual negotiation was now the way to ensure labour discipline; industrial relations had been placed on a formal footing. It was, therefore, only fitting that the law should also reflect this transformation.

4

From custom to economism: the redefinition of industrial relations

THE NEW GAME

The search for a new, more secure, basis of industrial discipline had caused autonomous regulation to be supplanted by a formalised structure of industrial relations. It had required that the possessive paternalism of the Master and Servant Laws be replaced with the equal contract of the Employer and Workmen Bill of 1875. And this same search also demanded that the bargaining relationship between employers and men be fundamentally re-defined. Men were no longer 'servants,' employers no longer 'masters' and the language and methods of those earlier conceptions were inappropriate to describe their new relationship. Thus, in what was probably the first business manual for the building trades, employers were urged *not* to work alongside the men, for that confused the true nature of the authority relationship. Employers' energies should be devoted to the efficient running of the business leaving direct supervision in the hands of the foreman.[1]

The dissolution of the paternal ties that popular conception had taken to characterise the unformalised system of industrial relations was a reflection of the logic of the new system which implied that the bonds between employers and workmen could be reduced to those of pure and simple economics. Such, for example, was the inference to be drawn from the new Labour Laws which defined the relationship between employers and employed as a commercial contract actionable like others for any breach. It was reflected too in the ease with which the intelligentsia consigned the wages fund theory of classical political economy to the dustbin of myth and, in its place, began to develop the relationship between wages and productivity. Expressing this new locus of contact was the comment of the *Builders' Trade Circular* in 1872 that: 'Our men in their bargaining with us have only the right to require that we shall pay them their wages and give them the opportunity of earning them.'[2] It was, of course, a supremely important paradox that as economics was beginning to be recognised as a more complex discipline than the natural, self-regulating models of the past allowed, economic man in all his naked simplicity was being resuscitated to explain the nature of work relationships.[3] But we need not be detained by this contradiction, for its results were to become readily apparent by the 1890s and its inadequacy was to become an enduring part of industrial relations under advanced capitalism. Of more relevance for our purposes is how this new conception of industrial relationships asserted itself and how it impacted upon the behaviour and activities of the working men themselves.

For this re-definition was not simply a matter of belief. It was also a matter for action. We have seen how 'customary' forms of behaviour were changed by the emergence of new structures to regulate the industrial relationship, and similar changes were to be experienced in the way in which the issues of industrial relations could be explained, justified and disputed. Others, of course, have addressed this phenomenon before – most notably Eric Hobsbawm and the Webbs. Both their analyses are in agreement that the essential result of this process was that worker behaviour became more appropriately 'modern' and economically oriented. The distinguishing mark of 'customary' worker behaviour was that it formulated demands without a relevant reference to the limits of the market place and relied instead (for example) upon 'traditional' standards of differentials, or upon the guild-like conceptions of the 'doctrine of vested interests.' The shedding of these kinds of assumptions to be replaced by purely market criteria is viewed as gradual and evolutionary. During the 1840s a 'partial learning' of the new rules occurred and the 'doctrine of supply and demand' replaced that of vested interests as the dominant characteristic of trade union policy; not until the 1880s was a full learning achieved and the 'collectivist' assumptions of the 'doctrine of the living wage' adopted by trade unionists.[4] But neither Hobsbawm nor the Webbs adequately explained how or why these changes occurred; nor did they provide a clear conceptualisation of where the process could be located in terms of working-class experience, although both tended to assume that it derived in the main from the working class itself.[5] Furthermore, the phenomenon is treated with a finiteness that failed to adequately reconcile the presence of 'economist' tendencies within a 'customary' structure of values and vice versa. Indeed, the very conception of 'learning of the rules of the game' implies that at some point workers either did not know how to play, or were playing under the assumptions of a false consciousness which had to be shed before they could become more fully aware of their true interests. In the neglect that has surrounded this general problem since Hobsbawm's seminal essay, it is apparent that there remains much that is difficult and problematical about a development that is central to understanding the history of modern labour. Our focus, therefore, will be to attempt to re-define the course these earlier masters have charted. In particular, we are concerned to place the transition to 'economism' within an explanatory conceptual framework; to follow its transformation of the terms in which certain issues were conceived; and then to re-assess the limits and meaning behind the rules of the new industrial relations game.

THE ECONOMISM OF THE SYSTEM

No particular mystery attaches to the impetus for this re-definition of the employer–worker relationship in building. The dynamic of the new system rested upon the twin pillars of hourly pay and formalisation, and economism was inherent within both of these features. Both separately and together, their imperatives served to define and allow economic issues as the only legitimate language of industrial relationships. As we have already shown, hourly pay expressed a new link between the wage, the work and productivity which would hopefully raise the 'efficiency' of the individual worker. Its purpose was to allow free rein to employers to alter modes of working so as to increase the rate of exploitation. Whether, in fact, it achieved very much in this respect is by no means certain. Perhaps it was no coincidence that the greatest gains in 'efficiency' in London can be roughly correlated with the formalisation of the new system in that city.[6] In any case its practical results are, for present purposes, beside the point. More important was the fact that hourly pay served to shift the bargaining emphasis decisively to an economic perspective. Because it tied the pay to the work, it ensured that any concession employers made was granted with more than just a glance at its effects upon productivity. It was this, for example, that lay behind the commentaries of the *Builders' Trade Circular* on the negotiations of 1872 in London where the central issue boiled down to the price that should be paid for overtime. The men demanded that it be high enough to abolish systematic overtime, the masters were anxious to ensure that this did not happen: 'Recognising as we do, their moral right to demand a moderate increase in wages and somewhat shorter hours of labour . . . we maintain that the masters have also rights for the men to respect and to recognise, and that they ought to meet concession with concession.'[7] If, as it was claimed, hourly pay 'has rendered the relations between them [employers and men] more intelligible, and therefore more easy of adjustment,' it did so because it could be used to clear away the customs of the trade that were so often merely hidden forms of restrictive practices.[8] And during the seventies the customs of grinding money, walking time, lodgings money and overtime were all to feel the cold breath of hourly pay's economic logic.

Stimulated by the connection that hourly pay drew between work and production, a new kind of attention began to be paid to the whole question of productivity.[9] This concern was, of course, far wider than building, but in most other industries it was accompanied by changes of an organisational and internal kind that mandated a more efficient use of capital resources. Such was not the case in building where the new interest in productivity owed more to the pressures of labour relations. Frederic Smith's business manual (entitled *Workshop Management*) for cabinet makers and building workshops reflected this new focus, but much of what he advised had been pre-figured by the masters of the north in the late sixties. When Smith wrote of the decline of the 'former' custom of allowing a few minutes' grace in the morning and of the need for punctual starting times, he merely intellectualised what the employers had tried to achieve by standardised hours and payment systems.[10] And when it was urged that careful attention be paid to the division of labour on the job to ensure the most efficient organisation of the work, this was merely a reflection of the new skills that were emerging to cause building to be rent with demarcation disputes.[11]

The traditional means of extracting higher productivity had been to drive the men harder. It was not without some significance, therefore, that one of the first to question the value of such methods was Thomas Brassey whose family business shared many features and problems with the building trades proper. Brassey is of interest more because he marked the end of one epoch than because he marked the beginning of another. One of the first of the 'captains of industry' to suggest that a high wage economy was a better approach to productivity than the traditional methods of long hours and low wages, his emphasis on the seduction of the greater earnings to be gained by pieceworking made him an early exponent of economism. It followed naturally from this recognition that the carrot might be a more effective source of productivity and authority than the stick and, thus, it is unsurprising that Brassey was an advocate of the integration of labour. As an original 'new model' employer, he was one of the first to acknowledge and publicly advertise the advantages of a trade union labour discipline.[12] But he failed to devise any new methods by which productivity could be increased or any new prescriptions as to how the cooperation of labour might be achieved. And he rested content with a reiteration of the value of pieceworking systems and the paternal profit-sharing of the Briggs Coal Company.[13] If Brassey himself had few new ideas as to how productivity was to be improved, it would be too much to expect more enlightened views from such organs as *Capital and Labour* which in the seventies was a mouthpiece for the large general contractors. But it is interesting to note that as the Great Depression begins, their attention is turned to the problem of productivity in a correct recognition (from their point of view) that 'what the necessities of trade require is, that ten per cent more work should be done at the same price.' Their answer to this conundrum, however, was no more adventurous than it had ever been: depress wages and lengthen hours.[14] It was, in truth, a reflection of the transitional nature of this period that the question of productivity should be so poorly and inadequately formulated. Although their practical strategies were more advanced than the opinion of *Capital and Labour* would lead us to believe, it was not until the 1900s that recognisably modern prescriptions began to issue from the mouths of building employers. By that time Brassey's admonitions about 'high' wages had been clearly learnt and the advice that was given to builders in the downturn of the early part of the twentieth century was to leave wages alone but to cut costs by attacking restrictive practices.[15]

If hourly pay forged a link between work, wages and productivity that was to lead employers to translate 'customs' into their pounds, shillings and pence worth, the formalisation of industrial relations pointed in precisely the same direction. Mutual negotiation can only occur on the assumption that both sides define issues in the same way. Only thus may compromises be reached and bargains struck.[16] Such imperatives held no place in the unformalised system of industrial relations. In theory no issues were bargainable even if the practice amounted to something very different. It was a reflection of this assumption of sovereign authority that employers often refused to meet with formal delegations but, like C. M. Palmer, met their men in open public meetings. And the use of intermediaries was a similar device to short-circuit recognition. Under the pressure of sufficiently powerful challenges, however, conceptions of what constitute managerial prerogatives are subject to accommodating re-definition; but this represents only a shifting of its limits and boundaries in order more effectively to assert its legitimacy. Mutual negotiation represented no threat to such prerogatives: it was, rather, an answer to the challenges that had called it into being. But mutual negotiation did signify a re-conceptualisation of the nature of managerial prerogative which was aptly illustrated by the 'authority of employer' clauses in the working rules of the new system.

No contradiction was implied by the co-existence of these clauses with the truly collective bargaining structures that were also erected by the same rules. A distinction was being drawn that there were certain issues and questions not subject to the bargaining process and although the nature of those issues was deliberately left imprecise, the implication was clear enough. Bargaining was legitimate if it translated into economic terms. The right of the men to set a price upon their own labour had always been the weak point of employers' claims to paternal authority and to admit that 'with the exception of the time question there was no other question that should be subject to the trade rules' took no great betrayal of conscience. Ideally, therefore, negotiations should be limited to wages and hours; the apprentice question, for example, 'is not one for a trade rule at all.'[17] Whether this was always practicable is, for the moment, irrelevant. Just as a complete unilateral authority had been unrealisable in the naturalistic state of industrial relations, so the actualities of this new

definition of prerogatives were a lot more complex. Underlying this re-
definition, however, was the basic assumption that for mutual negotiation
to work this fundamental distinction had to be recognised. Even if, as was
obviously true, grievances were not always or simply about the economic
reward for work, it was only in this way that they could legitimately be
articulated. Certain authorised issues – specifically wages and hours – had
now been explicitly admitted to the bargaining process; others had been
implicitly rejected: 'Wage demands, unlike aspirations for workers' control, are culturally defined as legitimate.'[18] It therefore followed that only
if the questions were defined in economic terms could a recognisable bargain be made. As we have already suggested, mutual negotiation was not
the only force that acted to encourage and stimulate the definition of issues
and relationships in this way.[19] But, for our purposes, the workings of
mutual negotiation was of most significance because it was at this level of
experience that the process may be seen in operation.

It was precisely because mutual negotiation would work to translate
relationships and issues into a matter of economics that the men were so
suspicious of its methods. Possibly because they had been the most
successful practitioners of autonomous regulation, the masons were the
most sensitively aware of the implications behind the employers' advocacy
of the new structures. The 'simplification' of relationships that was
implied by hourly pay and formalisation would serve to remove the kinds
of trade rules with which masons had traditionally protected themselves.
The Manchester masons' opposition to hours and arbitration was a reflection of this understanding: 'It [hourly pay] would remove the necessity
for . . . any rules . . . except one, and that was to settle the price per hour,
and that could easily be done by this pet scheme of arbitration, so that by
the acceptance of these two points, they left themselves completely at the
mercy of their employers and the arbitration.'[20] Usually the men were not
so perceptively articulate as this: the 'confusion' that was noted amongst
the Manchester carpenters in 1869 may, in part, have signified a dimmer
recognition of the same dangers. In their arbitration of that year, however,
they were soon to be brought face to face with the economist realities of formalisation. For a brief moment the different perspectives of arbitrators and
men were revealed when Kettle began to probe the reasons for the suspicion
of hourly pay. The following dialogue illustrated the cross-purposes at
which both were speaking. Not having learnt the rules of the new game,
the men were arguing from a 'traditional' standard of living perspective in
contrast to the masters' and Kettle's focus on productivity. The men
wanted a reduction of hours without hourly pay to provide more opportunities for 'improving' leisure-time activities. To Kettle's reply that this
could be achieved by working fewer hours, they responded that this would
mean a wage reduction:

Kettle: 'So you want to be paid for hours you don't work?'
Men: 'No, we think our present wages are what we are worth. We think 32/-
really little enough to live on; and we hold this argument on behalf of the
whole body of men in Manchester.'
Kettle: 'I understand it. It is all in a nutshell.'[21]

Agreement was then secured by Kettle extracting a promise from employers not to reduce wages in winter, and in return the men accepted hourly pay.

By its mere presence, by the vocabulary that was used and by the perceptions and prejudices of involved outsiders like Kettle, formalisation presented a set of intangible pressures. Inherent within the very structures of the system, its economist tendencies remained often unspoken. Only occasionally can we see it working both positively and negatively to discourage techniques that aimed to control the work process. One such example, however, was the Huddersfield carpenters' arbitration of 1873 which refused to consider the men's objections to piecework because it was a question that fell within the authority of the employers.[22] Another example of the distinction to be drawn between legitimate and illegitimate issues was provided by the London carpenters' movement of 1872. Advocating the principle of mutual negotiation, the employers refused to discuss the men's desire for the abolition of piecework, a ban on overtime or the creation of a code of rules. But they were willing to negotiate on the questions of prices and hours. In comparison to earlier strikes, the issue became not one of the right of the men to demand an hours reduction, wage increase or steeper rate for overtime, but the price to be paid for such concessions as each side was willing to make.

The tension in Manchester carpentry that led up to the year-long conflict of 1877 may also be seen in the context of the clash between the work control aspirations of the men and the economism of the formalised system. Since 1875, the arbitration awards had been greeted with general dissatisfaction by the men. Not only did these awards insufficiently recognise their true economic position, but they also failed to allow the trade protection the men desired. In October 1876, this dissatisfaction climaxed in the presentation of rules that were a direct assault upon the economist logic of the system. In addition to a wages increase, artificial light was to be prohibited, walking time boundaries extended, there was to be three days' pay or notice for discharge, covers provided in wet weather, apprenticeship rules tightened and arbitration abandoned.[23] The employers, aware of the difficulties that existed between the Amalgamated Society and the General Union, stubbornly resisted these demands and the intervening depression effectively broke the strike. The men returned to work with a reduction of wages, an increased number of working hours and no restrictive rules.[24]

But even when the different imperatives of the men and the system were not resolved by conflict, the mere working of the procedures themselves served to induce an economist mode of behaviour upon the men. At the Birmingham bricklayers' arbitration of 1875, for example, Kettle refused to allow restrictions on the summer hours because only 'by making hay while the sun shines' could the men mitigate the irregularity of employment caused by hourly pay. Such a view, of course, was directly opposed to the work-sharing purposes of hours limitation and it stimulated an individual competitiveness among the men that could only serve to weaken their collective position. It was, therefore, hardly surprising that the following year the bricklayers made an unsuccessful attempt to remove the arbitration clause from the rules.[25]

A similar example is provided by the 1891 arbitration of the London carpenters' and joiners' demands for increased wages, reduced hours, and restrictions on piecework, sub contracting and overtime. The award, by the president of the RIBA, addressed only the hours and wages issues and failed to allow any increase in wages. But a clever linkage was forged between an increased overtime rate and changes in the periods of winter and summer hours which served to foster overtime work in order to maintain wage levels. An extension of the weeks to be worked on winter short time stimulated overtime for it meant that: 'Our men will find that for working the same number of hours in winter as they do in summer, will earn more money. We want to discourage overtime as much as possible.'[26] It was critical to control overtime in summer in order to provide more work for the winter months. To shorten the summer period was to enhance the temptation of overtime in order to maximise earnings during the fine weather. But, equally, as the passage quoted above suggests, the same applied to winter where more money could be earned by working extra hours in the mild autumn and spring weeks. The tendency of the award to encourage overtime in both seasons had, therefore, inverted the original purpose of the men to control the practice.

The formalisation of the bargaining process, therefore, accentuated and developed its economic focus. But formalisation could not recognise the legitimacy, indeed the desirability, of mutual negotiation without also addressing the problem of conflict. If regular bargaining was now to become the only acceptable mode of stabilising relationships, it followed that provision needed to be made for bargaining to collapse without throwing the whole process of mutual negotiation into question. Under autonomous regulation, systematic bargaining had been marked by precisely this problem. Whenever tentative contacts had been established they were generally ruptured by the failure to reach agreement and the outcome of a strike was left to decide the issue. Simply because there had been no procedural rule-making process, mid-Victorian commentators had not really known how to conceptualise industrial conflict. They tended to resort, therefore, to sanctimonious homilies on its futility or, if they were employers, to brand it as evidence of the 'dictatorial' tendencies of the men.[27] The no-strike clauses before arbitration and conciliation that appeared in the working rules of the early seventies were an expression of the changed assumptions that lay behind mutual negotiation because they implicitly recognised the legitimacy of conflict. There was no anticipation that strikes would dissolve under the new system, only the expectation that they could be controlled and reduced. But it was clearly necessary to provide a rationale for conflict that would enable it to be reconciled with the legitimacy of mutual negotiation and formalised relationships. Out of this need the theory of conflict was transformed from a matter of authority to one of economics, as it was only in economic terms that conflict could now be justified. And because this rationale quickly became a consensual definition some details of its emergence are worth our notice.

Some mid-Victorian writers on industrial affairs had occasionally attempted to assert that strikes were really, or should really be, about wages. Thus, in a pamphlet written at the time of the Preston cotton spinners strike of 1853, the issue had been squarely put:

When . . . you think that circumstances justify you asking an advance, ask it . . . If you like, *refuse* your labour till your claim is granted . . . [But] you have no right to ask for more than *wages* . . . He who provides the work, has a perfect right to say what that work is to be done, and to lay down the rules under which it shall be done.[28]

Similarly, in a comment on the 1859 building strike it had been remarked that: 'It is merely a commercial crisis; a mode of readjusting the value of labour from time to time; a question of pure science . . . No value . . . can be stationary . . . and wages must frequently be revised to suit changing demand . . . How . . . can this be practically ascertained except by striking?'[29] But in building, at least, such views flew in the face of what the masters and workmen knew to be the case under an unformalised system of industrial relations. All the while there were no other means of determining the conditions of work save by autonomous regulation and strikes then such advice ignored the realities of industrial conflict as a pure struggle for control. Once the structures changed, however, and the definitions with them this conception of conflict rapidly assumed a dominance that has still to be displaced.

A telling example of this re-definition of conflict may be seen in the contrast between the employers' handling of the strikes of 1859 and 1877–78 in London. Unlike 1859, and following the precedent of 1872, the question of whether or how negotiations were to be conducted never arose in 1877. Indeed, the strike hardly interrupted the smooth continuum of meetings between the employers' association and the union representatives. Gone, too, was the language of unilateral authority; no blanket accusations of dictation were made and no 'document' was introduced. The dispute was treated purely as a question of economic science:

At the commencement of this unhappy business it was a question of supply and demand, and on these grounds and those only have we fought the question. The masons said that the supply was not equal to the demand . . . the masters . . . set about ascertaining where the supply was in excess of demand, the result being that between 400 or 500 men are now on their way to this country [from Italy and USA].[30]

A violently anti-workmen journal reported that 'the masters look upon the present dispute . . . as a resistance . . . to the efforts . . . to force them to pay a larger sum in wages than they considered the work to be worth.' Perspectives of 'tyranny' had not, of course, disappeared; but they had been interestingly re-formulated to reinforce the legitimacy of the new structures. 'Union' tyranny was no longer the main irritant to the masters' authority: it was the uncontrolled activities of the local shop stewards – wrongly identified as 'officers' of the union – whose 'coercions and restrictions' made it 'impossible to carry on one's business.' For the other officials, employers had nothing but praise. And in the agenda for negotiation, the employers sought to secure from the union a commitment to curb the restrictive activities of the rank and file.[31] These new targets of employer censure were symptomatic of the emergent disciplinary function of unions which we shall address in another chapter. What is central to our present theme is to note how the logic of mutual negotiation and formalisation had secured not only a re-definition of conflict but also that of managerial rights, trade union roles and the legitimate areas of economic bargaining. This new view was well-expressed before the Royal Statistical Society by Jacob Waley who pointed out that employers must abandon their paternally autocratic pretensions and admit the right of the unions to speak on questions:

On which a workman has a right to be heard . . . his pay, his hours of labour, the salubrity of the factory in which he works . . . but . . . they are bound not to admit the interposition of the Society as to any matters not immediately connected with the remuneration, health and comfort of the workman . . . Those whose means keep industry going, and who run the risks . . . must be left to control the discipline of industry.[32]

In a broad sense, then, economism was a reflection of the logic of the new structures and styles of industrial relations that had emerged out of the crucible of the 1860s. A new context had been created which contained a place for trade union bargaining and defined the legitimate point of contact between the men and the employers as the determination of marketplace relationships between the two sides. Even if these new delimiters were frequently ignored to make a rigid adherence of this definition both impossible and unrealistic,[33] the difference with the past lay in the fact that relationships and issues could be treated as if they were purely economic in content. There were times, as in the 1890s, when the employers were forced to accept restrictions that did abrogate their prerogatives and discipline but there now existed strategies beyond a head-on authority conflict with which such challenges could be met.

When employers wish to introduce innovatory methods and systems, they frequently resort to the lure of increased economic benefits. Indeed, it is during this period that we may see the first application of this 'modern' technique. The offer of a higher wage in return for hourly pay, we may recall, was one of the anomalies that fuelled the Manchester carpenters' suspicions of the whole business in 1869; and in the 1870s, the booming prosperity of the industry made the ready granting of economic concessions an even greater practical possibility. It was the combination of these circumstances with the triumph of the system in 1869–70 that accounts for the relatively easy diffusion of hourly pay in the seventies.[34] Strikes over wages remained a low proportion of total strike activity, but wages themselves continued to climb.[35] There was a certain irony in the fact that even the Manchester bricklayers and masons experienced a scale of increase never seen before. Between 1870–77, the bricklayers saw their wages rise by over 30%; and the masons, whose wages had risen by 11% during the sixties, gained an extra 26% over the first seven years of the next decade.[36] But the immediate wage gains that were attained were not the only way in which the propitious circumstances allowed the advantages of the new system to be accentuated. Under boom conditions, the greater freedom that hourly pay offered to the employers accrued also to the men. Less money was lost for late starting, men could leave at a moment's notice to accept more remunerative employment and, consequently, there was a diminished need for the kinds of protective 'customs' associated with the day system. The series of reasons given by the Middlesbrough masons when they decided to adopt the hourly system in 1875 allow us to glimpse the alliance of forces that encouraged the dominance of the hourly method of wages payment during the decade. They explained:

From the time of the first general inauguration to the present time the hour system has slowly advanced, and is now nearly the general mode of payment throughout the building trades. Finding this to be the case, we have thought it policy to ask for its adoption in our local rules, instead of, as heretofore, resisting its introduction . . . seeing that it has worked well wherever it has been introduced, especially in regard to the amount of time saved through being enabled to start at the half-hour . . . instead of losing, as at present, a quarter or a half-day . . . through being late in starting time. Another special advantage . . . [will be] by having a fixed time during the winter months for starting and leaving . . . instead of . . . the vague time of from daylight till dark . . . It is such a source of petty tyranny and discontent . . ., that we have thought it time that some means were devised to put an end to this intolerable source of dissatisfaction.[37]

But it was not simply the fortuity of economic circumstance that associated the new system with enhanced economic advantages. A rudimentary form of productivity bargaining was inherent within the new system itself and may be seen from the very moment of its inauguration in the compensatory concessions that were offered for its acceptance. The Birmingham carpenters' rules of 1865, for example, from which restrictive practices had been removed, also saw wages rise by over 2s per week – on the assumption, that is, of stable working hours. And the rules of the two following years saw similar increments all of which reinforced the viability of conciliation and arbitration.[38] Similarly, smooth passage of the hourly system amongst the Leeds masons was secured in 1876 when a wage increase combined with a guaranteed winter wage was accepted in return for the new method.[39] Because of the link that hourly pay established between wages and work, it also suggested the modern tactic of buying out restrictive rules and customs whose rationale the system had undermined. There was an early illustration of the tendency of hourly pay to transform customs into a simple monetary formula in London when, in 1866, the plasterers were offered a higher wage for an end to the practice of employers paying the lodgings fee. When the Hull joiners demanded the Saturday half-holiday in 1867, the masters indicated their agreement was conditional upon the implementation of hourly pay and, similarly, the London employers in 1873 responded to a wage demand by offering to trade this for abolition of the overtime rate.[40] These particular efforts at productivity bargaining were unsuccessful; but they were ploys whose logic was inherent within the tendency of the new structures to make explicit the economic nexus around which industrial relations were now focussed.

More successful and precise examples of the same theme, however, are to be found in the masons' trade where it now became accepted practice for the employers to offer to trade economic benefits in return for the surrender of the worked stone rule. At Bristol in 1872, a reduction of hours was bargained against the rule; at Darlington in 1873, restriction of worked stone was dropped in return for a large wage increase of 3s per week; and at Doncaster the combination of an hours reduction and wage increase secured abolition of the rule in 1876.[41] The Manchester rules of 1875 provide a clear illustration of the tension that existed between economism and restrictive practices and how in the context of the seventies that tension could be resolved by substantial economic gains. The state of trade in the city was good and in the sixties this circumstance would have been the basis for an expansion of restrictive rules. Indeed, in its original demands for restrictions on piecework, apprenticeship, the erection of sheds and a change in the notice time for alterations, the masons' negotiating package reflected the remnants of this bias. In the event, however, none of these demands were achieved. They seem to have been surrendered for an increased rate of overtime pay and a substantial wage increase which the men somewhat defensively claimed afterwards to have been 'the chief feature in our application.'[42]

Given the context of the forces that we have outlined above, it is unsurprising that the seventies were marked by a general decline in masons' restrictive practices.[43] But this decline stood at odds with the economic conditions of the decade and had such practices been solely a function of economic circumstances and opportunity this would not have been the case. The seventies reveal this interesting pattern precisely because the viability of such restrictions is also affected by the structural characteristics of work and the surrounding system of industrial relations. Paradoxically, the tendency of the industrial relations structures to de-legitimise the restrictions of the seventies was accentuated by the possibilities that the boom allowed for greater economic benefits. Such benefits had also advanced during the sixties but within the totally different context of an unformalised system without mutual negotiation. By the mid-seventies this pattern had been replaced by one which encased gains and losses firmly within a regularised set of negotiation procedures and structures in which wages and hours were not merely one issue amongst many but the main issues against which all else could be bargained. The decline of restrictive practices was not simply, therefore, a function of the masons' defeats in the northwest – critical though those defeats were in establishing the legitimacy of the new structures – but was also a function of the positive operation of the new structures as they became the accepted means of governing relations between employers and men.

For the masons, however, the character of industrial relations in the seventies is a true reflection of the 'transitional' character of the decade. It presents an amalgam of the old and the new with the latter slowly securing, as if by osmosis, its dominance. In many places outside those towns that had been the cockpit of the crisis of the late sixties, restrictive practices were still current. Piecework, worked stone restrictions, the working of overtime only in cases of emergency, the maintenance of apprenticeship ratios, of walking time and shed requirements could all still be found.[44] And it took the long trough of inactivity that began in the late seventies to destroy (for a time) the final remnants of sixties' restrictionism so that by the eighties not only had hours been lengthened and wages decreased but all surviving restraints upon overtime, worked stone and piecework had also been removed.[45] Similarly, it was not until 1873 that there was a noticeable increase in the number of towns on the hourly system or with conciliation structures. But by the mid-eighties the former was universal and the latter – unnecessary for employers during the depression – was to revive with added force in the 1890s.

But, from what has been said about the new styles that were coming to govern industrial relations, it should be clear that the extent of the change cannot be gauged simply by the survival of certain features of the 1860s. For it is obvious that the trend of events was moving away from the kind of restrictions on employers' authority that had marked that decade. The Manchester, Liverpool and Birmingham rules illustrate the point: the decisive change that followed the defeats in those towns was not reversed in this period. Indeed, the effects of the defeats were reinforced and safe-guarded by the economist bias of the industrial relations structures that were in place and by the opportunities of the boom. Restrictive practices and an increase in the men's sphere of control were not, of course, to disappear for good. But when they revive in the 1890s it is under markedly different circumstances whose roots lie in this transitional period. What we witness in the 1870s is not so much a resolution of the 'problem' of authority at work as the beginnings of new devices and stratagems with which it is attacked.

Productivity bargaining as a means of diminishing restrictive practices was one such expedient which appears for the first time as a consistent and self-conscious employer artifice. Nor should this occasion any surprise. Under the informal system of relationships which denied the possibility of negotiations within a permanent structure of institutions and procedures, productivity bargaining had been infeasible. Within the new structures it was hard to avoid. And its emergence reflected not only the awakening awareness of a modern conception of industrial efficiency, nor simply the accident of hourly pay's logic, but also the dimensions of authority that lay behind the crisis of the late sixties and the system that it spawned. Late-nineteenth-century employers may not have had at their disposal armies of personnel advisors schooled in the study of human relations industrial sociology, but they hardly needed to be told – even if they didn't intellec-tualise the point – that productivity bargaining reclaimed 'authority over areas which [previously] came under the control of particular groups of workers.'[46] Whatever benefits productivity bargaining may hold for workers – and in the seventies they were of no mean order – its central pur-pose remains to diminish the control that the workforce is able to exercise over the work process and thus allow managers greater freedom to 'manage.'[47] Neither is this perception peculiarly modern. It is to be found in a pregnant exchange drawn from the Newcastle shipwrights in 1851 when their industrial relations were in the process of being formalised. Responding to the employers' attempts to 'buy out' the restrictions on the number of feet to be caulked per day with the higher wages promised by pieceworking, the shipwrights pointed out:

Their character was involved in the work being well done, and . . . it was their duty to caulk vessels properly, whatever order they received from the employers. To this it was responded [by the employers] that the men ought only to obey the orders and look to the interests of those who paid them their wages, leaving the other question to be settled by the dock-owner and ship-owner. [But to accept the employers' demands, the ship-wrights replied, would be to] lose the means of protecting and advancing ourselves.[48]

Productivity bargaining, thus, followed naturally from the replacement of paternal definitions of authority with those that emphasised the supremacy of the market relationship. Beyond the precise measurement of this relationship, the authority of employers was supposed to reign supreme. It was the purpose of the new structures to provide the market-place where haggling over the bargain could occur. But this very fact also presumed that those structures would protect the re-formulated definition of authority. In practice we have seen that this was achieved in various ways; the new structures would rule certain issues as illegitimate; the process of arbitration focussed solely upon what it was believed economic circumstances would allow; the vocabulary of mutual negotiation inevitably biassed the reduction of grievances to an economic formula. But the transformation of the terms in which issues were perceived was an implicit projection of mutual negotiation itself and there was seldom a clear recognition that a 'customary' definition was about to be replaced by an 'economist' one. Only infrequently is it possible to identify a clear and precise encounter between the two opposed definitions and the systems they implied. The significance of 1869–70 in Manchester was in large part composed of the sense of profound change that pervaded those events. But such a confrontation – which even at the time was uncertainly discerned – is a rare exception to a process that was often intangible and natural. Whilst it is, therefore, an unavoidable necessity to over-schematise the mechanics of transition from custom to economism, this should not be taken to imply a linear movement from a state of innocence to one of corruption. Masters and men had made their economic calculations under the unformalised system; wages had always been the most significant quantitative issue of dispute. We are not, of course, concerned to argue the sudden appearance of an economic nexus between masters and men; the language of economic definition was not peculiar to the new structures. But the universalistic application of this definition and the transmutation of its sphere of influence to compose the total essence of the authority relationships at work was a critical new twist to an old story.

All this is precisely how it should be. One historical phenomenon does not follow another in quick and ready succession. The 'new' does not come pre-packaged ready to replace the 'old' on the shelves of history's supermarket of products but struggles in an era of transition to free itself of the shackles of the past until its own legitimacy is unquestioned. Only then can it begin to build and re-shape its area of responsibility in its own image. In the context of our present concerns, the 1870s to the 1890s were that time of transition after which the new definitions were absorbed into the dominant culture and reflected in the vocabulary and discussion that composed the dialogue with the subordinate elements. But for a dialogue to occur it needs to be based upon certain common assumptions and terms which may portray only a partial aspect to the reality of the relationship between the various parties. It is not to be assumed, therefore, that our categories of 'customary' and 'economist' as they describe concrete modes of behaviour are fixed immutably in time and place. Labour history has suffered too much from simple-minded conceptions of the linear progression of men and movements. And it is not our intention to compound those errors with the suggestion that 'economism' followed on and, in all respects, re-placed 'custom' as a meaningful description of worker behaviour.

The heart of the transformation was the substitution of a new paradigm of constructs within which the issues that arose in the workplace were to be translated, listened to and settled. This new economist paradigm – a lot less honest than the customary paradigm of autonomous power – did nothing to dissolve the essential struggles for authority and power that were the very substance of issues between employers and men. But it did allow those issues to be endowed with a superficially different nature that provided the opportunity for a common resolution of contentious questions. The emergence of economism represented an attempt to resolve the essence of industrial relationships into a simple economic equation and it complicated, therefore, rather than simplified these relationships; for it treated the shell as if it were the kernel. To trace the transformation of certain issues from customary to economist paradigms does not mean, therefore, that we are witnessing a change in the essence of those issues. The process is that of the creation of new methods and strategies with which the issue is mediated through the filter of the industrial relations system. But this does nothing to diminish the significance of the process, for it is crucial to understanding the future dynamics of industrial relations and conflict. This is true largely because it is through tracing the process of re-definition as it affected the discussion and conception of certain issues that we are able more adequately to interpret the historical meaning to the idea of 'learning of the rules of the game.'

CUSTOM AND ECONOMISM:
GRINDING MONEY, OVERTIME AND WORKED STONE

Carpenters' grinding money – the time allowed carpenters and joiners to sharpen their tools at the end of a job – was one of those customs whose basis and rationale were undermined by the economic logic of hourly pay. The customary charge of one quarter of a day's pay expressed the autonomy of the craftsman's work. But it was a charge that bore no relation to the economic worth of the transaction, was based on no real assessment of the value to the employer of men possessing tools that were ready for work. In a sense, too, it was a charge one employer made upon another because it inflated the wages bill after the actual job had been completed. And if, as was reported, hourly pay increased the number of short hirings, then much of the custom's advantage to the employer disappeared. Within the new definitions, it could be defended only as an 'old privilege' that was clearly at odds with the imperatives of hourly pay and the economic standards of judgement imposed by mutual negotiation.[49] Until the introduction of these new methods, therefore, the tradition and its standard remained unquestioned. Indeed, it was one of those substantive issues which, under appropriate conditions, the unformalised system allowed the men to push forward.[50] But it is significant that once hourly pay was introduced into London – the town for which we have the best information – the privilege began to be challenged. An attempt by Jackson and Shaw to abolish the custom in 1866 was successfully resisted but it showed which way the wind was blowing. The prevailing situation after 1861 was somewhat confused but it would seem that a drive in 1864 to reduce the time to two hours was an effort to generalise what was already the common allowance. Charles Matkin, for example, claimed in 1875 that, 'Previous to 1861 the time allowed was a quarter of a day – when the hour system came into operation it was altered to two hours.'[51] The employers agreed with this, pointing to the different circumstances of the custom under the new system of payment:

It thus appears that the custom of the trade since men were no longer engaged by the week is not to give grinding allowance – in time or money, if the men leave of their own accord or are discharged for incompetency or misbehaviour – nor generally if the men work for less time than a full week . . . The custom so far as it existed before 1872 was generally modified with the introduction of the hourly contract system.[52]

Court cases on the issue resulted in contradictory verdicts. Some, such as one in 1864, upheld the old standard but others, noting the logic of hourly pay, ruled that 'it would be most unreasonable to allow grinding money when the hiring was an hourly one.'[53]

If hourly pay threw the custom into confusion and doubt, the formalisation of industrial relations in the city allowed the twin pressure of mutual negotiation to be brought to bear. Following the agreement of 1872, some employers refused to continue the custom because it had formed no part of the settlement.[54] Indeed, by the mid-seventies it was reported that out of 103 firms surveyed only one third granted the 'official' two hours, another third gave one hour and the rest refused any kind of time or monetary payment. And in the summer of 1875 the employers' association began an effort to obtain the one-hour standard – and that only if the employer considered it necessary. It was reported in June 1875 that 'during the past few months the employers have been trying their utmost to do away with the two hours' custom, and establish in place of it one hour only.' For their part, the employers drew attention to the 'inefficiency' associated with the custom, claiming that: 'It is a very general complaint that the indulgence is systematically abused – that men who received two hours notice immediately therefore cease working and either leave the work, or by idling about interfere with others.'[55] United in a traditional trade movement, the men successfully defended the two hour standard – although it surely remained as partial and insecure as it had been since the beginning of the sixties. It was during the depression of the mid-eighties that the final demise of the old standard was achieved when mutual negotiation obliged the men to bargain on the basis of the employers' valuation of the custom. In the summer of 1887 it was agreed that one hour's time and money be allowed for the grinding of tools.[56] Elsewhere in the country the evidence is even more scanty than that for London. But there seems little doubt that the same decline in the customary arrangement was a general experience. It was reported from Edinburgh, for example, that by the late eighties grinding money was seldom given because of the short notice received by the men and that 'there was scarcely any jobs now where a grindstone was kept.'[57]

What happened to grinding money was a particularly good example of the 'modernisation' of a custom, an illustration of the more subtle ways in which autonomous regulation was broken down. But grinding money lay ancillary to the theme of control over the work; it was more a symbol of the workman's sphere of independence than a central bastion of their autonomy. The case was different with overtime, whose status and methods of restriction underwent a similar kind of transformation during this period. Under unformalised industrial relations the question had been whether overtime was to be worked at all and discretion for this decision had been largely exercised by the men. Once the issue had been subjected to the influences of hourly pay and formalisation such fundamentals were removed from consideration and the contest became how much was to be charged for a practice that would be worked at the discretion of the employer. Overtime was converted from a disincentive on the employer to an incentive for the men.

The importance of overtime lay in the relationship between extended working hours, over-exploitation and the distribution of work between the men and throughout the seasons. If it was to be worked at the discretion of the employers it would be a powerful weapon with which conditions and wages could be attacked. Extensive overtime working, it is still reasoned, means less work for more men, more unemployment and a weakened collective unity. In building, it was particularly important to control hours of work during the summer months: the light and fine days tempted employers and men to work beyond the normal day but for the men to pay the consequence of unemployment and short time during the winter.[58] Control of overtime was, therefore, central to control over the productive process and was an important part of the official and unofficial collective activity of the men during the pre-1870 period. Overtime rules were commonplace in the union rule books, but informal activity was also widespread. In 1852, it was reported to be a 'peculiarity' of the Edinburgh masons that on hearing the signal to cease work, their mell would descend to deliberately miss the chisel. So opposed were masons to overtime working that the *Royal Commission on Trade Unions* heard how 'they have refused to work on to clear away scaffolding from a market-place though they knew . . . the space was wanted.'[59]

Whatever form collective resistance to overtime assumed, its central characteristic was to restrict the conditions under which the employer could demand that it be worked. The exaction of a higher price for extra hours was a natural and integral part of these disincentives but it was combined with definitions that determined the specific circumstances under which overtime would be allowed. Thus, the masons' rule books deprecated the practice but recognised that certain conditions may dictate its necessity. The local branches were left to decide what constituted 'necessity' which they tended to restrict to cases where an accident, breakdown or other unforeseen emergency occurred.[60] Thinly disguised behind these restrictions there lurked the objective of a total abolition of the practice. This, of course, was the purpose of rigidly prescribing the conditions under which it could be worked; for they allowed judgements to be drawn between systematic and justifiable overtime. It was only once these definitions were broken down and replaced by a sole reliance upon the deterrence of a higher rate that overtime was transformed from a contingency circumstance into its modern role as a natural and permanent addition to the work week. Under the old system, however, employers were restrained both by the higher price and the normative definitions; the seduction of increased earnings for the men was enjoined by the convention that it be worked only under special conditions and union branches did not hesitate to discipline those who ignored these limits.[61]

The question of overtime, then, was dominated by the themes of restriction and abolition. The only trade to deviate from this pattern were the painters who suffered particularly from seasonal unemployment and who, on certain jobs, were willing to work an extra two hours at ordinary rates in summer to make up for lost time in winter. More typical were the

Manchester masons in the 1840s who constantly urged an extensive assault on the problem, pointing to their own experience when 'it was entirely put down in this town for two years, and would still have been so, had it not been for men coming from other towns, and working in direct opposition to our bye-laws.'[62] Similarly, the 1866 Derby joiners' rules allowed overtime (at a higher rate) only in cases of necessity, but they explained that 'if it could be dispensed with altogether [it] would prove beneficial to both employer and employed.' And the Bolton masons, whose rules of 1868 allowed overtime if specific cause could be shown to make it necessary, claimed that 'our motto is to do away with overtime if possible.'[63] These sentiments continued into the seventies when it was already common for control of overtime to have passed into the employers' hands. The Barnsley masons struck against the practice in 1871, the Birmingham masons claimed that their 1876 rules had effectively abolished it, and in Droylesden and other towns attempts were made to change the wording of the rule from 'necessity' (a loose term which in the context of the seventies allowed the employer to make the definition) to that of 'emergency.'[64]

This particular frontier of control was, like all others, in a state of almost perpetual movement and it is impossible to gauge the extent to which the men were able to realise an effective control over the issue. But it seems to be clear that by the 1860s the scope of the men's control had attained limits not reached before. The carpenters of Scarborough, for example, in 1865 made overtime optional at the discretion of the men and the Ashton lodge of the General Union claimed the right to decide whether each case could be considered a justifiable emergency.[65] It is certainly true that by the late sixties employers were sufficiently constrained by the overtime rules to include it among the restrictive practices they wished to see abolished. The right of the employer to initiate overtime working was an integral part of their efforts to change the structure of industrial relations during that decade. And wherever they were victorious in their contests with the men, the rule was changed to require that it be worked at the employers' request.[66] But, as with the other developments that we have been tracing, the transformation of overtime was not solely the result of the localised employers' victories at the decade's end. As important were the constraints and necessities imposed by hourly payment and the new system of formalised relations. Thus, there is a strong correlation between the spread of hourly payment in the seventies and the exaction of a higher price as the sole device to restrict overtime working.[67] Nor was this mere coincidence. Leaving aside for the moment the intangible effects the masters' victories of 1869–70 might have had upon the formulation of the overtime rule, the fact was that hourly pay engendered a different game which required a different set of rules. The uncertainties and insecurities that were created by the hourly system forced the treatment of overtime into a different mould. Under the collective unity that had been stimulated by the day system, qualitative restrictions against overtime had been a viable and appropriate policy. But, as we noted earlier, the foundations of that unity were shattered by hourly pay. Even if the full effects of that system were mitigated, the threats posed to the whole range of customary work experiences were sufficient to question the viability of policies that rested upon their presence. Outright prohibition or restriction through 'necessity' were, thus, less realistic strategies to control overtime than one based upon that condition common to all the men of the standard wage per hour. This was particularly true because, as we have already noted, one of the effects of the hourly system was to enhance the significance of the standard rate and the normal day as protective devices that were also legitimate bargaining issues. Under these circumstances the exaction of a higher price for overtime working became the most opportune form of restriction available.

In addition to this, there were the economist pressures implicit in mutual negotiation. As with other customary modes of restriction, formalised bargaining made it impossible to justify the tactic of prohibition. Such a strategy had suitably conformed to the logic of autonomous regulation where unilateral rule making had been the norm. But mutual negotiation allowed no room for such autonomous activity and the wage was, thus, the only legitimate method of control. It was with a realism born of the new circumstances that the Manchester masons in 1875 proudly exalted the economism of their new rules. The men's explanation of the resolution of the overtime question suggests the kinds of pressures that were operating: 'Owing to the great amount of overtime worked in this locality, we made a standpoint to stop it if possible and sooner than the good feeling which exists between them and us should be disturbed, they [the employers] conceded us Rule 4th. which is time and a half for the first two hours and double time after.'[68] Examples drawn from Birmingham and London may be taken to illustrate neatly the powerful influence exerted by the combination of hourly pay and formalisation. Prior to the Birmingham discharge note strike, the carpenters and joiners held the characteristically traditional attitude on overtime. Opposed 'to any amount of overtime, even at the rate asked for,' they restricted its use by the customary blend of a higher price in conjunction with the limitations that it be worked only in cases of emergency or breakdown.[69] But the introduction of the new style of industrial relations in 1865 saw an end to these assumptions; the restrictions on overtime were among the constraints abandoned in return for a conciliation and arbitration system. In their place, the employers were free to request overtime on any occasion and the only contentious question remained the price to be paid.[70]

The secret of the rapid triumph of overtime's economist definition in

Birmingham lay in the unity the employers forged between hourly pay and formalisation as a condition for ending the dispute. The experience of London in the sixties revealed the importance of the connection; for the strength of abolitionist sentiment in the city survived the introduction of hourly pay until mutual negotiation made it an irrelevancy. Several movements in the 1860s aimed to control systematic overtime and, although their success is problematical, the masons did claim to have asserted a unilateral prohibition on the large sites associated with the re-building of Whitehall. And, in 1870, the carpenters began to press for a code of rules whose central purpose was to 'annhilate entirely that bug-bear overtime.'[71] With the emergence of mutual negotiation in 1872, however, the range of possibilities was immediately transformed. The carpenters demanded a level of overtime pay which they knew would be effectively prohibitive. The employers, of course, refused to talk about prohibition and adamantly resisted a rate which would have amounted to the same thing and make economic nonsense of the hourly system. Once negotiations were entered into, concession was bound to be met with concession. The masters gave a little on hours and wages, the men gave a little on piecework and overtime. The result was an improvement in hours and wages and an overtime rate which failed to discomfort the employers but left the rank and file very dissatisfied.[72]

It would be a mistake to assume from this, however, that attempts to control overtime more completely through customary devices sank without trace in the sea-change of industrial relations that occurred in the seventies. Like most other restrictions it took the Great Depression to effectively remove the final vestiges of sixties restrictionism. Neither then, of course, had such efforts disappeared for good. In the 1890s and in the period from 1911 to the First World War there were notable revivals of customary techniques of control. The Liverpool masons, for example, in 1896 and again in 1911 made attempts to tighten their overtime rule from that which specified it be worked at employer's request to one which limited it to 'accidents' or 'necessity.'[73] In 1902, the London bricklayers made it known that they 'objected against all overtime as this prevented many men obtaining employment,' and most of the cases brought before the carpenters' conciliation board in 1911 concerned work group attempts to control the practice. In 1912, the plasterers proposed to allow overtime only in emergencies and the masons suggested a tightening of restrictions which would have prevented it except in cases of breakdown or other unforeseen interruptions to the work. And in 1911 the abolition of overtime became an official policy of the London Building Industries Federation.[74] Similarly, in the early nineties it was reported that the Edinburgh masons, once again, worked little or no overtime; and the ship-joiners and shipwrights were also reputed to exercise a very tight control over the issue.[75] But there are two things to be said about this renewed drive to control overtime by traditional means. In the first place, both in the nineties and in the years before the First World War it was part of a widespread revival of work control efforts by the men which we shall address more fully in subsequent chapters. For the moment, we need only note that the defeat of autonomous regulation in the seventies had done nothing to alter the fundamental struggle for control over work that dominated the workplace. But, secondly, that struggle was now complicated by the presence of an industrial relations system which by this time had moved far beyond the rudimentary structures of the seventies to a more perfect maturity.

Herein lay the critical difference. Restrictionist techniques had harmo· nised with the structures of autonomous regulation whose values were those of an admitted search for power and authority; but they were incompatible with a system which denied the struggle for power and substituted in its place the higgling of the market. The vocabulary of customary control was not the language of the system of industrial relations and its assertive efforts were dealt with accordingly. It was the business of this new system to translate control aspirations into pounds, shillings and pence – to prevent, if possible, their admission into the rules governing employer–worker relationships. Seldom transmitted, therefore, into 'official' policy, these customary techniques could only be exercised, as they were at Fawley in the 1950s, as the informal and illegitimate rules of work groups outside the purview of the system. From this perspective, the prohibition of overtime had ceased to be a principal objective of the men: indeed, it is interesting to note that restrictions on overtime in the nineties did not grow to the same extent as those on other issues such as piecework. And, although restrictionism was occasionally to surface, it failed to find expression in the rules that emerged from the negotiating process. For the most part, overtime had become a part of the regular work of the week and the economist formulation dominated its discussion. By the 1890s, then, the bias in the treatment of overtime had shifted to make it just another economic issue between employers and men. The Wolverhampton masons proudly announced a new rule on overtime in 1892: 'The masters have been in the habit of doing anything they liked in this respect, and no extra pay whatsoever' but there was now an additional charge for overtime working.[76] In an ideal world the London bricklayers of 1902 would have wished for the total abolition of overtime, but the practical realities of mutual negotiation dictated that this remain an ideal and not be admitted as a bargainable issue. Indeed, by this time the rules of the OBS itself reflected this: their sole condition for overtime was that it be paid at the recognised rate. Similarly, although from 1911 London building workers were to reveal strong abolitionist sentiments, at no point during the previous twenty years had they found their way into the official negotiations which had translated these sentiments into demands for a higher rate.[77]

Rules controlling overtime were an annoyance employers would rather live without but masons' attempts to prohibit the importation of worked stone were an outrage. We have seen how this had been a prime target of the employers' campaign against 'tyranny' in the sixties and the object of productivity bargaining in the seventies. It was unlikely, therefore, that this customary rule would remain untouched by the emergency of economism and, like overtime, the techniques to restrict worked stone were transformed during the nineties. Superficially, the content of the change was simple and unremarkable. The customary restriction had proscribed from a given town any stone worked or dressed elsewhere; the economist rule stipulated only that prepared stone could not be introduced from an area where wage rates were lower than those of the locale where it was to be used. Despite the employers' efforts, and buoyed by the slow spread of the new structures and the economic activity of the decade, the worked stone rule retained a widespread presence in the seventies. Like many other restrictions, depression was to be the most effective handmaiden of the masters' desire and from the late seventies until the early nineties the rule was to be found in few, if any, of the working rules. With the economic recovery of the industry in the nineties, however, the prohibition of worked stone began to be re-asserted to form the main issue of conflict in the decade.[78] The reasons why this should have been so are obscure. It is probable, however, that the restrictive effects of the rule were highlighted by the enhanced popularity of stone-cutting machinery and quarry-prepared stone whose viability had been encouraged by the cost-cutting economic stimulant of the depression.[79] Indeed, the decade had opened with a long and bitter strike at Cardiff in 1892 in which this question had played a central role. Although no formal settlement was reached on this issue, the employers secured a *de facto* right to use imported stone which was officially recognised in 1898 when it was agreed that the economist rule would prevail.[80] By that time, however, the old rule was facing its critical test in a decisive confrontation with the employers of the northwest.

It remains unclear precisely where the origins of the economist rule lie. It is likely, however, that they are to be found amongst those in the stone-masons' union who were responding to the new realities of hourly pay and mutual negotiation. Indeed, it was no coincidence that apart from the employers the earliest condemnations of the old rule emanated from London where there never had been a worked stone rule and where any attempt to introduce one would certainly have been defeated by the size of the city. But it is probable that London's attitude had something to do with the hourly system, for those towns where hourly pay had been imposed in conjunction with the demise of restrictive rules also tended to turn to the new economist formulation.[81] More clearly than the other examples we have examined, internal divisions within the union were to play a crucial role in the transformation of this particular issue. Divergent attitudes amongst the lodges was one aspect of this division. As early as 1869, some London lodges, reflecting public disapproval of the prohibitive rule, had pressed for its abolition because it was protectionist and violative of free trade.[82] With the revival of militancy on the issue in the 1890s, they led the assault from within the union. It was absurd, the Battersea and Hammersmith lodges argued, that Liverpool stone should be blacked in Birkenhead, 'they are for all practical purposes, one town . . . with the same rate of wages throughout . . . Our Birkenhead brothers could easily cross the river to work if they did not . . . find it on their side.' Then there was the strike supported by the Society against working stone in Huddersfield which was to be fixed in Doncaster; the standard rate was the same in both towns and the union had, thus, spent some £140 'fighting against ourselves.' The London branches proposed to initiate the remedy for these anachronisms by amending the customary rules presented for ratification by Llandudno to read 'no stone from underpaid districts to be brought into the town.'[83]

A few years later, on the eve of the critical contest of the decade, the Bury lodge returned to the charge. Since the employers were determined to attack this question, they argued, and since the same restrictive purpose would be better served by the economist formula, it was proposed that the Society should allow worked stone to move freely into any town provided it did not originate from a lower paid district.[84] But on this occasion, the 'modernisers' argument did not go unanswered. The Manchester and Ratcliffe lodges re-asserted the traditional case in an interesting rebuttal which the Webbs would have done well to note. Their argument made the point that the question of the standard rate was itself intertwined with that of authority over work:

If it [i.e. working of the stone] is done is these yards here, we have control over the system of the employer . . . [In, for example,] the down-trodden town of Warrington . . . we are anxious for some big jobs to come out there to give it a chance with the rest of us, but what is its chance with the towns of Liverpool and Manchester if we allowed the contractor to work the stone here and send it into Warrington, thus, employing only a few Warrington fixers for a job that should employ 60–80. This would defeat any chance of increasing the rate of wages, or any betterment.

In fact, they argued, the contrary was the case: the economist policy doomed low-paying regions to remain under-employed because it gave the employer complete freedom to take work out of the town and put it where he pleased. When the question was put to the vote – and in what was to be the last victory of the old rule – the Society overwhelmingly endorsed the Manchester position.[85] By this time, however, the new rule was gradually strengthening its hold: Bury, Halifax, Dewsbury, Huddersfield, Newcastle and Liverpool were all reported to have adopted it early in 1898. More important, the employers were now preparing to strike a concerted blow at those towns of the northwest where the old rule was most strongly entrenched.[86] Uniting their town associations into a district federation, the large employers of Lancashire and Cheshire gave notice that they intended the abolition of the worked stone rule. On 2 May 1898 a partial lockout was enforced that lasted in Manchester until the end of July.[87] When it ended the old rule had suffered a decisive defeat and as part of the settlement the new economist rule had emerged victorious.

Certain similarities exist between this contest and that of 1869. Both were critically important in legitimising a new definition of employer-employee relationships; and in both cases Manchester was the arena in which the issue was ultimately resolved. But there were also important differences, not least among them that in 1898 the Society was seriously split. Even within the northwestern districts of the union there was something less than unanimity in support of the prohibitive rule. The London Kennington lodge argued for those who adopted a 'progressive' opposition to all such customary devices: 'We should drop our protective crotchets . . . As we have lived to see over the artificial light, and the hours question, it was but phantoms we were fighting, although we ruined our Society more than once in doing it.'[88] In spite of this, however, it is important to realise that the economist version of the rule was championed by a very small minority of the lodges. At most, a mere dozen or so had adopted it by this time and only the virtue of hindsight allows us to see them as the wave of the future. That this was to be so must be attributed to the major difference with 1869 which lay in the division between the Union Executive and those who were resisting the employers' offensive. In the contests of the late sixties, the attitudes of Harnott and the Executive were an irrelevancy that could have no impact or significance on the course or outcome of the dispute. They neither claimed nor possessed any real authority over local branch autonomy in trade matters. But such was not the situation by 1898 when the Executive had acquired a power and authority that made its attitude and intervention of crucial importance in deciding the result. In this respect, the transformation of the worked stone rule provides an illuminating example of the role official structures played in the destruction of custom and the triumph of economism.

The Executive refused to sit idly by whilst the struggle in the northwest was fought out. Once the lodges in the area had recorded a decisive majority in support of retaining the prohibitive rule, delegates from the Executive Council went into action. Thinking 'it wise to go outside Manchester and practically commence a crusade against the worked stone rule whatever shape or form it took,' they travelled first to those towns which seemed willing to accept the economist formulation. Their arguments were unabashedly 'progressive': they pointed out that the old rule was condemned by public opinion; they claimed that it was antagonistic to machinery; they asserted that it enhanced the cost of production and led, therefore, to 'commercial suicide'; and, finally, they expostulated, 'can we withstand the commercial evolution of our time?' But wherever they went they found themselves 'crusaders against – with the bulk of our members we have contended with – a conviction that was firmly rooted in their minds.' By the middle of June, however, and after a month of such efforts, 'the change of opinion on the worked stone rule . . . was slowly but surely coming about.' Thanks to the labours of the Executive delegates, a general lockout was avoided and Manchester isolated by surrounding lodges who had succumbed to the combined pressures of the union and employers. The denouement followed a meeting of the Lancashire and Cheshire Federation of Master Builders with the Executive delegates and representatives from some of the affected towns. The compromise economist rule was accepted and imposed by Executive fiat upon those towns, like Lancaster, who were still inclined to resist.[89]

Just as the crisis of 1869–70 had not immediately effected the universal institution of hourly pay, so it was not the nature of this mini-crisis that the new worked stone rule should immediately be enacted everywhere. Nottingham, Wolverhampton, Harrogate and Derby, for example, maintained the old rule (whether continuously or not is unclear) until 1912. But by this time such towns were in a distinct minority.[90] Employers, of course, would have preferred to have had no rule at all – and they used the economic downturn of the early twentieth century to achieve this temporarily. But if rule there had to be, it was infinitely better to have one that was only minimally restrictive and where the opportunities for evasion (who was to know whether the origin of the stone was a lower paid district or not?) were considerable. Neither should it be assumed that the economist rule possessed no advantages for the men. The new rule was undoubtedly more realistically 'progressive' than the old; it signalled an end to the rigid, guild-like assumptions which aimed to maintain the isolated self-sufficiency of each town's trade. By its emphasis upon the standard rate, the rule may have been a partial stimulant to the organising efforts undertaken by the union in the years immediately preceding the war. It may also have contributed to the rising tide of syndicalist consciousness that spread throughout the building trades at this same period. Certainly by 1912, socialists within the union were arguing that the 'economist' rule's emphasis upon the standard rate provided the only sensible basis for collective action. But if all this was true, it was also due to the failure of the rule to achieve the anticipated result of naturally working to raise wages in the quarry towns. For when the issue re-emerged again in the years just prior to 1914, the voice of prohibition was practically non-existent and the debate revolved around the virtues of the economist strategy as opposed to those who argued that the Society's efforts would be better spent in direct organisation of the quarry workers to improve their standard rate.[91]

But these are all imponderables that are beside the point. The struggle over the issue in 1898 had legitimised a new view of the question and had effectively transformed it from a problem of authority and control to one which placed the matter safely within a purely economic context. Because of the way in which the system of industrial relations had changed, the customary prohibition could no longer form the basis of a viable strategy. Not only were the employers opposed to the restriction of authority implied in this formulation of the issue so, too, were critical elements of the Union who found it impossible to defend before the bar of mutual negotiation – thus, the kinds of arguments used by the peripatetic executive delegates during their 'crusade.' The compromise rule illustrated the point; this form of the rule was viable precisely because its economism was within the realm of possibility allowed by the industrial relations structures.

LEARNING THE RULES OF THE GAME

Some of the questions that arise from previous treatments of this general problem may now be seen to be resolved. By the end of the century there had been a distinct shift in the methods of trade unionism away from what the Webbs termed the doctrine of vested interest and Hobsbawm called 'custom,' towards an economist asking what 'the traffic would bear.' But neither of these earlier accounts adequately explain this shift. At one point Hobsbawm suggested a deliberate slackening of output at the end of the Great Depression only to doubt its presence in the next paragraph but to revive it later on as a reason for declining profit margins.[92] Did regressive piece systems come first, or did the emergence of a new 'economic' working man call these systems into being? Similarly, the Webbs' schema of a three stage trade union development, each one more economically rational than the last, is, at best, a broad sociological categorisation of the policies of trade union structures which in itself tells us nothing about worker behaviour. It is clear, however, that the answer to the question of causation lies in the changing structures of work and industrial relations. Hobsbawm's partial learning of the rules of the game signified the early formalisation of industrial relations in engineering and cotton that followed the demise of their traditional structures and systems in the 1840s and 1850s. The complete learning that occurred thirty to forty years later reflected the extension of that formalisation to a much greater portion of the working class. But, in addition, we are now better able to deal with a related and perhaps more important aspect of this question which will allow us to obtain a more accurate perception of how extensively and in what respect the game was learnt. It is a logical implication to be derived from the arguments of both Hobsbawm and the Webbs that 'customary' man was now replaced by 'economic' man. The assumption is that workers at last began to act as they were always supposed to behave under capitalism by asking what the traffic would bear (either in terms of money or a minimum standard of life) and regulating effort according to the payment (either by restriction of output or by other devices such as reductions in the normal day).

The problem with this over-schematic conceptualisation is not simply that it can be faulted on points of detail: the Webbs, for example, exaggerated the increased difficulty of late-nineteenth-century apprenticeship regulation and were much too eager to write off ca' canny as a degenerated form of the doctrine of vested interest. The major drawback, however, that derives from a linear division between 'customary' and 'economic' working man is that it prevents us from a proper appreciation of what learning the rules of the game really means. For it is in the tactics, strategies and, most of all, in the verbalisations that were used to express worker demands that the rules of the game changed, and not (as the Webbs and Hobsbawm claim) in the demands themselves. It is for this reason that all three kinds of the Webbs' trade union 'assumptions' may be found at all periods of trade union history. To take a very simple example; it is obvious that restrictive practices have not withered away under the 'collectivist' (and now 'corporatist') policies of the modern labour movement. Similarly, the car workers of contemporary Dagenham, or the modern supermarket clerk of the Retail Clerks' Association in America, insist as fiercely as did the old craft artisan upon their vested interest in the property rights of their jobs.[93] Old forms are not displaced but co-exist within the new. It is the context in which they are translated and mediated that is different. We have earlier remarked upon the similarities that may be detected between the description of worksite practices in the 1966 *Cameron Commission* and those of our period. What was different was that this modern work group activity occurred within a system that made provision for worker grievances and that action outside that system was, therefore, illegitimate and would be received with a combination of hostility and attempts to strengthen the 'official' structures to better contain and control such 'unofficial' activity.

The same kind of perception must apply to other issues such as the demand for a normal day. The Webbs suggested that the increased importance of this issue was a response to the declining viability of the assumptions of vested interest and that it pointed to the growing collectivist aspirations of the workers.[94] But this missed the point; for the normal day had always been of central concern to the workers. It was for this reason that there were struggles over artificial light in the 1840s, for this reason (in part) that the hourly system was resisted, and why efforts to reduce hours of work were a continuing feature of worker demands. There was nothing peculiar about the late-nineteenth-century unions' insistence upon enforcement of the normal day: the men had been fighting that battle for many a long year. Definitions of a normal day might change and new strategies might be demanded to protect it. But, most of all, its importance is enhanced because it becomes one of the few legitimate demands that the structures of industrial relations will allow. When the masons demanded a 48½ hour week in the 1860s, they did so as an expression of a wider expansion of their power. When the eight hour day was demanded by the London building workers at the beginning of the 1890s, it was as a defensive measure to slow down the intensity of work and to establish a common rule of minimum standards. As such, this re-definition of the normal day signified its emergence as one of the few devices that could be legitimately broached to combat the exploitative methods of work that had grown out of the chaotic work arrangements of the 1880s. Similarly, as we have seen, the standard rate had always been an important trade union device – even in the period dominated by the doctrines of vested interest and individualistic supply and demand.[95] It becomes more important only in the sense that people other than workers now began to accept its legitimacy and that structures had emerged (e.g. powerful unions) whose raison d'être was to argue for and maintain it. Nor was there anything new about the demand for a 'minimum standard of life' whose echoes may be heard throughout the literature of the struggles of the 1830s. What else was it but this being expressed in 1833 when the men spoke of their reduction 'from a condition of comparative comfort to a condition of distress.'?[96]

And so it is, also, with the idea that 'customary' workers 'did not apply market criteria to the measurement of their efforts.'[97] Just as the conception of traditional differentials does not disappear once the new rules have been learnt, neither was there anything new about assessing what the 'traffic would bear' or restricting output to influence the flow of that traffic.[98] What had changed was the terms in which the assessment could be made and the rationale that could be used to justify it. To take a very obvious example, building workers had always known that the most appropriate time to press demands was the spring and summer; the relative decline in winter strikes owed more to a changed method of industrial bargaining than it did to a new 'economic' consciousness that these were inappropriate months for industrial action.[99] They knew also about maximising earnings through reductions of hours and if overtime changed its character this was not the result of an increasing economism of worker perception but that of new limits within which they could operate. And we have quoted enough examples to suggest that workers also knew the advantages that derived from a slackened effort. It was the means of assessing and justifying these kinds of calculations that constituted the new rules; there was no new revelation of the necessity for the calculation itself. Here, for example, was the pertinent way some class-conscious painters of St John's Wood did their 'traffic' sums in 1864:

> The men could plainly see that they were entitled to their reasonable demand from the fact that the employer's profits on the trade was enabling him to keep a carriage to ride about in from job to job (a very different position to that which he occupied a few years ago, when he was at the bench knocking a jack plane about).[100]

Unlike the spinners of the 1850s, the boilermakers of the 1870s, and by the 1890s most other unions, these men did not have the services of a cadre of technicians and experts to do their sums for them or to remove any suggestion of class conflict from the equation. But on the basis of observed knowledge about the state of activity in the trade, they were making a rational economic assessment in the way available to all building workers.

It is similarly the case with the customary expression of the work relationship as involving 'a fair day's work for a fair day's pay.' As Hobsbawm has pointed out, this has little in common with the economist conception of buying in the cheapest and selling in the dearest market. But that customary notion neither excludes such a conception nor is it inherently an 'uneconomic' way of expressing the wage relationship. As it is today, the 'fair' wage level was judged by reference to a variety of factors which included what workers thought they could get for their labour in relation to certain standards of comfort and traditional differentials. What is more important, however, is that 'a fair day's work for a fair day's pay' goes beyond the monetary aspect of the work relationship. It suggests an integrity, dignity and autonomy that transcends the fact of wages pure and simple; it suggests a 'customary' independence, a certain equality in the control over working arrangements. As such, this expression was, indeed, appropriate to the time when 'custom' dominated work arrangements for it was precisely this context that was removed from legitimate consideration by the new rules of the game.

At the heart of customary industrial relations lay autonomous regulation and it is not useful to associate 'uneconomic' behaviour with this fact. As we have suggested, economic assessments were made as to what the traffic would bear but they were made in different ways than they were later to be computed. Under autonomous regulation the game had not revolved only around such calculations; they remained integral to its content but were an inseparable part of the implicit assertion that work arrangements were as much an independent responsibility of the men as they were of the masters. This was the tussle that lay at the bottom of the new kind of class conflict that comes with industrialisation, for such a claim was incompatible with the needs of this new form of extended capitalism. But it was the genius of the new economist definitions of industrial relations to separate that authority context from the assessments as to wages, hours and conditions which now stood subject to a purely economic bargain. It is for this reason that the changes we have traced in the definitions of overtime and worked stone are so significant. With the emergence of mutual negotiation and proto-modern conceptions of managerial authority which denied the legitimacy of autonomous regulation, these issues could no longer be discussed within their traditional work control context. Thus, attempts to resolve the London overtime question in both 1872 and 1891 left the men dissatisfied because they failed to meet the demand that the price should effectively prohibit the practice. The 'language' of the men and of the system was different: one wanted prohibition, the other a compromise which would not admit the legitimacy of this aspiration. Similarly, the Clyde shipbuilding joiners were locked out when their efforts to control overtime threatened to extend beyond the simple economic device of the higher rate. Employers had no objection to an overtime wage; what they resisted was the 'inefficiency' implicit in the joiners' insistence that overtime one day result in short time the next and that any hours over the short-time period be worked at overtime rates.[101]

It has been an obvious failing of the previous historiography to adequately explain how it is that the triumph of the new game has done nothing to diminish the continuing presence of old, customary strategies which aim to control the work. Resistance to piecework, speed-ups, the abolition of overtime, restriction of production, even support for the old worked stone rule continued to appear long after they had been subjected to the economist device of compensatory higher wage rates.[102] At certain moments, such restrictive practices may be bought out only to reappear in new or old guises when the conditions are appropriate. In this sense, then, there was an incomplete learning of the rules of the game which testified not to the 'traditionalism' of workers but to the continuing relevance of work control as a central manifestation of class conflict. But traditional devices were not unaffected by the new game; they were transmuted in two separate ways. In the first place, it was possible to adapt and refine the economist techniques themselves so that the essential aim of control was retained. The absorption and control of overtime at Fawley so as to serve the purposes of 'customary' regulation provides a clear illustration of this process in action. Engineers, also, quickly learnt to control regressive piece rates, and it may be that the diminishing hostility of the shipyard boilermakers to piecework represented a similar kind of adaptation.[103] Often, these adjustments must have demanded changes in organisational forms, of which the enhanced importance of unions was a significant outcome. Nor should we ignore the immediate benefits that may be secured from the new devices of economism. But we know virtually nothing about how these kinds of changes occur, nor of the conditions necessary for their successful manipulation.

For our purposes, the second way in which customary responses to the economism of the system were transmuted is more important and, perhaps, more common. Because such practices as the control of overtime and restriction of production stand outside the paradigms of discussion allowed by the industrial relations system, they are driven 'underground,' transformed into 'informal' and 'illegal' practices. Within an otherwise smoothly working system, these practices play a dynamically active role presenting a constant challenge to the system which may eventually become an explosive critical mass. As we shall see, it was this tension that characterised the industrial relations system of London – and on a broad scale the whole country – from the 1890s. Dependent upon buying out grievances and the economist comprises of mutual negotiation, the system was incapable of resolving the 'customary' form assumed by the opposition to sub-contracting, overtime or non-union men. The eventual result was the full-scale crisis of 1914.

The process of learning the rules of the game was, therefore, rent by the fundamental and irresolvable paradox that the game could be both played and not played at the same time; that the rules could be learnt and not learnt. Modification in the structures of work (like regressive piece systems or hourly pay) and changes in the structures of industrial relations (the emergence of mutual negotiation) had altered the rules. In the sense that workers learnt to live under, adopt and manipulate those structures they had clearly learnt how the new sport could be played. But, at a deeper level, the game was rejected, the necessity to play by its rules questioned. For the problematic effect of the new rules was that they imposed an economic rationality that could not address the enduring problem of how the authority at work was to be divided. The tendency of the system as a whole – with its attendant intellectual rationales – was to deny that the question even existed or, when pushed, to arbitrarily distinguish legitimate economic issues from illegitimate ones of managerial prerogative. From the 1890s onwards it was obvious that the tension so created lay at the heart of much industrial unrest. Whereas the cotton spinners' union, for example, responded to the speed-ups of the 1880s by demanding higher wages, the tendency of the rank and file was, by restriction of output, to resist them altogether.[104] Thus, there was a conflict created within the working class itself between abiding by the rules and departing from them, a conflict that signified the dichotomy between workers as they functioned as proletarians and workers as they functioned as 'citizens' within the system of industrial relations.[105] This was a division that could exist both simultaneously and at different stages in a working man's career; it was conditioned by the particular role he was playing at any particular time. Thus,

it was very probably true that officials of the building unions in London
from the 1890s informally encouraged the men to take unilateral action
against non-unionists.[106] But this did nothing to prevent those same men
from negotiating restraints upon such work group action when they were
wearing their 'official' hats as trade union mediators within the local conciliation system.

It is in terms of the distinction to be drawn between the 'official' institutions which represented the working class within the industrial relations
system and the rank and file acting outside the limits of that system that this
division may best be understood. And it was an important aspect of the
growing separation of these two entities during this period. The system
itself did not work to prohibit overtime, nor prevent speed-ups: indeed, it
was willing to pay a higher price to encourage them. It would not ban
worked stone, nor deal satisfactorily with non-unionism and it insisted
upon translating customs such as grinding money into their economic
worth. Action taken against those and other problems would generally
have to be informal and illegal – sometimes winked at by union officials in
their 'unofficial' capacity, at other times disciplined by these same men.
At the level of the 'official' structures and institutions, however, the rules
of the game were fully learnt because it was just these rules that formed
the basis of mutual negotiation and bargaining. In their official relations
with employers, unions learnt to speak the language of asking what the
market would bear, basing their requests upon the scientific calculations
of economic logic. This was a task unions, as institutions, adopted with
alacrity. It was, after all, the function that legitimised their existence; and
this tendency had always been present within trade unions. Officials had
always tried to advise the men on the correct and incorrect way to behave,
when and when not to strike. But this had remained of no significance
until they became an estate within the realm of an industrial relations
system where their terms of reference were purely economic.[107] Thus it is
that we see the masons' union working to 'teach' the men of the northwest
how the worked stone issue must be played under the new rules. It is,
therefore, at this 'official' level only that we may meaningfully speak of a
learning of the rules of the game.

The rest of this book will be concerned with the implications of this
bifurcated learning process. For it was a result of the changes that we have
been following that the whole problem of industrial relations and conflict
assumed its 'modern' more complex form. The nature of that complexity,
however, may be reduced to the tensions that were now extant between
the three parts of the emergent system of industrial relations – the men, the
unions and the employers. And the character of those tensions was the
friction that was created between the struggle for control and the structures and institutions of industrial relations whose purpose it was to disci-

pline and tame that struggle. Within this tension, the unions played a crucial role as the mediators who had, indeed, learnt how to participate in the new game but who were hard put to convince their constituent rank and file that it was one worth playing. If, ultimately, the tensions of the system proved irreconcilable – which is not to say that they were insurmountable – this was inherent within the logic of a system that aimed to establish its legitimate authority upon the basis of translating the grievances of class conflict into those of an economic fine tuning.

5

Conflict and control: the creation of an industrial relations system

THE NEW SYSTEM

The formalisation of industrial relations had marked a sort of half-way house between the individualism of autonomous regulation and the collective responsibility of the mature systems that were to emerge in the years following the end of the Great Depression. As we have indicated, the process of transformation was slow and, in reality, the institutions of formalised industrial relations endured somewhat insecurely whilst their quality remained characteristically very 'informal.' Many of the conciliation boards that had grown out of the 'craze' of the sixties and seventies disappeared in the depression of the eighties. And in London the mutual negotiation that had been established in 1872 remained a matter of quiet, unceremonious and irregular contacts between the officials of the employers' association and of the unions. Not until 1892 was a permanent committee of the Central Association of Master Builders created to handle the on-going, day-to-day negotiations with the unions; and only in 1896 did systematic conciliation structures begin to emerge. This experience was typical; it was the nineties that saw the seeds of formalisation blossom into a recognisably modern system of industrial relations whose extent and comprehensiveness clearly distinguished it from the structures that had dominated the previous twenty years.

In the first place, there was a sharp expansion in the number of collective agreements which regulated industrial relations in the industry from just over 100 in 1890 to around eight times that number in 1910.[1] But the really significant feature of these agreements was not their quantity (estimates of which vary) but the fact that increasingly they were drawn into an interlocking, pyramidal structure of local and district boards which in 1905 was capped by the creation of National Conciliation Boards for the whole country.[2] At each level arbitration could be introduced, and throughout the whole system the regulatory responsibility of the particular units of the employers' associations and the unions was fully recognised. In this respect building was no different from the similar systems that emerged during these years in the engineering, shipbuilding, printing, railway and textile industries – all of which followed the same basic pattern.[3] At the local level of building's industrial relations system were the joint standing committees whose function it was to settle individual disputes which did not affect the general interest of the trade. Then came the local conciliation board on which all trades were represented and whose function it was to adjudicate on wages, conditions of working and local demarcation disputes. In any conflict this was the first court of appeal but should it prove unable to resolve the issue, the case was referred to the Centre Board made up of the district representatives of employers and unions. If the intervention of this body failed to reach agreement, the matter went to the National Conciliation Board composed of the national officers of the National Federation of Building Trades Employers and the unions who were the final arbiters in any dispute. At each level, while the procedures were being worked through no stoppages were supposed to occur; only if the National Board failed to resolve the issue could a strike or lockout be legal. Thus, not only did the scheme possess a complete coverage – the formation of the National Board brought in those places which still did not have local systems – but it was also more sophisticated and centralised, more specific and precise than anything which had existed before.[4]

But the growth of this system cannot be seen simply as the natural consequence of enlarged worker and employer organisation, as a result of the greater sense of solidarity and apartness that characterised each group.[5] The relationship between the system and employer–worker organisation was complex and dialectical but it was clearly true that the impetus for organisation derived as much from the habit of collective bargaining as did the latter from organisation. That habit had been established in the formalisation of the seventies as a response to particular disciplinary needs, and the extension of this formalisation into a mature system built upon the foundations laid in the earlier period. In its turn, however, the growth of this mature system was evoked by the specific needs of the nineties and, in particular, by the obligation to address the problem of industrial discipline in a more complete way. The means by which this could be done lay to hand but their scope needed to be expanded, refined and properly systematised. Only in this sense was the progression from formalisation to a modern industrial relations system evolutionary. Had the dimensions of industrial relations not been changed from the seventies through the nineties then, as happened in chain and box-making, the state or some other outside agency would of necessity have stepped in to answer the needs of industrial discipline and to create such a system.

The necessity for more comprehensive structures also demanded a more corporate organisation amongst employers and men. Concurrent with the system's growth, therefore, employer and worker organisations change their form to better fulfil their allotted roles within the system. The General Builders' Association, for example, had approximated more closely to a traditional voluntary association – linking individuals with common interests – than it did to a modern employers' organisation. Its focus was primarily local and, whilst it exercised a very loose coordination of branch activity, its main function was to serve as an informational clearing house. But it played no organisational role in the local structures of industrial relations that emerged from the endeavours of its individual affiliates. When the National Association of Master Builders replaced the GBA in 1877, its deliberately national focus was symptomatic of the direction in which things were moving but its initial purpose of assisting the efforts of local masters' associations to resist the men's encroachments remained basically the same as the earlier body.[6] The circumstances of the 1890s – the revival of work control, the growing sphere of responsibility given to industrial relations structures, the increased importance of procedural rule making – demanded, however, that organisation be more tightly integrated to the procedural structures themselves. The consequent changes in the organisational structures of the employers' associations included the growth of district federations to serve not merely as agencies of coordination but also to occupy a central role in negotiating with the men.[7] Lancashire masters, for example, had long been used to cooperating on an informal basis but until the middle nineties were still grouped mainly in the unit of their town associations. Only in 1898 did a district federation emerge that was to become one of the centres of the national system.

In any industry other than building, it would be a simple matter to identify the problems posed by the 1890s which required that industrial relations be organised on a secure and permanent institutional basis. The structural shifts in the economy and society, the new international relationships in the world economy (both of which had begun in the 1870s) demanded that British society become more 'efficiently' organised to compete with the challenges of a multi-lateral world.[8] It was a central preoccupation of this period, therefore, to search for better systems of discipline which would enable these challenges to be adequately met. The radius of this search was hardly confined to industrial relations but it generally returned to the pivotal location inhabited by discipline in industry. Speaking of the iron and steel industry and, in particular, the conduct of its managers, *The Economist* noted in 1906 how:

The problem of trade is, primarily, the problem of cheap and efficient production ... It is not too much to say that, so far as labour costs are concerned, an entirely new policy has recently been adopted. More practical and alert managers and foremen – 'six o'clock' managers – are now controlling our works and workers. The old methods of slackness and family influences which have hitherto cursed British industry, have been well-nigh abolished. There has recently been a speeding-up all round.[9]

But even if we bear in mind the impact large-scale capital movements might have made upon the industry, building was hardly an industry critical to Britain's world-wide economic performance. Nor would it be deeply influenced by the problems associated with that performance; complaints about foreign-made, machine joinery are about the only echoes we hear of the predominant economic fear of the period. Nevertheless, the fact that there is such a close concordance between the building industry and others in the creation of industrial relations systems is no quaint, irresolvable paradox. Indeed, it serves to reinforce the decisive impact of these wider economic shifts upon social organisation as a whole and to underline the central importance of social discipline in the years from 1890 to the First World War. But our attention must be directed to the specific problems posed by the nineties – and beyond – that served to call forth the industrial relations structures that we have sketched above. And to do this for building may shed some new light upon the wider phenomenon of which it was a part.

WORK CONTROL AND UNIONISATION

As with other industries, the early part of the 1890s saw building revive from the mysterious economic malaise which had cast such a pall over the previous twelve years. In Birmingham, S. B. Saul tells us, land bought cheap in the eighties was now developed as money for mortgages suddenly became plentiful enough to usher in a decade or so of high activity. Indices constructed by other economic historians show that, with minor variations, this was no quirk limited to the Midlands but was characteristic of the nation as a whole.[10] On this basis, the men occupied a stronger bargaining position than had been possible for some time. In trades like plastering there was a real labour shortage; over the industry as a whole, opportunities were good enough to encourage a thirty-five per cent increase in the labour force. Unemployment fell from around 8% in 1887 to under 2% in 1890 and remained below average until 1901 when it again began to climb.[11] In Manchester, for example, these conditions saw carpenters' wages rise by 12%, masons by 15% and bricklayers by 14%. Throughout most of the decade wage advances were secured with relative ease; of the plasterers, it was claimed that 'the masters did not regulate wages but the men themselves.' Carpentry was marked by a similar ascendancy. In London, an early example of the wages drift phenomenon was achieved by local work group activity improving upon the advances negotiated in 1892 and 1896. Indeed, one of the factors which inhibited the CAMB from a coordinated offensive against the men was the evidence continually before them of employers acceding to wage demands that went beyond the accepted rates and made outside of the official channels of negotiation.[12]

The improved position of the men was faithfully recorded by the Chief Correspondent of the Labour Department who in 1895 began to note the consistent ease with which the men secured their demands. In that year it was remarked that in most cases the men were partially successful; in 1896 that 'the workpeople were most successful in obtaining their demands in the building trades,' and in 1898 that 'one of the special features of the strike statistics of the last years has been the remarkable preponderance of results described as "in favour of workpeople" in the building trades as compared with any other industrial groups.'[13] The masons' strike statistics to the end of our series confirm these assessments and show a distinctly higher victory rate for the 1890s than for the total period – although for the building trades as a whole the picture is decidedly more mixed.[14]

Table 15. *Masons' strike results by year 1890–96*

Year	No.	Men victorious %	Employers victorious %	Compromise %
1890	23	70	13	17
1891	27	89	0	11
1892	40	77	15	8
1893	26	81	8	11
1894	26	89	8	3
1895	21	71	29	0
1896	28	85	11	4
1836–96		75	20	5
1890–96		82	11	7

If we examine the results for specific strike issues we may see that the men were particularly successful not only in enforcing wage demands but also in the categories of conditions of work and craft enforcement. These two are of interest because they reveal the nature of the men's expanded frontier of control during the 1890s. And the distribution of issues over the period serves to illustrate the importance of craft enforcement as the major bone of contention with the employers.

The prominence of craft enforcement conflicts reflected the revival of the worked stone issue which over the period 1890–96 composed two thirds of all craft strikes, 21% of the total strike population and whose pattern of results precisely mirrored that of the larger category. Indeed, the success rates in this category underlined the tensions that surrounded these issues and, in particular, emphasised the necessity that employers secure some resolution of the worked stone question. This also is the significance of the high success rates within the conditions of work category for, as we have seen, these issues (meal hours, sheds and walking time in this period)

Table 16. *Masons' strike issues by result 1890–96*

Issue	No.	Victory %	(1836–96)	Failure %	(1836–96)	Compromise %	(1836–96)
Wages	27	77.8	(69.0)	3.7	(22.3)	18.5	(8.7)
Hours	6	66.7	(70.3)	33.3	(23.2)	0.0	(6.5)
Organisation of work	13	61.5	(75.7)	7.7	(19.8)	30.8	(4.5)
Conditions of work	26	92.3	(81.7)	7.7	(14.6)	0.0	(3.8)
Control over labour	34	79.4	(77.7)	20.6	(21.6)	0.0	(0.7)
Craft enforcement	53	90.6	(80.4)	7.5	(17.8)	1.9	(1.7)
Working rules	26	61.5	(72.0)	19.2	(12.1)	19.2	(15.9)
Other	1	100	(75.0)	0.0	(15.0)	0.0	(10.0)

Table 17. *Masons' strike issues 1890–96*

Issue	No.	%	(1836–96)
Wages	32	11.9	(31.1)
Hours	7	2.6	(7.7)
Organisation of work	24	9.0	(9.9)
Conditions of work	35	13.1	(11.4)
Control over labour	49	18.3	(19.8)
Craft enforcement	88	32.8	(14.2)
Working rules	31	11.6	(5.5)
Other	2	0.7	(0.9)

were those which typically revived at a time when the men were pushing their frontier of control forward. The Swansea masons, for example, were by no means unique in seeking the availability of sheds but went further than most in demanding that they be equipped with a toilet.[15] Whatever the case in other trades, the evidence for this craft does not suggest any marked decline in trade rules but, on the contrary, that they were being more rigorously enforced in the nineties. Masons' working rules similarly reflected this increased sphere of control over the work. Not only were restrictions re-imposed upon methods of working such as piece and sub-contracting and upon practices such as overtime and the importation of worked stone, but these were frequently achieved using the traditional methods of control.[16] In those places where the rules had remained basically unchanged since the crisis of the sixties, attempts were made to abolish the ancient edifice of employers' victories. Thus, in 1892, the Birmingham masons attempted to prohibit piecework and worked stone and to remove from the working rules the 'authority of employer' and arbitration clauses.[17]

Unlike the sixties, however, the plasterers had replaced the masons as the most troublesome of the trades. Aided by the shortage of craftsmen in the trade, plasterers directed much of their militancy towards maintaining this insufficiency and locally their restriction of apprenticeship seems to have been quite effective. In London, for example, they refused to work with unindentured boys, and the question of apprenticeship limitation occupied a prime place in the schedule of employers' demands presented to the men in 1899.[18] The arrogance of the Liverpool men in 1897 provides a symptomatic – if extreme – illustration of plasterers' militancy during this period. Not only were employers faced with demands for a wages increase, apprenticeship limitation, an extension of the boundaries of their work to include cement flooring and unlimited access to the works by their delegate, but they also requested that employers should purchase their buckets because 'as one of the deputation stated they could not wear a decent coat and carry a bucket.' This was hardly the language of a beleaguered craft group and it was small wonder that the employers stigmatised the plasterers as 'the most impudent and independent class of men in the building trade.'[19] But plasterers were not alone in their efforts. In some places, carpenters and bricklayers imposed similar controls upon apprenticeship and by the end of the nineties the efforts to control the labour supply and impose other sundry restrictive rules were common laments to be heard at meetings of employers' associations. When the National Federation of Building Trades Employers gathered in London in 1901 the local masters – who as usual were not plagued by the same kinds of problems – were treated to a catalogue of the restrictions experienced by their peers of northern England in their dealings with the masons and joiners. 'In London,' enviously commented a Huddersfield employer, 'it appeared there was no obstruction, no interference . . . no restrictions.'[20] But London, as we shall see, had its own brand of the same set of difficulties.

Against this background of a revived control over the productive process by the men the obsession of the period with ca' canny and restriction of output begins to make sense. By the nineties the new concern with productivity first nurtured in the seventies had germinated into a fully-aroused imperative to harvest the benefits promised by the 'second industrial revolution.' In highly capitalised machine trades such as engineering, boot and shoe and shipbuilding, the task was to harness labour power effectively to the new and mechanical techniques of working, but in building, where technological changes were not nearly so pervasive and where organisational changes in the structure of the industry were minimal, the problem of productivity did not reflect the imperatives of a new stage of capitalist development. More a repetition, at a new level, of older themes of work control, the problems of ca' canny and productivity in this trade are best understood within the dialectical interplay between freedom and control. Indeed, it is the failure to place the problem of restriction of output within this context of discipline at work that has allowed some historians to disregard the reality of the issue. It is certainly true that the sensational alarmism of Edwin Pratt's articles on restriction of output concealed the deeper constraints that contributed to the productivity problems of the period but, equally, there was nothing chimerical about the restraints ca' canny and other devices imposed upon the employers' power to organise his business around increased production and output.[21] The attention devoted to the problem was in no way misdirected for it was symptomatic of the relationship that underlies much of the history of the period between the need for social discipline as an essential pre-condition of an efficient profits performance.

Because the basic dilemma remained the same, the treatment of this problem in the 1890s was accompanied by many of the same traits that marked the similar concerns of the 1860s. This was true even down to the mistaken identification – which paralleled Mault's accusations against the unions – that Pratt made of ca' canny as a function of the 'concerted policy' of the 'socialistic' new unions and their 'trade union agitators.'[22] But just as Mault's prejudices should not blind us to the cognitive value of his case, so it is also hard to deny the central accuracy of Pratt's argument. If read correctly, the evidence suggests the truth of his assessment that restriction of output was practised on a widespread, if often informal, scale. As an illustration we need only look to the extensive presence of restrictive rules whose design and nature were deliberate impediments to the productivity and output of the men. But it is possible to go beyond these formal expressions of work control to illustrate the same theme. Thus, G. T. Jones concluded that in the London building industry – where restrictive rules of the kind found in the north were absent – 'the effort put in the full week's work began to decline in the nineties' so that between 1890 and 1910 the overall efficiency of the worker fell by 14%.[23] For reasons which will become apparent, the problem of restriction of output was most severe in bricklaying. Although precise figures must be treated with caution, it would seem beyond dispute that a general standard of 300–400 bricks per day were lain in comparison to the employers' ideal of 1200 and to the 600–800 that had been standard twenty or thirty years earlier. On London County Council jobs the rate was recognised to be a precise three hundred and thirty and when Westinghouse built a factory at Manchester in the nineties their managers, accustomed to 'American methods,' were astonished by the languorous working pace of the men.[24] Industrial action to enforce slower speeds occasionally surfaced; no doubt more detailed searches could find additional examples. The London employers, for example, had cause to notice a strike of bricklayers in 1893 against two non-union men who were working at a faster rate than the rest of the work group. Nor was bricklaying the only trade so afflicted; at least one strike of carpenters was directed at men who were hanging doors too quickly. And when in 1897 the National Association of Master Builders discussed the pressing need for extending piecework it was because the men only gave 'the smallest possible amount of work for the largest amount of wages.'[25]

As in the 1860s, restrictive rules and the deliberate restriction of output were of central concern to employers because they signalled a denial of the 'discipline,' and end to the 'freedom,' employers needed if they were to cope with the realities of the industry. But parallels between the two decades can only be drawn so far; the forms may have been similar but the context and structures of those forms were very different. In their broadest significance and import, the major developments within the labour movement of the nineties were a defensive response to the shifts that had occurred during the Great Depression to break the 'negotiated' equanimity of the mid-Victorian relationship between labour and the dominant classes. Building upon the twenty years of transition between 1870 and 1890, the period saw a rearrangement, a re-negotiation of relationships and the emergence of a new consensus in which the Labour Party, the unions and their role within the industrial relations systems played a vital role. This was true at all levels of working-class experience and in the building industry (in common with other industries) restrictive rules and ca' canny were a far more ambiguous expression of the enlargement of worker power than they had been in the sixties. It was not just the case that established or emergent structures of industrial relations blunted and mediated, in an economist way, the clash between freedom and control. It was also the fact that the restriction of output was a defensive–offensive response to the general attempts to increase the pace of work that marked the eighties and nineties.[26] In more mechanised industries this was inextricably associated with the technological changes of the period which permitted an increase of exploitation through new techniques such as regressive piece rates. But, in building, such methods were not applicable and so employers turned to older, more prosaic styles that had been common in the 1830s and 1840s. In particular, they turned to sub-contracting for labour only and the restriction of output that was visible in bricklaying reflected the deep permeation of this system of work in the trade. Similarly, the presence of these methods was to be a major reason why bricklaying was a main focus for the developments in industrial relations structures during the period.

Although such methods as labour-only sub-contracting were inherent to the chaotic competitiveness of the industry, they derived an added stimulus in the eighties and nineties from the pressures of labour costs. During the depression these costs had remained stable in absolute terms but had risen as a proportion of total costs because the price of materials had tended to fall. With the continued decline in the cost of materials during the nineties, this problem was greatly accentuated because it was accompanied by a 20–30% rise in the labour portion of the total cost burden.[27] And, in addition, the employers had to contend with a workforce which achieved some success in its efforts to impose restrictions on output. The compulsion to circumvent these restrictions and to restore the full 'freedom' employers needed was, therefore, irresistible. Employers could not afford to surrender the right to use sub-contracting or other methods that would stimulate greater productivity and, whereas in the eighties the men had been in no position to withstand such methods, by the nineties they were able to combat and even control such modes of working. The conflict and consequences aroused by this particular weapon of employer discipline was a re-cycled version of the familiar themes of freedom and control; but it was a rendition that occurred at a more acute and complex level. Habits of mutual negotiation and the presence of rudimentary industrial relations structures, for example, made it impractical for employers to mount the same kind of counterattack that they had launched in the sixties. More important were the different contours that the struggle for control now assumed. In the 1860s the confrontation had been an undivided contest between masters' prerogatives and men's restrictions; now that issue was partly transposed on to the divisions within the working class itself and its form was to be the question of the employers' right to employ non-union labour. Indeed, this particular issue was to occupy a central place in the evolution of an industrial relations system; and since it provides an interesting example of the relationship between the imperatives of work structure and the creation of systems of industrial relations, it is critical that we examine its content with some care.

The general decline in working conditions forced by the depression had been most clearly displayed by the expansion of sub-contracting. Particularly manifest in London, it was by no means confined to the metropolis.[28] By 1890, however, sub-contracting was virtually universal in London bricklaying and plastering but it afflicted all trades seriously enough to induce the London United Building Trades Committee to attempt its prohibition in municipal contracts. And, in the same year, a deputation from the building unions twice petitioned the Royal Institute of British Architects to declare against the practice.[29] The men were largely unsuccessful in these efforts, but worksite attacks on the system were a constant problem for employers and may have contributed to a decline in the method. Nevertheless, the evidence suggests its continued presence throughout the whole decade and after 1900 it clearly experienced an unrestricted increase.[30] In the early nineties the bricklayers claimed that 'the system has got so bad that . . . [we] have resolved as a body that . . . [we] will not work for sub-contractors'; and in 1896 they endeavoured to obtain rules that would forbid the system. To the *Royal Commission on Labour*, the plasterers pointed out that 'we do not object to a man if he is a *bona fide* contractor finding his own materials taking the work direct and doing it, but . . . this system of these men doing the labour only is what we object to.'[31] Even the London carpenters, who were traditionally divided on the question of piecework – those in the poorer districts accepting it as a fact of life, those in central London opposing it – made its abolition a central demand in 1891 and 1896. Thus, in 1892, the Amalgamated Society, which had formerly confined its rules to a condemnation of the practice, introduced a rule prohibiting both piecework and sub-contracting.[32]

Its effects so well described by Tressell, the objections to sub-contracting remained what they had always been. Through its tendency to encourage scamping, sweating, speed-ups and task-master pieceworking, it was both a symbol and an agent of the inability of the men to maintain decent standards of wages and conditions: 'Sub-letting practically means this; that the same amount of work is squeezed out of four men by a scamping system that would in the ordinary way be got out of five men . . . to do that the men are compelled to adopt various methods of slighting their work.'[33] In addition, by the nineties the system encouraged the spread of new techniques and materials that devalued craft skills and allowed the substitution of unskilled labour. The masons, for example, claimed that as a result of competitive cost pressures to rush and scamp the work, machine-made stone was often used in place of the prescribed Portland. In plastering, not only was putty used to water down the plaster but new substitutes that were developed for faster work had caused the traditional plaster mixers to be displaced by general labourers.[34] The impact of these various technological changes on the skilled crafts was a complex matter. Stone-working machines, reinforced concrete and new plastering materials led not so much to a destruction of old skills as to an increased specialisation and sub-division of those skills. They provided the structural basis for the demarcation disputes that marked the period from the late seventies and, more importantly, they fostered sub-contracting by their division of the work into new and specific jobs for specialists. By the 1890s, then, sub-contracting had become even more firmly linked to the imperatives of general contracting than it had been before. Extensively used by all large builders in London, attempts by the men to secure rules prohibiting its usage were constantly and successfully resisted.

The new-found importance of sub-contracting for labour, however, depended not only upon the time-worn evils that it brought in its train but also upon the extent to which it appears to have altered employer–men relationships. Some time between the seventies and nineties in London it had occasioned the emergence of a quasi-independent class of foremen who served as labour contractors to the large employers. The relationship of these foremen to the general builder was frequently shrouded in mystery. Employers liked to claim that they were permanent employees delegated to find the men but in fact they were more likely to be task-masters paid a lump sum by the builder to get the work done. In plastering, it would seem that the master plasterer was being converted into this kind of labour contractor; only twenty per cent of plasterers were employed directly by the general contractors and it was in that trade that the problems of who was and who was not a 'real' foreman were sharpest. There is little doubt that the function of the foreman was undergoing an important re-definition in the industry as a whole. We can hear echoes of this in carpentry where the point was made that the old nomenclature of a 'man who never takes his coat off' was increasingly unsatisfactory.[35] Employers were beginning to take literally Frederic Smith's injunction to leave all day to day operations solely to their foreman.

Although the foreman had frequently possessed the power of hiring and firing and, since the Parliament strike, had enjoyed responsibility for the speed of work, their lines of authority had invariably derived exclusively from the employer. But through their role as the direct employer of the labour force, the power of the foremen was now greatly increased. This, at least, was the implication of all the evidence before the Charity Organisation Society's *Special Committee on Unskilled Labour* where it was reported that 'the men are not engaged by the firm at all . . . they follow the foremen' who generally employed a stable core of permanent men and for the rest depended upon a network of patronage and word of mouth: 'They [men] will usually come to you and say "I was working for so and so" mentioning, as a rule, a man that you personally know . . . They are unknown in a way, but they come with a half recommendation.' In the big companies, this direct employment of labour was the fief of the 'general foreman' – described by one of Cubitt's managers as the 'real employer' – whose responsibilities were explained in this way: 'You have a leading man in charge who is called the "General Foreman." He engages the men, and they are under his supervision. If the builder or the employer sent the men there the foreman would simply "pooh-pooh" it and have nothing to do with them, or they would be sent away at the slightest excuse.'[36] Thus, new categories of supervisors had emerged – the general foreman in bricklaying and managing foreman in plastering – who did not fulfil the foreman's traditional role of a superior, over-looking craftsman; a new authority relationship had been established with these men as task-masters under whose aegis all the problems associated with sub-contracting were magnified.[37] Such men were particularly evident in bricklaying and plastering, but they were also to be found elsewhere – the very nature of the function tended to make it disrespectful of all craft boundaries – and whole buildings could be erected using their services: 'A builder will employ a person to undertake the erection of a building, the builder providing the plant and materials, financing the person employed on measuring up the work each week so that payment may be in accordance with results.'[38]

The system amounted to a new way of working; it was so pervasive, so much a permanent part of the structure of the industry that it complicated the means by which fair and decent standards could be judged. The best index of judgement thus came to be union membership which, for the first time, signified a real distinction between different methods and conditions of work. Affiliation to a union now implied something more concrete than it had done in the past, for it was an explicit statement about the circumstances under which men were willing to work. A new unity was forged between unionism and work control because it was only upon the secure foundations of an expanded union membership that the system could be restrained or controlled and its consequences mitigated.[39] But the distinction between union and non-union, fair and unfair methods of working was fraught with ambiguities and, as the difficulties that were experienced in formulating a satisfactory definition of the difference were to illustrate, the matter was anything but simple. At one level, the relationship between union and non-union men retained its 'traditional' characteristics. In a broad sense, the unions continued to play their traditional role – if on a more extensive stage – as the arbiters of minimum conditions which were often recognised by the non-union men. Indeed, it was constantly asserted that unionists had no objection to the 'genuine' non-union man. The *Building Trades News* (the organ of the London unions), for example, claimed in 1895 that 'from the unorganised workers in the building trades support may always be relied on in any steps which the unions see fit to take for the general good.' And, in response to the employers' demand for a no-disability clause which would allow them to employ whomever they liked, it was asserted that: 'The non-unionist who is merely a non-unionist requires no such "protection" as is here contended for . . . But at the "blackleg" and the fraudulent competitor in the labour market, the organised workmen claim to draw the line.'[40]

The distinction that was made here between the 'non-unionist' and the 'blackleg' pointed to the nature of the problem. It reminds us that the term 'blackleg' had another, much older, meaning than that of a man who broke a strike call – something which union men had been known to do. For the term also referred to a turf or gambling swindler. Those who took piece-work as foremen in order to chance making a quick and easy windfall, or those who were willing to accept the degrading methods of work he offered were 'obnoxious' for this reason, that they were perpetuating an 'unfair' system of employment and work. In itself 'non-unionist' was not necessarily pejorative, but it was becoming more so because it was increasingly diffi-

cult to distinguish between the genuine non-unionist whose beliefs pre-
cluded membership in a union and the man who was willing to undercut
and destroy minimum standards. Thus, the word most frequently used to
describe such men was 'obnoxious,' a vague term which had the advantage
of being more acceptable to employers but which avoided the fact that
unionism was increasingly the most certain way of determining where a
man stood. Thus, the attempts to define who or what was 'obnoxious' to
the union men was laden with irresolvable difficulties because the dividing
line between the two sectors of working – the 'honourable' and the 'dis-
honourable' – was in constant motion. One employer who asked his carpenters what it was that made a man obnoxious was answered in the form
of examples, such as working overtime at the ordinary rate – something
many men may have been prepared to do during bad times.[41] Furthermore, sub-contracting had always been unreservedly obnoxious but,
equally, it was also conducive to a certain kind of social mobility and
today's union man was often tomorrow's managing foreman. It was even
known for foremen to seek the support of their union to obtain a promised
bonus from an employer for getting the work finished on time.[42] Thus,
employers' attempts to persuade the unions to define exactly which men
they found obnoxious were always met with evasive and unsatisfactory
replies. In the plasterers' negotiations with the National Association of
Master Builders in 1899, for example, the employers pressed the union for
a precise definition: were the non-union men they objected to defaulters or
foreign plasterers? But the men would go no further than a formula which,
in addition to defaulters, included 'other men who have shown themselves
to be specially objectionable to union men.'[43] And, as an illustration of the
difficulties of definition there was the person of Sam Wright whose specific
case engaged the attention of the conference. Although the 1899 agreement
had established that union men would work peacefully with non-unionists,
the plasterers of Messrs Colls refused to return to work until certain men –
including Wright – were discharged. To the men, Wright was not only a
strike breaker who had worked during the recent dispute, but 'obnoxious'
because he was a 'unionist defaulter who has been an unfair employer in
the London district for a number of years.' Wright was clearly an example
of a sub-contractor who, at one point, had also been a union man. But to
the employers, he was a genuine non-unionist whom the men were obliged
to work alongside.[44]

A more extensive degree of union membership, however, would avoid
those kinds of ambiguities, for it would ensure that men like Wright could
be adequately controlled. Dominion over the foremen was a way of regulating the conditions under which the men worked and it was for this reason
that plasterers had traditionally expected their supervisors to be union
members. In 'respectable' shops outside London this was still very largely

the case and it was just this issue that was to plague the London trade in the 1890s.[45] Indeed, it was the attempt of the plasterers to realise their policy of forcing union membership upon these men that occasioned the lockout of 1899 and around which the largest part of the negotiations of that year focussed. The employers' intransigence on this issue was well-founded, for the plasterers' strategy would destroy the value of the whole system of labour sub-contracting and considerably enhance the power of the men. All the time the foreman's role was that of an expert workman whose authority derived solely from his dependent relationship to the employer, the case was fairly clear. Working plasterers could claim him as one of their own and at the same time recognise that he had a duty to the employer with which they allegedly did not interfere. But the managing foreman was a completely different animal and when the employers raised the issue of their foreman's membership in the union it was with the specific intention of exempting these labour managers from the prescription:

As to ordinary foremen, I do not see why he should not be in the union . . . [But] we object to any man being compelled to join the Union, and more especially, any whom the employer has put in charge of other men . . . If he is under the control of the men that he is intended to superintend it is not possible for him to do his duty to his employer.[46]

Partly because the labour shortage in their trade allowed them more easily to impose union membership on the men, the plasterers tended to focus their efforts on the foremen. But there were no shortages of available men in the easily learned trades of bricklaying or carpentry. In these trades, therefore, attention was largely directed to expanding union membership amongst the men and both carpenters and bricklayers were markedly more aggressive than the other trades in union recruitment during the 1890s. The OBS and the ASC&J each launched membership drives in 1892 and the latter expanded the London district boundaries to better control the suburbs in 1894. For this same reason, both trades initiated and led in the formation of stronger sectional and trade organisations like the London Building Trades Committee and its successor the London Building Trades Federation whose activities were largely devoted to the problem of sub-contracting.[47]

Union membership thus attained a new kind of urgency during this period which served to shatter the traditional cooperation that had existed between the two sectors of the labour force. We should also note, even if we are unable to develop the point, that this division was only one of a series of important forces that acted to fragment the working class along new and different lines during these years. The eruption of fierce demarcation disputes was another, comparable agent of fragmentation which also rested upon changes in the structure of work. But a further source of enhanced tension between union and non-union men derived from the new-found strength and respectability of the unions themselves, and tension between unionism and non-unionism had made its first appearance from the moment that industrial relations were formalised. In 1876 the *Bee-Hive* remarked upon 'a growing disinclination of unionists to support non-unionists in the case of a strike' initiated by the unorganised men. H. A. Turner noted the same phenomenon amongst the textile unions and attributed it both to the impact of the 1870s depression which 'forced the unions to tighten up their organisation' and to the creation of the Weavers Amalgamation in the mid-80s which increased the 'pressures [for unionisation] . . . working up to a regular campaign in the early years of this century.' And, in 1892, coincident with the last of the traditional trade movements in London (where union and non-union had cooperated in an uneasy partnership), the ASC&J, for the first time, introduced a legal procedure for striking against non-union men.[48] These early manifestations of the growing separation between union and non-union men reflected the existence of rudimentary formalised structures. By their very presence these institutions enhanced the significance of union membership, for the unions were the organisational basis of representation within the system. Furthermore, because the effect of formalisation was to superimpose levels of decision making that went beyond the workplace to the town and, occasionally, the district, an institutional expression of unity became of more consequence than it had been before. If agreements were to stick, they had to represent the collective will of the largest possible number of men; if disputes were to be resolved they had to be channelled through the proper and permanent structures. These circumstances also sharpened the need for 'union discipline'; and unionist objections to working with non-unionists in trade movements owed much to their lack of commitment to the cautious and legal styles of action demanded by the structures. Once these early structures had matured into the fully developed system of the post-1890s procedural and substantive collective bargaining arrangements, their tendency to underscore the distinction was greatly accentuated. This was especially true because their emergence coincided with (and was a response to) changes in the imperatives of the workplace situation which served to mandate union membership as an index of the nature of working conditions.

It was this fusion of the structural and institutional imperatives to union membership which helps to explain the nature and characteristics of the breakthrough in unionisation that occurred from the 1890s. The intricate roots of this expansion have been subject to few illuminating analyses and obviously differed from trade to trade; it is clearly necessary to distinguish between the breakthrough achieved by the new unions and the steady and solid (though in many ways no less spectacular) enlargement of membership attained by the older, craft organisations.[49] The seemingly sudden widening of consciousness that betokened the creation of formal unionism where none existed before had, of course, been preceded by a long tradition of informal organisation which was no longer adequate to serve the needs of the workers.[50] But in those industries with a previous culture of union organisation the situation was somewhat different and more complex. Not only were changes in the structure of work mandating union membership but the presence of the unions themselves and the institutions of industrial relations were also variable factors that need to be recognised in any consideration of the mechanics of union growth. These were trades where the particular stimulants to organisation were able to build upon long-standing cultural and social prescriptions of the value of union membership and, in this respect, their pattern of growth was more secure than that of the new unions many of whom, it is well-known, had faded away by the late nineties.

But given these considerations, we then have to ponder a very curious phenomenon. It is a little-regarded fact that, in spite of the broad wave of unionisation from the nineties, the old unions continued to be plagued with the same kind of oscillation of attachment that we noted in the mid-Victorian era. Between 1900 and 1910 there was a substantial leakage of membership from the building unions that is at odds with the contemporaneous power and importance attained by those unions in society as a whole. The bricklayers, for example, lost 15,000 members, the carpenters and masons 10,000 each, and the plasterers 4700.[51] And although this leakage did nothing to destroy the role that the unions were already playing as corporate parts of the industrial relations systems, it does suggest two very important themes. In the first place, it emphasised how the normative pressures to join a union derived largely from the workplace situation – with its attendant lessons for where historians of unionisation should direct their scrutiny. Even within these traditionally organised trades, the social and cultural habits and pressures that favoured union affiliation were evidently insufficient to block a veritable flood of lapsed members. Like that of the sixties, the growth of the nineties reflected the augmented power of the men which interacted upon changes in the structure of work to make union membership an expression of collective solidarity and work control. Once this workplace situation changed for the worse, as it did after 1900, a large proportion of this membership crumbled away. In the face of adverse conditions and abridged economic opportunity, union membership was a less meaningful expression of solidarity because there was a diminished ability to control the work. But if membership patterns continued to respond to these kinds of forces, this was beginning to matter less and less to union stability and importance. Unions had achieved additional vitality from sources that were external to their membership. Moored securely to their function within the industrial relations system and deriving an amplified resilience after 1910 from government social policy, these fluctuations were less significant to union strength than they had been in the period when unions had been denied these extrinsic benefits. It was ironic that the institutional imperatives to union membership – first evident in the 1870s – really began to take root in the early twentieth century just at the moment when there was a recrudescence of the old pattern of membership fluctuation in bad times. But, for our purposes, its importance lies in the relevance it suggests of the workplace situation for understanding changes and developments in the structures of industrial relations. And this is true not only for the growth of unions themselves but for the evolution of industrial relations systems in the period as a whole.

WORK CONTROL AND THE SYSTEM OF INDUSTRIAL RELATIONS

The convention of irregular mutual negotiation and contact between organised employers and men that had composed the rudimentary structures of industrial relations in London since the 1870s were soon exposed as inadequate to cope with the renewed militancy of the 1890s. The carpenters' movement of 1891 marked the final instance of this transitional phase of informal collective bargaining methods and the sectional demands of the following year led to a conference with all trades to settle virtually uniform conditions upon the industry. The general trade agreement that resulted was important because it was the first negotiated with the whole body of the unions and it marked their institutionalisation as sole bargaining agents for the men: nothing more is heard, for example, of securing non-union representation at the bargaining table. Signifying this shift, the employers created a Standing Trades Committee of their Association whose job it was to maintain regular and permanent contacts with the unions to settle any minor disputes that might arise.[52] The machinery was, therefore, in place for future refinements and extensions and the masters were not long in pressing them forward.

The 1892 agreement had covered only wages and conditions; it had said nothing about non-union labour and within a year the constant complaints about the 'ill-discipline' of the men – and especially the bricklayers – had led the employers to hanker for 'a central authority [of all the unions] without whose sanction no strike shall be called.'[53] Underlying this call for the strengthening of union authority there lay the inadequacy of the existing structures to deal with the newly emerged problem of strike activity against non-union men. When employers claimed that the 'distinct understanding' of the 1892 agreement had been that there was to be no distinction between the unionist and the non-unionist, they merely expressed the traditional reality of cooperation between the two sectors that was no longer functional. In fact, the settlement had not formally addressed the problem at all, but if the trade was to be covered by comprehensive agreements then this issue, too, would have to be faced. Thus, it was explained that: 'Matters went on smoothly for some time until attempts were made to compel employers to discharge non-union men, and these . . . became so intolerable that this association felt that the time had come when what had always been an honourable understanding must be put in the form of a written and definite agreement.'[54] The employers were deterred from openly raising the issue because 'owing to the state of trade the Committee did not wish to enter into any controversies with the bricklayers,' but by late 1894 the rules were due for re-negotiation and the problem had grown so serious that it had to be confronted.[55]

It was George Trollope, who for four years had been struggling with a strike against non-unionists at his Claridges' site, who first suggested the answer to this dilemma. He proposed that a 'no-disability' rule be instituted which would allow employers to hire any workman – union or non-union – that they wished. Although this was not the first time such a rule had appeared in building (nor was it confined to that industry alone) its central role from this point onwards in employer–worker relationships testifies to the different elements that composed industrial relations and discipline in the 1890s.[56] A no-disability rule would secure the sanction of the union for the employment of non-unionists and in return furnish a commitment from employers that men would not be victimised by virtue of their union affiliation. But the no-disability clause was not simply a response to growing unionisation, it was far more a reflection of the specific needs of employer authority that emerged as a consequence of the structural changes in the industry and the disciplinary problems they had created. This was revealed from the very moment of its inception in October 1894 when it was coupled with the demand that demarcation disputes should be decided by the employer and, more importantly, that the right of the employer to sub-contract be specified in the rules.[57] The lengthy negotiations which followed revolved solely around this link between the need for some sort of non-interference procedure with the right to sub-contract, and failure to reach agreement on this issue was the major reason why the rules were allowed to lapse in 1895.[58] Grounded in the fact that non-unionism was now virtually synonomous with sub-contracting for labour only, the connection between the two issues was obvious. A linkage such as the employers proposed would not only leave them free to sub-contract, it would also save them from the harassment of strikes against the men who worked the method. For their part, the men wished to expressly prohibit sub-contracting and so it is likely that there was an element of negotiating gamesmanship in the employers' presentation of their optimum desires. Indeed, once serious bargaining had begun, and after several fruitless meetings in the first half of 1895, an honourable compromise was reached that the working rules remain silent on the sub-contracting question. As B. L. Greenwood – a prominent member of the CAMB – pointed out, having no rule was preferable to one which prohibited or limited the system.[59] But this concession did nothing to abrogate the 'constantly recurring strikes' over the non-union question. Indeed, the silence of the rules on the matter of sub-contracting accentuated the necessity to find some way of resolving this issue. Without a procedure to handle cases of 'obnoxious' men, this silence would serve to aggravate the problem by merely inciting further strike action by the men. In the final phase of the negotiations, therefore, the employers insisted that this question be readdressed; and it was in response to this particular need that the creation of a Conciliation Board began to be seriously discussed.

The idea of a Conciliation Board had been first mooted by the OBS as a rejoinder to the employers' original set of demands. At that time it had been coolly received by the Central Association which was hoping for a simple no-disability clause that would have allowed them maximum discretion in who they employed. More importantly, however, the suggestion for a Board had been decisively vetoed by the ballot of the London bricklayers in 1895. Nevertheless, during the negotiations that followed the concession on sub-contracting, the proposal was revived (it would seem) by the employers and it now became their prior demand that the no-disability clause be linked to that of the creation of a Conciliation Board.[60] It is easy to see why this should have become the employers' position: a Conciliation Board provided the means by which strikes over obnoxious men could be delayed and resolved without disruption to the work. Furthermore, since the rules had nothing to say about sub-contracting, arguments before the Conciliation Board – which at this point was limited solely to questions arising from the no-disability clause – would revolve around the difficult meaning associated with the definition of 'obnoxious' and thus allow employers a maximum flexibility in negotiations. In addition, there was the disciplinary advantage to be gained by ranging the employers' authority with that of the union against recalcitrant men.

Because the union had already proposed a Conciliation Board, the only problem was to get them to agree that the Board should be limited to and have specific authority over this issue; and it was here that the limits of the no-disability clause became critical. In his letter opening the way for the eventual compromise, Batchelor (General Secretary of the OBS) drew the familiar distinction between non-unionists and obnoxious men and pointed out that 'we do not object to work with non-unionists.' The employers accepted this definition and, in direct contravention of the votes of their membership, the union in return agreed that a Board be established whose authority was defined in these terms:

If application be made to any employer by the Central Committee of the OBS to discharge any workman on the ground that such workman is obnoxious, and the employer refuses . . . no strike shall be sanctioned, but the question shall be referred to the Board of Conciliation. Provided that no such application shall be made in consequence of such workman belonging or not belonging to any trade society.[61]

This same clause was then presented to the plasterers who rejected it, to the masons who accepted it and to the carpenters and joiners whose initial rejection was followed by successful negotiation which obliterated the distinction between obnoxious and non-union men.[62]

The emergence of a system of Conciliation Boards and procedures (whose authority was greatly extended in the early 1900s) in the London trades was, thus, a disciplinary response to the tensions created by the dominance of labour-only sub-contracting in the city. Many of the same considerations applied to the emergence in 1899 of a national set of procedures to govern employer–worker relationships in plastering. But in this case the issues were somewhat broader than those affecting the other London trades and although the capital was to be the cockpit of struggle, it was only because the problems of the London employers were a more acutely visible version of those common to the country as a whole. There was a national focus to the problems in plastering that reflected their ambitions as the most aggressive purveyors of restrictive rules and practices. Indeed, the relevance of a national confrontation had been recognised by the London employers as early as 1896 when, following the plasterers' rebuff of a local Conciliation Board, the Central Association had approached the National Association of Master Builders with the suggestion that a united challenge be mounted against the men on the question of apprenticeship limitation. Mindful of the power of the men, however, the provincial associations had snubbed this proposal. Not until the success of the closely observed engineering lockout of 1898 had proved the viability of an attack upon the work control power of the men, did the builders set out to replicate the victory of the Employers' Federation of Engineering Associations. Throughout 1898, the London employers worked to secure an agreement with the National Association and in November their efforts were capped with success when a concerted list of demands was formulated which if unmet were to provide the *causus belli* for a national lockout.[63] Designed to prohibit and discipline work control by the men and to create an orderly procedure for the resolution of conflict, this schedule of demands covered the six issues that presented the greatest challenge to employer authority. It proposed an end to the coercion of foremen into the union, that there be no limitation of apprenticeship, no blacklisting or boycotting of firms, an end to attempts at achieving a closed shop, that all demarcation disputes be decided by the employer, and that conciliation be accepted prior to a strike.[64] Nor were the employers prepared to be conciliatory.

The London lodges had voted in August 1898 to withdraw their demand that all foremen be unionists but retained their insistence that those who worked as plasterers join the union. It is hardly surprising that this concession failed to divert the employers from their determined confrontation. If men like Sam Wright were any guide, the distinction was a false one because such men were alternately working plasterers and sub-contracting superintendents of labour. Once in the union, they would be subject to union discipline and should they try to leave to be transformed into sub-contractors they would become 'obnoxious' union defaulters and the potential object of strike action.

At the end of January, an attempt in three London firms to enforce union membership on the foremen provided the opportunity for the employers to present their schedule of demands.[65] Failing to secure a satisfactory response from the union, the lockout was declared at the beginning of March. But, except in London where over 1200 union men were dismissed and foreign plasterers imported to work with non-unionists, its effectiveness was limited and inconclusive.[66] Outside of the capital city only about one fifth of union men were actually deprived of work and the support the plasterers received from the other trades led the master plasterers of the north to press for an extension of the lockout to other sectors of the industry. Nevertheless, at a series of conferences in April and May, an agreement was reached which essentially gave the employers what they wanted. Definite restraints were placed on certain aspects of work control which were to be guarded and enforced by a structure of conciliation. A formula was devised which defined as obnoxious 'defaulters and other men who have been shown to the employer to have made themselves specially objectionable to the union men.' Agreement was reached on apprenticeship, there was to be no blacklisting of firms which adhered to the rules, and a hierarchy of local, regional and national joint committees was established through which conflicts could be appealed whilst the work continued unhindered by stoppages.[67] However unsatisfactorily these structures were to function – and there were further conferences in July 1899 and April 1904 as a consequence of the reluctance of the rank and file to abide by the agreement – they provided a basis upon which to build and extend the system. Indeed, this agreement was to form the model for the erection of national structures to cover all the trades.

In what was to prove a premature offensive against restrictive rules, the summer of 1899 saw a tentative move in this direction when the National Association used the support of the other trades for the plasterers as the excuse for a general lockout. But the series of demands delivered to the men at a conference held in July to resolve the conflict revealed the true nature of the employers' intent. Known as the Yorkshire Manifesto, these demands were virtually identical to those presented to the plasterers; and, as the employers' journal pointed out: 'The real issue, so far as the employers are concerned has always been the unsatisfactory character of the conditions of working. The various settlements throughout the country were not unappreciated. It was the unwritten practices which they had determined to strangle.'[68] Even more than the plasterers' lockout, however, this general offensive achieved only a limited success. Its impetus had derived from the Yorkshire Association who seem to have dragged the other employers unwillingly in their wake – the London association, for example, was opposed to widening the conflict in this way. In places like Leeds, the lockout was ineptly prosecuted with the employers attempting a version of the rolling lockout by dismissing one quarter of the men only then to be faced with a strike of the remaining seventy-five per cent.[69] And this was not so much a stratagem as a reflection of the widespread lack of unity on the advisability of a confrontation. By November, the Hull Master Builders Association which had been chosen to lead the struggle, were bemoaning their being 'left alone to struggle for [our] . . . very existence.'[70] In fact, this was a trifle over-dramatic, for the Hull employers were unique in securing a notable victory over the power of the men. Throughout the nineties the building workers in that town had been pre-eminently successful in imposing their rules upon the employers. Indeed, 'such was the strength of the Hull Building Trades Council that master builders who had infringed its rules were ordered to appear before a trade union court where they were fined.'[71] And the Hull unions had secured a virtually complete organisation of the men – at the beginning of the dispute 95% of the labour force were unionists. By the time the strike petered out in the late autumn, however, over a thousand strike breakers had been imported and about 45% of the workmen were non-unionist. And by the summer of 1900 it was reported that thirty-five shops in the town were completely staffed with 'free labour.'[72]

In spite of its varied success, this lockout was significant because it revealed once again the conditions that dictated the creation of an industrial relations system. The bricklayers had responded to employer complaints about unwritten practices by proposing a National Conciliation Board modelled on their London experience. But, following the pattern of 1896, the employers had refused to consider this suggestion until the work control issues outlined in their Yorkshire Manifesto were addressed. Their reticence was understandable; employers were willing to talk about conciliation structures and procedures only if the men were either defeated and submitted to their imposition, or, more intricately, if such a system was accompanied by some resolution of authority issues – as it had been in the plastering trade. Without the installation of procedures for resolving such issues as obnoxious men and apprenticeship ratios, a national conciliation system would have been of little value to employers in 1899. For a moment, it seemed that this would be achieved when officials of the OBS accepted virtually all the prior demands of the Yorkshire Manifesto – an indication of how far the unions were prepared to go in pursuit of a conciliation system. But this acquiescence was decisively rejected by the rank and file and so the whole matter was dropped. Despite the presence of pliant union officials, the employers were negotiating from a position of weakness. At this moment the worksite power of the men stood at its zenith; the Yorkshire Manifesto was designed to demolish that power and only on its ruins could a conciliation board hold any attractions for employers. With the rank and file rejection of this plan, any further discussion of a board was rendered futile because its work would be hampered by the lack of any clear definitions for the critical issues upon which it would be called to adjudicate. Nevertheless, this episode did mark a step in the direction of such a system. The idea of a National Board was accepted in principle and the groundwork for its structures laid in the agreement between the employers and bricklayers to encourage the extension of conciliation procedures and to establish a standing committee whose responsibility would be to act as an informal arbiter in the settlement of disputes.[73]

Had the employers been able to peer into the future they would hardly have bothered with their abortive general offensive of 1899, for a depression was imminent which would enable them to achieve their ends with relative ease. The building boom ended in 1901–2; in Birmingham, banks refused to lend on the deposit of land deeds. Unemployment which stood at around 4% in 1903 reached nearly 12% by 1908; short-time working was widespread: in 1905 only 40% of London building workers had a full week's employment; union membership and strike success rates tumbled.[74] Not until 1911 did the industry revive and, just as the depression of the late seventies and eighties had seen the efficient removal of restrictive practices, so, too, did that of the early twentieth century. Unlike that earlier period, however, there was a wider recognition of the advantages of using the depression to encourage improved productivity. Whilst the classic pattern of wage reductions and increased hours had by no means disappeared, it was accompanied with the tendency to maintain wage levels and to reduce the work week. Indeed, between 1900 and 1909 a larger proportion of building workers gained a reduction of hours than experienced a decline in wage rates.[75] Of course, this still meant a reduction in the wage, whose rates remained steady, but it did signify a change of emphasis by the employers towards a more productivity-oriented strategy whose origins we have noted in the 1870s. Most particularly, this could be seen in the advice that was frequently tendered to take advantage of the depression to remove restrictive practices but to leave wages and hours untouched. Thus, early in 1901, just as the boom was beginning to break, the National Federation of Building Trades Employers (as the National Association of

Master Builders had become) urged its members to focus on the restrictions
of the men: 'They were prepared to pay good wages for competent men,
but they wanted the trade freed from some of the restrictions with which it
was unjustly hampered.' And these sentiments were not confined to the
national officers of the Federation, they were echoed in the following year
by the President of the Manchester and Salford Master Builders. Indeed, in
that same year, the Birmingham carpenters' and joiners' rules maintained
wage levels in return for a reduction of the dinner hour, no apprenticeship limitation and a requirement that no stoppages occur until the conciliation procedure had been followed through.[76] Six years later the same
employers decided against a reduction of wages 'in the hope that the
operatives would recognise the friendly spirit in which the notices were
given to secure alterations which it was believed would be generally
advantageous.'[77]

By the end of 1907 the employers' journal could smugly remark that
'it is quite a long time since we have had to report any changes in the
working conditions affecting the building trades.'[78] And behind this bland
complacency there lay the steady deterioration in restrictive practices that
had occurred since the early years of the new century. In 1905, for
example, the masons of Bradford could prevent neither the widespread
employment of non-union men nor the imposition of longer working hours
than the rules formally allowed. Nor was this experience in any way
unique. Resistance to piecework and sub-contracting became less credible;
the London carpenters and masons made unsuccessful protests to the
master builders' association about its extent and the plasterers were forced
' "to watch men competing against one another in taking piece work for
labour only." ' In all parts of the country, masons' working rules were
denuded of those clauses which prohibited these methods of working.[79]
But neither were these the only 'privileges' that disappeared from the
working rules. Undirected though it was by any national offensive, the
attack on work control followed the same pattern in all localities. A
package of demands would be presented which included the removal of
rules on apprenticeship, walking time, worked stone, a reduction of meal
hours and sometimes an extension of the work day. Amongst all the trades,
restrictions on overtime work disappeared. The 1890s had seen the men
arrogating 'to themselves the right to decide which are cases of necessity,'
but that right now became the employers' prerogative to demand that
overtime be worked on request.[80]

In addition to these familiar results of an oscillation in the balance of
power, the employers used the depression (as they had not used that of the
seventies and eighties) to expand the methods of the industrial relations
system. The opportunity was seized to impose the no-disability rule –
which was sometimes only accepted after lengthy strikes – and to secure

more complete and precise conciliation procedures. Thus, at West Brom-
which and Newcastle in 1902, the employers imposed a full hierarchy of
such structures from local joint committees to a Board of Trade arbitrator
appointed under the provisions of the 1896 act. Elsewhere, courts of arbitration were set up or more extensive conciliation procedures established.[81]
Just as the first origins of formal industrial relations structures may be
found in the defeats of the northern workmen in the 1860s, so the National
Conciliation Board emerged from a context in which the employers were
able to announce that 'they had been able to combat these troubles [over
restrictive practices] almost entirely.'[82] When the Yorkshire employers'
association initiated discussions with the unions in May 1904 that were
to result in the creation of the national system, they could do so in an
atmosphere that had been largely cleansed of the restrictive power that
the men had been able to wield in 1899.[83] It was a fitting climax to these
trends that the National Board was established in May 1905.

A NEW SOURCE OF AUTHORITY

The national system was designed to provide a complete structure of decision making in the industry. By investing the system and its component
parts with the sole authority to resolve issues and conflicts that arose between employers and men, the practice of the national structures amounted to something more profound than merely the sum of trends that had
begun with formalisation. It is true that many aspects of the industrial
relations system had been pre-figured in the characteristics of the earlier
stage and formalisation had clearly been an essential pre-condition for this
later development. But formalisation had been built upon and altered
precisely because it was hardly systematic enough, because it was too
incomplete to answer the pressing needs that began to present themselves
around the 1890s for a tighter discipline in industry. A whole series of
complex changes demanded that formalisation be transformed into a truly
modern system, the most general of which was the recognised need for a
more efficiently productive society whose imperatives pressed more heavily
in the nineties than they had before. Thus, the system grew dialectically
and out of a related context whose parts we separate simply for convenience and not because they existed in a disparate reality. The structures of
formalisation themselves, for example, had been agents of dialectical
change, stimulating unionisation and organisation and, therefore, advancing the level at which future formations would develop. When the
problems of the nineties emerged, the casual negotiation by responsible
deputations or occasional arbitration by the peripatetic outsider were
clearly inadequate for the constant monitoring demanded by such issues
as non-union labour. What this implied was that the system provide a

new source of authority whose edicts would ensure a smoothly functioning industrial discipline. In building – and in all the other large industries of the economy – this system was not, therefore, simply a warmed-over phase of formalisation. The question was no longer merely one of loosely controlling the discipline of the men, nor of destroying the dominance of autonomous regulation – for those functions formalisation had served its purpose and done its work. The problem that now presented itself was more drastic in its implications than that. For the new unity of employer–union authority that composed the industrial relations system was intended for a regulatory function that may seem primitive by today's standards but which bore more in common with the contemporary scene than it did with its predecessor. In particular, the system was designed to remove decisively all decision making away from the workplace and into the formal and neutral procedures where calm would prevail and reasonable solutions would result.

It would, therefore, be a serious mistake to view this industrial relations system as a one-dimensional retreat of managerial prerogatives towards a more open framework of consensus rule. From one perspective the process did involve a re-negotiation of the relations between the working class and its employers which gave the Labour Movement a status and role that it had not achieved before. And in this respect it represented a formal gain for the working class as a whole. But this, of course, was not the only consequence that flowed from the creation of the system and it both begs the question of the content of that re-negotiation (of what was bought and sold) and fails to recognise the ambiguities and complexities of the process. The retreat from managerial prerogatives provides one hardly unimportant illustration of these complexities. In return for the concession to bargain thoroughly throughout the system, the employers gained a concrete realisation of the re-definition of industrial relations that had begun in the 1870s but which was now backed up by a full panoply of legality and authority in which the unions played a vital role. The bargain over the 'obnoxious' men question illustrates the point. Superficially, this might seem to have been a considerable gain: the men were recognised to possess a say in the nature of the workforce. But, more precisely, it was the union within the industrial relations structures who had this right; the men could only make a negative appeal after someone had been hired. Neither the men nor the union were given any meaningful power over managerial prerogatives to say who was hired or fired or to mandate, for example, a closed shop. Only after the employer had exercised his right to hire whom he pleased could an appeal be made. Furthermore, the men had *always* possessed a negative sanction over the composition of their workmates and we have observed the masons exercising this right in the control over labour strikes of the 1860s. Now, however, that right was systematised but with these differences: the men were not permitted to strike, they were no longer the party who could actually make the decision and they were expressly prohibited from basing their appeal on the question of unionisation. Thus, if we could construct a differential calculus of prerogatives, it would show that the major consequence of this re-negotiated bargain was the restriction and abrogation of the power and prerogatives of men at the workplace.

The paradigms that governed the exercise of workplace power by the workers underwent a qualitative change during this period. As an absolute, the power of the workplace remained – these systems in no way resolved the problem of industrial discipline, only raised it to a new level. And it was more the results that could be expected to accompany workplace activity than the simple act of defiance itself that was affected by the removal of authority from the workplace into the system. In an industrial action it now became necessary for men to consider the reaction their activity would engender not only from employers but also from those institutions that were to sit in judgement upon the issue – institutions which included their own unions. Power relations, the possibilities for industrial action, the technical rights and wrongs of an issue now became immeasurably more complex and problematic to assess. Instant stoppages were now prohibited; demarcation disputes were no longer a matter for autonomous regulation by the men nor, as they remained in shipbuilding, for resolution between the crafts; employers now gained a legitimate say in the boundaries of work not only while the procedures were being worked through but also by their presence on the joint committees that made the awards. A similar point is illustrated by the case of some bricklayers who, in contravention of the Society's bye-laws, were working an extra hour at the ordinary wage rate. With union support the Board found in favour of the employers' right to allow the men to work until 6 p.m. if they so wished – even though it seems clear that those who refused (mainly union men) would be discharged.[84] When the bricklayers at one of Higgs' sites in Battersea ignored the procedures, failed to inform the union for presentation of the case before the Board and struck work for an extra 1d per hour, the employers urged the union to order the men back to work before the Board would consent to hear their case. Although the union replied that 'it would be useless . . . to attempt to do this as the workmen would not listen to them,' neither did they pay strike pay and after a week of this impasse the men in fact returned to work and allowed their case to be considered by the Board.[85] Similarly, there was the case of an evidently 'obnoxious' sub-contractor working for the Veronese Fibrous Plaster Company in 1901 where, on the managing director's admission, the men were in a position to force the issue should they choose to strike. Following the procedures, the union took charge of the case and brought it before the Board which found in the company's favour.[86] The men had, in effect, suffered a needless defeat; if they were to strike – as they threatened to do – they would have received no sanction from the union. Indeed, quite the reverse would have been the case; the full weight of the legitimate procedures and institutions would have been brought to bear against them. To this extent, then, the conciliation structures served to legitimise and extend the very system of work that had called them into being.

But if our differential calculus would show power devolving away from the workplace, it would also show it accruing into the hands of the union whose role was now integral to the successful workings of the whole system. It was the unions who were participating in any power sharing that might be involved but it was a power that was to be exercised *over* the men. Of course, the system depended upon a union authority that was viable and effective, but the system also worked to enhance and legitimise that authority. Thus, in the London bricklayer's conciliation procedure of 1896 it was specified that any application for the dismissal of 'obnoxious' men must come from the Metropolitan Central Committee of the Society, and each subsequent extension of the procedures involved an extension of union authority.[87] The 1896 conciliation rule had originally been confined solely to the application of the no-disability clause, but in 1900 it was modified to cover all disputes. In accepting this alteration, Batchelor gave the employers an assurance that in all cases they would deal neither with the lodges nor, presumably, with the local Central Committee but only with the Executive.[88] And by 1905 the Boards were handling in this manner all and any disputes that came their way. Concurrent with this came a strengthening of the no-stoppage rule. Until 1905 there had been no obligation on the union to take action if the rule was violated, but they now accepted a wording which clearly placed any violations outside union rules. Henceforth, men who broke the rule were not merely acting illegitimately, they were in legal conflict with their union.[89]

These systems offered considerable benefits to institutional unionism which made them more appreciated by the officials than by the rank and file. It is instructive, for example, to note the minimum of discussion that accompanied the adoption of the 1905 scheme, which was propagated by a union officialdom clearly concerned to manipulate opinion with all the weapons at its disposal. It is very important for labour historians to realise how a seminal event such as this may represent so very few collective wills. When they wish to argue a potentially unpopular policy, union bureaucracies (and by this time we may accurately use the phrase) are never reluctant to dwell upon their organisational weaknesses and the following argument from the masons was typically used by all the unions in their selling of the national system. The OSM pointed out that the uncertain state of the law made strikes a dangerous trade policy and that over the past six years:

We cannot congratulate ourselves on the beneficial results of strikes . . . therefore, it is clear, that as a means of securing benefits for our trade, strikes have lost their ancient powers, no doubt largely due to the formation of powerful employers associations throughout the country . . . coupled with the altered conditions under which trade disputes have to be conducted in order to keep clear of the law.[90]

Losing members and short of money, the unions had been thrown a life-line by the employers which they were determined not to let drop. It should hardly be a matter for surprise that very little was revealed in the union journals of what was afoot, or that the scheme itself – like the analogous ones in shipbuilding – was very much the work of the officials of both sides. Indeed, the first announcement of the plan to the carpenters come in July 1905 when a circular was hurriedly distributed to the branches repeating the arguments of the mason's society, demanding an immediate vote and allowing no opportunity for debate. When the votes were reported in August a clear majority was recorded but only about 16% of the union had bothered to register their opinion. Under these circumstances there was some justice in the complaints that members had been given neither adequate time nor information to make such an important decision. The Stockton branch spoke for many when it voted against the proposal as a protest 'against the way in which this question has been put before the members.'[91] For the moment the issue that had been raised here lay dormant, but in later years it was to move beyond the limits of protest and into revolt.

These new structures signified that a third force composed of the diad of employers and union had entered fully into industrial relations. And this implied that the unions be more than just a mouthpiece of the men's wishes; it demanded that they move nearer to a position of neutrality whose loyalty was balanced between their constituents and the system whose decisions they helped to arrange. It is very important to emphasise that, in this respect, union officials were not engaged in a conscious, underhanded sell-out but were responding – as a bureaucratic, professional elite – to a perfectly honest series of realities and possibilities. From their perspective, the benefits these systems offered far outweighed the disadvantages.[92] It could legitimately be argued, for example, that the no-disability clause protected unionists from charges of intimidation when they raised objections to certain men.[93] And this was perfectly true, but there was a price to be paid for this advantage which lay in the procedures to be followed to effect these objections. Despite the fact that the problem of non-union men was largely a problem most suited to rank and file discretionary judgements, decisions as to who was objectionable were not to be made by those on the spot and strikes were prohibited while the procedures were in motion. Not only were the rank and file the best immediate judges of who was and who was not a genuine non-unionist, but they were also the party which would ultimately ensure that the definitions were enforced. Immediate strike action was not simply the traditional weapon of the building workers, it was also the most powerful. It was just this reality, however, that the conciliation structures were devised to subvert and the kinds of tensions that this created for unionism were illustrated by the experience of the London Building Trades Federation.

The Federation had been established primarily to coordinate action against non-unionism. But rather than leading the men, the Federation soon found that its main task was to restrain their zeal. Its insistence that all requests for action be channelled through its own authority structure and its condemnation of informal action were all too frequently ignored. The best the Federation could do was to issue warnings that 'we cannot in any case recognise men taking upon themselves to turn out on their own initiative against non-union or "Free Labour" men' and then sit back and watch some Homerton carpenters make: 'A successful stand against the introduction of "Free Labourers" and [secure] . . . their removal after a three days' strike. In this case action was taken by the men on their own initiative and strike pay was granted to pickets only.'[94] There were similar problems concerning the duties and actions of the ticket stewards who, as officers of the Federation, were the source through which all requests for federated action were to be channelled. But the stewards' lines of authority were more likely to flow towards the work group than towards the Federation and they tended, therefore, to be more militant than the Federation desired. Thus, it was a significant illustration of the ambiguity of the Federation on the whole question of non-union labour that its rules did not require a weekly or monthly show of its membership card. But it was an equally significant illustration of the importance of union membership to the men that in many cases they enforced this show regardless of the rules.[95] By 1895 the Federation was so embarrassed by the difficulties this was causing with the employers that it began to issue admonitions against the aggressive pursuit of its own unionisation policies: 'We consider it an excess of duty for a Federation Steward to take upon himself the inspection of cards during working hours and to follow this up by giving instructions to the men on the job . . . When information of an important nature is to be conveyed to the men . . . we can, as an Executive Council, arrange for this to be conveyed by a responsible and duly appointed person.'[96]

In the negotiations with the bricklayers in 1895 and the plasterers in 1899 the same dilemma was revealed. The unions were prepared to adopt a conciliatory attitude on the question of working with non-unionists and both assured the employers of their reluctance to sanction strikes against these men. But, as Batchelor pointed out with disarming frankness in 1895, 'he was not prepared to put that in writing.' At one point in the plasterers' negotiation, William Deller, the general secretary, indicated that he was willing to accept a monetary guarantee to ensure observance until his generosity was repudiated by Hennessey, the London district organsier.[97] The divided loyalty of the union officials between the system and their members was reflected in their Janus-like pronouncements on the subject of non-unionists. To the membership Deller cautioned in 1899: 'We must, in a sense work with him [the non-union man] for a time to obtain his entrance fee,' but to the employers they pointed out the impossibility of a specific commitment because they could not 'maintain the effective control of their unions, for their members as a body would never sanction such a proceeding.'[98] Indeed, the lack of control over their membership on this issue was revealed by the unsatisfactory results of the agreement they did make in May 1899. The National Association of Master Builders reported that it was 'receiving by every post almost from all parts of England the identical complaint that, in spite of the agreement, the unionists still refuse to work with the non-union men.'[99]

The agreement was, indeed, being widely ignored. Many branches had refused to return ballot papers and the continued boycotts against non-unionists in London, Nottingham, Manchester, Leicester, Oldham and elsewhere illustrated that the majority vote for the agreement was virtually meaningless.[100] As an example were the plasterers of Bromley who, before resuming work, demanded the removal of all the non-unionists. The employers refused, claiming – quite correctly – that 'we had agreed to work with these fellows,' but the branch secretary 'declined to accept that interpretation, and declared that all non-unionists were to him objectionable.'[101] These kinds of difficulties necessitated a second conference in July which failed to resolve the problem and a further conference was held in 1904 concerned largely with the same questions. The rank and file had evidently created a stalemate on this issue, but in no way did this affect the main body of the system created in 1899; indeed, in 1904, at the union's suggestion it was further extended.[102] The aftermath of the plasterers' agreement had revealed the central weakness in the system: the officials 'had acted fairly, and he [i.e. President of the National Association of Master Builders] was sorry their example had not been followed all along the the line,' but 'Mr. Deller did not appear to have put his statements to his men as forcibly and as plainly as he might have done.'[103] What was being hinted at here was plain enough: a new kind of authority system required a new kind of power structure to enforce its mandates.

These systems of industrial relations had grown out of the twist given to the problem of industrial discipline by the first emergence of a real distinction between union and non-union men. But they were of little value if they were to be rendered ineffectual by the same problem. If the industrial relations systems were to be viable, then the institutions responsible for their functioning had to possess the necessary power to ensure recognition of their authority. This was, of course, a wider problem than building, and applied in every industry where these kinds of schemes were erected. It was, after all, the purpose and result of the engineering lockout and of the boot and shoe conflict of 1895 that the authority of the 'official' procedures and channels be strengthened. And it is important to realise that, in this respect, these schemes complemented rather than contradicted the main drift of the celebrated court cases of the decade. Both were equally significant aspects of the 'employers' counter-attack' of these years which went far deeper than a simple-minded anti-unionism, and whose end goal was not to destroy union organisation but to define its disciplinary responsibilities. Thus, although it is tempting to regard the offensive through the courts as a punitive weapon of class warfare, it was, in fact, a profound attempt to provide recognised lines of responsibility and authority for the consequences of trade actions. It was for this reason that the court cases were mainly directed at those industries where collective bargaining was already established and where the major problem was how to ensure compliance with its decisions. Cases like *Trollope v. LBTF*, which attempted to make boycotting and blacklisting conspiracies to injure, or *Lyons v. Wilkins* and *Charnock v. Court* which made picketing more difficult were direct parallels to the provisions of the various agreements which restrained the 'ill-discipline' of the men. But they were accompanied by those like *Temperton v. Russell* which introduced the issue to be climaxed by Taff Vale of the responsibility to be exercised by the union over their membership.

This two-pronged character of the legal battles reflected a similar kind of duality in the character of the industrial relations systems. Whilst, on the one hand imposing constraints upon work control possibilities, they also demanded that a tighter and new kind of discipline be exercised by unionism. Underlying the varied strategies with which employers faced the working class in its industrial life, there ran a thematic unity that sought discipline through stimulating the more perfect organisation and accountability of the working class covered by collective bargaining systems. Such a task could hardly be left to the law alone. Fighting industrial struggles in the calm atmosphere of the court room was a convenient way of avoiding conflicts whose outcome – in building, at least – was far from certain, but it was also slow and its results were at times contradictory. And, in the final analysis, the law could not mandate the viability of industrial relations systems but only encourage and sanction currents that already flowed from the voluntary partnership of unions and employers to regulate the trade. It was upon this cooperation that the vitality and feasibility of these systems ultimately rested; and it naturally followed that each side should be equipped with the necessary power and authority to ensure the success of these new systems of industrial discipline.

Among employers' associations this presented no particular problems; by 1905 few employers of any consequence stood outside the master builders' associations, and the conditions negotiated were those acceptable to the largest employers of labour. The unions, however, presented a more difficult set of obstacles to the exercise of collective responsibility. Trade unionism represented wider and more diverse groups of individuals; the course of its historical development had been more complexly determined by 'organic' roots in its particular community. And, most important of all, from their history, unions had acquired a very different pattern of authority structures than those demanded by collective bargaining within industrial relations systems.

6

The growth of union power

The most significant feature of working-class history at the end of the nineteenth century was the full legitimation of the traditional function of unionism to collectively protect and improve the conditions of work and standards of life. But, as we have already suggested, this re-negotiated relationship between the working class and its employers bestowed a mixed legacy. As equal members fully participating within collective agreements, the acceptance of unionism was conditional upon its adoption of a partial responsibility for the preservation of work discipline. The role of the union as enforcer of industrial discipline – implicit in the creation of formalised collective bargaining – became explicit with the conception of an industrial relations system and it now joined in necessary fellowship with the traditional agency of the union as a collective association for the common good. Nor was there any contradiction in the partnership of these two functions: indeed, they existed in symbiotic harmony. For unionism could now perform its meliorative work only within the structures of industrial relations and only with an observance of the discipline demanded by those structures.

The degree to which the unions assumed their new role as agents of industrial discipline varied, of course, from trade to trade. It depended upon the nature of the agreements that covered an industry, the extent to which the unions were able to develop the necessary internal authority structures, the nature of the work itself and even upon the personality of the key officers of the union and, in particular, the general secretary. In the building industry, for example, the national agreements emphasised procedural rather than substantive rule making, the tradition of local union autonomy was very strong, the labour force mobile and transient and these conditions governed the extent to which the unions were required (and able) to exercise a direct power of discipline over the men. Where, as in shipbuilding, the collective agreements centralised decision making a union like the United Society of Boilermakers and Iron and Steel Shipbuilders endeavoured to assert an intensive discipline over its members. Conditions in most other industries – including engineering, mining and building – did not allow the autocracy characteristic of the

198

Boilermakers' Union to be inflicted upon their men.[1] And although the divergent execution of this kind of union power was important in understanding the variant contours and intensities of the rank and file militancy that resulted, it hardly affected the general trend. Wherever collective agreements had come to govern an industry, the impetus to a union responsibility as an agent of industrial discipline was to be found.

Unionism had always possessed an inherent tendency that pointed in that direction. The support proffered trade unionism in mid-Victorian times by the 'new model' employers and certain segments of the intelligentsia was predicated upon the stability and discipline that characterised union men in comparison to non-unionists. But this species of discipline had reflected the internalised, collective self-discipline of autonomous regulation; it had proclaimed those working-class virtues of self-respect, sturdy independence and respectability that found their most perfect expression amongst the mid-Victorian aristocracy of labour. Since its origins, for example, the Boilermakers' Union had always insisted that employers be treated with honesty and fairness. Fines were imposed for bad work and an early rule had forbidden the use of 'improper' language to an employer, and although there were occasional complaints that such rules were 'framed in the interests of the employers,' their spirit was that of the self-reliant craftsman whose dealings with his employer were those of a man-to-man freedom.[2] Furthermore, this kind of discipline proceeded from an internally derived cohesion that was not conditioned by external sources of authority. Within union government the organs of central authority were primitive and weak, they exercised little influence over the local behaviour of the men. Union control of insurance benefits remained a disciplinary weapon whose sanctions never seem to have been used.[3] General secretaries possessed virtually only one weapon – that of an uninfluential exhortation. Formal procedures and systems demanded an entirely different kind of discipline, however, and one which derived its authority from sources that were external to the workplace or the work groups and its power from the hierarchy of institutions which composed the structures of industrial relations.

THE UNION AND WORK DISCIPLINE

Honoured as they usually were by the presence of a local notable, the early attempts to achieve industrial discipline through formal procedures were based upon the assumption that their inherent moral authority would suffice to secure a ready adherence to the working arrangements they devised. Indeed, many of the formal structures of that early period worked adequately enough in this manner.[4] But the creation of permanent conciliation machinery raised inescapable questions about internal autho-

rity structures within unionism itself.[5] And it was as an early expression
of this relationship that the *Bee-Hive* addressed the matter in a couple of
interesting articles in the mid-1870s. The first suggested a connection that
was to be revived at each moment of crisis from the 1890s to the present
day, and illustrates how contemporary tensions are, in fact, enduring
themes of labour's history. It proposed that unions be endowed with a
corporate legality that would enable collective bargaining to be enforced
through the courts and envisaged that a fund be available to compensate
employers for breaches by the men. Employers would then 'contract with
the union as [a] capable and responsible agent to supply labour and fulfil
conditions to ensure fulfillment [*sic*], or pay the penalties for breach of
contract . . . The union in its disciplinary government of its own members
will be the capitalists' best guardian.'[6] A year later a long article expressed
in unmistakably modern terms the need for a positive union control over
the men. It took the case of some iron workers who had recently been
reminded by Daniel Guile that they had no power to strike without permission of the Executive, and went on:

The members of trade societies ought not to require being reminded that their
associations are every day becoming more and more important in their bearing,
not only on the interests of the trade to which they belong, but on the interests of
the country generally. It is absolutely necessary . . . that all irregular and unautho-
rised action should be abandoned, that all local disturbances should be avoided . . .
[The men] in obedience to the advice of their leaders must prove that they are
capable of acting in good faith.[7]

It was the formalisation of industrial relations that began to move the
meaning of union discipline beyond collective self-control towards a discipline that was externally defined. Some of the first to express the implications of formalisation for union discipline were the London building employers during the 1877–78 masons' strike who urged the union to restrain
the autonomy of their stewards. But this aspect of the *quid pro quo* involved
in the creation of regularised procedures only emerged fully blown with
the more sophisticated systems of the 1890s. Indeed, if the promise of these
systems was to be fulfilled, it could hardly have been otherwise; and it is,
therefore, unremarkable that at the first general trade negotiations between the London unions and the employers this issue of union discipline
was defined for the first time in circumstances and terms that were, hence-
forward, to be characteristic: 'Possibly . . . these two strikes [of plasterers
and bricklayers at Colls] have not been ordered by your union; but you
must bear in mind that if you have the power to order a strike or to come
and negotiate with us, you certainly have the power to keep your people
in order.'[8] During the lengthy wrangling between the plasterers and the
NAMB on the issue of 'obnoxious' men in 1899, B. L. Greenwood pointed
out that: 'You have the means of bringing your individual members into

line when you want to and . . . of compelling obedience to your own rules.
Surely it is not proper for you to keep throwing the responsibility on the
individual members.'⁹ From the first creation of conciliation procedures
for London, it was a deliberate policy of the employers to encourage
unions to acquire and enforce a greater authority over their memberships.
To the plasterers, for example, it was suggested that the delegates to the
proposed joint committee of 1896 have full powers – unanswerable even to
the Executive – to make its decisions binding; to the same men in 1899 it
was argued that a monetary guarantee for the observance of agreements
'will strengthen the hands of your executive . . . Will strengthen your control over your own members.' And in 1900 the carpenters were urged to
fine or expel any members who breached the conciliation procedures.[10]

These kinds of pressures were hard to resist and, as we shall see, the
unions do acquire an increased power over their members during this
period. For the moment we may merely contrast the vigour with which
the plasterers' union dealt with the problem in 1910 as compared to 1899.
As we have already shown, the 1899 agreement was seriously dislocated by
a widespread refusal of the men to return to work. This was particularly
acute in Manchester where a deliberate boycott of the large contractors
jeopardised the viability of the compact reached with the employers.
Deller accepted responsibility to try and get the men back to work but his
efforts were largely unsuccessful and six months passed before the issue
was resolved. By 1910 – with the habit of national conciliation legitimised
by a national board – a more punitive policy was feasible and, once again,
it was the men of Manchester who were involved. They had struck work
without following the conciliation procedures and the union – whose credibility was more clearly at stake than it had been in 1899 – condemned
them, ordered them back to work and promised that 'if the men refused
. . . others would be supplied in their place.'[11]

Because it was upon the industrial relations structures that the importance of unions in society rested, each extension of the system placed an
additional and heightened responsibility upon the unions for making them
work. Nor was this phenomenon to be found only amongst the old-
established craft unions: an illuminating example was provided by the
experience of the Liverpool dock unions. By 1911 a cartelisation which
ended rate-cutting competition had enabled the big shipping companies
to overcome one potent source of profit instability, but the absence of
labour discipline continued to imperil this agreement and the employers
sought to reduce the incidence of strikes by accepting collective bargaining. Through recognition of the unions 'it was intended that the hand of
the union officials in disciplining the rank and file would be strengthened.'
Without any effective form of internal authority, however, this new-found
union power was seen to be meaningless, and, following upon a large

unofficial strike in August 1912, the unions were handed a share of control over the labour supply when the joint committee on which they sat was given authority to issue or refuse registration tallies for work. The Birkenhead men soon encountered the force of this new authority when their strike against the agreement was broken by union-imported blacklegs.[12]

By the early twentieth century this kind of union discipline had become so important that employers were prepared to use the lockout to enforce its credibility. This, for example, was the purpose of the 1910 shipbuilding lockout when the employers were 'incensed at the number of sporadic strikes, and the absence of control over their men which the executive of the boilermakers appeared to exhibit.'[13] And it was the case, also, with the London building conflict of 1914. Early in that year, the NFBTE had pointed out that working arrangements were meaningless unless backed up by disciplinary powers against 'members of unions which had . . . resorted to strikes instead of at first referring the dispute to conciliation.' When three successive attempts to find a formula that would allow the unions to impose a disciplinary penalty upon the men had been rejected by ballots of the rank and file, the employers began to think in terms of a national lockout. As the secretary of the employers' federation explained to his counterpart in the General Union of Carpenters and Joiners:

This action has become imperative in consequence of all reasonable suggestions for a settlement put forward by the accredited representatives of the employers and operatives having been rejected by the London operatives . . . It is obvious that if a section of your society . . . can successfully breach agreements that have been entered into [after all formal requirements on either side have been complied with] . . . then no agreements throughout the country will any longer be a safeguard to the trade.[14]

In other words, only through an employers' lockout could union authority be established over the men.

Although the impact that systems of collective agreements had upon the meaning and content of union discipline was general and all-pervasive, the forms that accompanied the emergence of the union as an agent of industrial discipline varied from industry to industry. The particular historical and structural conditions within given industries played a major role in determining not only the types of agreements and procedures developed but also the nature of this new union discipline. In terms of its industrial structure, for example, shipbuilding provided about as great a contrast with building as could be found. The industry was concentrated into two major centres, its ownership structure was heavily oligarchic and certain of its crafts achieved virtually total unionisation. All this enabled the industry to be covered by comprehensive and specific collective agreements that could be closely regulated and which, in their turn, required a tight exercise of union discipline – particularly in those parts of the industry most densely unionised. Precisely because shipbuilding was in these ways so different from building, it is of considerable interest to our study, for it enables the demands the industrial relations system placed upon the union discipline of the United Society of Boilermakers to be seen more sharply than is the case elsewhere. To a certain extent, the example of the shipbuilding industry and particularly the person of Robert Knight are stereotypical images of the argument that we shall make; it is the virtue of stereotypes, however, to express general themes and tendencies whose details may, in other instances, need modification but which nevertheless stand as expressions of a wider reality.

Ever since the early 1880s, Robert Knight (General Secretary of the Boilermakers' Union) had worked to develop the habit of mutual negotiation beyond the local focus it had reached in the 1870s to a regional level where the executive officers of the union could play a permanent and predominant role.[15] This was finally achieved in the course of the northeast coast strike of 1886 which revealed the advantages of district negotiations enforced by union discipline. When, by a large majority, the lodges rejected the first results of negotiations and refused to grant the deputation full authority to settle, the Executive began to exert its powerful influence. With the undoubted knowledge of Knight, the district delegate arrived at a unilateral agreement with a company outside the employers' association; it was made clear that strike pay would be withheld until negotiations were conducted on terms devised by Knight (which proposed a larger reduction in pay than had yet been offered by the men) and until the deputation had been invested with full powers to settle. Knight's role in this strike had been larger than in any previous dispute – from the beginning of the conflict he had held private informal meetings with the men and the final terms clearly reflected his influence.[16] To this episode was traced the 'better understanding [with the employers] . . . on the North-East coast,' which brought the 'society . . . to believe more and more in Boards of Conciliation as opposed to the old-time method of the strike' and prepared the way for the completely formalised agreement of 1894.[17] Nor was it coincidental that this period marked the flowering of a coyly flirtatious relationship between Knight and the large employers. When Lifton House, the new headquarters of the Society, was opened in 1890, owners were conspicuous in their attendance and lavish praises were shuttled back and forth between Knight and the captains of the industry.[18]

A recognition of the importance that the 'new style' of union discipline had attained was the attention the union suddenly began to pay to the problem of absenteeism. Previously, the question of lost time had not been subject to the reproval of union officials but from the late-eighties hardly a month went by without some discussion of the issue in the Knight-controlled Monthly Report. It first appeared in December 1888 when it was reported that employers had complained about members who worked only half a week and disciplinary action was threatened against a Hebburn gang who were sporadically working at a job for which they had received an advance. In April 1889, the members were reminded that rules existed to fine 'misconduct' towards employers and that this rule was going to apply to absenteeism.[19] But the problem persisted throughout the nineties and by the end of the decade it was reported that Palmer's men lost an average of 28% of their working time. This stimulated an agreement with the northeast firms which divided the disciplinary responsibility between unions and owners. The employers were to gather the evidence against miscreants and the union would serve as the court of justice, convicting or reprieving the offender from the mandatory 5s fine.[20]

By this time the union's role in such matters had been formally recognised by the northeast coast agreement of 1894 which represented the fulfillment of Knight's cherished dream for long-term accords to regulate the trade. It was, however, significant that the agreement should emerge when both union and employers direly needed the stability such an arrangement could bring. The absence of a formalised system of conflict resolution had hampered the union's ability to control the 'illegal' disputes that plagued the late-eighties and early nineties. Employers needed relief from these same problems because the organic composition of the industry's capital was shifting to an increased ratio of constant capital per worker which made time losses more expensive and control over labour costs more important.[21] The northeast coast agreement promised a partial answer to these difficulties. Its provisions included a stabilisation of wage fluctuations to 5% every six months, an agreement on apprenticeship, machinery, and overtime, and it established a procedure which allowed small disputes to be settled by the men and employer, a standing committee for local disputes and executive level conferences for conflicts irresolvable at these levels.[22] There were to be no stoppages pending settlement of disputes and only a committee of union officials and employers was permitted to resolve disputes above the yard level. It was a reflection of the already powerful nature of the union's internal authority structure that this agreement was imposed in the face of an intense hostility from the men it was to govern. Sensing this antagonism, the union submitted the agreement to the whole Society – who approved it by some four thousand votes – rather than just to the northeast district where it was overwhelmingly rejected.[23] But this repudiation carried little impact and the agreement seemed to work fairly well: the frequent breaches were amicably settled by the union 'with the exception sometimes of the men concerned upon whom we . . . put heavy penalties.'[24]

But the 1894 compact was nothing as compared to the Shipbuilding Trades Agreement [STA] of 1909 and its supplement of 1910. These

agreements marked the industrial relations system in shipbuilding as, perhaps, the most comprehensive then in existence. Modelled on the northeast coast agreement, they covered all the trades and created a national
machinery for the negotiation of all issues and the settlement of all disputes
between the executives of the unions and the employers.[25] To ensure that
the system worked smoothly, the unions were handed a virtually total
authority for the maintenance of work discipline. If time was lost at a
particular yard a representative of the union accompanied by a representative of the firm went immediately to interview the men and: 'If it was
found that they had no legitimate reason for being off work, other than
deliberately laying off and obstructing the work, we fined the men so
much per hour or per day . . . for all the time that they were off beyond
one day in the week . . . the penalty went automatically on.'[26] Between
1910 and 1913 this procedure was used incessantly: 'We have had hun-
dreds of our members found guilty in terms of our rules for these breaches.'[27] Thus, the agreements effectively denied any legitimate authority
to the men in the yards to resolve disputes. All problems had to be communicated to and channelled through a union officer: 'If any man has
any difficulty with his employer he is to report it to the Society . . . he is
not at liberty to leave his work. If he is dissatisfied with anything, no
matter what it is, he must report it to the nearest branch official who will
try and settle it.'[28] In addition, should the point in contention be a
general one, those parts of the system closest to the men – the yard consultations and local joint committees – could be bypassed and the matter
shipped immediately to the central conference of the executives. By including repair work in its coverage, the STA ended the traditional autonomy of the work group to decide the piece rate by 'all standing at the
top of the dock or outside of the dock, until their price put upon the work
is conceded.' Because no stoppages were allowed, piece workers were unable to exercise their traditional means of controlling the price by striking,
nor would they know how much they would be paid until the procedures
had been gone through. It was small wonder that the agreements occasioned a prolonged and bitter resistance.[29]

Rank and file hostility to this displacement of power and arrogated
authority was, of course, a central constraint upon the unions' effective
fulfilment of their disciplinary role.[30] Balanced uneasily – and never sure
when the tipping point would be reached – between their obligation to
deliver the material goods to their constituents and the disciplinary restraints to the employers, union officials were inevitably led into stratagems of discretion and manipulation, although even this by no means
guaranteed the acceptance or ultimate effectiveness of the agreements.[31]
The boilermakers' rank and file refused to renew the STA in 1913 and the
three-fold rejection of agreements to end the London building workers'

lockout of 1914 signified a climactic and symbolic flight of chickens to the roost. To this question of the problems of squaring the rank and file we shall return, but the unions were also faced with attempts to fortify their disciplinary function in ways that challenged their institutional independence and threatened to draw them into relationships they had no general wish to consummate. This was the case, for example, with the much-discussed question of investing collective agreements with legal enforceability. The *Royal Commission on Labour* had raised this possibility to the status of a public debate and a majority of its members were inclined to support a change in the law which would enable unions to enter into contracts with a liability to be sued. This was no iconoclastic position. Culminating in Taff Vale, the court decisions of the decade pointed in the same direction and right up to 1914 it continued to be canvassed as a solution to the seemingly irresolvable problem of rank and file militancy. Nor should it come as any surprise that the idea found considerable support within the Labour Movement and especially among its intellectuals. As a member of the *Royal Commission on Trade Disputes,* Sidney Webb suggested to an astonished Sir Benjamin Browne that unions would be in a better position to conclude agreements if they were endowed with a legally binding power over the men.[32] Such a view was, of course, fully consistent with the Webbs' corporatist image of an 'efficiently' organised society, but by 1913 it was persistently raised at the Industrial Council where it found widespread favour amongst employers and a general opposition from the unionists.[33]

In addition to legal enforceability, the idea of a monetary guarantee found widespread support as a device to ensure the maintenance of working agreements and to secure the viability of union discipline. From 1899 the building unions were continually pressed by the employers to adopt this scheme and it was to occupy a prominent place in the employers' prescriptions for the ills of the industry in 1914. Each time it was suggested, however, the unions resisted the idea as subversive of their carefully hoarded financial stability and their rather shaky institutional credibility.[34]

But there was often a certain ambiguity in the unions' resistance to schemes that promised to result in disciplinary benefits. The monetary guarantee was relatively easy to reject, but the potential contained within the Taff Vale decision was considerably more seductive. Just as opposition to the Criminal Law Amendment had taken some time (and persuasion from the Positivists) to gel, so many within the Labour Movement had at first welcomed the Taff Vale ruling. As Ernest Aves pointed out, ' "they perceive the necessity for stricter discipline and for more centralised executive authority" '; and in their original draft of a Trades Disputes Bill, the Parliamentary Committee left it open for trade unions to be sued. But once it was realised just how much money this would mean, the mixed blessing of Taff Vale became fully apparent.[35] Not only did it muddy the limits of trade union action by leaving so much to the discretion of judges, it also posed a fundamental threat to the union's institutional survival and to avoid that peril the officials were willing to live with the militancy of their rank and file.

Taff Vale, the monetary guarantee, and legal enforceability were the natural change from the price to be paid for the rights and authority that unionism had acquired within the systems of industrial relations: their menace lay in their efforts to push the unions' disciplinary function into more constrained and inflexible rules than they were prepared to countenance. In this, the unions showed themselves wedded to a pluralistic ideology of interest group individualism which was based upon a recognition that credibility with their constituents could be sustained only by a voluntary assent to the rules of the game. In this, too, their reflexes were more acute than those of the Webbs and unions were, in this respect, the staunchest defenders of liberal pluralism that late-Victorian and Edwardian society had to offer. Just as they have always resisted external attempts to reform their internal structure, so at this period they were perfectly willing to undertake the job of special constable of the workplace but had no wish to be transformed into paid policemen of the State. Power they were prepared to accept, but only if it left their essential voluntary status untouched. This was the problem with legal enforceability and, ultimately, with the trend of the court cases – that both tied the unions to rules and relationships that were not subject to a voluntary bargain. The unions' power rested upon the important function they performed within the industrial relations system, but it was a function they had freely acceded to and helped to define and which provided them with a certain flexibility – they could always withdraw – that was essential to the voluntary relationship in which they stood to their constituents. Those efforts to force the unions to a logical extension of their voluntary role were resisted not only because of their contrary ideological presumptions but also because their implications would undermine financial stability and the contractual credibility of the institution with its members. In this period, therefore (as until the recent past), the struggle to match union responsibility with union power was a struggle played out within the unions themselves.

RESPONSIBILITY AND POWER: INTERNAL AUTHORITY STRUCTURES

In part, the efforts to impose external canons upon the internal behaviour of unionism was a reflection of the inadequacy of rules devised within unionism to ensure a proper attention to the terms of collective agreements. The demands for a new style of union discipline were not necessarily equalled by the suitability of the internal authority structures of the unions themselves. Changes in the nature and structure of union government were, therefore, a pre-ordained consequence of the growth of industrial relations structures because, as V. L. Allen has remarked, 'The introduction of national collective bargaining was not timed by the trade unions to coincide with their ability to undertake it . . . Their organisations were loosely knit and they had to set about adapting themselves to their new conditions.' Beneath this rather bland formulation, which views the adaptations through the deceptively neutral prism of the imperatives of increased efficiency, there lies a rather more complicated process.[36] And at this point it may be as well to explain what seem to me to be some of the analytical weaknesses of the way in which this story is usually confronted. To begin with, however, I should explain that I intend to leave out of this account any detailed consideration of the Webbs, whose model of trade union development consists of so many different interlocking parts that it is impossible to do critical justice to any one aspect without being led into consideration of the whole. Such a task would be decidedly out of place here, partly because most later accounts amount to little more than a re-statement of their assumptions and more especially because I hope to return to that question at another time in another place.

In most accounts, it is the link between the emergence of national collective bargaining structures and changes in trade union government in the post-1890 period that is usually emphasised. And whilst it is obviously true that the creation of national systems demanded that the unions be internally equipped to the task of administering them, this focus ignores the very important developments experienced during the previous twenty years. Between 1870 and 1890 changes in union rules which asserted the supremacy of executive over local authority and displaced the temporary and informal authority structures that had previously governed trade disputes with those of the union were obviously the fertilised soil within which bureaucratisation could take root and agreements like the STA and National Conciliation Board could flourish. These changes established the framework of an extended union authority which provided the basis for the power that unions were to exercise after 1890. It would be a mistake, however, to see these developments as merely transitional, as simply preparing the groundwork for heightened union control and discipline demanded after the 1890s. They were of historical significance both in that respect and as a response to the imperatives demanded by the emergence of formalised industrial relations after 1870. And because formalisation was itself shot through with informal structures (such as the uncodified procedures that developed in London), so the changes within the internal authority structures of the unions were ambivalent and incomplete. But although it took the creation of a truly regularised system of industrial relations to complete the development of internal union authority, formalisation had forged the first need for internal authority structures to marry responsibility with power.

The general treatment which this problem has received, however, is not simply a matter of failing to get the chronology right. More serious has been the seeming failure to view these various developments as part of a total perspective of change whose elements complemented and sustained each other. When Clegg, Fox and Thompson correctly identify the two most important changes in union government as being the trend towards more representative executives and institutions and the increasing bureaucratisation of the union structures, they fail to point out that these changes were integrally and necessarily related. Indeed, it is strongly implied that they stood in a contradiction to each other whose force was only avoided because 'the [full-time officers] did not obstruct reform.'[37] But there was no necessary contradiction: the new structures of authority secured their legitimacy by these very alterations in the methods of government. It was hardly surprising that in spite of more representative democracy in union government the influence of full-time officials was increased rather than diminished, for it was precisely those representative structures that they both dominated and from which they derived their authority. The power ties, for example, of the carpenters' and bricklayers' district secretaries in London were clearly with the executives and the bureaucracies, but it was the district committees composed of men working at the trade which provided them with at least part of the legitimacy of their actions.

It is a similar kind of conceptual inadequacy that led H. A. Turner to argue quite eccentrically that the period sees a trend away from the centralisation of power and towards a dispersion of authority to the localities. As James Hinton has demonstrated for the engineers – upon which Turner largely based his argument – it was precisely the national agreement of 1898 that provided the Executive with its weapon for exerting a control over the local autonomy of trade policy.[38] It was, of course, true that the period saw a renewed assertion of local control but this was a function of the tension that resulted between attempts to enforce executive authority and local resistance to these encroachments. Furthermore, what needs to be stressed is that authority and its diffusion was now defined by the executives and that, whatever the decentralising forms were, they were responsible in the first place to the 'union' and not to the rank and file. Legitimate rank and file power and the limits to that power were derived from agreements and structures that were very largely beyond their control. It derived from agreements made at a national or regional level between executives of unions and executives of employers. Rank and file

activity – and the limits to that activity, on strike movements for example –
were circumscribed by rules that made them answerable to the executives
and was also contained by collective agreements that defined the procedures for settling disputes. In this context the proliferation of local committees did not mean more local control, for the rules of the game strictly
codified their responsibilities and power within the system; it meant,
rather, the legitimisation of enhanced power and authority for the centre
and for the bureaucracy.

As we have already suggested, before the 1870s most significant efforts
for the improvement of working conditions occurred outside of the institutions of unionism and, indeed, most of the important trials of this earlier
period were conducted in the face of union hostility.[39] But this was not
simply a reflection of the strength of local autonomy: the primitive democracy that the Webbs analysed was much wider than they seemed to
appreciate and signified that decision making flowed from alternative
sources of authority to the union and derived its legitimacy from democratic structures that owed little to unionism. Authority for the conduct of
trade disputes and for bargaining rested solely with the rank and file. In
the days when the distinction between union and non-union was of little
significance, the sovereign authority was 'the trade' as a whole gathered
in mass meeting. The organisational structure of (what I shall call) traditional movements reflected this; they were separate and distinct from any
union organisation that might exist and, just as the movements themselves
emanated from organisational efforts in a few shops which brimmed over
to a district or town, so the sources of authority flowed upwards from the
mass to the leadership.[40]

A typical form of trade movement organisation was for delegates from
all the shops in a town to be elected (sometimes different ones for each
meeting) to form a delegate committee. In larger towns like London an
executive would be selected from that body – the Conference of 1859 – to
run the strike or negotiate with employers. At all times these delegates
were responsible to their rank and file constituents (to whom they frequently referred back for mandates) and to the 'aggregate' trade meetings
which were the supreme arbiters in the endorsement or rejection of
negotiating postures and bargaining offers. Thus, in 1853, the London
carpenters elected fifty-four delegates who represented some 3000 men to
decide upon a 6d per day wage increase. When the masters rejected their
memorial, the first of several general trade meetings was held to determine
the next step and the delegates seem to have met fairly frequently to report
on the progress of the movement. Later in the year a Metropolitan
Carpenters' and Joiners' Association was formed to maintain the advances
secured and press for the abolition of systematic overtime but the centre
of action lay in the shops. Although permission to strike was supposed to

be obtained from the delegate committee, this was merely a formality to keep them informed as to what was happening, for no sanctions were to be applied against those who failed to secure permission. And, in fact, the men at Myers who led the successful strikes to secure the advance left work on their own initiative.[41]

When the Liverpool carpenters and joiners wanted to secure an advance of wages in 1865, they created an informal organisation with shop stewards in each shop to collect the levy for the movement and presumably (the report in the *Bee-Hive* is not explicit about this) formed a delegate committee in whose hands the direction of the movement rested. Representatives of the Amalgamated Society tried to persuade the men to join the union but they were rebuffed.[42] The same pattern was true of the London carpenters' movement of the same year. Delegates were selected at shop meetings, were mandated by the meetings as to the advance that should be demanded and then met centrally to implement their constituents' policies. At each delegate meeting there was a continual referring back to the wishes of the shop floor meetings and a continual polling of the mandate granted by the rank and file.[43]

Leadership, too, took a different form; it was of a purely 'unofficial' character and its links to unionism remained tenuous. In 1859 all the members of the Conference were men working at their trades and as Howell (a union member of only one year's standing) remarked in his *Autobiography*, 'most of the official work of the strike was done by men who had no official position or paid position in the union.' Similarly, in the London movement of 1872 – which was the last where these traditional features could be seen in their purity – no union leader was to be found on the Amalgamated Building Trades Committee. The deputation to masters in June, for example, included only one union official, the rest being delegates from some of the biggest shops.[44] As one would expect, individual union men were frequently to be found in prominent positions within these movements. Charles Matkin, later to be an official of the General Union of Carpenters and Joiners, was secretary to the Short-Time Committee of 1872; and in Potter, Cremer and Howell, the 1859 movement produced a host of men who were later to achieve positions of prominence. No doubt their involvement in these movements enabled their names to become known and provided them with a kind of career ladder into union or other Labour Movement work, and this applied also to large conflicts in the provinces – one thinks of John Prior and John Burnett.[45] But their union connections were not the context within which leadership activity was exercised and equally typical were men who did not progress to celebrity status. Henry Noble of the masons in 1859 – always a prominent figure in mid-century trade activity – and Charles Shearman of the bricklayers in 1872 – a long-standing foe of Coulson –

were examples of this pattern. The career of John Kennedy, carpenter and member of the ASC&J, was representative of the men who performed leadership roles in these traditional movements. Active in trade affairs since the 1840s, he served as treasurer to the 1859 and 1872 movements and was an original member of the Central Board of Carpenters in the 1860s and the United Trade Committee in the 1870s whose treasurer he was for ten years. For men like Kennedy, union membership was a re-flection of personal commitment and sturdy independence; his leadership career owed nothing to his institutional attachment and, apart from a brief pamphlet in the Webb Collection, he has sunk without trace to posterity.[46] The nature of this kind of traditional leadership was differ-ently conceived; it rested upon no institutional base outside of the trade meeting. In the London movement of 1865, for example, the chairman-ship of the delegate meetings changed with every meeting and in 1872 the deputations to the masters were re-elected each time a negotiating session was agreed upon.

Thus, the 'unofficial' character of leadership within these traditional trade movements was not merely reflective of the lack of any permanent union bureaucracy to perform this role: it was also an expression of the different authority relationship in which they stood *vis-à-vis* the rank and file. Leadership roles were firmly and unequivocally tied to the mandates of the rank and file and it was from this alone that the 'leading men' (the phrase itself is revealing) derived their authority.[47] Until unionism derived a power and legitimacy outside of the rank and file mandate, Thomas Carter's admonition to the Liverpool employers in 1846 expressed a stark reality that was illustrated again and again: 'There is no reason [he said] why you are to suppose that the managing men [of a society] can either lead or drive the general body whichever way they please.'[48]

Nor was it only in a nominal, organisational sense that authority flowed from the mass base upwards. The sovereignty of the trade meeting ex-tended beyond a simple ratification of the results of a deputation; it reached into a control over the very details of each negotiating posture. This was true at the branch level as well as in the occasional mass move-ment. General meetings were held to monitor conditions in the various shops, to draw up the broad conditions of the working rules (which were then framed by committees selected by the meeting), even the content of letters to be sent to employers was decided in this way.[49] The 1846 strike illustrates the point. After nine weeks a meeting was arranged between a deputation which included Carter and the masters. They agreed upon a settlement that provided for withdrawal of the document in return for a promise from the men not to interfere with the freedom of labour and to drop the reduction of hours question. Contrary to the masters' assumption, however, the deputation had no power to settle and although ' "the leaders and the secretary did all they could to secure assent . . . the general body felt so indignant at being kept in suspense for nine weeks . . . for a foolish document which the masters ultimately abandoned" ' that they rejected the settlement and refused to go back until the question of hours and wages was settled.[50]

When the Manchester carpenters struck in 1857, the architects suggested that arbitration be used to reach a settlement. Although this question had already been considered by a meeting which numbered one third of the men, the strike committee replied that an issue of such fundamental importance could only be decided by the whole trade. Two days later a trade meeting was held which rejected the proposals but after eight weeks a similar meeting revived the issue and named an arbitrator.[51]

The 1859 movement illustrated the difficulties faced by attempts to coordinate and 'lead' traditional trade movements that involved thousands of men. And in this conflict we may glimpse for the first time the inherent tension between attempts at centralised leadership and rank and file sovereignty. The negotiating posture of the Building Trades Conference was determined by shop ballots whose unsatisfactory results and lax administration illustrated the workshop focus of the movement and caused the leadership the frustration of responsibility without power: 'Mr. Noble wished to know how they were to get the numbers correctly if they gave the men voting papers they would not vote and if they called a special meeting they did not attend and he hoped the conference would lead [?take] them this evening for his trade was getting tired.'[52] At an early stage in the Conference proceedings when the masters had refused to meet a deputation, Potter – in the unfamiliar guise of a centraliser – had proposed that instead of adjourning for a month to get the opinion of the trades on the next step, 'we should be prepared to suggest certain steps for their approval.' This idea was rejected and the Conference decided to consult their constituents for instructions.[53] As the subsequent course of the conflict illustrated, the masters were quite right to ignore the Conference. It had little power or authority, was in no position to decisively influence the course of events and although it possessed some voice in the resolutions to be presented at mass meetings even this was subject to delegate meeting approval. When the Conference unconditionally withdrew the Trollope strike, the men remained out against the document and about the only positive influence exercised by the body was the propaganda function of arranging district meetings which were chaired by their appointed delegates.[54]

The supremacy of rank and file control over negotiations was reflected also in the Birmingham dispute of April and May 1864. When a conference of delegates and masters took place at the beginning of May the men's delegates were not empowered to accept anything and 'the discussion

M.U.A.M.—H

turned on entirely the order of proceedings and the powers of the delegates.' The masters 'required . . . that . . . the representatives of the men should also pledge themselves to accept the decision of the meeting' as to whether all matters in dispute be submitted to a conference of masters, architects and men, but the masons, plasterers and labourers refused and the carpenters (encouraged, perhaps, by Applegarth's presence) and bricklayers agreed even though they do not seem to have been so empowered. Negotiations broke down over this issue and when they were resumed again the carpenters' delegation was not empowered to settle although the bricklayers were.[55] In the same year, the Leeds carpenters' attempt to secure a code of rules revealed a similarly close attention to the negotiating process by the rank and file. The trade had been called together to discuss the need for rules; a committee was appointed which submitted its draft to a mass meeting. When the masters made their reply, the committee responsible for correspondence with the employers 'was increased by a delegate sent from each shop to inform the . . . committee . . . of feeling in the shops; each delegate brought with him a paper signed, with very few exceptions, by all the men in the firm.'[56]

Slightly more is known about the structure of the 1865 carpenters' movement in London. In the middle of June, 70 delegates met to receive the shop ballots on the wage increase to be demanded and the results were sent by letter to the employers. When their reply was received the delegates returned to the shops to see whether the men were willing to accept the masters' offer. As the majority were unwilling, each shop was then free to present a memorial so informing the employer. At Cubitt's the presentation of the memorial was met with the reply that the masters would not reconsider; a shop meeting of all the men was called which made the decision to strike after the dinner hour. This sparked off a combination of the strike in detail with the rolling strike and after about two weeks the masters offered a compromise which the delegate meeting referred back to their shops who voted to accept.[57] One year later a deputation was appointed to explore the possibilities of gaining an extra $\frac{1}{2}$d per hour but they were 'to have no power to agree without having first consulted the general body of delegates.'[58]

Nor was this structure of authority peculiar to building. John Gast was reflecting the same relationships when in the 1820s he had talked of each London shipbuilding yard being a 'sort of republic in itself, governed by its own rules and . . . regulations; we do not interfere in any one yard.' When the Sunderland shipwrights agreed to a Court of Arbitration in 1853, so alien was the idea of confidential negotiations that two men from each yard were to have the right to sit in on its deliberations.[59] In view of the strong group orientation of the work, it is unsurprising that until the 1880s the same theme dominated boilermakers' trade movements but it serves to remind us how it was external forces that stimulated the highly centralised power that came to characterise their union.[60] In the Tyne strike of 1875, for example, mass meetings elected strike committees, delegations possessed no power to settle and for virtually the last time rank and file authority was unalloyed.[61]

The traditional structure of authority relationships began to be challenged once industrial relations were formalised. All the while autonomous regulation dominated relations between employers and men, there was little incentive for representatives of the men to be made accountable. The defeat of one side made the agreement reached tenable until the next round of struggle. But once mutual negotiation and a formalised way of arriving at settlements became the norm, then accountability was a critical imperative. Conciliation boards played an important role in this process by separating the rank and file from their traditional control over negotiations. Rupert Kettle always made it a cardinal rule to 'satisfy myself that men came with open minds and with a full power to finally determine the question, that they are not merely delegates, but that we meet as a deliberative assembly.'[62] Cognisant of the same need, employers saw accountability as a central facet of their efforts to bring order to the labour force and the issue first emerged as employers determined to formalise relations with the men. The experience of May 1864 had brought the lesson home to the Birmingham masters and when they launched the discharge note conflict later in the year, accountability was a main intent of their purpose. One of the first resolutions to be passed by the GBA expressed the intention that all disputes be resolved by an equal number of masters and men who would possess full power to settle. Similarly, in 1868, when they were attempting to force the masons into the formal structures, accountability was again a major theme: 'The men always expressed themselves very glad to hear what the masters had to say; but they were unable to concede or accept anything except such terms as had been decided by their lodge . . . The only way of saving the trade from such abuses was by arbitration.'[63]

The decline of rank and file control thus followed as an inevitable consequence of formalisation. In Edinburgh, for example, a joint committee of the Scottish society and the ASC&J had been established in 1884 but, until the formation of a conciliation board in the early nineties, its authority remained tenuous. At certain times the joint committee was permitted responsibility for initiating action, at other times their advice was rejected until an aggregate meeting had been called and on further occasions the rank and file insisted on a certain programme of demands.[64] Early in 1890 aggregate meetings agreed to the suggestion (by the chairman or secretary of the branch) to push for a board of conciliation, interest in the issue then flagged until suddenly in November the board was announced. From that moment through the yellowing pages of the minute books can be hazily discerned a struggling resistance to the inevitable demise of rank and file authority. In September 1891 the committee were denied power to settle working rules but it seems to have made little difference, for in January 1892 the joint committee recommended acceptance of the boards' rules and amidst 'bitter and angry discussions' over the unsatisfactory nature of the agreement the 'officials' won the day. A month later a resolution to dispense with the board was defeated and by the end of the nineties the battle was won. There were few, if any, aggregate meetings, all control over dispute negotiations rested in the hands of the joint committee and conciliation board.[65]

It is clear that a similar experience may be found in Manchester with the formalisation of relations in that town in 1869. Following the carpenters' acceptance of the masters' proposals, a United Trade Committee of the unions was established which rapidly secured responsibility for negotiations and settlement of disputes. Within a year rank and file authority had asserted itself when the ASC&J branch repudiated the terms negotiated by the committee. But when a shop meeting at Edward Johnson's works tried to exercise a work group control over its hours, the United Trade Committee promptly declared any action which originated from such meetings illegal. From this date, the kinds of questions – such as walking time disputes – which would previously have been the subject of informal work group action were now referred to the joint committee.[66]

In most cases the sources allow the process we have been describing to be seen only in its bald essentials, but a more exact and precise example of the emergence of modern principles of negotiation, of the transference of authority away from the rank and file and into the hands of leaders unhampered by delegate mandates, may be seen in the London movement of 1872. Beginning in the usual way of such trade movements, delegates representing 5000 men met and appointed a committee to draw up a memorial for presentation to the masters which was then approved at various district meetings. When the masters refused to meet a representative group of the men it was decided 'at committee and district meetings and confirmed at Delegate meetings' to prepare a strike in detail on June 1. Subsequent to this, a deputation selected to meet with the masters' association was ordered to neither 'refuse or accept any proposals by the masters' committee, but to report the result of their interview to a special delegate meeting for its consideration.'[67] It was this question of the power of deputations to settle negotiating details that dominated the dealings between the masters and men. At the very first meeting after the strike had broken out, before the Amalgamated Committee was formed and whilst the movement was still largely a carpenters' affair, the masters raised this issue and the men pointed out that they 'had no power and must convene a meeting of Delegates to obtain the necessary authority.'[68] Getting this authority proved to be no easy matter and for some time control remained in the hands of the men. A delegate meeting on June 13 addressed the issues of the strike and determined the negotiating posture to be taken by the deputation: they were to have no authority to agree to general arbitration (which had been proposed by the masters), or to nego-tiate on hours or wages but they could discuss the terms of arbitration on the question of whether there should be a code of working rules. A meeting of the deputation and the masters' committee then took place at which it was proposed to submit wages and hours to arbitration and to discuss the question of working rules. The delegates were reluctantly forced to reject this resolution but 'it was the opinion of the Deputation that if time were granted that the Delegates [from the shops] would certainly accept the resolution.' The masters – pursuing what would appear to have been a consistent strategy of trying to strengthen the hands of the deputation – agreed to postpone their threatened lockout and the deputation, in their turn, agreed 'to recommend the acceptance of their [i.e. masters'] resolu-tion presented to us today as a fair and reasonable way in which a settle-ment . . . can be arrived at.' This was an implicit challenge to the authority of the delegate meeting over negotiations and the challenge was immedi-ately accepted. At a delegate meeting the following day it was decided that the adopted negotiating posture be submitted to a shop ballot and on 18 June at a 'specially convened meeting comprising a full repre-sentation of the trade' the ballots were returned to show an overwhelming repudiation of the deputation's position. Reflecting the delegates' unease at the deputation's willingness to negotiate on the basis of the employers' proposals rather than those of the men, the meeting would not permit the results to be personally conveyed to the masters and insisted that reply be made by letter.[69] The lockout was subsequently declared for 19 June.

When negotiations resumed at the end of July, they did so within the context of an increasingly weakened and disunited trade movement. The masons, bricklayers and painters had joined with the carpenters to form the Amalgamated Building Trade Committee soon after the lockout was declared. Unbeknownst to the others, however, the masons conducted their own negotiations and reached a settlement at the beginning of July and the masters opened their shops on these terms – which were very similar to those eventually arrived at. Within the Amalgamated Com-mittee, there were clear differences of opinion between the carpenters and painters and by the beginning of August the confusing disunity was be-ginning to affect the carpenters themselves. The machine joiners were being offered $9\frac{1}{2}$d or 10d per hour by some employers and it was reported that they were fast returning to work. But for a month, between the end of July and the end of August, the central obstacle to a settlement was the continuing refusal of the rank and file to surrender their control over negotiations.

At the end of July it seemed that this problem had finally been overcome. A deputation met the employers on 26 July and agreed that negotiations should open the next week with the men's representatives having full power to settle. The following day a mass meeting which was evidently well controlled by the leadership seemed to accede to this position but subsequent trade meetings of the carpenters and bricklayers refused to award this power to the deputation. And although a compromise on the nine and nine demand was offered, the masters rejected any further negotiations until the deputations secured the right to settle.[70] Finally, in the middle of August, when it was clear that the impetus had gone out of the movement the masters got what they wanted. At a carpenters' delegate meeting it was resolved that 'a deputation [be] appointed to act in conjunction with the committee with full powers to settle the dispute.' But even at this late date, it is clear that the deputation was very anxious to cover its rear; agreement was reached on 27 August, but 'not without considerable reluctance on the part of the deputation who, before finally acceding, consulted with our [delegate] committee.' On 29 August the bricklayers, too, accepted the inevitable and indicated their willingness to send a negotiating committee.[71] The employers had gained an important victory. Not only had they avoided the men's desire for restrictions on piecework and overtime and blocked the development of a code of rules, but they had also secured the principle of negotiations with responsible representatives. 1872 was claimed to be the first time, for example, that the masons had invested a delegation with full negotiating powers and the suspicion that surrounded the way this had been done was a major reason why the bricklayers were reluctant to grant similar powers to their deputation. A meeting of the bricklayers' strike committee – which included non-union men – called to endorse the settlement saw some 'warm discussion' on the manner in which the agreement had been reached: 'Mr. Shearman charged the committee with effecting a settlement without taking a full vote of the trade.'[72]

Once formalisation was achieved, the old authority structures began to crumble. By way of example we may note the declining importance of the aggregate meeting whose authority – once supreme – ebbed away in the face of mutual negotiation, conciliation boards and joint committees. In Edinburgh and Glasgow, for example, it was gradually transformed from the initiator of action to its modern role of sanctioning or rejecting decisions already made;[73] and in London the events of 1872 dealt a death blow to its sovereignty. The ASC&J, for example, retained the London aggregate meeting as the sole source of determining opinion until 1874 when it was argued that the size of the district persuaded the general council to transfer its function to branch delegates elected to a delegate committee which alone possessed the right to determine the opinions of members. As befitted a more 'primitive' organisation, the General Union did not follow suit until the early nineties when their district committee's recommendation to abolish the annual aggregate meeting was approved by a vote of members.[74] In other trades too the same trend can be discerned. Amongst the boilermakers, the last aggregate meeting in Liverpool was held in 1875 and the district delegate held no regrets: 'Aggregate meetings,' he told the Webbs, 'are "aggravating" meetings and [anyone] with a gift of the gab will carry the meeting.' In 1882 the Executive of the union warned that shop meetings 'were illegal, unconstitutional and contrary to the rules . . . All resolutions passed at such meetings were not binding . . . All business . . . must be transacted at duly-convened lodge meetings and in no other means.'[75]

Into the vacuum left by the decline of one kind of authority structure there moved the union. A few weeks after the 1872 strike was settled, correspondence had already begun between the CAMB and the Amalgamated Society on how the agreement was to affect the dinner hour custom. The unions came to play a more central role in the organisations designed to continue agitation for the original ninepence and nine hours demand and a code of rules. When a further strike seemed imminent in 1873 the ASC&J told its members that they would receive union support – 'a support which they did not receive during the struggle of last year' – and the reasons for this were not hard to seek, for it was from the ASC&J branches that the initiative and leadership now came. Thus, at a traditional delegate meeting the union committees shared the platform with the elected shop delegates, the meeting was dominated by the unionist chairman (E. Harrison, soon to be a general councilman) and it approved a resolution identical to that passed by the union lodges the previous day. In the negotiations that followed, the deputation – which this time contained a majority of known union men – were not hamstrung by the necessity to continually refer back to delegate or mass meetings.[76] And when, in 1893, the OSM made a feeble attempt to revive rank and file control over negotiations the employers quickly 'repudiated the suggestion that representatives of the union should attend a conference without the power to settle questions . . . such a policy had never been accepted by this Association since its establishment in 1872.'[77]

But if the unions were to adequately fill the displaced role of the old structures, it was necessary that the traditional flow of union authority from below be reversed and that local affairs and disputes be subject to executive control. This process occurred between 1870 and 1890 and although we treat it as a discrete, internal phenomenon, it must be seen as another filament in the web that was being woven during these years to incorporate the unions into a recognised estate in society. The end of autonomous regulation necessitated the demise of old structures of authority and the birth of the new was fostered, for example by changes in the law on trade unions which encouraged their internal authority to shift towards executive organs. It was neither ironic nor coincidental, therefore, that the decisive extension of executive authority in the ASC&J should occur in 1872 when it became a union rule that members seeking new privileges were obliged to forward all particulars to the Council who would then decide whether to grant or deny permission. If the employer failed to comply with the demand, the branch then had to return to the Executive for further instructions and under no circumstances would strikes be allowed either for new rights or in defence of old privileges without union sanction.[78] But the origins of this rule are also of some interest, for it was first promulgated in January 1865 and its entrance into the rule book delayed until the uncertain legal position of unions was resolved by the act of 1871.

The exact genesis of the rule derived from Applegarth's experience during the discharge note strike in Birmingham. On his return from an ill-fated visit to the town – where his intervention had been met with cat-calls and jeers and his advice to return to work resented and ignored – Applegarth set about constructing a case for more executive control. In spite of the fact that 'on the question of strikes and their management our rules are silent,' the Birmingham men were upbraided because: 'The Council had no knowledge that it was the intention of the men to strike at so short notice, neither did we think that any branch would pledge themselves to strike without first acquainting us with their intentions.' With no sanction from the rule book, the strike action was claimed to have been illegal and disapproving snorts were made about the way benefits were being paid.[79] Although it is indeed likely that Applegarth was concerned about the dangers this kind of trade action posed to union finances, it was surely a strange coincidence that the first attempt to assert executive control over a local movement should turn on a conflict whose purpose and outcome was to formalise industrial relations. Nor was it probable that Applegarth was unaware of this connection. Indeed, his attempt to induce a return to work had occurred at the very moment when the masters' plan to establish formal structures in the town was being jeopardised by the intransigent demand of the men that the discharge note be definitively withdrawn. Certainly, his experiences in Birmingham could have left little doubt in Applegarth's mind of both the need and dangers of executive action and the delayed promulgation of the rule probably owed something to rank and file resistance. The Manchester branch, for example, was quick to protest against this assumption of executive authority with the reasonable suggestion 'that the opinion of the members ought to be taken on so important subject as the Council only lately stated that they were not there to alter the rules but to enforce them.'[80]

Similar trends could be seen in the other building unions. Although some right of executive intervention had always existed in the Operative Bricklayers' Society, the balance of power had invariably rested with the branches. Edwin Coulson's intervention in the Wolverhampton strike of 1865 had persuaded the delegates to suspend the strike and offer arbitration, but his intercession had been resented and more often he restricted his activities to checking the legality of the strike or the state of the payment books. Indeed, his visitations seldom merited much notice and on at least one unpropitious occasion an empty hall was his only audience. The rules of 1871, however, decisively tilted the balance towards the Executive who gained the right to settle any strike on whatever terms they saw fit, the power to order the branch secretary to cease payment of strike benefit, and the authority to appoint executive delegates whose wide-ranging licence of investigation and intervention extended even to negotiating between the employers and members.[81] By May 1872 these powers were being used to close a strike at Gloucester but, more typically, they lay dormant until the 1890s.

Like the OBS, rank and file control over strikes in the Operative Stonemasons' Society had occasionally been tempered by the assertion of executive responsibility. The 1849 rules, for example, required branches to consult with the Central Committee even when established privileges had been infringed but in 1852 this restriction was removed. In 1862, the Central Committee gained the right to investigate all applications for permission to strike but merely to gather information and most delegates it appointed were local men with no ties of power to the executive.[82] As we have seen, the restraints imposed upon work group action by the rules of 1871 marked the first questioning of the propriety of unimpeded local autonomy, but the decisive transition to enhanced executive control came with the rules of 1881 which granted that body the power to intervene in a dispute they believed to be futile or detrimental to the Society's interests. Two council members could be dispatched to any district to negotiate or investigate and on their report the Executive Council could recommend to the General Council that the strike be closed.[83] The same trend towards more executive authority was reinforced by the second aspect of the 1881 rule change. In spite of the more complex procedures that the 1871 rules had established for striking against infringements, responsibility for such action still resided in the hands of the branch members. The rules of 1881 shifted that responsibility away from the branch. A rule analogous to that of the carpenters was introduced which made application to the Executive necessary before any action could be taken against proposed alterations in working conditions. Irrespective of the fact that the prevailing code of rules may have been ratified by the Society, permission now had to be sought by a vote of all members to resist infringements in the same way that had always been demanded for improvements in working conditions.[84] And whilst this procedure might seem to have been de-centralising (*vide* Turner) and democratising (*vide* Clegg, Fox and Thompson), it not only worked to slow down the tempo of industrial action but also to inject the Executive into the process through the influence on the vote their recommendation would carry in the *Fortnightly Returns*. The right to strike against infringements and to receive automatic support was a right held by the men since the formation of the union; it was one of the bastions of local autonomy but it had now been diffused to the whole society with the Executive as arbiter of local interests.

The passage of these kinds of changes was usually eased by the special circumstances under which they occurred. We have noted how the rule changes of 1871 were conditioned by the defeats in the north, the divisive effects of public opprobrium of work control rules and, perhaps, the pending changes in the law. In 1881, it was the carefully encouraged fear of union bankruptcy that allowed a transformation to be accomplished that thirty years before would have been unthinkable. And although it was true that the Society had seen its finances denuded first by the 1877–78 strike and further threatened by the depression, the restraint on expenditure that this demanded did not necessarily imply the growth of executive authority that resulted. The union had, after all, been bankrupted before without experiencing these kinds of changes and the expansion of executive authority at this point owed far more to the demands that were beginning to be placed upon the union by collective bargaining than it did to the preservation of financial security. In fact, the third of the rule changes of 1881 had adequately addressed the problem of union finances by tightening the conditions under which dispute pay would be granted.

At the other end of the industrial spectrum, a similar rearrangement of authority and power relations was in motion. Although the United Society of Boilermakers and Iron Shipbuilders achieved an unenviable reputation for centralised control and dictatorial general secretaries, both were children of the 1870s. The Webbs – by no means blind to Robert Knight's labour boss idiosyncrasies – had nevertheless lovingly dwelt upon this 'most powerful and best conducted of English trade societies . . . [in which] popular control has sunk to a minimum.'[85] And whilst there was far more workplace control by boilermakers than the Webbs cared to admit, it was undeniably true that the sanctions at the disposal of the officials were quite formidable. But it had not always been this way. Since its inception, the power of the Executive had been strong on paper but weak in practice. In the sixties, it was common for branches to act first and seek permission afterwards and there were many examples of lodges acting ' "in open defiance of the Executive," ' distributing strike pay contrary to their orders and failing to heed exhortation to seek increases by negotiation.[86] Concomitant to this was the casual way in which the Society was run: no annual reports were issued in the middle 1860s, a copy of the 1863 report was found wrapped around $\frac{1}{2}$ lb of butter and the report for 1868 was but a single leaf. Not until 1872 – a year after Knight had become general secretary – were regular monthly and annual reports issued and not until 1873 were any records kept of General Council Meetings.

The changes begun in the early seventies were a consequence of the inadequate state of the Society, the personality of Knight and, most importantly, the growing desire of the employers for a more stable system of industrial relations. For it was one of the consequences of the 1871 dispute that the employers of the northeast began to turn to the union as a responsible agent for the men and it was at this point that autonomous regulation in shipbuilding (and probably engineering) shaded into formalised bargaining relationships. Although the story remains to be unravelled, it is probable that its elements included a changing economic structure of the shipbuilding industry which necessitated a changed style of industrial relations and the lesson of 1871 that union negotiation could bring a badly needed labour discipline to the industry. In any case, Charles Palmer was typical of the capitalists in the area in experiencing a conversion of attitude from one which dictated hectoring lectures on the futility of combinations in 1864 to waxing lyrical on the virtues of union negotiation in 1872.[87] In an appropriate *pas de deux*, the union's structure of internal authority began to change. A fierce battle with the Tyne district in 1876 established the principle of executive control over both the District Committees and District Delegates. Led by the district officials, the men engaged in a piecework dispute refused to heed or implement Executive orders to negotiate and return to work. A national ballot narrowly upheld the right of the Executive to control branch distribution of strike pay and finally, under the threat of its own resignation, the Executive demanded and obtained a majority vote of the Society for the dismissal of the District Committee and the delegate.[88] Never again were District Committees or District Delegates to act as rank and file leaders in defiance of Executive wishes.

The 1880 rules reflected the victory: 'Both committee and the Delegate shall be under the control of the Executive,' by 1884 the Executive had claimed a sole responsibility to authorise any strike action and, as we have seen, two years later during the strike of 1886 the Executive effectively smashed any remaining rank and file control and secured the *de facto* right to actively intervene to resolve strike issues.[89] Finally, in anticipation of the collective bargaining structures to be erected in the mid-nineties, the rules of 1890 placed a further brake upon rank and file activity by the creation of a voting procedure for 'every question likely to lead to a dispute where the funds of the Society are likely to be affected' which in 1895 was extended to common piecework disputes. These rules reinforced the disputes procedures of the collective agreements to slow the pace of industrial disputes and allow the Executive to interpose for a settlement.[90]

The right of executives to actively intervene in strikes and to supersede the local men in negotiating a settlement was an important part of the growing armoury of union power over its members during this period. In the case of the Amalgamated Society of Carpenters, it would seem that the practice grew in an *ad hoc* manner, legitimised by the increased authority the Executive acquired in 1872. The first instance of the use of Executive delegates as mediators, for example, is to be found in September 1869 when, acting with no authority from the rule book, it was reported that: 'Previous to the last quarter the E.C. did not as a rule send a delegation to branches engaged in disputes with their employers, but a few months ago they decided to do so, and it has been attended with the most beneficial results . . . it has been the means of speedily restoring a good understanding between the employers and workmen.'[91] And the first recorded usage of the new rule of 1872 was directed against the Newcastle branch in 1874. This branch had committed 'numerous violations' which included conducting their agitation by general trade meetings and allowing themselves to be overruled by democratic votes of the non-unionists. The members were denied benefits, ordered to submit various questions to arbitration, accept the employers' wage offer and, to ensure their compliance, the General Secretary and Chairman of the Executive Council were dispatched to the city. It may have been this episode that led the Sunderland branch to publish a resolution of protest against this kind of 'interference' by the Executive, but only after 1890 did such intervention become a widely used sanction against the branches.[92] Thus, in September 1896, the Dublin carpenters – on strike, interestingly enough, against the introduction of the hourly system – saw control taken out of the hands of their managing committee and unilaterally closed by the Executive. Like the men of Newcastle, the sins of the Dublin carpenters lay in the democratic authority structure of their trade movement. The managing committee were totally fettered by rank and file control: 'They were not empowered to make a single offer towards effecting a settlement, but were simply message carriers between the men and the employers.'[93]

In the OSM, too, it was only in the nineties that the rule giving the Executive power of intervention began to be commonly used.[94] We have already noted its role in the worked stone strike of 1898 in Manchester, but the first important exercise of this authority was to be found in the masons' and joiners' strike at Cardiff in 1892. For the masons, this area was reputed to be their best organised district and both trades were confronted by employers determined to destroy restrictive rules. Control of the strike was initially vested in the rank and file who resolutely refused to grant negotiating powers to their deputation.[95] By May, two months after the outbreak of the strike, Chandler and Matkin were in the town trying to reopen negotiations for the carpenters in the face of rank and file resistance. And by the beginning of June the weight of their efforts and advice had prevailed to effect a settlement that included withdrawal of the piecework rule in return for the abolition of the masters' authority clause. This seems to have ended the carpenters' strike, although not before the 'widespread dissatisfaction which exists [with the settlement]' had delayed a return to work.[96] But the masons continued to hold out for another year until their executive dispatched an investigating delegation which closed the strike and abandoned the efforts to retain the restrictive controls of the men over their work.[97]

By the early 1890s, then, the unions were poised to assume the role that a fully-fledged industrial relations system was to demand of them. The previous twenty years had seen the balance of authority within the union tilt decisively against the membership in favour of the executive; it had seen the displacement of the traditional leadership which sprang from the base of a given movement; and it had seen the demise of the authority of the trade and its replacement by the union as the responsible agent for the conduct of trade movements. But as we have insisted before, the period before 1890 was transitional. Preparatory to their role as agents of labour discipline, the unions were engaged in readjusting their governmental structures but the potential contained within these changes was not fully realised until the 1890s because the external stimuli of a mature industrial relations system were not present. Thus, it was still possible for Robert Last, long-serving General Secretary of the General Union of Carpenters, to be discharged by a vote of members because of his failure to adequately support the Manchester strike of 1877–78.[98] The 1870s and 1880s saw, therefore, an intermingling of the old and the new which did not finally result in an unalterably new synthesis until the 1890s. To illustrate this, it might be useful to look at the London carpenters' movement of 1891 where the old and the new could be seen in uneasy partnership but where, also, the dominance of the new was clearly foreshadowed.

The traditional aspects of the movement of 1891 were represented by the marked cooperation between union and non-union men and the continuing deference to rank and file authority. The decision to press the 8 hour and 10d per hour demands were taken by shop and job delegates and endorsed by a mass meeting at the Exeter Hall which instructed the United Trade Committee ' "in consultation with the shop and job delegates to take such steps to enforce the demands" ' by strikes in detail. Authorisation to extend the strike was granted only by the shop and job delegates, and the assertion of rank and file control over negotiations was never far from the surface. Thus, at one meeting a resolution was passed that the 'central committee might negotiate with the Master Builders' Association but it was thoroughly understood that there must be no settlement until an aggregated meeting of the trade had been called.' And the United Trade Committee continually referred back to the district aggregate meetings to get their decisions endorsed.[99] But the very presence of the United Trade Committee suggested that the aggregate meetings were not unchallenged for control of the strike. Unlike the Conference of 1859, or the Amalgamated Committee of 1872, the United Trade Committee was composed solely of representatives from the societies and the evidence suggests that the initiative flowed from the Committee rather than from the shop delegates or mass meetings. Most resolutions, for example, were proposed and seconded by union men – although non-unionists frequently spoke in support; the leadership were all prominent unionists and clearly dominated by those – like George Dew and William Matkin – who were officials. Decisions on strike policy seem to have been uneasily balanced between the rank and file shop delegates and the United Trade Committee. Thus, the decision to extend the strike was taken by the delegates, but the details of when and which men to withdraw seems to have been the responsibility of the Committee. When the employers made their demand that non-union men be included in the deputation (which, in contrast to 1859 and 1872, was initially composed only of union men) the shop delegates wanted an aggregate meeting to elect four men with full powers but the United Trade Committee caused special meetings to be held to elect non-unionists to the deputation.[100]

Furthermore, the manner in which the strike was settled illuminated the decline of the traditional authority of the rank and file and the ultimate dominance of modern styles of leadership. It was, for example, the recently formed London Building Trades Committee (a joint committee of all unions) which invited the arbitration of the Royal Institute of British Architects; a trade meeting had passed over an earlier suggestion of arbitration and had instead voted in favour of extending the strike. The acceptance of the highly unfavourable award in October revealed all the characteristics of a 'responsible' union leadership. Both R. Day and Francis Chandler (Chairman and Secretary to the ASC&J) were in attendance when the award was discussed in private deliberations by the Committee. No aggregate or delegate meetings were called to end the strike but telegrams were sent to the districts announcing that: 'Arrangements Satisfactory. Men to return to work tomorrow.' In their notice to the supporting unions, the United Trade Committee claimed that 'acting on behalf and with the consent of the trade, [the United Trade Committee] have mutually agreed to . . . the proposed code of working rules.'[101] But this consent was belied by the last meeting of the traditional shop and job delegate meetings which, contrary to the advice of Day and Chandler, passed a resolution disapproving of the award. It was too late. The arbitration was binding and backed by the unions; the bifurcated authority systems that controlled the strike had been divisive and confusing; many men had already returned to work.[102] As we have seen, the following year the employers moved to more completely systematise industrial relations and by 1896 the last traces of any effective rank and file authority had completely disappeared.

The movement of this year was a union not a trade movement. From the very beginning only the ASC&J and three other carpenters' unions were involved in negotiations, no pretence was made at a rank and file control over the strike – there was not even the presence of a United Trade Committee. No aggregate meetings were called to formulate or endorse policy, balloting was restricted to union members, and even their opinions could be safely ignored – as was illustrated by the continued negotiations over the no-disability rule after it had been rejected by the rank and file. There is some uncertainty as to how the strike was called off, but the best evidence suggests that the Executive of the Amalgamated Society signed the agreement and declared the strike closed without the bother of a ballot.[103] The legacy of 1872 had now truly come into its own.

RESPONSIBILITY AND POWER: INTERNAL POWER STRUCTURES

The bureaucratisation of trade unions that was well under way by the mid-1890s, was no mere abstract search for 'efficiency'; nor was it, as the Webbs strangely suggested, simply a consequence of the administrative need for centralised finance.[104] As we have endeavoured to demonstrate, the shifting authority relations within the unions was consequent upon the demands of formalisation and the creation of a system of industrial relations. But it was one thing for the rule books to legitimise these new authority arrangements, or for the general secretary to exert his influence to override the wishes of rank and file, and it was quite another for such authority to be effectively exercised on a permanent basis. It was the job of the bureaucracies to consummate the relationship, to provide a substance to the authority that now resided in official hands.

What we call the bureaucracy – never adequately examined for its origins and growth – was a miscellaneous and confusing collection of committees, personnel, and institutions whose spheres of authority and relationships with those above and below them are seldom clearly delineated or precisely defined. But it is clear that the characteristic feature of these edifices was to provide an internal power structure whose domi-

nant tendency was to protect and to wield the institutional authority recently acquired by the officers of the union. Authority now flowed downward from the leadership bodies and it was a major – though by no
means the only – function of the bureaucracy to ensure its jurisdiction.
Power relations remain, of course, extremely complex phenomena to
analyse; so much depends upon the particular circumstances within which
they operate and upon the role of such intangible quantities as 'influence.'
It is clear, for example, that within the branch there had been a decline
in rank and file influence but to what extent this was true and in what
circumstances it could change are unclear. Part of this development had
been due to the conveyance of responsibility over many matters from the
branch itself to the district, joint, or managing committees.[105] It is at
branch level that these questions are most problematic, for the extent to
which branches were integrated into the bureaucracy varied from case to
case, even within unions. It is, therefore, inevitable that what follows will
be considerably over-simplified, but focussing upon three or four cases
typical of the wider tendencies of the period should serve to minimise that
risk. The new internal power structures assumed two somewhat different
forms. There were the new personnel whose function was to act as agents
of union authority and discipline and whose power and responsibility –
even when they were elected – derived solely from the executive. And,
secondly, there were the new institutions of union authority which were
sometimes elected, frequently staffed by full-time officials, and which encompassed a wide range of different shades of power and responsibility
with some being much closer to the rank and file than others.

We have already had occasion to note the growing practice within the
building unions for disputes to be subject to the intervention of executive
delegates and, although we have no way of knowing how many or how
frequent such interventions were, we may be fairly sure that after the
1892 Cardiff strike they characterised virtually every major dispute. But
although this remained the prime form of executive control over local
disputes, it was supplemented (or in some trades replaced) by full-time
officials whose title of 'organiser' belied their multiplicity of duties. The
carpenters first introduced this office in 1893 when the Amalgamated
Society appointed six and the General Union created the post of national
organiser.[106] Not until the 1912 rules revision did the masons follow suit.
In both trades, however, their duties were the same: they organised districts where the union was weak or non-existent, they prodded sluggish
districts and lodges to greater efforts and, most importantly, they served
to mediate disputes or remove causes of friction with employers. Their
authority derived from the executives and their reports became an important and prominent item in each issue of the union journal.[107] A typical
example of the organisers' work may be taken from the ASC&J *Monthly*

Report for June 1895: 'I met the employers at Harrogate and made them, with the consent of the men, a modified offer.' Then it was off to Rotherham where he recommended acceptance of the employers' offer and on to Pontypridd to improve organisation. At Bishop Auckland 'we decided on a very necessary trade movement, and I have endeavoured to extend the Bradford Managing Committee District in a direction where men hug their chains of slavery and think it noble.' Finally, to the Isle of Man and then back to home base of Liverpool.[108] The extent of this kind of bureaucratisation depended upon union finances and there were some fluctuations in the numbers of organisers throughout the period – even the boilermakers had to reduce their district delegates in the mid-1880s. But even if they were an occasional rather than a permanent feature of union structure they represented a new layer of official interventionism in the localities' sphere of authority.

The best example, however, of these new agents of union authority is to be found in the boilermakers' office of district delegate. Created in the 1870s – the first ones were quartered in the northeast, London and on Merseyside – they were elected officials who served as the 'local officer of the council at Newcastle . . . responsible to the Executive Committee.'[109] In the days of Robert Knight, when the Executive rotated every six months, this meant fealty to the General Secretary, and Knight did everything in his power to ensure that district delegates did not form too close an attachment to their district. They were generally strangers to the area, private correspondence with Knight was encouraged, and any unsuitable nominees were certain to face abusive propaganda in the monthly reports preceding the election.[110] Nominally under 'the supervision of the District Committees' – attending its meetings only when invited – the actual relationship appears to have been the other way around, with the delegates overshadowing and controlling the committees of elected workmen. In Liverpool, for example, it was the delegate who told the secretary when to call committee meetings, claiming to the Webbs that without him they would be ' "fish out of water!" '[111]

The district delegates were quintessential agents of industrial discipline and they illustrate perfectly the relationship that emerged at this time between collective bargaining, union power and control over the labour force. It is significant that they were frequently recruited from amongst the foremen and at least one of their number went on to work for the employers' association.[112] The delegate's prime function of course, was the settlement of disputes and employers quickly learnt the advantages of dealing with a direct line to Knight; their well-known praise for the union's discipline was explained by a Hull employer to the *Royal Commission on Labour*:

In cases of dispute we almost invariably write to Mr. Knight . . . if the local [district] secretary cannot or will not deal with the matter as we think he should . . . Mr. Knight sends an officer to the district, a delegate generally, who takes up the matter, and the whole thing is dealt with promptly . . . we have always found them most conciliatory in their methods and firm with their men.[113]

Almost universally, the delegates enjoyed good relations with the employers. In the nineties the South Wales delegate claimed that he alone settled all the disputes in the area, the Hull delegate 'smooth[ed] over friction and prevents disputes' and the Webbs were most impressed by the Liverpool delegate who 'walks in and out of yards and is on [friendly?] terms with the employers.' Especially in times of good trade, their work was of considerable benefit to the men, for they could serve as permanent adjusters of piece rates and save gangs the time and trouble of stopping work to negotiate. This kind of work, however, only served to increase their power and by 1910 there were instances of the delegates exercising a total authority over the distribution of overtime working.[114]

The position of the district delegate was in many respects unique, the kind of power and authority they wielded was not to be found in other unions – least of all those in building. But the building unions were advanced in other respects and, particularly, in their highly developed institutions of union authority. By 1914 the individual building unions were honeycombed with a complex system of branch, district, joint, and managing committees and above these were the various inter-union structures of cooperation and coordination. Both kinds of organisation were responses to the imperatives of union power and authority. Particularly interesting in this regard is to trace – albeit scantily and without total satisfaction – the London carpenters' United Trade Committee from its origins in the late sixties to its metamorphosis as the London Management Committee of the Amalgamated Society of Carpenters and Joiners in the early 1890s. It was generally the case that, when a trade movement folded, the delegate committee that had coordinated the effort was also disbanded. But in July 1865 when the carpenters compromised on their 8d per hour demand they decided to maintain their delegate committee to prepare for a renewed effort in 1866. For at least a year the committee maintained a permanent if shadowy existence and it is possible that it fed directly into the 1872 movement. At the conclusion of that dispute, it was similarly decided to preserve the Carpenters' Advance of Wages Committee – which was what the group of nine delegates was called – to monitor the settlement and press for the full demand again in 1873. Within a year the name had been changed to the United Trade Committee and it would seem that this signalled the deepening involvement of the ASC&J in the city's industrial relations, for in that same year a union rules revision provided for the creation of such committees to coordinate action more effectively in towns where there were other societies.[115]

It took some years before the London United Trade Committee was fully integrated into the union structure but its history in the 1870s emanated from the tussle between its rank and file origins and its union destiny. Not until the middle seventies did the union successfully assert an unchallenged dominance over the Committee; non-union men were elected in 1874 and, although in 1877 its secretary and chairman were important unionists (one of whom was Francis Chandler), the following year saw the traditional elements regain their dominance. Thus, the officers of 1878 were not prominent unionists (indeed, they may not have been union men at all), and a wages movement initiated by a traditional delegate meeting was condemned by the ASC&J because the opinion of their branches had not been sought.[116] Since 1875, the Executive had endeavoured to bring the Committee under its control, first by denying it power to institute legal proceedings in defence of trade privileges, or to initiate trade movements, and then by asserting that the Committee was responsible to them alone:

There is a party in London desirous of securing for the London branches all the laxity and freedom from restraint enjoyed by local societies . . . Our rules provide for the establishment of a Committee, subject to the supervision of the Executive Council; they desire to constitute themselves as a Council, independent of all control, whose decisions are only to be registered and endorsed by the Executive Council.[117]

By 1877 the Executive had won its point. In that year the disallowance of a United Trade Committee prohibition on piecework was upheld by a majority of the London delegates and complete victory was attained when it became the duty of the secretary of the senior branch to call delegate meetings, take minutes and forward all material relating to the United Trade Committee to the Executive.[118]

Concurrent with the creation of this dependent and subordinate relationship to the Executive, the branches began to complain about the Committee's imperialism. Neither were these two developments unrelated, for coincident with the 1873 rule and name change the Executive asserted the Committee's authority over decisions that had previously rested with the branch.[119] Resistance from the branches to extensions of the Committee's authority was strongly flavoured with the 'traditional' concern for rank and file control but, in a curious twist, they looked to the Executive as the protector of branch autonomy. Thus, the Paddington branch claimed that the purpose and mandate of the United Trade Committee had been perverted:

Elected . . . to act in concert should circumstances arise in trade matters, so as to bring such a movement to a successful issue . . . [it] was never intended to be kept in continual operation . . . when there has been no business whatever but what could and ought to have been done in the branches . . . We . . . recognise only one authority, and that is the Executive Council.[120]

With the withdrawal of the General Union from the Committee in 1878 over the piecework question, it became a sole preserve of the Amalgamated Society so that by 1887 it could be claimed that 'all business ever transacted by that body has been such as only concerned the Amalgamated Society of Carpenters and Joiners.'[121] It is surely this history that explains the Committee's ambiguous relationship to the delegate and aggregate meetings of the 1891 trade movement and it was appropriate that the final absorption of the Committee into the union structure should follow the demise of the last movement where traditional elements played an important role and be coincident with the full recognition of unions as bargaining agents for the men. In 1892 all the pretence that it was a trade committee was abandoned and its name changed to the London Management Committee of the ASC&J.[122]

At the same time similar institutions were created in other unions, although whether they derived from analogous rank and file roots is not clear. The Metropolitan Central Strike Committee of the OBS, for example, grew out of a committee elected from the branches in 1890 to draw up a code of rules and its initial responsibility was to organise for a wage increase and hours reduction. The Central Committee conducted negotiations with the CAMB in 1892 and assumed a wide freedom in its consent to a postponement of its wages and hours demand which led to a stormy attempt by the rank and file to assert their authority. At a meeting in Hyde Park, 'the most disorderly scenes were witnessed' when the General Secretary (who had been a member of the negotiating team) and the secretary of the Central Committee were 'shouted down, abused and vilified.' When an agreement was finally reached with the employers, the Executive affirmed the Central Committee's authority over branch autonomy with an order that all questions on wages and hours must be referred to the Committee: 'This order practically suspended the Branch Committees . . . as far as working rules and wages were concerned, and therefore nearly the whole of the work of these Committees devolved upon us.' Enforcement of the settlement lay firmly in the hands of the Central Committee and, although there were twelve strikes undertaken without its permission, these paled in comparison to the six hundred visits the Committee paid to the various sites and jobs.[123]

Contemporaneously with the erection of these kinds of internal structures of power and authority a parallel set of intra-union structures was being created to provide a firmer basis for official union cooperation. Two such institutions require our attention – the London Building Trades Federation [LBTF] and the London Building Industries Federation

[LBIF]. Both these organisations are sometimes taken to represent a rank and file force intended to transcend sectionalism and stand in opposition to official unionism.[124] In fact, as the origins and officials of both organisations show, they were bastions of official union power which served as local adjuncts to central union authority.

The LBTF arose from a 'feeling . . . among the leaders of all the unions in London that something more was necessary' than the London United Building Trades Committee that had been formed in the late 1880s to press for trade union conditions in government contract work. The Federation was governed by delegates appointed by the various unions and George Dew, an organiser for the Amalgamated Society, was its Secretary – a role he had also performed for the United Building Trades Committee and, before that, for the United Trade Committee. The LBIF emerged from similar circumstances and Dew again served as Secretary accompanied by Stennett who in addition to his work as Chairman was the District Secretary of the London ASC&J.[125] Attempts to coordinate official union activity inevitably brought these organisations to assert a control over rank and file activity and we have already had occasion to note the efforts of the LBTF in this direction. In its attempts to exert its authority over the non-union issue, the Federation represented yet another device to channel power and responsibility into the official structures of trade unionism. It was, therefore, no coincidence that its career came to an abrupt end when conciliation structures that could better perform the same function were implanted for most of the trades in 1896. Similarly, the Federation as an instrument of the large unions was revealed in its attitude to sectionalism – which, in reality, it did very little to overcome. Thus, because of the hostility of the OBS, the small slaters' union was refused affiliation and the East End painters were advised to 'amalgamate with . . . one or other of the larger Unions at present in existence.' And the LBIF not only prohibited sympathetic strikes but constantly showed itself hostile to the syndicalist desire for one big building union.[126]

The stance adopted by the LBIF during the course of the 1914 lockout revealed its true nature and purpose, its subordination to official union authority, and its distance from the policy aspirations of the rank and file. In March, it proposed a settlement which contained punitive clauses for the trade unions to enact against their members similar to those found in the Shipbuilding Trades Agreement; in April, it committed the unions to secure adherence to the agreements ' "to the utmost of [their] . . . disciplinary power," ' and agreed to the cessation of its site ticket inspections upon employer request.[127] Once the national executives adopted the leading role in negotiations, the Federation loyally followed in their wake. It ignored pressure from the rank and file to live up to its claims to be the sole negotiating agent of the London building workers and endorsed the settlement reached by the national officers. Following the rejection of this third set of proposals, the Federation betrayed its own rhetoric about unity and sanctioned its own break up by resolving that each trade arrange individual settlements.[128] And, finally, as befitted an 'official' body, the Federation consistently refused to subject itself to rank and file control or to heed their resolutions on negotiating positions. It continued to accept the no-disability clause in spite of the clear evidence that this was a major cause of rank and file dissatisfaction; it refused to recall a delegate meeting that had been adjourned in February; it denied a request to convene a delegate conference to lay down policy for the conduct of the strike; and it declined to allow representation from the rank and file district lockout committees.[129] There is every reason, therefore, to believe the accuracy of Jack Wills' characterisation of Federation policy: 'Although the dispute has been in progress three weeks, the rank and file have not been taken into the confidence of the leaders and the conduct and policy of the dispute has been entirely in the hands of the officials of the Federation.'[130]

We may view the significance of the 1914 conflict from several different angles. From one perspective, it revealed with frightening clarity the ruined authority of the official power structures; their thrice-made recommendations to return to work were ignored, their negotiations rendered meaningless; of necessity, their meetings were frequently held in secret. But that side of the story – the explosion of tension between officialdom and the rank and file – we leave until the next chapter. From a more immediately relevant – and by no means contradictory – perspective, the events of 1914 also showed the durable reserves of energy available to the various structures of union authority and power. If it was true that the men could not be forced back to work, it was equally true that they could be denied any possibility of victory. Crudely put, if the officials chose to negotiate on terms which the rank and file rejected (and such was the case) then the likelihood was that it was merely a matter of time before the strike be settled on terms defined by the negotiators. Only the official structures possessed the recognised right to bargain and negotiate, and however disdainfully out of touch with the rank and file they showed themselves to be there were no easy avenues through which rank and file change could be directed. Apart from the local strike committees, who had no role in the negotiations, there were no structures to ensure rank and file input to discussions that were conducted in the rarefied atmosphere of the National Conciliation Board. Rank and file sanction of the legitimacy and power of the official structures rested upon the slender thread of acceptance or rejection at the ballot box and there was a limit to the number of repudiations that could be voted. By the third ballot of June 10, it was apparent that the constant presentation of virtually the same terms of settlement was beginning to whittle rank and file resistance away. Ultimately, there were few alternatives open for the rank and file but to accept official unionism's authority and legitimacy. Only in July and August (seven months after the conflict had begun) were plans set afoot to create a syndicalist-inspired union. But even in the steamy summer of 1914, the success of such a venture would have been problematical. Thus, whilst at one level 1914 exposed the failure of those authority structures that had grown out of the systematisation of industrial relations, it, paradoxically, also revealed their monolithic, granite-like indispensability. Fuelled by their role within the system of industrial relations, they generated a power unto themselves and they could run a certain and long distance without having to heed the rank and file. There were, of course, limits to the space they could so travel; limits that were not (and are not) subject to precise measurement but which may have been on the horizon in 1914. As historians, however, our interest lies not only in this expression of a familiar and eternal dilemma for trade unionism but primarily in the circumstances that entailed this perilous journey.

7

Anatomy of crisis: the rank and file and the system

For reasons that are not hard to seek, George Dangerfield's imaginative reconstruction of the divisive forces that were loose in pre-First World War Britain has never been improved upon.[1] Dangerfield recognised, even if he didn't fully explain, how the tensions of the period reflected a struggle for dominance between contesting values, systems and structures of authority. The various 'revolts' of those years were not meaningless and inchoate reactions to hot summers or worlds that were in danger of being lost, but fierce and violent debates about what kind of society Britain was to be and how and by what principles she was to be governed. The House of Commons was not treated to the spectacle of Herbert Henry Asquith's tears because Liberal conceptions of decency or gentlemanly behaviour (never really a feature of the British upper classes) had been abandoned, but because he realised that the forces opposing his conception of how society should be re-ordered were powerful enough to selectively block and deny their realisation. The behaviour of the House of Lords was not simply that of a puppet in the hands of Mr Balfour nor was it a new and more exciting fox-hunting course for the 'backwoodsmen' but a real field of action where one set of theories about society met in head-on collision with another. Workers did not turn sullenly unresponsive to their leaders or to Sir George Askwith's endless patience simply to protest their falling real wages, nor to express a mindless militancy of incomprehensible dimensions but because they knew what they wanted and weren't getting it. These issues and 'revolts' were all but different versions, at different loci of tension, of the same conundrum of whose authority and which principles were to govern. Far from being the 'concidental' aggregate that has been suggested, they were all linked together to create not just the *sense* of 'an impending clash' but the *reality* of a society in crisis.[2]

This was a crisis of authority of far greater dimensions and far more uncertain potential than the crisis which ended the age of equipoise and some of the reasons why this was so will become apparent throughout the course of this present chapter. But it was due, in part, to the overriding presence of very deep and serious intra-class divisions that continually threatened to break into open warfare. The political divisions and the women's revolt were, at bottom, squabbles of varying intensity and moment within the dominant class (which is not to belittle their importance) who seemed incapable of devising a new consensus for their resolution.[3] It was true, also, that the labour unrest was largely an internal phenomenon and, like the other revolts, was conditioned by deep forces of fragmentation within the economic and social structure whose roots traced back to the 1890s.[4] What made the revolt of labour more serious than the rest, however, were not the local demarcation disputes that had been a permanent feature of working-class industrial life since the 1890s, but the fact that alone of all the classes the working class possessed a greater sense of class isolation and solidarity that pronounced their revolt to be the most insolvable of all. For if it was true that certain aspects of working-class culture and politics in the period from the nineties manifested an 'enclosed and defensive conservatism,' it was equally true that the alienation and separation so induced were the breeding grounds for revolt.[5] And, in syndicalism, the revolt of labour was unique in the possession of a militant, forward-looking ideology of change.

Aside from Dangerfield, interpretations and explanations of the labour unrest fall into basically three categories. First, there are those who apply a crudely reductionist framework of inter-generational tensions and economic trends. Thus, Phelps Brown relegated rank and file militancy to some variant of youthful indiscretion – an argument which if applied to the House of Lords would presumably attribute their rejection of the budget to gerontocratic senility. The Cambrian Coal Dispute, for example, revealed nothing more amongst 'the younger men [than], a blazing anger, a bitter determination to enforce new claims'; the seriousness of the unrest derived from the mysterious fact that 'something had come over people: they were divided into irreconcilable camps.' Underlying all this and giving it force was the check to real wages that had occurred from 1909.[6] Henry Pelling is somewhat more sophisticated in his argument. But he, too, denies that there was anything more to the unrest than a responsive reaction to enhanced bargaining power caused by a decline in unemployment with the further implication that the militancy of this period was comparable to that found at similar periods of mass unionisation in the seventies and eighties. The greatest blunder of these kinds of interpretations is that they fail seriously to confront the uniqueness and the content of the militancy of the period and assume the sufficiency of a bluntly inadequate economic and mechanistic explanation that would shame the most vulgar of Marxists. Never eager, it would seem, seriously to face the possibility of something more than a conservatively contented working class, syndicalist support is counted, found wanting and thus dismissed as being of no importance at all.[7]

Yet it is clear that 'the mood [of the times] was one that needs to be

explained by more than reference to a loss of spending power on the part
of the working class as a whole, or to a heightened political militancy on
the part of a few spokesmen.'[8] And this brings us to that interpretation of
the unrest which would see it as a puzzled and contradictory response to
the rapidly changing structures of life and behaviour which:

> Threw men and women back upon tradition for psychological shelter, while at the
> same time forcing them to discard the very habits of mind and action they needed
> to sustain themselves. Confused by the challenge to traditions . . . working-class
> men and women were not at all sure what to do. Some contented themselves with
> doing little or nothing. Those who did something, did many apparently contra-
> dictory things at once.[9]

The problem with this elegantly argued thesis is to throw *us* back to
Dangerfield in the sense that it, too, views the militancy as the product of
a society in motion whose destiny seemed uncertain because its passengers
could neither control nor comprehend its direction. Furthermore, like the
economic interpretations, it impedes any understanding of the unrest
beyond a single – and unacceptable – category of psychological confusion.
In fact, if we focus purely upon the phenomenon of working class militancy, the internal evidence of discussions in union journals about conciliation, amalgamation, executive despotism and the like make it very
difficult to accept an analysis that posits bewilderment as a fundamental
attribute of working-class society. If we take a document like *The Miners'
Next Step* as an example of the expression of that militancy, it is the
articulate precision, the commanding ideological grasp that must impress
itself upon us.[10] In terms of its comprehensive range, *The Miners' Next
Step* is, perhaps, an extreme example but the aims and purposes which it
addressed were anything other than unique in the trade union world of
the day. Indeed, I would go further, and assert that an argument could
be made that working-class consciousness – political, economic and
social – attains a clarity of comprehension and understanding during
these years that it had not possessed since the days of Chartism.

   For if the conservative hold of tradition lay at the heart of the unrest,
if the unrest was simply a catalytic reaction between modern change and
working-class conservatism and passivity, then we are hard put to explain
even the presence of syndicalism. Historically, the clash between 'modern'
and 'pre-modern' strata of experience produces ideologies that are
genuinely backward-looking which syndicalism clearly was not. What is
more crucially debilitating about this thesis, however, is that if the working-class past is regarded as a static force – as a psychological crutch upon
which a crippled working class lent for support while the disturbing
modern world swept by – then the possibility is implicitly closed off that
the unrest possessed specific historical roots within an on-going historical
continuum. To the extent, then, that this kind of approach to the problem

fails to reconcile countervailing facts and tendencies, it has not moved us beyond the weak conceptualisations that characterised the Dangerfield thesis. For although Dangerfield was correct to link the labour unrest to the other revolts of the period and although he has a great deal of value to say about the period as a whole, in the end the revolt of labour, like that of the women and politicians, is a response to the ethereal and spiritual 'strange death' of Liberal values. In fact, there was nothing very strange about the revolt of labour if it is seen as a response to the corporatist society that was being erected.[11] Which brings us to the third and most useful of the interpretations of the unrest.

In a significant recent book on British syndicalism, Bob Holton has drawn attention to the importance from the 1890s of the increasingly oligarchic composition of a capitalism more concerned and better able than ever before to manipulate and control the labour force, the related changes in technology which in some areas undermined bargaining power and led to the search for new ways to assert that power, and the increasingly corporatist social welfare policies of the state which aimed only incidentally at a better life for the working class and primarily at diffusing and containing labour militancy.[12] This general view – to which must then be added specific, local factors – was, of course, anticipated many years ago by G. D. H. Cole and, to a lesser extent, by Carter Goodrich. Cole, for example, quite clearly recognised that the self-conscious meaning of labour militancy was that it challenged the very assumptions upon which authority and legitimacy in industry rested:

It is the first awakening [he wrote] of a new and positive demand, of a nascent philosophy which needs formulation and interpretation. Behind the new industrialism is the germ of the demand for the real control of industry by the workers, for an 'Industrial Democracy' that shall mean not merely Trade Union management, but the real superintendence of industrial processes and conditions.[13]

But it is ironic that the major failing of all the historiography of the subject began with Cole and Goodrich. For whilst both made convincing analyses of the content of the militancy, neither seemed fully to appreciate the historical process of which it was a part. Carter Goodrich, perhaps, came the closest to this appreciation but his otherwise excellent account is marred by an excessive present mindedness which relegated the earlier struggles for work control to the 'negative' realm of defensive craft custom. Cole, too, cannot have been totally unaware of the historical dimensions of the phenomenon but when he rightly perceived the non-union question as the most notable sign of the syndicalist spirit, he seems to have regarded this as a new development and failed to enquire into those earlier historical periods when this issue had attained a comparable prominence.[14] In a similar manner, he recognised the importance of the challenge to discipline and management that marked the unrest but regarded this as something new, about which there had been no earlier ambiguity and which 'had till quite recently been supposed, by masters and men alike, to be spheres in which the employers' authority was unquestioned.'[15] More by way of qualification than criticism, the same general point may also be applied to Holton whose central purpose – which he completely vindicates – is to free us from the conventional and sterile view that syndicalism was neither indigenously a part of, nor significant to, the British working-class experience. But because his primary focus is on the years immediately preceding the war and because his reference to earlier years is only to trace the growth of syndicalist organisation he, too, does less than justice to the historical process that allowed the labour unrest to emerge in the form that it did.

But this criticism is especially pertinent to those theories that search for meaning in the 'malaise' of society or the stranglehold of tradition upon the working class. For they involve an abstraction of the unrest from its historical roots and imply that the conservative drag of tradition impeded an adaptation to the needs of the time. In fact, the key to understanding the unique character of the unrest lay in the perfect symbiosis it represented between past and present. It was from the interaction between the challenges of the present and the traditions of the past that the labour militancy emerged; it was precisely because the past infused the present that the labour unrest gained its particularly threatening and purposeful force. Tradition in no way bred confusion about contemporary developments but was, rather, a central and vital ingredient to understanding and grappling with new realities. Only on the basis of their particular histories of work control struggle could those militant segments of the working class (and, as Holton has shown, they covered the whole spectrum of industrial experience) actually make their journey. There was nothing new about the issues that formed the core of militancy's attention and anger; all were to be found in some form or another at earlier periods. What was new were the impediments to the realisation and articulation of those issues – impediments which included the trade unions, economist collective bargaining and, ultimately, the corporatist social welfare state. Their presence lifted the old, 'traditional' struggle to a new level of experience, transformed it from a struggle at the workplace to one which finally had to confront national structures and institutions. This was why the militancy was unique, why it cannot be patronisingly dismissed as just another stage of simple union militancy, why its significance cannot be gauged by the measurement of statistical indices of any sort.

The labour militancy grew out of the historical struggle for work control; it was that same struggle writ larger than before because the obstacles it had to confront were more immense than those of previous days. The national perspectives of industrial relations inevitably lifted the contest out of isolated local foci into the realm of the nation as a whole. In its industrial setting, then, tradition fused with, informed and heightened a militancy that was stimulated by the contemporary context. But in order more properly to understand the dynamic that created the labour unrest, it is necessary to locate it precisely within those structures that formed the reality of the contemporary world and the transforming links between past and present. And it is here that the themes of corporatism are of most interpretive use, for they enable us to comprehend the central benchmark of this period's militancy which was to be in revolt against the very institutions and procedures that represented the Labour Movement's achievement. From the growing disillusionment with Labour Party policies to the commonplace rejection of officially negotiated industrial agreements, all sections of the Labour Movement experienced some variant of this problem. Nor was this alienation simply a function of natural divergence inherent to the collective organisation of diverse and competing groups and strategies. What raised it above those kinds of mundanely simple precepts was the depth of its intensity – as manifested by the ideological presence of syndicalism – and its contribution to, and coincidence with, the wider and general crisis in British society. The revolt of labour was a revolt against the institutions and tactics that worked for the incorporation of labour into society and although that must not be taken to imply a continuously high level of self-conscious action, it is only within that general analytical framework that we can make any real sense of the phenomenon. In the industrial sphere, it was the first time a crisis of capitalism had been accompanied with a demonstration of the modern dilemma of collective bargaining systems: that is, the inherent contradiction between their labour management function and their inability to address the central issues that created the need for that function. Sooner or later, the economist articulation of worker aspirations and the economist focus of industrial relations systems run into the basic reality that industrial struggle is a struggle for control and authority at work; the strain that results between the image and the reality cannot forever be contained and ultimately threatens to reveal the illusion for what it really is. It was this point of consciousness that had been reached in the labour unrest.

THE STRUCTURE OF MILITANCY

The basis of labour militancy lay in the fact that, for a variety of conjunctural reasons, this period saw a climacteric collision between the disciplinary impulses of the industrial relations system and work control. Richard Hyman has explained the essence of the problem in terms which precisely describe the process at work in Edwardian England:

The ordinary employee, perpetually subject to the oppressive and exploitative relations of capitalist wage-labour is always liable to overturn some aspect of existing 'industrial legality.' The union's function is to 'keep the faith' . . . It is precisely at the point when existing structures of capitalist domination are under pressure, when the frontier of control is being forced forward, that the potentially conservative role of trade unionism, as the defender of industrial legality, is a most serious danger.[16]

An exhaustive study of this relationship in American steel and auto industries has conclusively shown how a piecemeal and successive rollback of work control gains that had been achieved in the early years of mass unionisation was a consequence of the creation of collective bargaining systems. Paralleling this decline of labour power over managerial rights and prerogatives was the enhanced status and influence of union leadership. Such developments as the replacement of strike enforcement with conciliation and arbitration rendered the rank and file increasingly dependent upon the union leadership; worker devices to restrict managerial decisions were rolled back with union participation. A division of responsibility assigned to the unions the job of problem solving whose function was not to challenge managerial authority but to ensure the smooth working of industry.[17]

We have already noted that, from the 1890s, a similar process was at work in Britain – this, after all, was the equivalent historical period to the late 1930s and early 1940s in US labour relations. But a direct parallel from that period might be useful to illustrate the kinds of frustrations that must eventually find an outlet. Once the boilermakers became enmeshed in a collective bargaining structure, there was a progressive negotiating away of apprenticeship restrictions. After some hard bargaining caused by the employers' desire for a removal of all limitations, the 1894 agreement set the apprentice–journeyman ratio at 1:4 in return for a union commitment not to enrol apprentices until their fourth year. And in 1901, for reasons that will remain obscure until the union opens its records, the leadership accepted the removal of this restriction. This may have been a wise or unwise decision, but its main interest lies in the way in which the agreement was bludgeoned through the union. On the first vote, the membership rejected the agreement but the union ordered a new referendum on the spurious grounds that too few votes had been cast. Only 3300 more votes were cast on this second ballot but the result was what the leadership desired and no more trips to the polling booth were necessary. Like the pattern noted by Richard Herding amongst the American unions and as with the collective agreements we discussed earlier this agreement weakened the workers' power whilst elevating that of the union. It was explained that 'it is not their [employers] intention to overstock the yards with Apprentices, and if the Boilermakers' Society finds it necessary to prefer a complaint respecting the number, this must be done through the Secretaries of the [union and] . . . the Shipbuilding Employers' Federation.'[18]

Even as it grew, then, the industrial relations systems were creating the conditions and spawning the unrest that was to detonate with such ferocity from 1909. The dispersion of legitimate power and authority away from the workplace and into the body of the corporate structures of the system created a vacuum into which 'shop systems of domination and resistance . . . [develop] in their own right.' These 'informal' groupings, characteristic of all collective bargaining systems, focus around work control issues, pose 'a continuous and growing challenge to managerial authority, and a source of industrial unrest' that explodes as violently against the unions as it does against management.[19] It was just this process that was involved in the growth of 'formal' workshop organisations in Britain from the 1890s: that is, from the moment that the contradiction emerged between union-oriented economist collective bargaining and the continuing reality of workplace struggles for authority.[20] Drawing upon the firmly established historical tradition of work group solidarity, it was during the 1890s that this tradition was obliged to express itself in formal organisation precisely because it was denied a recognised and authoritative position within the union or industrial relations structures.

The growing prominence of the shop steward was one manifestation of this development. Although the office had existed for many years before, it was only at this point that it added to its other duties the role of representative of rank and file interests against those of the official structures.[21] In building, where they were known to the rule books as early as the 1840s, we may see the first glimmerings of their modern role during the masons' strike of 1877–78, but formal rank and file organisation does not seem to have begun until 1911 with the creation of a syndicalist Consolidation Committee whose main support derived from the London bricklayers.[22] Unlike the engineering stewards, who were integrated into the union structure in 1917, those in building have only recently attained official recognition.[23] In shipbuilding, the boilermakers' district delegates were inhibited by their subordination to the Executive to ever develop into rank and file leaders. But the very nature of their work had accustomed platers and riveters to work group organisation and coincident with the growth of executive power in the early eighties complaints began to be heard about 'inner circles' who 'meet in the yard and decree what shall be the price paid on certain jobs, which has been in some cases exorbitant.' By the early 1900s, these 'platers' socials' became formalised into Vigilance Committees about which one would like to know more. On the Clyde, for example, the local Vigilance Committee was reported to have 'abused' officials, distributed circulars, survived the amazing smears levelled at it in the Monthly Reports, and successfully defied executive attempts to secure its dissolution.[24]

This flurry of rank and file organisation extending throughout industry was of great significance in understanding the historical dynamics of the labour unrest. It represented that synthesis of past and present which gave the militancy its portentous force; for these organisational efforts signified a challenge to the established authority systems that was based upon an older tradition of work group activity which aimed to exert a control over the productive process. Like the wider, less organised militancy of which they were a part, formal rank and file organisation came into being at the point where the 'traditional' aspirations of the workforce were being denied or restrained by the system. And it was precisely here that the relevance of the past infused the present with a revolutionary force because, in the contemporary context, those traditional aims could not be achieved without an alteration and re-arrangement of the whole structures of industrial relations and – potentially – those of the whole social system. The case of the Durham miners' opposition to the eight hour day can be seen to illustrate the point. Like the non-union issue in building, resistance to the three-shift implications of an eight hour day had a long tradition behind it whose rationale was based upon its threatened disruption of the miners' ability to control safety conditions, wage levels and division of time between home and work. But the traditional nature of the issue spoke only to the eternity of the tussle for authority in the pits and the influence that transformed the question from its 'traditional' context to one that led to an attack upon the authority structures of the union was the workings of collective bargaining itself. As with the Shipbuilding Trades Agreement of the same year, negotiations were carried out in secret; when the agreement was published it was found that the Executive had reversed its previous policy without seeking any mandate from the rank and file and had accepted the eight hour day. These inescapable features of 'responsible' union negotiation combined with the face workers' traditional resistance to any weakening of their ability to control working conditions and led ineluctably to a rank and file revolt against the Executive and the union itself.[25]

Like most such revolts, this one failed. But that is decidedly beside the point; its importance lies in the disclosure that it was exactly the interaction of the past upon the present that permitted militancy to move beyond the limited aims of opposing this or that wage settlement or conciliation decision towards an attack upon the whole system that made those decisions. The hostility to conciliation, the concern with non-union men, the rejection of executive authority were not isolated, discrete outbursts of an inchoate, dispersed militancy. All were integrally related, and seen to be related, as different parts of the same problem: how were the rank and file to re-assert their control and authority over decision making at the point of production (as over the labour supply) or at the point of the bargaining procedures (as in the conciliation boards)?

It was, of course, precisely because of the nature of this dynamic that syndicalism attained a relevance and importance far transcending any judgements to be made by the counting of heads. G. D. H. Cole got it exactly right when he wrote that:

Of real syndicalism there is in England practically none; of an impulse which, unless we consent to the inaccuracy, we must leave nameless, there is a great deal, and it is so important to emphasise the unity that we do not for a moment boggle at the perversion . . . There is a unity to be disentangled, if we do not exact too great definiteness or too much self-consciousness.[26]

That self-consciousness was to be found at many different levels of appreciation. It would be foolish to expect an articulate formulation of consciousness in every dispute or at every moment when its essentials were present and neither would any test of this sort provide the slightest insight into the quality of labour militancy. But it was the implicit presence of this consciousness that composed the ominous and intangible element to industrial disputes that men like Sir George Askwith struggled to grasp, the better to tame.[27] *The Miners' Next Step* obviously represents a very advanced point in the scale of articulate consciousness but that document is critical to any appreciation of the relevance of syndicalism to the militancy, for it was a clear enunciation of the direction in which many workers were already marching. In its proposals for a democratisation of union structures, it expressed the realisation that the struggle for control over work could now be achieved only by a total rearrangement of authority relationships within the system.[28] Through conciliation the system not only slowed a full harvesting of the fruits of collective bargaining potential, it also ensured that any resolution of issues was achieved by procedures that effectively denied the rank and file a decisive authority over the institutions of their own power – i.e. the union bureaucracies. Syndicalism directly addressed this structural dilemma. In much the same way that Owenism had provided an ideological mediation between the struggle for work control as it faced the new system of general contracting, so syndicalism provided the same role for that same struggle in its modern context. Like Owenism, it enabled that struggle to widen its focus, to envisage a control that went beyond the local efforts of the 1860s to threaten the stability of the industry itself. And just as the struggles of the 1830s were infused with an Owenite 'spirit,' it is for this reason that the unrest before the First World War breathed with the temper of syndicalism.

If it is clear that the labour unrest marked the climax to the historical contradiction inherent in the systems governing industrial relations, the moment of the climacteric – 1910–14 – was the product of the conjuncture of these broad contradictions with specific and transient economic conditions. Indeed, in themselves, these local forces revealed the failure of collective bargaining's inability to deliver to the workers the full rewards of their enhanced workplace power. Whether consciously acted upon or not, the failure of money wages to keep pace with the cost of living could not be ignored or unrecognised by workers – especially when it was combined with the dramatic decline in unemployment rates from 1909.[29] This decline signified a revival – in building, at least – of the opportunity for an expansion of the men's sphere of work control. The 1911 London working rules negotiations reflected the renewed pressure from the men to exert a control over the work: they were the first attempted revision since 1906 and were characterised by efforts to restrict overtime, worked stone, piecework and to abandon the conciliation rule.[30] On a national scale, the masons' rules resembled those of the 1860s and 1890s with the reappearance of restrictions – often in a solely 'economist' guise, however – on apprenticeship, piecework, sheds, walking time and overtime.[31] But this revival in worker power was now forced to confront fully the restraints of the system: it was significant that in 1913, when unemployment was at its lowest point for years, over 80% of disputes in building were resolved by compromise and, as the events of 1914 in London were to show, the system could not grant the most fundamental demands of the workers. Militancy grew and developed from those points where the restraints of the system of industrial relations met the attempts to realise the potential work control power contained in the basically favourable economic circumstances. In building (and the industry was not peculiar in this respect), there were two areas in particular where this dichotomy was sharply revealed – in the continuing struggle over the non-union issue and in the growing recognition of the adverse results of conciliation procedures. Together these issues formed the most significant components of the labour unrest in the industry.

THE CONTENT OF MILITANCY

Efforts to assert rank and file control over the labour supply were common to those periods when the men's sphere of authority was being extended. We have seen how in the 1860s, for example, this issue was the most important cause of masons' strikes and how in the 1890s it was central to the creation of an industrial relations system in London. Its prominence in the period leading up to the First World War did not necessarily signify a new kind of work group hostility to non-unionists – we have already noted the ambiguities of that question – but more a chafing against the removal of this issue out of the hands of the rank and file into the conciliation structures. Furthermore, it was one of the remaining issues where the men could most reasonably demonstrate their militancy; resistance to attempts to expand their membership base merely served to reveal the contradiction in which the unions were placed by their role within the industrial relations system.

In London, the existence of a non-union sector was formally recognised in the working rules. Elsewhere the rules were seldom that precise, but the matter was a national issue. Clause seventeen of the National Conciliation Board rules allowed any subject to be discussed at the request of one of the parties and attempts by the unions to get the non-union issue exempt from this provision were adamantly resisted by the employers.[32] But it was in London – where the structures were the most highly restrictive on this question – that the main tension of the issue was focussed. From the very inception of the rule in 1896, there had been rank and file resistance to its provisions and in 1905 the carpenters and masons attempted unsuccessfully to remove the issue completely from the authority of the conciliation board. Indeed, a new rule of that year which committed the unions to discountenance any strike against non-union men was extended from the bricklayers (to whom it had previously solely applied) to all the trades.[33] By 1912 and 1913, the rule was the central impediment to the smooth operation of the city's industrial relations system. Rank and file pressure was strong enough in 1912 for the carpenters' leaders to propose – somewhat half-heartedly – a repeal of this aspect of the conciliation rule. Its maintenance in the rules of 1913 occasioned a large strike of plasterers in May and caused the bricklayers to reject the working agreement.[34] Resistance to the no-disability clause was one of those issues that allowed the militancy to move beyond a single issue eventually to confront the principles upon which the industrial relations system was based. The rule was frequently cited as one of the ways in which trade unionism had been 'disarmed' by conciliation.[35] Because the question had been placed under the authority of the conciliation boards, rejection of the clause itself led directly into a consideration of the role and functions of conciliation procedures and rules and the part played by the unions within them.

Although there are no numerical indices of the extent of hostility to conciliation, it is very evident that from 1909 those who advocated withdrawal from the procedures set the terms of the debate. Indeed, 'debate' is too strong a term: apart from the occasional executive defence of the schemes (usually on the grounds that they prevented sharp reductions of wages) the paucity of support for conciliation is striking.[36] But it is also important to note that the demands for withdrawal usually referred specifically to participation in the national scheme; attitudes towards the local structures were more ambivalent. There were those who stated bluntly that 'conciliation and arbitration boards are formed for the purpose of fixing the degree of robbery between a parasite class and a working class,' and who hoped that soon 'we shall be enabled to place our just demands before employers without these time-serving devices.'[37] Such sentiments presumably derived from committed syndicalists; but whether those who wished to withdraw from the national scheme would have maintained the local structures is not clear – the experience of London and other evidence suggests that they would not. In any case, this was never a viable option; a return to a local system implied a different set of union structures and authority relationships. And, ultimately, it was this that comprised the significance and meaning of the hostility towards conciliation boards. Complaints about the system could not merely rest on one narrow cause – that it was slow in making awards, or that its decisions were too frequently adverse.[38] The situation was now too complex for those kinds of set-backs to be seen in an isolation that was, perhaps, possible when conciliation was purely locally based. The national system committed the unions to enforce both the no-strike rule and the final settlement; it contained an inbuilt bias against any one group of men through the cross voting in the National Board by trades not involved in a particular case. It was, therefore, impossible for hostility to focus on the specific problems of non-unionism or conciliation without branching out to a wider offensive against all the authority structures of the system.[39]

The case of the Hull masons affords a pertinent illustration of this tendency. In 1911 they wished to withdraw from the Northern Centre Board not only because of the delay involved in settling disputes, but also because their delegates had voted against the unanimous wish of the lodge on the question of worked stone. The delegates were, of course, acting as responsible leaders were supposed to act and they could expect to receive the support of their Executive. But what this did was to force the Hull masons to address both the perversity of the Board and the authority relationships within their union that could allow such a state of affairs. Even more telling was the experience of the Derby lodge which in September 1913 mounted a campaign to take the Society out of the national scheme because of the restraints it imposed on freedom of action. Opposition from the Executive to this proposal was immediately forthcoming: the only amendment was one moved from the headquarters lodge and articles were written by Organisers attacking the Derby proposals. From this point things seem to have gone from bad to worse. In late 1913, the Derby lodges repudiated conciliation procedures and were censured for their irresponsibility by their district organiser. They replied in kind, pointing out that they were not syndicalists but had been denied support from officials in their struggle against an attempt to make the working rules binding until May 1915: 'From start to finish he [the organiser] but put the case for the masters and tried to bring about a settlement at any price.' The Lodge had, therefore, been forced to confront an executive and bureaucratic authority that was repressively heedless of the wishes of the rank and file. Ultimately, the wielding of such authority could only serve to radicalise the men and, in a microcosmic image of the process that must have been repeated thousands of times to compose the militancy of the period, the Derby masons were eventually driven to the syndicalist conclusion that brought them into a full opposition to the whole system: 'A fighting trade union never dies, a peaceful one . . . goes to sleep and its members forget what trade-unionism is . . . A peaceful decision in a dispute may appear to save money, but . . . you will find that members run out of it easier, whereas a hard fought fight . . . stiffens the backs of the workers.'[40] The lesson must have been all the more imposing because the men finally won the battle against the combined forces of the employers and the union.

It was inevitable, therefore, that conciliation should not remain the only target of hostility. Entrapped by conciliation and no-strike clauses, with their unions as the under-keepers, the men were led to focus their particular attention upon the roles and actions of their unions and executives. The carpenters and joiners (whose hostility to conciliation was, perhaps, the strongest of all the building trades) had reached a clear appreciation of this relationship by 1911. The point was made in one resolution that: 'Our Society, being founded on democratic principles, it should be ruled and governed by the members as a whole, and not be a few who are self-appointed, such as our representatives on the National Board are at present.'[41] But letters and resolutions were of little avail against the arrogance of power in the Amalgamated Society. In 1912, it was reported – and not denied – that the union had participated in changes in the conciliation procedures that violated union rules and that although this was recognised by the Executive there had been no thought of consulting the membership. In 1913, the union went even further when its General Council ordered the Executive not to grant trade benefits until all conciliation procedures had been worked through and elevated any conciliation decision into the status of an executive order.[42]

The constant reminders that the rank and file were barren of legitimate authority and power occasioned a dialectical response that issued in the slogan and practice of 'direct action.' Standing in complete opposition to the 'time-serving' devices of the system, direct action expressed the traditional form of industrial action in the industry which aimed at success by the sudden and total paralysis of jobs. But direct action was more than just the translation of traditional methods into syndicalist prose; it couched in a modern guise the continuing relevance of autonomous regulation and negotiation by imposition to the conditions in which the men found themselves. Given the presence of no-strike clauses, procrastinating conciliation procedures, immovable and unresponsive industrial relations structures, autonomous regulation was, in fact, the only viable alternative open to the men. An assertion of autonomous regulation, however, now implied something more than it had done in earlier days, for it involved confronting the union as well as the employer. In its claims for a share in the control of the productive process, autonomous regulation had always contained a radical, incipiently revolutionary, core which the contemporary escalation in the price of conflict allowed to become extant. Its revival in the form of direct action represented the impact of the present to politicise and radicalise tradition and, conversely, the adaptation of the tradition to fit modern circumstances. Syndicalism was the vocabulary which translated autonomous regulation from a limited expression of resistance to managerial authority to a radical challenge to the whole gamut of established authority. Thus, it was possible for an article on the delays and failures of the conciliation boards to end by asserting that: 'By direct action we can bring pressure to bear upon the capitalist class without the aid of intermediaries of any description . . . working in concert we can bring about the expropriation of the capitalist class.'[43]

It was inconceivable that the unions should respond favourably to this kind of pressure. If, in many ways, the story of official union behaviour during these years seemed to run directly counter to the interests and wishes of the men, this was not because officialdom was cynically selling out their rank and file but because they responded to the different imperatives demanded by the role and responsibilities prescribed for unionism within the system of collective bargaining. Only 'primitive' unions like the Manchester Operative Bricklayers – who had maintained their 'purity' by side-stepping the gaderene rush to bureaucratic centralisation of power – could complacently regard the demands for more rank and file control, for an end to collaborationism and for a revival of autonomous regulation in a syndicalist mien.[44] From most other unions a different general response could only have been ensured by a different structure of authority relationships along the lines suggested by the South Wales Miners' Unofficial Reform Committee, or the various proposals for an industrial union in building in which executive members would be clearly subordinated to rank and file mandates. As it was, the unions were bound to offer a formidable resistance to any reorganisation that pointed towards a re-assertion of rank and file authority; their legitimacy and authority rested upon the role that they played through precisely those institutions that were under attack.[45]

The ability of the unions to resist rank and file pressure was, of course, as much a reflection of internal power relationships as it was an echo of the numerical strength of rank and file dissatisfaction. But neither did the unions stand entirely alone. In their efforts to meet dissident rank and file pressure, they were generally assisted by the employers – as the London negotiations of 1912 and 1913 which focussed largely around the future of the conciliation boards may be seen to illustrate. Reflecting the increased power of the men, the notices of alterations submitted to the LMBA in March 1912 aimed to make the rules more restrictive than they had been since the 1890s and among those submitted by the carpenters was a demand for the abolition of the conciliation rule. The employers' bargaining response was to offer the inducement of a substantial wage increase but to make it contingent upon a reinstatement of conciliation and the preservation of the unrestrictive nature of the rules. And at the final bargaining session, it was Samuel Stennett (secretary of the London district of the Amalgamated Society) who moved acceptance of the conciliation clause – although he was opposed by at least two of the other members of the men's deputation. This time productivity bargaining paid off; the 1d increase was accepted and, now that the carpenters had settled, precisely the same tactics could be used with the other trades. The masons' delegation accepted the proffered extra penny on the wage in return for the surrender of their proposed worked stone rule.[46] One year later, the same pattern prevailed with the OBS. Like the carpenters, rank and file pressure had forced the union to move reluctantly towards an abandonment of conciliation. At the end of 1912, under pressure from the employers, the chairman of the London district had agreed that the matter should be discussed again by the men and two months later a ballot vote reaffirmed an earlier decision to end conciliation. When negotiations were resumed in March 1913, the employers once again made a generous wage offer in return for maintenance of the conciliation rule and this was eventually accepted by the union.[47] Whilst the precise outlines are not clear, the evidence strongly suggests that rank and file opinion was overruled by the leadership who – even in the union supposedly most disposed towards syndicalism – were clearly determined to keep the conciliation rule intact. Not until the end of 1913 did rank and file pressure force the bricklayers' union to abandon this policy and formally announce their intention to withdraw from the London and National Conciliation Boards. But it is worth noting that even after this vote, and during the course of the 1914 dispute, the OBS continued to participate in the National Board's discussions.[48] A similarly determined loyalty to the conciliation structures may be detected in the NAOP whose members struck for a wage increase and the removal of the no-disability clause in May 1913. Askwith was called in to mediate and a settlement was eventually reached which granted a $\frac{1}{2}$d wage increase and – on the initiative of the union – attempted to improve the efficiency of the conciliation rule by shortening the time in which appeals should be made to the Board. Neither of the men's demands had been met and because they rejected the offer the executive stopped paying strike benefit. Even after a national vote had supported the London rank and file, the union continued to withhold strike money and compounded their injury by denying the legal costs of men arrested for picketing.[49]

Whilst many of the details are unclear, these episodes revealed the gulf that existed between the rank and file and official unionism as a result of the inter-relationship that prevailed between union power and the unions' role and function within the industrial relations system. For the union to bow willingly to rank and file pressure to abandon conciliation and the no-disability rule would be to destroy their usefulness to employers. It would also signify an end to their credibility as agents of collective bargaining. More than this, however, the maintenance of the conciliation and no-disability rules was critical to the preservation of the established union structures themselves and any accession to rank and file demands on those issues would have opened the door to changes within unionism's own systems of internal authority. Trade Unionism was structured around the *quid pro quo* of discipline in return for the right to bargain and any return to a modern form of autonomous regulation (which was the implication of rank and file desires) would require a different kind of union structure. Ultimately, therefore, all these questions were tied together in an endless chain; to open one link would be to unravel all the others.

It was because of these connections that the parallel competition between amalgamation and federation as alternative strategies to achieve a closer organisational unity in the industry was so significant. Amalgamation became a syndicalist code word – to be found in mining and engineering as well as building – for the creation of one Industrial Union where executive power would be at a minimum and rank and file authority supreme. Federation was the 'official' answer to the demands for tighter cooperation and meant the forging of closer institutional links between union bureaucracies by the duplication of the various layers of officialdom. Demands for amalgamation were, in a sense, the logical culmination of rank and file dissatisfaction with the structures and policies of unionism, a token of the seriousness of the rank and file militancy of the period and bespoke the totality of the threat to the whole system of industrial relations. Amalgamation was the organisational counterpart to calls for direct action and the abandonment of conciliation because it connoted the relationship between dismantling both the established procedures of industrial relations and the existing authority structures within unionism. The fierce resistance to schemes for amalgamation from official unionism rested not so much on the feared loss of bureaucratic jobs but more on the fact that a reversal of authority relationships within the unions – a return to the days when rank and file authority was supreme – was an integral part of its nature.

Support for amalgamation resided almost entirely within the rank and file; and, although its historical significance does not depend upon any numerical assessment of the extent of this support, virtually all the evidence suggests that serious opposition came only from the officials.[50] From 1910–11 resolutions favourable to amalgamation recurred with embarrassing frequency in the union journals. A masons' ballot in 1910 had approved the principle of amalgamation but the Executive refused to act upon the issue; in 1912 a committee of the union issued a report calling for an Amalgamated Building Workers Union but it received little notice in the *Journal* and was ignored by the officials.[51] As is well-known, the movement was strong enough to secure official support in the OBS but its tendentious nature was illustrated by the failure of the union to implement amalgamation policies.[52] In the only clear vote on the issue by the whole building trades there was a clear majority in its favour. Official opposition had prevented this vote from being put to the painters' National Amalgamated Society and the General Union of Carpenters but rank and file pressure forced a reversal of that policy. When the leadership of the Amalgamated Society of Carpenters decided to drop the question in mid-1913 they were again forced to re-consider by rank and file protest. and the 1911 Parliamentary Committee resolution of support for industrial unionism was achieved in the face of Executive opposition at a meeting where the officials had lost control to militant rank and file delegates.[53]

It is necessary to insist upon this extensive rank and file support for amalgamation because some historians have tended to downplay its significance and force. Even Postgate, who was by no means unsympathetic, argued that apathy amongst the rank and file was a major factor in the ultimate failure of amalgamation and Pelling has gone one better by virtually denying the movement any importance at all. Thus, on the national ballot of the unions in 1912, Pelling has this to say: 'Only [*sic*] eleven [unions] . . . agreed to hold ballots on the subject; and . . . only one – the Builders' Labourers, who had most to gain – showed a majority in favour which would have been large enough to satisfy the legal requirements of amalgamation.'[54] But it should be recognised that those unions who refused to take ballots did so because the officials did not choose to hold them, that two of them were eventually forced to reverse themselves and that none of the large, important unions were amongst this group. Furthermore, the failure to achieve a two thirds majority is hardly evidence of insignificant support. All the unions who voted recorded a majority in favour of amalgamation, the two thirds requirements was an arbitrary standard imposed by trade union law designed to hamper just this kind of development. Since when did an expression of the general will in a representative democracy demand anything more than a simple majority? The same inadequacies surround 'apathy' as an analytic concept to explain the failure of amalgamation. In the light of the traditionally low levels of participation in trade union ballots, the 36% poll achieved by the 1912 scheme was a more than respectable figure which compared most favourably with the 16% recorded in the Amalgamated Society's vote on the National Conciliation scheme. At what percentage point, we might ask, does apathy transmute itself into enthusiasm? Apathy has never been a notable brake upon union policies if they are perceived by officials as in the union's interest and if amalgamation had been so perceived it would have triumphed, no doubt to be celebrated by future historians as testimony to the wisdom of the union leaderships.

The problem with these kinds of arguments is, on the one hand, their erection of idealistic criteria which when unmet are taken as proof and, on the other, their one-dimensionality. To treat the ballot of 1912 or that of 1913 (which achieved a 22% poll on a revised amalgamation scheme) or to view the movement in isolation from the power realities and leadership policies is to miss the whole point. Militancy did not exist in a neutral environment separate from the reactions of the union power structure and it was this context that determined the course of the movement. Amalgamation could not have been achieved without a re-ordering of the structures of power and authority within unionism and a rearrangement of the industrial relations systems and it was for this reason that the weight of the official structures was ultimately thrown against the movement. The strategy of the leaderships, however, was seldom one of direct confrontation, for there were differences of opinion within the leadership structures themselves – differences which were a factor in the ability of syndicalism to obtain such a strong footing in the OBS and in the passage of the 1911 Parliamentary Committee resolution. But the main trend of leadership was clear: the demand for amalgamation could not be ignored but it could be controlled and countered by alternative proposals for schemes of federation.

Federation had long been an official strategy to reinforce union stability by linking together institutional structures to achieve a greater degree of coordination without surrendering individual authority or interfering with their internal structures of power.[55] Proposals for a closer federal unity had first emerged in the 1870s as a response to the creation of national employers' associations and the initiative which always derived from the leaderships was just as commonly rejected by the rank and file.[56] Federation, therefore, was a tactic that stood to hand to be used against the demand for amalgamation before 1914 and its significance in these years lay not in its role as a half-way house to amalgamation (which was how it was often presented) but as an alternative which would strengthen the power of union officialdom. As Geoffrey Phillips has remarked of the

Triple Alliance of 1914: 'It was designed specifically to control and discipline such [syndicalist] militancy . . . The second clause of the constitution . . . stipulated that "the cooperation of the joint organisation shall not be called upon . . . unless and until the matter in dispute has . . . received the endorsement of the National Executive . . . concerned." '[57]

The opportunity to reassert the panacea of federation arose in the confused aftermath of the 1912 and 1913 ballots on amalgamation. The limited success of the first ballot caused a delegate conference to be convened whose job it was to devise a scheme that would reconcile support for the principle of closer unity with the opposition that continued to be offered from the officials. The results of their deliberations were issued in July 1913 in conditions that were hardly propitious for success. The Executive of the ASC&J refused to conduct the vote in their union because the scheme required them to relinquish their shipyard and foreign memberships; and the masons' executive declared the vote invalid because of the low poll. In addition, the scheme itself was badly formulated and although there was a majority vote in favour of the proposals to implement amalgamation, the sparsely furnished benefits section was rejected outright.[58] The lower vote of 1913 was, thus, more probably a reflection of the inadequacies of the scheme than an indication that the tide of support for amalgamation was ebbing. But it allowed the leaderships to regain the initiative for federation.

Under pressure from its rank and file, the Amalgamated Society was forced to re-consider its opposition to closer unity. And in November 1913, it put forward a scheme for a National Building Trades Federation which audaciously proposed the creation of one big union bureaucracy. A legislative council was to be elected from the general councils of the unions, an executive from the executive councils of the member organisations, and the district committees of the Federation were to be drawn from the managing committees of the various unions. It was not surprising that a scheme which envisaged the duplication of official union institutions should meet with the approval of a conference of officials held to consider the proposal in October 1913. And it was equally unsurprising that the scheme should be rejected by the memberships when it was voted on later in the year.[59] By this time, however, the London lockout was pending and the issue fed into the accumulated resentment with official policies that marked the crisis of that year. In the meantime, official unionism had scored a notable victory. By procrastination, by persistently offering alternative schemes of Federation, the leaderships had effectively blocked and out-manoeuvered the sentiment and support for a true amalgamation into one big union. Without undermining the bases of their power and position, the unions could act in no other way, but the consequence was to lead progressively the rank and file to a realisation that it was the system as a whole that would have to be challenged. The sentiment of a militant rank and file was well-summarised by a mason who wrote in 1912: 'We know something about the men who are going to rebuild our Society, if it gets rebuilt, but those men are not officials . . . The trade union movement is bled white by officialdom.'[60] As many syndicalists realised, such sentiments could ultimately mean a challenge to the whole economic and social system but it must be admitted that at whatever level the challenge was mounted the in-built power of those who controlled the machinery of organisation was capable of absorbing many blows and the match was heavily weighted against the proponents of change. It mattered that the rank and file were difficult to control but how much did it matter, and at what point did 'ill-discipline' pose a real threat to the survival of the established structures? The situation was clearly serious enough for the State to initiate a substantial involvement in industrial relations and the fame of Sir George Askwith rested upon his ability as the embodiment of the State to patch and bandage established procedures and institutions.

There is no doubt that there was a crisis of unionism during these years that deserves to be explored further than is possible here – a crisis that focussed around its inability to control its members adequately. The State threw the occasional life-belt in the shape of mediation or, perhaps, the National Insurance Act which greatly expanded membership in certain unions and greatly increased their potential authority. But alienation from the policies of official unionism took many different forms: the overall decline in building union membership throughout the period from 1900 was one; another was the increased difficulties noted by 1912 in recruiting members; and the wide-scale appearance of rank and file organisations was an already-discussed third.[61] Against these varying degrees of alienation and protest, however, stood the monolith of unionism, conciliation, and collective bargaining procedures and behind that stood the somewhat cracked edifice of the State. The Clyde Vigilance Committee certainly made the lives of boilermakers' officials difficult but neither it nor any similar organisation ever effected a transformation of power within the union.[62] It is important to realise that this cannot *simply* be reduced to the inherent strength of officialdom. Loyalty to the union was a complex and contradictory sentiment that demanded dissent and revolt against oft-times duplicit policies but which also, and on most occasions, required an ultimate acquiescence. Reinforced by the awareness that organisationally there was nowhere else to go (for this reason the militants of South Wales mining rejected dual unionism), this dichotomous loyalty was the reason for the often noted reluctance of the rank and file to dismiss long-serving officials.[63] Paradoxically, the men were probably more prepared to exercise such sanctions against 'unofficial' leaders simply because their power was quite unambiguously conditional upon rank and file authority and did not possess the same latitude of loyalty that derived from a long-standing institutional attachment.[64]

But the meaning, significance and seriousness of the crisis in unionism did not ultimately lie in the difficulties that were strewn in the path of those who challenged the assumptions upon which it had gained its legitimacy and respectability. The fact that syndicalism did not triumph, that unions were not democratised, that union power eventually survived shaken but intact, is all very fundamentally beside that particular point. Indeed, it was in those facts that the true nature of the crisis resided; for in spite of the power they possessed, in spite of the sophisticated procedures and institutions they operated, the unions and the system of industrial relations were evidently failing to do the job that they were set up to accomplish. They were incapable, it seemed, of resolving the fundamental conflicts that they had been devised to resolve; they could not contain the struggle for control over work; they did not ensure the observance of 'reasonable' and 'rational' procedures; and they could not maintain, therefore, that industrial discipline so needed by British capitalism from the 1890s. The irony of it was that every effort to strengthen these institutions of industrial peace merely heightened the contradictions and tensions inherent in the whole system. The alienation between the boilermakers' union and its rank and file only became a consequential theme after the 1894 agreement, but the subsequent answers to the problem of discipline in the Edinburgh Agreement of 1908, the Shipbuilding Trade Agreement of 1909 and the Supplement of 1910 merely served to accentuate that alienation. Indeed, so much was this the case that the boilermakers were scheduled to withdraw from the agreement in September 1912. The same was true in building. Conciliation as a problem-solving device worked at its qualified best all the time it remained a local authority system; once it became a national system in 1905, the greatly increased formal authority and power of the unions were ultimately nullified by increasing rank and file resentment at the remoteness of decision making.

Finally, then, the significance of the crisis lay in the simple fact that the system was not working. The challenge to the survival of the system of industrial relations (if not, ultimately, to the whole social system) lay both in the implicit fact of its breakdown and in the explicit resentment at the authority relationships that reposed within the system. It is still not clear whether the worst was over by 1914, or whether the challenge had reached its rapid climax in 1912 and that the storm had been weathered. It is unlikely that 1914 marked a greater quantitative challenge to stability than 1912, but it is equally unlikely that nothing more would have been heard of the themes we have been tracing.[65] For the tensions that produced these problems and conflicts were now to become secular to the system, rising and falling in intensity over the decades, never going away, never being 'solved' and each time that the game moved out of the workshop into the national arena, it was played out at newer and higher levels with stakes that were greater than at the times before. The ability of the social and industrial system to absorb and contain these periodic challenges to its stability is a story that requires the attention of historians of the twentieth century. But, for the moment, that is not our concern. We must return to 1914 and specifically we must focus on the building trades of that year. For if the climacteric challenge was reached at different times in different industries, in building 1914 represented a consummation of the themes not only of this chapter but also, in a sense, of this book. It is, therefore, necessary to conclude by an examination of the pertinent features of the London lockout of 1914.

THE CLIMAX OF MILITANCY

The lockout and strike of 1914 represented a tipping of the tightrope balance that unionism had to walk between persuading its memberships to accept unpopular decisions and policies whilst maintaining their credibility within the system of industrial relations. It marked the realisation of the problem that had been articulated by building union officials in London at the very moment of their full recognition as agents of collective bargaining:

It will be altogether useless for us to go back to our constituents and report to them to this effect [i.e. a year delay in the wages advance], because we . . . should just merely be deposed – they would take proceedings on their own lines and would have nothing to do with us anymore . . . We have incurred a great deal of odium by adopting the line of policy which we have done already . . . We have got enough to do to square them on that score [i.e. 9½d per hour instead of 10d] without having to square them with regard to anything else.[66]

The events of the two years previous to 1914 and, in particular, the last six months of 1913 revealed that the system as a whole was slowly grinding to a halt. Meetings of employers, unions and conciliation boards might continue to follow their normal schedule but increasingly they bore little relationship to what would actually happen at the worksite; quite simply, their writs no longer ran. Between May 1913 and January 1914 there were at least forty-eight strikes in London: all were unofficial and, as far as one can judge, all violated the conciliation procedures.[67] There were seventeen strikes affecting twenty firms against sub-contracted non-union labour and 'nearly all these cases have occurred without notice being given either to the employer or to the LMBA.'[68] Although there was some feeling amongst the employers that certain union officials were not as innocent in these matters as they claimed, the unions' protestations that they were powerless to do anything about these conflicts were generally recognised to be true. Throughout the last part of 1913, there were frequent and constant meetings between the employers' association and the unions where the same theme was echoed again and again. 'What was the use of an Agreement if the parties thereto repudiated responsibility for control of its [sic] members,' the plasterers were asked in September 1913. In the same month the OBS confessed that 'the officials had no power over their members' in respect to the non-union question. The masons' union, too, was unable to retain a control over their members on this same matter:

The whole of this trouble has arisen because individual members, or groups . . . have felt themselves at liberty to take exception to the presence of non-union work-men in the same employ . . . regardless of the agreement existing between their unions and the Employers' Association . . . that no exception shall be taken . . . and also that, to avoid stoppage of work, any dispute shall be brought before a Conciliation Board.[69]

The lockout – which the LMBA had resolved to declare unless they obtained a guarantee that strikes would cease – was about a loss of control by both the unions and the employers and it is hardly surprising, therefore, that the first three months or so were dominated by the employers' presentation of the document and the demand for a monetary guarantee against strikes over the non-union issue. Both were attempts to ensure the reassertion of *union* discipline: 'The employers had no desire to permanently adopt the principle of individual guarantee; it was only adopted whilst a collective guarantee was withheld.'[70] It would be a great mistake to regard the document as either the central issue or as designed to 'do injury to the fabric of trade unionism.'[71] The last thing the employers desired was a collapse of official trade unionism. Indeed, it was just the fact that this collapse had taken place that led them to the lockout as a way to revive the credibility of the official union structures. Any notion that employer policy was motivated by a crude, simplistic anti-unionism is quickly disabused by the constant contacts between employers and unions that were maintained in the period whilst negotiations were in abeyance and by the immediate withdrawal of the document and monetary guarantee once the unions had agreed to a system of fines against those who breached the rules.[72] 1914 is, therefore, very different from the earlier lockouts that we have had occasion to notice. All were about authority and control and all occurred when industrial discipline had broken down, but none of the earlier instances had involved the reassertion of union control and authority.

The real arena of struggle in 1914 was between competing conceptions of industrial authority and discipline. The employers and unions were concerned to reaffirm the legitimate authority of the established

procedures and structures and were obliged to confront a rank and file
searching to assert their sovereign authority. The different paradigms
proposed by the rank and file revealed, once again, the inter-marriage of
past and present. The almost eerie revival of hostility to the contracting
system and the efforts to secure direct labour contracts betokened no
harking back to the golden days before 1833 but, rather, the enduring
persistence of this form of the class struggle.[73] And it was hardly surprising,
therefore, that the forgotten tradition of autonomous regulation should
also re-emerge from the shadows of the past to play a central role in the
dispute. Cole and Mellor articulated the issue as it appeared to take shape
when the national lockout loomed near in July:

As a result of the threatened lockout there will come a united claim from the
organised workers in the building industry for absolute freedom of action on any
job . . . to down tools against their worst enemy – every disability clause must go.
In future the men must work on the strict understanding that it is their right to
decide what kind of man they shall count as fit to associate with.[74]

But this same sentiment had been expressed from the very beginning of
the dispute in January when a delegate meeting resolved that the autocratic behaviour of the employers had voided all rules and that the
workers should therefore formulate their own conditions of work. District
and Management Committees were called upon to appoint sub-commit-
tees to draw up rules 'that will be . . . the means of governing all in the
industry . . . [The opportunity now existed] for the men of all sections to
make arrangements for their own work, without considering the opinions
of others. All desired improvements can now be made without the interference by the capitalists or by Trade Union officials.'[75] Such an attitude
on the part of the rank and file ensured that the alienation between the
unofficial organisations represented by the Consolidation and local disputes committees, and the official organisations represented by the LBIF
and national executives should be complete. It similarly ensured that this
separation went beyond a merely negative rejection of official authority
to an attempt to change the authority structures themselves by the reassertion of rank and file control over negotiations and decision making.
Autonomous regulation – direct action – demanded no less and thus the
stage was set for the tussle that marked the whole course of the dispute
between the efforts of the rank and file to subordinate the official structures to their authority and the stubborn refusal of the officials to so
surrender their power.

A meeting of branch delegates on January 23 (one day before the lockout was declared) had formulated the basic and unchanging demands:
the no-disability and conciliation clauses were to be abolished, card
stewards were to be recognised, delegates were to have access to any job,
the LBIF was to be the sole negotiating agent, and overtime was to be

abolished.[76] Since these demands would have meant the effective dismantling of the existing industrial relations structures, the unions proved unwilling to place them at the centre of negotiations and a mass meeting of February 20 condemned a recent conference of unions and employers in terms that were to be familiar until the war put an end to the conflict: 'The officials had no mandate from the men on strike to meet the masters, and it was the men who had the power of decision.' In early March a group of Bermondsey carpenters issued a manifesto urging that 'power and control of the dispute [be placed] in the hands of the rank and file.' And a few days later the Consolidation Committee met to pass a series of resolutions on negotiating postures and suggest that full control of the dispute be given to a central strike committee of delegates from the various local disputes committees.[77] These proposals were brought forward at the next meeting of the LBIF and although there is some indication that they were nominally adopted, they were soon abandoned because on March 16 the LBIF effectively surrendered its weakly asserted claim to be the sole representative of London building workers and acquiesced in a special meeting of the National Conciliation Board with two extra delegates from each union to represent London.[78]

From this point suspicion of the Federation was as great as that accorded to the national executives and it boiled over into open rejection at the beginning of May when the Federation abandoned its demand for an end to the no-disability clause and supported the assumption of complete negotiating authority by the national executives. There was an immediate flurry of rank and file meetings and condemnations: 'Any proposals agreed to by the LBIF should be demanded by the rank and file to be submitted to a fully representative meeting of delegates,' read one resolution. The LBIF, it was claimed, was attempting to force 'on them . . . rules as the basis for negotiation without first . . . submitting the same for the approval of the members.'[79] The disputes committee of both carpenters' unions demanded that 'our Societies be not represented at Friday's conference . . . [and] that the Compiling Committees' code of rules be submitted to the members before any meeting of employers and operatives takes place.' Calls made for the Federation to re-convene the adjourned rank and file conference of March and recognise its authority were rejected on May 14 and the next day when the unions and employers attempted to meet in secret, they were greeted by demonstrators who carried banners inscribed: ' "Warning to Officials. No Surrender." ' A rank and file conference was held on May 22 at which the original list of demands was reaffirmed.[80] The round of negotiations that occurred in June followed the same pattern: LBIF support for the settlement negotiated by the executives, rank and file condemnation of its content and of the refusal to heed their opinion, and repeated calls for a delegate conference to take control of the crisis.[81] When, at the end of June the Federation 'sanctioned its own break up' by recommending sectional settlements, it provided a critical impetus to the gathering movement towards dual unionism. For the rank and file this was merely the last straw. It was pointed out that the Federation had persistently refused to recognise rank and file opinion; repeated refusals had greeted all attempts to secure 'representation of the rank and file on any constructive committee'; and the local disputes committees had even been denied the power to call men out.[82] Thus, a delegate meeting was called for July 16 to 'discuss their demands prior to a settlement taking place' which repeated the conditions formulated in January and this position was subsequently confirmed at a mass meeting attended by seven thousand men from which officials were deliberately excluded. At the same time the Consolidation Committee began to make preparations for a conference that was held in Birmingham at the beginning of August which established the Building Workers' Industrial Union.[83]

These attempts to place work control issues at the centre of the bargaining and to assert rank and file authority over the negotiations made not one iota of difference to the various settlements that were offered to the men in April, May and June. Each one failed to address the issues that concerned the rank and file and amounted to little more than attempts to find words and phrases that would secure acceptance of the very procedures of no-disability and conciliation that lay at the heart of the trouble. Indeed, all three aimed to strengthen the official channels and structures. In March, for example, the LBIF had stood willing to accept a disputes procedure which would have obliged a trade union to secure compliance by supplying an injured employer with blacklegs. Although this was not included in the proposed settlement, it illustrated the direction the officials were moving. And in the settlement negotiated on 17 April the authority of the Conciliation Board over all disputes was confirmed, a disciplinary clause was included which committed the unions to secure compliance with all mutually negotiated decisions, and the employers retained the right to refuse ticket inspections on their jobs. On 23 April, a rank and file ballot overwhelmingly rejected this settlement by 23,481 to 2021 votes.[84] A second round of meetings and discussions then ensued which on 18 May resulted in another set of proposals. The main features of these proposals were a slightly more liberal ticket inspection clause, a watered-down version of the no-disability clause and the retention of the full authority of the Conciliation Board. Like the first settlement, these proposals were also rejected – this time by a margin of four to one.[85]

At this point the national executives of the unions and the NFBTE moved decisively to assume sole command of the negotiations from the incapable hands of the London unions and employers. They quickly

reached agreement on a third set of proposals which were the most un-
compromising of all in their treatment of rank and file demands and
illustrated the determined solidarity of unions and employers to strength-
en the official structures of the industrial relations system. Constant access
of trade union officials to employers contrasted with the restrictions that
remained on rank and file ticket inspections; the disciplinary clause of
April was reintroduced; the no-disability clause was included in modified
form; and, most important of all, the conciliation system was extended to
'include all questions arising between the employer and the trade
unions.'[86] An all-out effort then followed to secure a favourable ballot
result. The national executives promised the employers that they would
withdraw support from the London men should the proposals be rejected,
they threatened a national referendum, and they made much of the un-
preparedness of the unions to face the nation-wide lockout brandished by
the employers. Even so, the men rejected the settlement by a ten thousand
vote margin.[87] But by this time – the middle of June – the situation was
about to be transformed by the agreement that was known to be pending
between the masons and the employers.

That it should be the masons who broke the hitherto unshaken united
front of the men was, for historical and contemporary reasons, unremarkable. Protected by their greater degree of craft skill, by their more
genuinely aristocrat-of-labour status which had only recently been jolted
by stone working machines, masons had never shared the will of the
carpenters and bricklayers for united action. They had been the first to
break ranks in 1859 and 1872 (on neither occasion had they been fully
committed to unity) and in 1914 they were the only group to consistently
vote to accept the negotiated settlements. Their six-month alliance was, in
fact, a remarkable testimony to a common interest that went beyond the
local interests of the trade, but by June there was a large majority of local
men prepared to accept the proposals.[88] The fact was that syndicalism
did not have the following amongst the London masons that it possessed
in the north because there had never been that solid tradition of restrictive
work control upon which it could build. On hearing of the settlement, the
Liverpool masons resolved to treat any London man venturing into the
northwest as a blackleg.[89] But the breakaway of the London masons was
also a reflection of the difference between their conditions of work and
those of the carpenters and bricklayers. Masons' work was to be found
almost entirely on the large sites where they were employed directly by
the large employers. Unlike the other trades, they were, therefore, more
able to control effectively the labour supply and were less affected by the
non-union question. But it also meant that they could not seek work
amongst the employers of the non-associated firms outside of the city
centre:

Their [labourers, bricklayers and carpenters] occupations favour them in obtaining short jobs, where a mason has no chance at all, and . . . their members are working peaceably around London, where they have no disability rule and can strike when they like . . . In most of the trades affected, their members have been able, on the smaller jobs, to have short spells of work during the dispute, but not so our members.[90]

Although this undoubtedly explains the readiness of the masons to conceive of a separate settlement, the actual impetus to seek negotiations came from a different source. Without the knowledge of the Executive – which supported the strike – the Society's general secretary called together the General Council on 22 June and they ordered the Disputes Committee to approach the employers for a settlement.[91] There may have been some resistance from the Disputes Committee to this command because it was only after a phone call from Williams (the general secretary) on 23 June that the Committee met and by a vote of 5 to 2 decided to bring the matter before the Management Committee of the LBIF. Responding eagerly to this incipient destruction of unity, the LBIF endorsed the principle of sectional settlements and negotiations with employers began on 26 June. The masons did not finalise a settlement, however, until they had unsuccessfully tried to persuade a rank and file joint trades meeting to recognise their special position and approve their action. In the meantime, just to make sure, the General Council had declared the strike closed and on 3 July a settlement was reached which basically followed the proposals that had been negotiated at the beginning of June.[92]

The significance of the masons' action went far beyond the epithets of traitorous villainy that were hurled in their direction. It created the opportunity for the unions to regain the initiative that had previously been denied to them. The first moves by the masons towards a settlement had coincided with the debate on the third set of proposals, had created serious divisions within the OSM and had reinforced the arguments for approval that were being trumpeted by the LBIF, the *Daily Citizen*, and the union officials. In the face of these pressures – which may explain the lower poll on the third ballot – the actual vote was a vindication of the critical intelligence of the men. But, in addition, the masons' settlement also served to legitimise the unions' support of the established structures of authority in the industry. Until this point, the official negotiations had borne no relationship to the issues that the rank and file were demanding they address. From the beginning, the struggle had revolved around the effectiveness and legitimacy of the industrial relations structures and it had quickly become apparent that the men were posing alternative systems of authority that would have shifted the balance of power into their hands. The unions, on the other hand, were casting about for ways to reassert the legitimacy of the recognised procedures and it was the masons' settlement that allowed this stalemate to be broken. To resist official negotiations and proposals now became more difficult. All the time the rank and file continued collectively and decisively to reject the proposed agreements, the credibility of alternative authority structures remained an issue which, at least, would have to be dealt with. It was for this reason, for example, that long after the first revelations of its status as a creature of official unionism had appeared, the men continued their attempts to convert the LBIF to their position.[93]

Because the Federation pretended to represent all building workers and, for a time, had pretensions to the role of sole negotiating agent for the men, it was the only 'legitimate' organisation which nominally recognised the unity of rank and file interests. If the Federation could be 'captured' – as the OBS had seemingly been captured for syndicalism in 1912 – it promised to be a potential rank and file beachhead into official union structures. But once the unity that had previously characterised the dispute was shattered, the official structures were automatically enhanced in power and prestige, official settlements legitimised, and the possibilities for the success of internal pressure for reform were much reduced. Only after the LBIF had proclaimed its support of the masons' settlement did all efforts to convert that organisation cease. The masons' settlement, thus, closed the door on internal reform and left open only that passage which led to the treacherous territory of dual unionism.

The settlement was important, however, in another, related respect. Not only did it legitimise the proposals that had been negotiated on 9 June, it also legitimised sectional settlements as a way of ending the dispute. The unions had been clearly anxious to bring the matter to a close since May but the collective unity of the men had denied the viability of sectional agreements.[94] The masons' return to work resolved that dilemma for the union officials and provided a weapon with which they could disrupt rank and file unity through sectional negotiation. It was a weapon eagerly seized. Without even waiting for the masons to reach an agreement, the LBIF on 24 June finally buried the last remains of any claim it might have had to represent the rank and file and passed a resolution which endorsed sectional settlements. And, throughout July, the officials of the various unions approached the London employers to make their peace – the bricklayers, as befitted the most syndicalist union – being the last.[95]

Under these circumstances the continued rank and file protest and resistance against sectional settlements was impressive but hardly auspicious. There was now a united front of employers and emboldened union officials to defy rank and file meetings and the rapid drift towards dual unionism. The General Union of Carpenters threatened to beat the men into surrender by submitting the terms it was negotiating to the whole Society; the ASC&J and OBS were negotiating without the endorsement of their rank and file; and the plasterers yet again rejected a settlement reached by their union. It was at this point that the final set for the confrontation was moved into place. On 27 July, the National Federation of Building Trade Employers decided to activate a resolution passed in May which provided for a national lockout and set the definite date of 15 August.[96] In the event that no general return to work had occurred by that time, the employers and the unions would together face the men.

As it turned out, of course, the contest was never joined because the war intervened to allow the full reassertion of official control. Claiming full powers to settle, the executives of the unions met on 6 August with the Executive of the NFBTE, agreed to the rules negotiated in June and declared the lockout closed.[97] In one final spasm of protest the carpenters' London Management Committee refused to sign the rules until the Executive of the Amalgamated Society secured a vote of the membership. This the Executive refused to do, suspended the Management Committee and:

Took over the management of the London District . . . Appointed Bro. A. G. Cameron, the London Shipping Delegate, as Chairman *pro tem*, and having ascertained from the employers that the signatures of the Chairman *pro tem* and secretary of the London District would be accepted on behalf of the local operatives, instructed Brs. Cameron and Stennett to sign the working agreements.[98]

Responsible men and legitimate authority had triumphed.

Although the war was soon to create its own conditions of industrial militancy, the immediate and overall effect of the holocaust that was about to begin was to provide an effective answer to the internal crises and challenges that faced British society. Social relationships were transformed, attention diverted away from internal problems. Encouraged by the almost unanimous support accorded to the war by the institutions of the Labour Movement, patriotism became the only acceptable virtue. What is important about the tale I have tried to tell in this chapter is not only what it reveals about the nature of the Georgian crisis but also that it was the first time that the contradictions of an essentially modern system of industrial relations stood exposed. Only by understanding the historical continuity that lay within those contradictions, only by seeing this particular stage of the contradictions as deriving from a firm historical tradition, articulating old themes in a modern vocabulary, can we really comprehend the labour unrest as yet another rendition of the struggle for control over work.

But it is important to realise that the war marked no finale to the themes we have been tracing in this chapter and book. One early, and somewhat primitive, stage of the struggle for control came to an end with the war and when that struggle again revived in peacetime, it was with a far greater complexity than anything encountered in our story. Neither the war nor the peace, the depression nor the post-1945 affluence have been able to resolve the tensions and threats that compose the continuing struggle for control over work. Indeed, the recent crisis of industrial relations in Britain has provided ample evidence of the relevance of this aspect of labour's history – even to the extent of revealing features within building that would be completely familiar to the men of the 1830s, 1860s and 1890s.[99] Our purpose, therefore, has been to demonstrate that no understanding of the course of labour history can be complete without a recognition of the central determinant of the struggle for work control. We have not been concerned to tell a story with an end but to suggest the beginnings and to trace the origins, mainly in one industry, of themes whose relevance is far wider than that of building alone and whose finale has yet, perhaps, to be played. By studying the struggle for control, by trying to understand its roots, its forms and its wider meanings, not only will labour history be enriched but we will be continually reminded that 'the disadvantage of men not knowing the past is that they do not know the present.'[100]

Appendix A
Masons' strike data 1836–96

Until the Labour Correspondent of the Board of Trade began to issue his *Reports on Strikes and Lock-Outs* in 1889, there was no systematic collection of strike statistics. The occasional enthusiast such as G. P. Bevan might cull the pages of *The Times* and other sources to arrive at aggregate estimates of conflict by industry but before the 1890s there exists no series of data upon which to base any statistical study of the many-sided nature of strike activity either in aggregate or specific trades. Partly for this reason and also because this study began with a focus on industrial conflict in building, it seemed desirable to try and develop a statistical series from the reports of strike activity that were entered into a special column in each issue of the stonemasons' *Fortnightly Returns*. It was thought that such a series would be particularly useful (and not only to this study) because, unlike most strike series which focus on aggregate trades and adopt the broad classifications of the government's series, it would provide a detailed data base for the study of such activity in one trade. And although the data have not been used as extensively as originally anticipated, it seems worthwhile to explain how they have been arranged and filed. At a later date, I hope to publish a small book that will lay out the full pattern of masons' strike activity as it is revealed by this data.

The series begins in June 1836 and ends in December 1896. Both dates were determined by the quality and format of the reporting of strike activity in the Returns. Before June 1836 the Returns were in manuscript that was difficult to read and the reports of strikes were inconsistent and scanty. Indeed, it was not until early 1841 that a separate column headed 'Strikes' appeared as a regular feature in the printed Returns with information that remained fairly consistent. Between 1836 and 1841, therefore, the data were haphazardly recorded with varying degrees of completeness in the body of the Return and in many cases only the mere fact of a strike occurring is recorded at all. In those cases (and this is a rule followed throughout the data collection) where no further information was given, I omitted to record the strike. Similarly, after 1896 the format of the reporting changed decisively for the worst and it proved impossible to continue to extract further data. Thus, there was seldom any information given on the causal issue, the numbers involved, or the result of the strike. The column seems to have merely served as a warning to masons to stay away from certain towns, sometimes accompanied with the scantiest bits of information. A typical entry from 1898 runs as follows: 'Keep away from South Shields as there is a strike pending there . . . Birmingham report having come to terms with their employers.' It would prove rather difficult to pick the series up with the official statistics where our series leaves off because the nature of the information was different and particularly in the specificity of the causes of dispute which in the Labour Correspondent's Reports were grouped into far broader categories than we have thought useful to devise.

The column 'Strikes' in the masons' *Fortnightly Returns* was based upon reports sent into the central office by the branches, its purposes were largely informational and there seems to have been no attempt by the various Corresponding Secretaries to lay down a regular format for a consistent reporting of the main features of each industrial action. Thus, the nature of the material made it inevitable that there be great variations in the quality of the data, for there was no consistent attachment to fixed categories of information. A fairly complete account of a strike in one place may be accompanied by only the barest mention of a conflict at another town. It is, perhaps, significant that the period when the data are fullest coincides with Richard Harnott's tenure of the office of Corresponding Secretary (1847–72) and after his death the quality of reportage begins to decline. Nevertheless, it proved possible to collect data on 2679 cases between June 1836 and December 1896 and at its best each report of a strike could contain information that fell into nine separate categories. The data collection was, thus, based upon what each strike report revealed about the following categories.

1. The date of the Return which recorded the strike was the first notation. Since the Returns were issued fortnightly, they were dated with the beginning and end date of the period they covered. Consistent with my usage in the footnotes, I took the final date on the Return as the reference point.

2. The town where the strike occurred.

3. The issue that caused the strike. In some cases it was clear that the actual issue over which the men struck was merely the spark and that there were other accumulated grievances. Where it proved possible to distinguish these cases a special notation was recorded to enable the identification of multiple cause strikes. But for the purposes of the statistics it was the spark issue that was recorded as being the causal issue.

4. The reports frequently cited the numbers of masons who were on strike at the beginning of the strike and, if the strike was mentioned in later *Returns*, there were occasionally references to the numbers remaining

on strike. In these cases identification of the decrease or increase of men on strike was made but for the purposes of our tabulation we have used the earliest recorded number as the size of the strike. There was no consistent distinction drawn between the numbers on strike (which could include non-union men) and numbers who were on the Society's funds (and who were more likely, therefore, to be union men).

5. If it was specified that union men were on strike, this fact was recorded along with any numbers that might be given.

6. Similarly, if non-union participation was identified, this was recorded along with any numbers that might be given.

7. The date on which the strike was closed or was settled was recorded where this was given.

8. The result of the strike was recorded as either a victory or failure for the men or a compromise.

9. A final column was reserved for any information that did not fall into the other categories but which might prove useful.

The data so collected were then coded into variables that generally followed the categories listed above and all the tabulations in the text used an SPSS programme. The variables so derived were as follows.

DAY, MONTH, YEAR

These are all separate variables derived from the date of the *Fortnightly Return* in which the strike was first mentioned and it also served as a reference point.

AREA

This variable is the registration division in which the strike was situated. I followed the divisions recorded in the 1891 Census but Scotland and Ireland were each accorded one number.

COUNTY

The county in which the strike took place. Again, the identification numbers of the *1891 Census of Population* were used with two modifications. The East, North and West Ridings of Yorkshire were combined to one identification number whereas in the Census they were accorded their own separate numbers. Second, as in the Area variable, Scotland and Ireland were each treated as one county because in neither case did there seem to be sufficient data to justify division into smaller units.

The town where the strike occurred was assigned a three digit number simply on the basis of their appearance in the data. Thus, the first strike recorded was in Armagh, Ireland and its identification number was, therefore, 001.

ISSUES

The classification of issues was the most important part of the data gathering and coding and it presented the greatest problems because of the lack of consistency in the descriptive categories. In some cases, for example, it was not immediately clear whether an issue should be placed in one category or another. Thus, when an 'infringement of meal hours' was recorded as the cause of a strike, should it be placed under an 'hours' issue or included as a category in its own right? In this particular case – partly because there were a substantial number of cases – they were given their own separate code number and not included in hours issues. To infringe on meal hours obviously meant an increase in the hours of work, but when the strike was specifically described as an 'infringement on meal hours' it suggested that the matter had as much to do with privilege and custom as it did with economics or hours of work. Similarly, when a strike was recorded for a 'Winter Wage Advance' this was distinguished from a pure 'Advance' (i.e. increase) of wages, for the former suggested a restoration of the *status quo ante* rather than an absolute increase in wages. In general, I tried to avoid the drawbacks of the usual classification of issues into broad issues alone because that tends to subsume all sorts of subtle differences between issues that may be similar but not the same. The classification of issue categories was kept as close to the data descriptions as possible rather than telescoping them into categories which would pervert their meaning to the strikers themselves. It is worth noting that only 1.5% of the cases recorded missing values for issues.

Thus, the issues were grouped into eight broad categories which were then sub-divided as seemed necessary and appropriate. Certain sub-divisions were themselves sub-divided into separate groupings but only the major divisions within each category are included here. The figures in parentheses record the number of cases in each sub-division.

a. Wages

Wage strike issues were divided into four major sub-divisions: 'Advance' (321), 'Reduction' (356), 'Period of payment disputes' (71), 'Maintain local standard rate' (80), 'Other' (21). It was decided not to include the 'Maintain local standard rate' division under 'Reductions' because this group was identified often enough to suggest a possible distinction. They could, for example, be strikes against attempts to reduce the rate per hour rather than the absolute wage and thus represent an attempt to get more hours of work for the same wage.

b. Hours

There were two basic sub-divisions in this category: 'Against an extension of hours' (101), 'For a reduction of hours' (72), 'Other' (25).

c. Organisation of work

This category included strikes over how the work was to be organised: strikes against 'Piecework' (180), against 'Sub-contracting' (79), strikes about 'Overtime' (11), 'Other' (1).

d. Conditions of work

Issues where the conditions under which the work was to be carried on were at stake: 'Meal hours' (113), 'Sheds' (70), 'Lodgings money' (10), 'Walking time' (69), 'Artificial light' (33), 'Other' (15).

e. Control over the labour force

This category included those strikes where the enforcement of collective standards of employment practice as they affected personnel was the issue. They were divided into two sub-divisions: 'Union membership or discipline' (440). Examples of this would be a strike over the enforcement of union membership, or the enforcement of union fines. The second sub-division was 'Employment division' (90) which covered, for example, strikes against foremen or the employment of blacklegs. 'Other' (11).

f. Craft issues

Strikes where the enforcement and/or protection of the standards of the craft were the issue: 'Demarcation disputes' (182), 'Violation of apprenticeship rules' (30), 'Worked stone' (162), 'Other' (13).

g. Working rules issues

Once working rules became common in the trade, the cause of a strike was often phrased in terms of attempts to maintain and/or establish new rules and the specific parts of the rules that were in dispute were unmentioned. For this reason amongst others, it was necessary to establish a separate category to include these strikes where the issue was to enforce or maintain new or extant rules. There were two major sub-divisions: 'To enforce old or establish new rules' (95), 'To maintain rules against infringements' (50), 'Other' (5).

h. Other

This category was to provide for miscellaneous issues that did not fall into the other groups. It totalled only 20 conflicts, 8 of which were recorded as lockouts.

NUMBERS INVOLVED

In 31% of the cases a figure was recorded for the number of men on strike at the first mention of the strike. In 2% of the cases a final figure was also provided. Figures were only included in this variable if there was no mention of either union or non-union participation.

UNION PARTICIPATION

If union participation was specified this was recorded as a separate variable.

UNION NUMBERS INVOLVED

If the numbers of union men involved either at the beginning or at the end of the strike were given, these figures were entered as a separate variable. In 55% of cases a beginning figure was recorded.

NON-UNION PARTICIPATION

NON-UNION NUMBERS INVOLVED

The same conventions as above were applied if it was specified that non-unionists were involved in the strike. In only 9% of cases was a beginning figure for non-union men recorded.

For the purposes of strike size tabulation in this book, however, the variables of numbers involved at the beginning, union men involved at the beginning and non-union men involved at the beginning were collapsed into one variable.

LENGTH OF STRIKE

This was always recorded in numbers of days. Where a fraction of a day (above one day) was involved, the number was rounded off downwards.

In 32.9% of the cases it proved impossible to calculate the number of days a strike lasted, usually because no mention was made of the end of a strike. Where no exact figure was given for the duration of a strike but where it was first mentioned as having erupted in one Return and then again in a following Return as having ended, an estimation of its length was made using the dates of the Returns themselves as the boundaries of the strike period. Although this involved an over-estimate of the length of a strike by assuming the strike ended on the day of the issuance of the Return in which it was recorded as having ended, this was probably balanced by an under-estimate from taking the date of the Return in which it was first mentioned as the date of its having broken out. For both beginning and end the margin of error could be as little as 2 (assuming two days for receipt of news, set up and printing of Return) and as much as 14 days. It is also important to note that frequently the length of the strike will have meaning only in that it represents the duration of time the shop was closed to union men. Thus, there was the case of a strike in York in January 1878 which involved five men and lasted until January 1879. The likelihood was that these men got other work and that the shop was not re-opened for one year.

RESULT

In cases where the result was not explicitly stated but where from the account of the terms upon which the men returned the result could be deduced it was entered as either a Victory, Failure, or Compromise.

GENERAL COMMENT

A general comment card was introduced where there was additional information included under Remarks in the data collection.

Appendix B
Wages fluctuations 1839–80

The following table was constructed from A. L. Bowley's 'Statistics of Wages in the United Kingdom during the last Hundred Years. (Part V) Wages in the Building Trades – English Towns,' Royal Statistical Society, *Journal* (June 1900). Its purpose is to support the case we have argued in the text for the considerable strength of the men's position in the 1860s and their ability to obtain big wage advances. As we have seen, the large increases that may be seen in some towns in the seventies had a rather different significance. I have not included all of Bowley's figures for all towns and trades but only those where there were fairly closely spaced figures spanning the forties to the late sixties and, ideally, into the seventies. The series is, of course, very patchy until the eighties and I have generally used only those figures where there is a comparison with years earlier than the 1860s. Thus, those towns and trades that have been excluded were those with insufficient data to provide useful comparisons.

It should be noted that most of Bowley's wages referred to the summer months and they tend to present, therefore, the best side of the picture. Where summer and winter wages have been given, I averaged the two for the base calculation. I have combined those figures where only one year is given with the next series of years – provided that the years followed on. Thus, where Bowley gave figures for 1864–65 and then 1865–69, I have compared 1864–69. Where a range of figures is given for a year I have taken the mid-point between the high and the low.

Trades	Town	Year	Total % inc/dec.	Average % inc/dec. per annum
Carpenters				
	Birmingham	1843–64	+ 6.0	+0.28
		1864–69	+14.7	+2.94
	Bolton	1843–64	+12.0	+0.6
		1864–69	+ 7.0	+1.7
	Burnley	1843–64	+ 8.3	+0.39
		1864–69	+ 7.7	+1.54
	Carlisle	1843–64	+33.0	+1.57
		1864–69	+12.5	+2.5
	Derby	1843–64	+ 4.3	+0.2
		1864–69	+16.6	+3.3
	Oldham	1843–64	+13.0	+0.6
		1864–69	+11.5	+2.3
	Preston	1843–64	+19.0	+0.9
		1864–69	+14.0	+2.8
		1869–73	− 1.7	−0.42
		1873–77	+25.0	+6.25
	St. Helens	1843–64	+27.0	+1.28
		1864–69	+ 7.1	+1.42
	Sheffield	1843–64	+12.5	+0.59
		1864–69	+11.1	+2.2
		1869–80	+ 3.08	+0.27
	Ashton-u-Lyne	1843–64	+10.4	+0.49
		1864–69	+13.2	+2.64
		1869–73	+21.1	+4.22
	Newcastle	1843–50	+ 5.0	+0.7
		1850–60	+14.0	+1.4
		1860–67/8	+12.5	+1.7
	Nottingham	1843–64	+13.0	+0.6
		1865–69	+21.3	+5.37
		1869–77	+31.1	+3.88
	Stockport	1843–64	+13.0	+0.62
		1864–69	+17.9	+3.58
		1869–77	+18.4	+2.3
	Macclesfield	1843–64	+ 4.3	+0.14
		1864–69	+12.5	+2.5
	Liverpool	1843–55	+12.5	+1.04
		1855–64	+ 3.7	+0.41
		1864–69	+10.7	+2.14
		1869–75	+18.2	+3.03
	Bristol	1858–60	+14.7	+7.35
		1860–63	+ 6.93	+2.13
		1863–69	+ 8.95	+1.79
		1869–77	+14.7	+1.84

Trades	Town	Year	Total % inc/dec.	Average % inc/dec. per annum
	Manchester	1839–49	+ 7.69	+0.76
		1849–59	0.0	0.0
		1859–64	0.0	0.0
		1864–69	+14.2	+2.8
		1869–77	+17.96	+2.2
Painters				
	Derby	1864–66	+ 9.5	+4.75
		1866–72	+13.0	+2.16
		1872–74	+ 7.7	+3.85
		1874–76	+13.9	+6.65
	Bristol	1858–60	+20.4	+10.2
		1860–63	− 7.5	− 2.3
		1863–77	+38.7	+2.76
Bricklayers				
	Newcastle	1840–50	+ 7.1	+0.7
		1850–60	+20.0	+2.0
		1860–67	+22.0	+3.14
	Manchester	1839–49	+ 5.5	+0.55
		1849–59	+10.0	+1.0
		1859–61	+ 4.76	+2.38
		1861–70	− 3.0	−0.33
		1870–77	+33.5	+4.5
Masons				
	Newcastle	1840–50	+ 7.1	+0.71
		1850–60	+ 6.6	+0.66
		1860–65	+12.5	+2.5
		1865–67	+11.1	+5.5
		1867–77	+26.6	+2.66
	Bristol	1855–58	+ 9.5	+3.16
		1858–60	+19.5	+9.75
		1860–63	− 1.8	−0.6
		1863–77	+33.3	+2.37
	Manchester	1839–49	+ 9.0	+0.9
		1849–59	+ 4.5	+0.45
		1860–70	+11.1	+1.1
		1870–77	+23.6	+3.37
Masons' labourers				
	Bristol	1857–60	+ 7.1	+2.36
		1860–63	+ 6.6	+0.94
		1863–77	+33.3	+2.37
	Manchester	1839–49	+ 2.9	+0.29
		1849–59	0.0	0.0
		1859–70	+16.6	+1.5
		1870–77	+15.9	+2.27

Appendix C
Formalisation and the seasonal distribution
of masons' strikes

One interesting reflection of the impact made by the formalisation of industrial relations was in the changing seasonal distribution of masons' strikes. The following table illustrates the changes that occur over the period covered by the data. Most noticeable is the definite tendency of winter strikes to decline and for those of the spring to increase. Summer strikes also show a tendency to increase and autumn strikes remain fairly steady.

Table 18. *Distribution of strikes by season*

	Winter	Spring	Summer	Autumn
1836–40	28.5	24.6	21.2	25.7
1841–50	28.0	31.2	20.0	20.7
1851–60	21.5	26.2	31.5	20.8
1861–70	21.9	27.4	25.9	24.6
1871–80	21.4	27.2	28.0	23.3
1881–90	19.2	36.4	24.2	20.2
1891–96	16.9	29.2	29.2	24.6

The decline in winter strikes and the growing importance of those in the spring may be further illustrated by shifts in the distribution of strikes by month and particularly in the declining importance of strikes in December and its replacement by May as the month with the highest percentage of strikes in the year.

Although there were some fluctuations in the significance of other months – for example, the tendency for November strikes to decline – it is for May and December that the shifts are most strongly accented. What these tables suggest is that around the 1870s a decisive modification of the traditional patterns of masons' strike activity occurred which moved it from a fairly even distribution throughout the seasons to one which began to focus on the spring – and, to a lesser extent, the summer – months of the year.

Table 19. *Distribution of strikes by month*

	1836 to 1840	1841 to 1850	1851 to 1860	1861 to 1870	1871 to 1880	1881 to 1890	1891 to 1896
January	3.9	7.9	4.9	5.5	5.7	6.4	7.3
February	6.1	5.4	6.0	6.0	9.8	9.1	3.8
March	10.1	13.3	9.0	7.9	8.0	9.1	3.8
April	8.9	10.2	7.5	7.7	8.6	9.6	10.0
May	5.6	7.6	9.6	11.7	10.6	17.6	15.4
June	6.7	7.1	11.7	9.3	10.2	10.7	9.2
July	7.8	7.0	9.7	9.6	10.2	8.7	9.6
August	6.7	5.9	10.0	7.0	7.6	4.7	10.4
September	4.5	7.9	4.6	7.0	6.2	6.2	8.1
October	6.7	4.4	5.5	6.9	6.5	4.7	10.0
November	14.5	8.4	10.8	10.7	10.5	9.2	6.5
December	18.4	14.8	10.6	10.5	5.9	3.6	5.8

The traditional pattern of strike action followed the broad seasonal fluctuations in the trade. The spring and summer were the time when advances in wages and conditions could be gained and the winter months the time when those improvements had to be defended by strike activity. The desirability of overcoming this cycle of insecurity had long been recognised by the men; the nine hours movement of 1846 had been justified partly on the grounds that it would even out the work and reduce the fluctuations between summer and winter that caused so much friction with the employers. One of the earliest attempts to secure six month notices for alterations had come from Harnott in 1860 because they were seen as a way to overcome this inherent insecurity of conditions.[1] But it was not until the 1870s that this old pattern was actually broken as far as winter strikes against reductions in wages were concerned. Table 20 shows quite clearly that strikes against reductions ceased to be a prominent feature of winter and were displaced into the spring months. It may also be noted that the pattern of strikes for increases of wages continued basically unchanged. This pattern of a decline in winter strikes against reductions may be seen even more clearly in Table 21 which shows these strikes in December as a percentage of total wages strikes.[2]

Thus, by the end of our strike series, it is clear that masons have virtually ceased to strike against reductions of wages in winter and are instead striking on that issue during the more advantageous spring months. At first glance, it might be thought that this change betokened a growing 'rationality' in stonemasons' consciousness, that it illustrated one aspect of a coming to terms with the economic realities of industrial capitalism.

Table 20. *Seasonal distribution of strikes against reductions and for increases of wages*

	Winter		Spring		Summer		Autumn	
	Red.	Inc.	Red.	Inc.	Red.	Inc.	Red.	Inc.
1836–40	51.0	0.0	10.2	52.4	4.1	47.6	34.7	0.0
1841–50	52.1	1.8	17.9	57.1	9.5	30.3	20.4	10.7
1851–60	41.4	1.3	14.4	47.3	11.3	46.8	32.8	4.5
1861–70	51.0	2.8	19.0	54.1	9.9	34.7	19.9	8.3
1871–80	29.1	1.3	21.3	31.5	30.0	60.5	19.4	6.5
1881–90	12.5	0.0	75.0	44.6	12.5	48.2	0.0	7.1
1891–96	25.0	6.7	50.0	66.7	0.0	26.7	25.0	0.0

Table 21. *Strikes against reductions in December as percentage of total wages strikes*

1836–40	26.0
1841–50	18.8
1851–60	9.4
1861–70	17.9
1871–80	4.0
1881–90	2.5
1891–96	0.0

Under any circumstances the winter was an unfavourable time to strike on any issue and to strike against a reduction of wages during that season was to fly in the face of the presence of an enlarged reserve army of unemployed and the lessened quantity of work available. But it is unlikely that this shift in strike activity may be attributed simply to a learning of the rules of the game that taught the futility of striking over wages in the winter. The disadvantage of winter strikes was obvious to workers and the problem of winter reductions had been commented on from the earliest days of our sources.[3] Furthermore, winter strikes on issues other than wages continued at generally the same rates throughout the whole period. This contrast is especially notable for strikes over conditions of work (which were also subject to employer attacks during the winter months).[4] And if the shift in strike patterns was due to a growing economic rationality this surely would not have been the case. If masons continued to strike against changes in the conditions of work during winter it was because those issues lay closer to the heart of work control and, unlike wages, once they were breached were more difficult to re-establish. Employers never willingly acceded to restrictions on walking time and the like and these 'soft' issues could be easily confronted in the winter. But employers were responsive to seasonal fluctuations in wages and it was a well-established custom for advances on the winter wage to be offered in the spring when the pressures of starting and completing the work began.

The decline of winter wage strikes and the increase of strikes in the spring were integrally connected through the changes that began to occur in the seventies in the nature of industrial relations. As we have seen, formalisation elevated the negotiation of working rules to the most significant role in the determination of working conditions and wages for the whole year. Thus, as the following table shows, strikes over working rules become statistically significant only in the seventies. Over fifty per cent

Table 22. *Working rule strikes as a percentage of total strikes*

1836–40	1841–50	1851–60	1861–70	1871–80	1881–90	1891–96
0.0	0.0	1.4	4.3	10.4	8.7	11.0

of these strikes occurred in the spring and 35% in the month of May alone. Most importantly, the wage rates were settled at this period, usually with a complex scale of different rates during the various seasons of the year. The traditional insecurity that had accompanied the absence of any formally agreed-upon winter wage rates was overcome by the negotiation of working rules. There was less likelihood of these rates being breached by employers because they were so precisely stated in the rules.[5] Thus, strikes over the determination of these wage rates were much more likely to occur in the spring negotiating season – and particularly in May which was the month when negotiations that had been continuing since January climaxed in success or failure.[6] As far as strikes for an increase of wages were concerned, this new negotiating procedure made little difference to the traditional pattern because the spring was always the most advantageous time for the men to impose their will and such strikes had always been common during that season. But it may be seen to explain the shift in strikes against reductions of wages from winter to the spring (see Table 20) and the increase in these strikes that occurred in May.

Table 23. *Strikes against reduction of wages in May as percentage of total wage strikes*

1836–40	1841–50	1851–60	1861–70	1871–80	1881–90	1891–96
1.3	2.0	1.2	5.0	4.1	5.0	7.7

Appendix D
Corporatism

I am acutely aware of the dangers and difficulties involved in using this term as it may be applied to the years 1890–1914 and particularly in the light of the complex and sophisticated use of the categories of 'corporatism' and 'collectivism' that has been made by Colin Crouch in his recent analysis of contemporary British industrial relations.[1] In our period his analytic category 'liberal collectivism' might seem more appropriate to describe the relationship of unions to employers and society because it is defined as 'subordinates' organisations offer no guarantees of discipline except in exchange for specific and precise concessions to the membership.'[2] But this does not adequately describe the disciplinary function of the collective agreements that we are dealing with where there was a far greater degree of permanent sanction than this implies and whose disciplinary role was accepted in return for the on-going concession to bargain. On the other hand the problem for us with Crouch's 'corporatist' categories is that they demand some State role, which in our period was rather weak. Yet there *was* a State role in this period even though it was not directed as it is today by firm policies, nor did it exercise a permanently coercive role. But its presence was manifested by Askwith, by Lloyd George's intervention in the railway strike, by the growth of the Labour Department and (what is of necessity ignored by Crouch) by the social policies of the State. Perhaps what is needed to encompass the nature of industrial relations system of this period is a new term: 'corporate liberal collectivism.' 'Corporate' because the disciplinary function of the unions was fully recognised as a result of their relations with employers within the industrial relations system and because this was a part of an increasingly recognised necessity to more tightly control and regulate all aspects of industrial production; 'liberal' because it subscribed largely to the voluntary nature of bargaining arrangements; and 'collectivist' because the system was based upon and stimulated organisation amongst employers and men.

So, I do believe we may use the term 'corporatism' without doing violence to the historical features of this period and without avoiding the kind of precision that sociologists (rightly – for their discipline) insist upon.

But this is a matter over which there should be more debate. It is necessary to bear in mind, however, that the corporatism of this period may not be equated with those varieties present in modern British society. But it is equally necessary to insist that the origins of the contemporary version lay in the species to be found in the late nineteenth and early twentieth centuries.

Notes

NOTES TO INTRODUCTION

1 On the inconsistencies that may be found in Pelling's work with regard to the central question of the role of socialists in the origins of the Labour Party see: Barbara Malament, 'The Origins of the British Labour Party: Some Interpretive Problems,' unpublished paper delivered to the Conference on British Studies, New York, 6 November 1976. Pelling's work is representative, of course, of both the strengths and weaknesses of this kind of labour history.

2 The exceptions are obvious: E. P. Thompson, Eric Hobsbawm, Royden Harrison are perhaps the most prominent. As early as 1960, Asa Briggs called for a movement away from the equation of trade union history with labour history see Society for the Study of Labour History, *Bulletin*, No. 1 (1960).

3 That of the possible 'discontinuity' in trade union development strikes me as being one such example, for which see A. E. Musson, *British Trade Unions 1800–1875* (London, 1972), Ch. 6 and *Trade Union and Social History* (London, 1974), Ch. 2.

4 Especially important in this revisionism have been John Foster, Gareth Stedman Jones, Perry Anderson, Tom Nairn, Robert Gray, James Hinton.

5 Henry Pelling, *A History of British Trade Unionism* (2nd ed.; London, 1972), pp. 94–7.

6 As already begun by Gareth Stedman Jones, *Outcast London* (London, 1971) and 'Working-Class Culture and Working-Class Politics in London, 1870–1900; Notes on the Remaking of a Working Class,' *Journal of Social History*, Vol. VII, No. 4 (Summer 1974). The recent trend towards local studies is a fruitful way to get into these kinds of question, as illustrated by Robert Gray, *The Labour Aristocracy in Victorian Edinburgh* (Oxford, 1976) and by Geoffrey Crossick, *An Artisan Elite in Victorian Society: Kentish London 1840–1880* (London, 1978). Although not overtly local in its focus, my work is analogous to these studies in its emphasis upon the importance of looking at the locality of the workplace.

7 Some of the History Workshop group at Ruskin College have produced important studies that focus on the workplace: see, in particular, Bob Gilding, *The Journeyman Coopers of East London*, History Workshop Pamphlets No. 4 (Oxford, 1971); and the two volumes edited by Raphael Samuel, *Village Life and Labour* (London, 1975) and *Miners, Quarrymen and Saltworkers* (London, 1977). Other volumes to appear in this series promise to be equally exciting.

8 Thus, John Foster, *Class Struggle and the Industrial Revolution* (London, 1974); James Hinton, *The First Shop Stewards' Movement* (London, 1973); Dave Douglass, 'The Durham Pitman,' in Raphael Samuel (ed.), *Miners, Quarrymen and Saltworkers*, Part 4; Keith Burgess, 'Technological Change and the 1852 lockout in the British Engineering Industry,' *International Review of Social History*, Vol. XIV, Pt. 2 (1969); 'Trade Union Policy and the 1852 lockout in the British Engineering Industry,' *International Review of Social History*, Vol. XVII, Pt. 3

(1972). Frank Wilkinson, 'Collective Bargaining in the Steel Industry in the 1920s,' in Asa Briggs and John Saville (eds.), *Essays in Labour History 1918–1939* (London, 1977).

9 It will be found that the tone of this book is very different from the portrait of building workers (particularly painters) that pervades the classic document by Robert Tressell, *The Ragged Trousered Philanthropists* (Panther Books ed.; London, 1965). Tressell's book is a marvellous description of the exploitation to be found in the trade but the mood and conclusions of the book must be seen in the light of the author's own ambiguities about his social origins and his deep personal despair. A very interesting study could be done to test Tressell's description of Hastings building workers against other evidence to be gleaned from the local newspapers and other sources. It is worth noting, for example, that Hastings was an early centre of painter's trade unionism, and in the 1870s had a sizable branch (about 70 members) of the National Amalgamated Society of Operative House and Ship Painters and Decorators. It should also be remembered that the book was written in the early 1900s, at a time of depression in the industry and that men such as he describes would not be willing to strike as the London workers did in 1914 for nine months. Between 1900 and 1910 the painters were the only section of the building trades which possessed a virtually stable union membership. For the details of Tressell's life, painstakingly unravelled by superb detective work see F. C. Ball, *Tressell of Mugsborough* (London, 1951) and *One of the Damned* (London, 1973).

10 See pp. 36–39.

11 Charles Tilly and Edward Shorter, *Strikes in France 1830–1968* (Cambridge, 1974), along with Tilly's other work, represents such an attempt. Their model of strike determination elevates political objectives and organisational strength to key roles and ignores the element of consciousness. There is much that is useful and much that is wrong with their approach. For an intelligent critique of this and other theories of long-term strike wave models see James Cronin, 'Times of Strife: Industrial Conflict in Britain, 1880–1974' (unpublished PhD dissertation, Department of History, Brandeis University, 1976) esp. Ch. II since published as *Industrial Conflict in Modern Britain* (London, 1979).

12 For a brief critique of the main trend of contemporary industrial sociology see Richard Hyman, *Strikes* (London, 1972), pp. 155–60.

13 It is generally true that labour historians have hardly begun to explore the relevance of industrial sociology for their discipline. My debt to the work of contemporary industrial sociologists will be evident throughout the book. I have found particularly useful the work of Richard Hyman, Alvin Gouldner – especially his classic *Wildcat Strike* (Yellow Springs, Ohio, 1954) – Allan Flanders, Alan Fox, Tom Lupton, and many others who are acknowledged in the notes.

14 For a study of the changing definition of industrial authority see Reinhard Bendix, *Work and Authority in Industry* (New York, 1956).

15 Carter L. Goodrich, *The Frontier of Control* (Pluto Press ed.; London, 1975). The re-publication of this classic is most welcome and illustrates the revived contemporary interest in this manifestation of the class struggle.

16 Similarly, the distinction for me between these terms and workers' control is that the latter represents the potential politicisation of work control into schemes for industrial democracy.

17 See pp. 105–15.

18 Perry Anderson, 'Origins of the Present Crisis,' in Perry Anderson and Robin Blackburn (eds.), *Towards Socialism* (Ithaca, New York, 1965), p. 25.

19 See Chapter 3.
20 There is, of course, much in mainstream traditional labour history that may be found to support the particular interpretation and arguments offered in this book. Thus, for example, H. A. Clegg, Alan Fox and A. F. Thompson, in *A History of British Trade Unions since 1889* (Oxford, 1964), p. 169 point out how national conciliation strengthened the unions and employers against the local branches. But it is typical of this kind of labour history that such themes are secreted away and never occupy the central role that they should and that the conclusions to be drawn from such insights are not consistently applied to interpret the material. Thus, this centralising function is not seen as a prime impetus of the movement towards national conciliation, nor is it developed to understand, for example, the changing nature of rank and file militancy.
21 Anderson, 'Origins of the Present Crisis'; Tom Nairn, 'The Nature of the Labour Party,' in Anderson and Blackburn, *Towards Socialism* and 'The English Working Class,' *New Left Review*, 24 (1964).
22 E. P. Thompson, 'Eighteenth-century English Society: class struggle without class?' *Social History*, Vol. 3, No. 2 (May 1978), p. 149.
23 Sidney and Beatrice Webb, *The History of Trade Unionism* (London, 1902), p. 1.

NOTES TO CHAPTER 1

1 J. O. French, *Plumbers in Unity 1865–1965* (London, 1965), p. 42.
2 E.g. J. Parry Lewis, *Building Cycles and Britain's Growth* (London, 1965); Brinley Thomas, *Migration and Urban Development* (London, 1972).
3 W. S. Hilton, *Industrial Relations in Construction* (London, 1968), p. 9 for figures from the 1960s. Those for 1851 are derived from the Census of Employment.

1960s	1851
80.6% firms employed 0–10 men	80% firms employed 1–10 men
15.4% firms employed 11–50 men	17.3% firms employed 11–74 men
2.1% firms employed 51–99 men	1.8% firms employed 75–149 men
1.8% firms employed 100+ men	0.7% firms employed 150+ men

H. J. Dyos has shown that in London there were no changes in the overall structure of the industry between 1840–70: 80% of firms built 6 houses or less – a figure which compares with Chalklin's findings for the eighteenth century. But in the 1870s–80s there may have been some shift in emphasis towards the medium and larger companies whose numbers rose more than the small firms and by 1899 3% of builders were responsible for 40% of London housing; but 60% was still built by the small men. See, 'The Speculative Builders and Developers of Victorian London,' *Victorian Studies*, Vol. xi, (Summer 1968), pp. 659–60.
4 R. W. Postgate, *The Builders' History* (London, 1923), p. 28. We shall have more to say about machine joinery at a later stage where it will be only too obvious that it is an area in need of research.
5 Raphael Samuel, 'The Workshop of the World: Steam Power and Hand Technology in mid-Victorian Britain,' *History Workshop Journal*, No. 3, Spring 1977.
6 A start has been made in this direction by the very important work of historians associated with Ruskin College under the inspiration of Raphael Samuel. In particular, see Raphael Samuel (ed.), *Miners, Quarrymen and Saltworkers* (London, 1977).

7 E. J. Hobsbawm, 'The Tramping Artisan,' in *Labouring Men* (London, 1964), pp. 35, 49. Patrick Joyce, 'Factory Politics in Lancashire,' *Historical Journal*, Vol. 18, No. 3 (1975), pp. 525–53.

8 G. P. Bevan calculated, for example, that there were 598 building strikes in the 1870s of which the carpenters contributed 187, belying the pacific image presented by the ASC&J, and the masons 151. See G. P. Bevan, 'The Strikes of the Past Ten Years,' Royal Statistical Society, *Journal*, Vol. XLIII (1880), pp. 35–54.

9 Keith Burgess, *The Origins of British Industrial Relations* (London, 1975), p. 138.

10 Postgate, p. 416.

11 We must avoid any discussion of the difficult question of whether and how much the problem itself was new or peculiar to the era of industrialisation. What does seem safe to assert is that even if it was not in and of itself new, the problem of industrial discipline now becomes a *central* feature of social relations and that only with industrialisation does it attain its 'modern' features, shapes and dimensions.

12 Douglas Knoop and G. P. Jones, *The Medieval Mason* (3rd. ed.; Manchester 1967), pp. 167, 180–2, 192–4, where it is suggested that the small-master system was given a boost by the re-building of London after the Great Fire. They also note that although forms resembling general contracting may be found at this period 'it is probable that the tendency was to limit the contractor to particular parts of a building operation.'

13 C. W. Chalklin, *The Provincial Towns of Georgian England. A Study of the Building Process 1740–1820* (London, 1974), p. 168.

14 *Ibid.*, pp. 170, 194. Carpenters and joiners enjoyed this position because their work was such that they had to be familiar with all stages of building work. For this same reason, in the early nineteenth century they were to be the group from which the general contractors in the northwest emerged and later in the century the favourite choice for the post of general foreman. See R. Campbell, *The London Tradesman* (London, 1747), p. 160; Master Builders, *Brief History of the Proceedings of the Operative Builders' Trade Unions in Manchester and the Consequent Turn-Out of the Journeymen Masons, Bricklayers, Joiners, Slaters and Other Trades* (Manchester, 1833), p. 8. For the carpenters' qualifications as foremen see *Building News*, 10 December 1869, p. 439, 31 December 1869, p. 492; Parliamentary Papers, *Royal Commission on Labour*, 1892, Vol. XXXVI, (c. 6795–III), Pt. III, ques. 18824.

15 Chalklin, p. 196.

16 J. H. Clapham, *An Economic History of Modern Britain. The Early Railway Age 1830–1850* (2nd. edition; Cambridge, 1930), pp. 162, 164 for the use of the term 'builder' as an entrepreneur first appearing somewhere between 1750 and 1800 and the effects of the collapses of 1816 and 1826 on the bankruptcies among small builders in London. The government's barrack building programme in the early years of the century may also have encouraged the system's growth because only six contractors built all the barracks. See Sidney Pollard, *The Genesis of Modern Management* (London, 1968), pp. 106–7.

17 Marian Bowley, *The British Building Industry* (Cambridge, 1966), p. 335; Hermione Hobhouse, *Thomas Cubitt: Master Builder* (London, 1971), p. 286 for Cubitt's other innovations such as his early use of machine joinery. A predecessor to Cubitt had been James Burton who erected over 900 houses between 1793 and 1803 by sub-leasing plots to small builders and supplying some of the materials and capital. But he did not directly employ the workmen. See, Dyos, pp. 648–9.

18 *Liverpool Standard,* 27 August 1833, p. 111.
19 See biography in *Master Builders' Associations Journal,* April 1899, p. 11; and *Bee-Hive,* 7 October 1876, p. 6 where it was claimed that Neill was secretary to the local Joiners' Society in the 1840s and in 1841 had urged members to contribute in support of the 1841 Parliament strike.
20 *Royal Commission on Labour,* ques. 18460.
21 In the 1859 lockout, for example, the 24,000 men locked out were all those employed by the 225 masters who employed more than 50 workmen. See National Association for the Promotion of Social Science, *Trades Societies and Strikes* (London, 1860), p. 66.
22 For an example see Friendly Society of Operative Stone Masons, *Fortnightly Returns,* 29 September 1853, p. 6. Hereafter cited as *Fortnightly Returns.* I take the final date on the Return as my reference point.
23 Master Builders, pp. 7, 9–10. For a similar statement from the painters see Master Tradesmen of Liverpool, *An Impartial Statement of the Proceedings of the Members of the Trades Unions Societies and the Steps taken in Consequence* (Liverpool, 1833), p. 20. Significantly, perhaps, no such protest came from the joiners.
24 Postgate, pp. 73–4.
25 *Liverpool Mercury,* 8 December 1833, p. 362 for a letter from a small builder who supported the union: 'I knew that the Union had been encouraged by the smaller masters against the great contractors.'
26 Italics added. These 150 masters employed 800 men. *Manchester Times,* 20 July 1833, 27 July 1833, n.p. There were also suggestions in 1846 that the small masters stood aside; thus, the jobs they controlled – like the Liverpool Dock works – were not stopped. See *Liverpool Mercury,* 5 June 1846, p. 271.
27 Parliamentary Papers, *Select Committee on the Bank Acts,* 1857, Vol. x, (220) Pt. 1, ques. 5466; N. B. Dearle, *Problems of Unemployment in the London Building Trades* (London, 1908), pp. 66, 82–4.
28 Clapham, pp. 163–4; Bowley, p. 334; Chalklin, p. 167.
29 Chalklin, pp. 169, 172, 232. In Nottingham, for example, between 1779 and 1801, of the 98 known builders 80 handled only one project and none more than three. In this period the only exception to this pattern was in Liverpool where the master joiners were already becoming prominent and more of them concentrated on speculation than their predecessors would have done. This, no doubt, was a precursor to general contracting.
30 *Ibid.,* p. 167.
31 H. J. Dyos, *Victorian Suburb* (Leicester, 1961), p. 125. The figures for Camberwell show how speculative activity was characteristic of the large and small firms. Of the 5760 houses built between 1878 and 1880, one third were built by only fifteen firms. But over 400 firms were involved in building Camberwell and about 50% of these had six houses or less under construction.
32 J. Parry Lewis, pp. 12–13, 57–9, 217–22, 230. The appearance since 1945 of the large-scale speculator using improved technical methods of 'mass production' has probably tended to make the industry less susceptible to these kinds of fluctuations.
33 *Select Committee on Bank Acts,* ques. 5414–17.
34 *Ibid.,* ques. 5242; Dyos, *Victorian Suburb,* p. 129.
35 *The Pioneer,* 9 November 1833, p. 74. See also an interesting pamphlet *In Contracting with Builders and Others, Beware* (London, 1851), pp. 7–8 for an attack upon competitive tendering which admitted 'all sorts of men to an equal chance with the fair and honest, and moreover give the worst man the best chance.' The anonymous author claimed that of 17 builders in a town of his

knowledge 7 had been ruined by taking contracts too low and another 6 had nearly shared that fate.

36 Knoop & Jones, p. 155; Parliamentary Papers, *Select Committee on Manufactures, Commerce and Shipping*, 1833, Vol. vi (690), ques. 1817.

37 Bowley, p. 335; *Select Committee on Manufactures*, ques. 4834–35 for a Liverpool sub-contractor who kept 300 labourers on hand and hired them out for 3s 2d per day, paying them a wage of between 2s 5d and 2s 10d.

38 *Fortnightly Returns*, 9 May 1839.

39 *Select Committee on Manufactures*, ques. 4787.

40 Parliamentary Papers, *Select Committee on Masters and Operatives*, 1860, Vol. xxii (307), ques. 856.

41 *Liverpool Mercury*, 13 September 1833, p. 291.

42 See W. S. Hilton, p. 28. Between 1960 and 1965 building firms contributed 13% of all bankruptcies. It would be interesting to know bankruptcy figures for the nineteenth century. See 'Bankruptcy Statistics,' Royal Statistical Society, *Journal*, Vol. xliv (1881), pp. 590–6.

43 *Building News*, 9 September 1859, p. 814.

44 *Master Builder and Associations' Journal*, 5 February 1913, p. 35, 6 August 1913, p. 33.

45 *The Sun*, 4 October 1841, morning edition, n.p.

46 *Liverpool Mercury*, 27 March 1846, p. 156 for a meeting of masters at which it was claimed 'all they contend for is, the liberty of employing workmen at such wages as may be mutually agreed upon without the unnecessary interference of a Club.'

47 *Liverpool Standard*, 27 September 1833, p. 111 for 'free labour.' The Manchester Free Labour Society was formed and supported by the master builders in 1869 to aid them in their struggle with the men of that year. See *Builders' Weekly Reporter*, 7 August 1869, p. 382; Manchester Free Labour Society, *Annual Report*, 1870. Edward Yates, a successful Camberwell speculator, was noted for 'his almost legendary personal inspections of the progress of the works.' Dyos, *Victorian Suburb*, p. 135.

48 *Liverpool Mercury*, 27 March 1846, p. 156.

49 Burgess, p. 138; Shorter and Tilly, *Strikes in France 1830–1968*, p. 206.

50 See E. J. Hobsbawm, 'Trends in the British Labour Movement since 1850' in *Labouring Men* for the best general statement of this position and its application to the British experience. John Foster's *Class Struggle and the Industrial Revolution* (London, 1974) has brilliantly applied it to Oldham and whereas his book may be criticised for being too rigidly Leninist much of his material is in fact an implicit refutation of the Leninist argument; for Foster demonstrates that it was precisely the workers' experience at work that led them to what he believes was a revolutionary consciousness. See also the very important and stimulating critique of Foster, upon which this paragraph partly rests, by Gareth Stedman Jones, 'Class Struggle and Industrial Revolution,' *New Left Review*, No. 90 who has pointed out that the industrial struggles of the 1830s and 1840s were about control of the productive process and not its ownership. And also on this theme see James Hinton's important book *The First Shop Stewards' Movement* (London, 1973).

51 For a critique of what is believed to be the 'workerist illusion' of studying work control as anything more than a limited form of defence see Jean Monds, 'Workers' Control and the Historians: a new Economism,' *New Left Review*, no. 97, (1976), whose criticisms of Hinton and Montgomery seem quite misplaced.

52 For which, of course, John Foster, *Class Struggle and the Industrial Revolution.*
53 Postgate, Chs. 3–4; G. D. H. Cole, *Attempts at General Unionism* (London, 1953).
54 'Why are we not worth 4s. per day now, as well as we were in days that are past?' asked the masons, see Master Tradesmen, pp. 5–7, 20.
55 Only carpenters' wages increased over this period. By 1834, perhaps as a result of these strikes and the concurrent revival of activity, wages were back to their 1825 level. See A. L. Bowley, 'Statistics of Wages in the United Kingdom during the last Hundred Years (Part v). Wages in the Building Trades – English Towns,' Royal Statistical Society, *Journal*, June 1900, p. 310. *Manchester Times,* 4 May 1833, n.p.
56 *Ibid.*, 29 June 1833, n.p.: 'Rebating boards, grooving boards and planks, sinking sash sills, rebating hot or greenhouse rafters, tenoning of every description, is the work of the joiner, not of the sawyer and saw-mills.' See also, Foster, p. 51 for attacks on a builder for the use of machinery in 1831 and 1832.
57 *Liverpool Standard,* 21 June 1833, pp. 34, 35. See Master Tradesmen, pp. 9–11 for a list of their demands which included legal apprenticeship, closed shop, foremen to be 'legal' plasterer, walking money, brush money.
58 Master Builders, p. 8.
59 London Master Builders, *Statement of the Master Builders of the Metropolis in Explanation of the Differences Between them and the Workmen Respecting the Trades' Unions* (London, 1834), p. 12.
60 Postgate, p. 87; Master Builders, p. 5.
61 Master Builders, pp. 7, 10.
62 *Ibid.*, p. 5; *Manchester Times,* 15 June 1833.
63 *Ibid.*, 29 June 1833.
64 *Fortnightly Returns,* 26 May 1837. Allen, it should be noted, had worked at Cubitts for nine years as a trade unionist. *The Sun,* 23 October 1841, evening edition. See also W. S. Hilton, *Foes to Tyranny* (London, 1963), pp. 74–5; Postgate, pp. 130–1; *The Builder,* 31 December 1853, p. 778.
65 I. J. Prothero, 'London Chartism and the Trades,' *Economic History Review,* 2nd series, Vol. XXIV, No. 24 (May 1971), p. 211.
66 OSM, *Narrative of the 1841–42 Parliament Strike,* to be found bound in the 1840–43 volume of the *Fortnightly Returns* and written by Thomas Shortt, the corresponding secretary. An interesting document whose language, until the end of the strike, was explicitly anti-capitalist and revealed a recognition of the deeper issues involved, e.g.: 'If the working classes wish to impose their conditions – if they would alter the system that makes one man so undeservedly rich and another so poor – they must . . . destroy the cause.' 'Avarice and despotism being essential in these days of competition and rivalry, to enable the distributors of our produce to wring from the working-men the means of superfluity and wealth.'
67 *British Queen and Statesman,* 7 November 1841, p. 8; *The Sun,* 15 September evening edition. T. J. Dunning investigated in great detail one of the accusations against Allen and found the men's case substantiated, see *The Sun,* 20 December 1841, evening edition.
68 *Ibid.*, 20 September 1841, morning edition.
69 *Ibid.*, 4 October 1841, morning edition. This claim was made, it should be noted, in a statement by the employers but its content is supported by other evidence which follows.
70 *Fortnightly Returns,* 26 May 1837. The men had won this strike, one of whose

demands was that Allen treat them with respect; Grissell and Peto were also the contractors on this job. For the claim that Allen invented chasing see *British Queen and Statesman*, 7 November 1841, p. 8.

71 *The Sun*, 20 September 1841, morning edition, 4 October 1841, morning edition; *British Queen and Statesman*, 14 November 1841, p. 8: 'The man had been in the habit of "scamping" his work; and then of neglecting to put his tool mark on it.'

72 *The Sun*, 29 October 1841, morning edition.

73 *British Queen and Statesman*, 24 October 1841, p. 16.

74 T. J. Dunning, *Trades' Unions and Strikes* (London, 1860), pp. 45–6.

75 *Weekly Dispatch*, 3 October 1841, p. 475.

76 *Ibid.; The Sun*, 20 November 1841, evening edition.

77 David Dunkerley, *The Foreman* (London, 1975); Alvin Gouldner, *Wildcat Strike*, p. 134 who puts the ambiguities of the foreman's relations with the men in this way: 'While it can be asserted that mutual expectations must have some degree of clarity, if the relationship is to be a stable one, no commitment need be made, however, to the precise amount of clarity which is required.' Thus, on the one hand, the men resent authoritarian foremen but, on the other, want to know the lines of authority. The only attempt at a historical reconstruction that has come to my attention is J. F. Clarke, 'The Foreman – a neglected figure in the history of industrial relations?' North-East Group for the Study of Labour History, *Bulletin*, No. 9, October 1975.

78 Place Collection, *Newspaper Cuttings*, Vol. 55. Cutting from the *Northern Star*, 27 November 1841.

79 *Liverpool Mercury*, 5 June 1846, p. 271; *Fortnightly Returns*, 18 January 1849, p. 5, 11 October 1860, p. 7, 25 October 1860, p. 5, 8 November 1860, p. 5, 20 November 1860, p. 8, 16 July 1863, p. 7, 5 September 1866, pp. 11–12, 19 September 1866, p. 11.

80 *Ibid.*, 27 September 1860, p. 7.

81 Postgate, pp. 97, 113. In 1846 hostility to contracting still surfaced and there was a proposal to form a company to undertake building work see *Liverpool Mercury*, 27 February 1846, p. 106, 22 May 1846, p. 247.

82 For narratives of these conflicts, both of which began as strikes and soon became lockouts see Postgate, pp. 135–7, 167–81.

83 *Liverpool Mercury*, 20 March 1846, p. 145, 3 April 1846, p. 162. The men retorted: 'What do we have to do . . . with the . . . Trade Unions in 1833? Are we responsible for the acts of men who are long in their graves?' *Liverpool Mercury*, 24 April 1846, p. 202. The masters even seem to have seen a recrudescence of the OBU in the pacific and innocuous National Association of United Trades which had offered to arbitrate.

84 Masters who acceded to the men's requests were 'destroying their own authority . . . by surrendering the entire controlling power [of the industry] to the secret mandates of an irresponsible body,' *Liverpool Mercury*, 17 April 1846, p. 190, 8 May 1846, p. 228.

85 *The Builder*, 13 August 1859, p. 528.

86 *Ibid.*, p. 540.

87 *Liverpool Journal*, 4 April 1846, p. 8.

88 *Ibid.*, 2 May 1846, p. 3.

89 *The Builder*, 11 February 1860, p. 92. This may have been the same man who told Howell 'that it was more through petty strikes that the masters associated and opposed the Nine Hours' movement, than through any fear of losing money by conceding those terms. They felt . . . they must take a stand

somewhere.' Operative Bricklayers' Society, *Trade Circular*, 1 June 1862, p. 87.

90 *The Builder*, 11 February 1860, p. 92. This Central Association is not be confused with the Central Association of Master Builders formed in 1872. The 1859 body grew out of the social and fraternal Builders' Society to whom the men had addressed their memorials. It did not survive the end of the lockout.

91 *Liverpool Mercury*, 27 February 1846, p. 106; Manchester Guardian, 14 March 1846, p. 7.

92 Candlelight working was one of the 'encroachments' that followed from the introduction of general contracting. For an earlier complaint of its increasing use see, Friendly Society of Operative House Carpenters and Joiners [the General Union], *Minutes 1837–1841*, p. 8. This strike probably decided the issue of working by artificial light – a means of extending the work day – because it seems to have been accepted after this date. Pauling and Henfrey were an example of the large contracting firms – they even owned brickyards which was fairly unusual at this period. Pauling was a vice-president of the Masters Association. For an interesting account of this strike see Friedrich Engels, *The Condition of the Working Class in England* (Stanford, California, 1968), pp. 338–52. For complaints that Pauling extended hours after this strike see Place Collection, *Newspaper Cuttings*, Vol. 58, p. 21. For a violent and fascinating confrontation the firm had with the local brickmakers see *Manchester Guardian*, 26 April 1843, p. 2, 20 May 1843, p. 6, 24 May 1843, p. 6, 19 August 1843, p. 5, 2 September 1843, p. 6.

93 *Manchester Guardian*, 21 March 1846, p. 10; *Liverpool Mercury*, 17 April 1846, p. 190; *Liverpool Journal*, 21 May 1846, p. 3; *The Builder* 1846, p. 188.

94 *Statement of Facts Connected with the Turn-Out in the Lancashire Building Trades* (Manchester, 1846), p. 24.

95 *Fortnightly Returns*, 25 December 1845.

96 *Ibid.*, 26 January 1843, 12 December 1844, 6 February 1845, 20 February 1845, 6 March 1845.

97 This series of strike statistics has been developed from 2769 masons' strikes reported in the *Fortnightly Returns* 1836–96. For a description of the series see Appendix A.

98 B. Weber, 'A New Index of Residential Construction and Long Cycles in House-Building in Great Britain, 1838–1950,' *Scottish Journal of Political Economy*, Vol. 2, No. 2 (June 1955), p. 131 where 1844–46 are shown as peak years in Liverpool and although the town was somewhat exceptional in this it was from there that the movement originated. See also A. K. Cairncross & B. Weber, 'Fluctuations in the Building Industry in Great Britain, 1785–1849,' *Economic History Review*, 2nd. series, Vol. IX, No. 2 (1956–57), pp. 288–97. For the impending collapse see *Liverpool Mercury*, 13 March 1846, p. 130.

99 Thus, see speeches at meeting of masters, quoted in *Liverpool Mercury*, 27 March 1846, p. 156.

100 F. C. Gillespie, *Labor and Politics in England* (London: Frank Cass, 1968), pp. 136–42; Postgate, pp. 167–79, Royden Harrison, *Before the Socialists* (London, 1965), pp. 3, 68, 259. There had been discussions amongst the London carpenters about amalgamating since at least 1852; see *Reynolds's Newspaper*, 4 January 1852, p. 14, 27 August 1854, p. 16 when the Metropolitan Carpenters' and Joiners' Association passed a resolution for an amalgamation of all London Societies and appointed a sub-committee to bring it about.

101 *The Builder*, 1 May 1858, p. 317.

102 *Ibid.*, 6 November 1858, p. 783.

103 *Ibid.*, 30 July 1859, pp. 498–9; Postgate, p. 171.
104 Clapham, Vol. ii, p. 455. In 1857 there had been an unusual amount of organisational activity and demonstrations amongst unemployed building workers which pre-figured the more celebrated events of the 1880s. See *Building News*, 9, 16, 30 January 1857, 13 February 1857, 3, 10 April 1857.
105 *Building News*, 16 April 1858, p. 409, 23 April 1858, pp. 432–4, 3 June 1859, p. 527; *The Builder*, 8 May 1858, p. 317.
106 Potter on machinery: 'They had seen that when a machine was . . . introduced to a shop, if a labourer could do the work he was put to it.' *Building News*, 30 April 1858, p. 460. There had been no mention of machinery in the 1853 movement. For strikes against the machine see: *The Builder*, 27 May 1854, p. 281; *Nottingham Review*, 28 April 1854, p. 4, 12 May 1854, p. 4, 16 June 1854, p. 4.
107 *Building News*, 16 April 1858, p. 409.
108 *Ibid.*, 4 March 1859, p. 221, 24 June 1859, p. 580; *The Builder*, 5 February 1859, p. 98; *Fortnightly Returns*, 25 August 1853, p. 5.
109 *The Times*, 12 August 1859, p. 10; *Building News*, 12 August 1859, p. 730, 22 April 1859, p. 389; *The Builder*, 28 January 1854, p. 45 for a claim that bricklayers succeeded in diminishing its extent.
110 *Fortnightly Returns*, 4 September 1856, p. 5.
111 *Building News*, 11 June 1858, pp. 608–10, 23 July 1858, p. 744.
112 *Ibid.*, 25 February 1859, p. 198. Evan Daniel, *A Prize Essay on the Reduction of the Hours of Labour* (London, 1859). But contrast this with Abraham White-head, *The Builders' Dispute in London* (London, 1859) where the machinery argument occupies the whole case, and with Potter's Address to the Building Workers of the Country for which see *The Builder*, 4 June 1859, p. 380.
113 *Building News*, 22 April 1859, p. 389.
114 *The Times*, 12 August 1859, p. 10; *The Builder*, 20 November 1858, p. 783. For the back-day system which was another grievance see *Building News*, 10 June 1859, pp. 546–7.
115 S. & B. Webb, *The History of Trade Unionism*, p. 217; Postgate, p. 171. This version appears to derive from that recorded in the Building Trades Conference, *Minute Book, 1858–1859*, 22 July 1859.
116 Thomas Brassey, 'On the Rise of Wages in the Building Trades of London,' Royal Institute of British Architects, *Sessional Papers* (1877–78), p. 175; *The Builder*, 30 July 1859, p. 500.
117 *Building News*, 22 April 1859, p. 389, 3 June 1859, p. 527.
118 These particular strike statistics have to be read all the time in conjunction with the other evidence; the small number of cases make them only a loose guide to the patterns of conflict.
119 Postgate, pp. 164, 168; Place Collection, *Newspaper Cuttings*, Vol. 58, Part 2, p. 73; *The Builder*, 25 October 1851, p. 681, 1 November 1851, p. 683, 6 December 1851, p. 772. The Myers strike was an interesting reflection of the needs for industrial discipline. He tried to abrogate the 4 p.m. Saturday from those who persistently absented themselves from work. The eventual com-promise was the men could lose 10 hours per week without losing the 'privilege.'
120 *Building News*, 30 September 1859, p. 587.
121 Building Trades Conference, *Minute Book*, 1 July 1859. For earlier ballots which had failed to show a majority for a strike see 15 April 1859, 24 June 1859.
122 The carpenters of the East End, for example, would do piecework, those of the West End would not.

123 Postgate, Ch. 15.
124 J. W. F. Rowe, *Wages in Theory and Practice* (London, 1928), p. 66. This even operated with the labourers whose differential to skilled men went back five hundred years. For an example of labourers striking to maintain the differential see *Birmingham Daily Post*, 8 April 1874, p. 4.
125 Foster, pp. 207–8.
126 Allen Flanders, *The Fawley Productivity Agreements* (London, 1964), p. 134.
127 M. A. Bienefield, *Working Hours in British Industry: An Economic History* (London, 1972), p. 5.
128 *The Builder*, 5 February 1859, p. 98. We must remember that these men had in mind a day without overtime. This, of course, was a problem, for the nine hours day would be reduced in effectiveness without controlling overtime. It is significant, therefore, that when the employers finally granted the nine hours in 1872, they determinedly resisted the men's desire for a prohibitive rate of overtime pay.
129 *Fortnightly Returns*, 26 January 1846, pp. 3–6.
130 Foster, pp. 108–11.
131 Sidney and Beatrice Webb, *Industrial Democracy* (London, 1913), pp. 330–1 for how a reduction of hours served to extend and strengthen the standard rate.
132 Tom Mann, *What a Compulsory 8 Hour Working Day means to the Workers*, Pluto Press Reprints in Labour History, No. 2 (London, 1971), p. 26.
133 *Liverpool Journal*, 11 April 1846, p. 2.
134 *The Builder*, 21 May 1859, p. 350; George Potter, *The Labour Question* (London, 1861).
135 *The Builder*, 11 February 1860, p. 92.
136 *Building News*, 27 May 1859, pp. 501–2; *The Builder*, 16 July 1859, p. 479.
137 *Ibid.*, 15 October 1859, p. 678, 19 November 1859, p. 763. Ayrton had also been active on behalf of the bakers in their strike against night work of this year. The employers submitted the union rules to Edwin James, QC and James Allen for their opinion as to their legality; none, of course, were found to be illegal.
138 *Fortnightly Returns*, 15 September 1859, pp. 6–7, 24 November 1859, pp. 8–9, 13 October 1859, p. 6 for hostility to Harnott's intervention.

NOTES TO CHAPTER 2
1 See Chapter 3.
2 On this see Lord Amulree, *Industrial Arbitration in Great Britain* (London, 1929), Chs. 7 & 9; Ian F. Sharp, *Industrial Conciliation and Arbitration in Great Britain* (London, 1950), Pt. 2, Ch. 1.
3 For the Wear shipwrights court of arbitration see: Royal Society of Arts, *Journal*, Vol. II, 1854; *Sunderland Herald*, 4 February 1853, p. 5, 11 February 1853, p. 5, 22 February 1853, p. 5, 4 March 1853, p. 5, 25 March 1853, p. 8, 8 April 1853, p. 5, 14 October 1853, p. 8. For the breakdown of the system see 21 July 1854, p. 5, 3 November 1854, p. 8, 17 November 1854, p. 7, 1 December 1854, p. 5. The major exception to this, of course, was the Nottingham hosiery board formed in 1860 for which see F. A. Wells, *The British Hosiery Trade* (London, 1935), Ch. IX.
4 W. L. Burn, *The Age of Equipoise* (New York, 1965), Ch. 5.
5 See Trygve Tholfsen, *Working Class Radicalism in Mid-Victorian England* (London, 1976), Ch. 6 for a good discussion of the role of the law in this respect.

6 *The Builder,* 24 November 1860, p. 756.

7 *Builders' Trade Circular,* 26 September 1872, p. 9.

8 Amalgamated Society of Carpenters and Joiners, *Monthly Reports,* September 1868, p. 238. This also suggests an interestingly ambiguous attitude to union membership and recruitment.

9 Allan Flanders, 'Collective Bargaining,' in Allan Flanders & H. A. Clegg (eds.), *The System of Industrial Relations in Great Britain* (Oxford, 1954), pp. 261, 262; H. A. Clegg, *The System of Industrial Relations in Great Britain* (2nd ed.; Oxford, 1970), pp. 4–5. The use of the term 'custom' in this sense is most inadequate for it implies a formless body of 'traditions' which operated on the sanction of ancient lineage. This, as we shall see, was not the way the system operated. But, like most other industrial sociologists, Clegg does realise the importance of worker regulation in determining these 'customs.'

10 We shall have occasion to note again how this change in the structure of industrial relations was only one aspect of a whole series of changes that occurred at this time which tended to the formalisation of relationships within society.

11 S. & B. Webb, *Industrial Democracy,* p. 173.

12 Hinton, *The First Shop Stewards' Movement,* p. 78; S. & B. Webb, *Industrial Democracy,* pp. 167–9.

13 John Cousins & Richard Brown, 'Patterns of Paradox: Shipbuilding Workers' Images of Society,' in Martin Bulmer (ed.), *Working-Class Images of Society* (London, 1975), p. 62; Tom Lupton, *On the Shop Floor* (London, 1963), pp. 114–15.

14 H. A. Clegg, *The System of Industrial Relations in Great Britain,* p. 27; Lupton, pp. 62–3.

15 Clegg, p. 21; Stephen Hill, *The Dockers* (London, 1976), pp. 43–55, for the extent of work group activity amongst unskilled dock workers.

16 Richard Hyman, *The Workers' Union* (Oxford, 1971), p. 192. It is also evident that long before unionisation, dock workers were operating similar kinds of work group associations, see E. L. Taplin, *Liverpool Dockers and Seamen 1870–1890,* University of Hull Occasional Papers in Economic and Social History, No. 6 (Hull, 1974); Stanley Mathewson, *Restriction of Output Among Unorganised Workers* (New York, 1931), p. 163.

17 H. A. Turner, *Trade Union Growth, Structure and Policy* (Toronto, 1962), pp. 85–9, 130.

18 See I. Boraston, H. A. Clegg, and M. Rimmer, *Workplace and Union* (London, 1975), which is a study of the relationship between work groups and the union in 14 different locales. For good historical studies of work group activity see the essays by Dave Douglass and Merfyn Jones in Raphael Samuel (ed.), *Miners, Quarrymen and Saltworkers,* Parts 2 and 4.

19 Lupton, pp. 2, 147–51, 174, 179–81.

20 Allen Flanders, *The Fawley Productivity Agreements,* pp. 64, 257–64.

21 *Ibid.,* pp. 139–40.

22 *Ibid.,* pp. 96–8, 129–30, 138–9, 144–5.

23 Edward Owen Evans, ' "Cheap at Twice the Price." Shop Stewards and Workshop Relations in Engineering,' in Malcolm Warner (ed.), *The Sociology of the Workplace* (New York, 1973), p. 98.

24 Clegg, p. 8.

25 Parliamentary Papers, *Report of a Court of Inquiry into trade disputes at the Barbican and Horseferry Road construction sites in London,* 1966–67, Vol. xxxvii (Cmnd. 3396). Even down to its red-baiting tactics this is a fascinating document,

testimony to the enduring nature of the themes of this book. There are even parallels to the 1841 Parliament Strike in the abusive foremen, the dismissal of men for bad time keeping (one of whom had been kept at home because his wife was pregnant), and the dismissal of a man who had been off work sick (see, pp. 83–5). More important is its evidence as to the growth of work group power at the worksites and the formalisation of that autonomous regulation through site committees.

26 Good examples are Edmund Potter, *Some Opinions on Trades' Unions and the Bill of 1869*, (2nd. ed. London, 1870), James Stirling, *Unionism* (Glasgow, 1869), J. Cranbrook, *On Wages in Relation to Trade Unions and Strikes* (Edinburgh, 1868).

27 H. W. McCready, 'British Labour and the Royal Commission on Trade Unions, 1867–69,' *University of Toronto Quarterly*, Vol. xxiv (1954–55), p. 397.

28 Parliamentary Papers, *Royal Commission on Trade Unions*, First Report, 1867, Vol. xxxii (3873), ques. 2979–97; Third Report, 1867, Vol. xxxii (3910), ques. 4522, 4616, 4724.

29 *Ibid.*, First Report, ques. 3120–25, 3205–11, 3227.

30 *Ibid.*, ques. 3218, 3239, 3363, 3364, 3369, 3373a, 3568.

31 Postgate, p. 456; S. & B. Webb, *History of Trade Unionism*, p. 492. Totals of the various trades are taken from the Census of 1871.

32 *Royal Commission on Trade Unions*, First Report, ques. 2968.

33 *Ibid.*, ques. 3389–449 for this interesting exchange between Mault and Harrison.

34 *Building News*, 29 July 1859, p. 688, 17 February 1860, p. 125.

35 *Ibid.*, 16 September 1859, p. 837. For non-unionist hostility to the Birmingham discharge note see *The Builder*, 21 January 1865, p. 50. For a similar pattern in 1914 see Postgate, p. 416.

36 Postgate, p. 172.

37 *The Builder*, 13 August 1859, p. 528: 'that even the very number of bricks to be put in a hod is restricted – that a bricklayer is never to lay down his trowel to lift anything with both hands, or work beside his master.'

38 Turner, pp. 122, 300.

39 *Glasgow Evening Post*, 7 April 1868, p. 3; *Bee-Hive*, 11 April 1868, p. 5; Nat. Ass. Prom. Soc. Sc., *Trades' Societies and Strikes*, p. 271.

40 *Bee-Hive*, 15 August 1868, p. 6.

41 *Royal Commission on Trade Unions*, First Report, ques. 1713; see also, *Select Committee on Masters and Operatives*, ques. 900. Howell himself is an example of this. He worked three years in London – some of the time as an 'improver' – before joining the union under the stimulus of the nine hours agitation. See George Howell, *Mss. Autobiography*, Vol. ii, p. 45: 'There was not then the same pressure to join a trade union ... But I always stood up for the full wage.'

42 E. S. Beesly, 'Trade Unions,' *Westminster Review*, Vol. 20 (October 1861), p. 534.

43 *Capital and Labour*, 25 April 1877, p. 228.

44 *Fortnightly Returns*, 10 April 1873, p. 11. See ASC&J, Maidstone Branch, *Minute Book*, 11 July 1866, for the fining of members for working during a strike.

45 *Newcastle Daily Chronicle*, 24 May 1888, p. 8. This was during a platers' helpers strike.

46 *Fortnightly Returns*, 12 November 1868, p. 7.

47 *Bee-Hive*, 24 June 1865, p. 5.

48 *Glasgow Evening Post,* 7 April 1868, p. 3. Only 20 men of the 317 who struck work on the first day were unionists.
49 *Bee-Hive,* 4 April 1873, p. 5.
50 *North British Daily Mail,* 7 June 1866, p. 2, 30 May 1866, p. 2, 31 May 1866, p. 2, 2 June 1866, pp. 2–3, 18 June 1866, p. 2, 19 June 1866, p. 2.
51 For which see E. Allen, J. F. Clarke, N. McCord, D. J. Rowe, *The North-East Engineers' Strikes of 1871* (Newcastle, 1971).
52 John Burnett, *A History of the Engineers' Strike in Newcastle and Gateshead* (Newcastle, 1872), p. 6. Gourlay had been a leader of the 1866 movement who had been dismissed by C. M. Palmer for his role; Nine Hours Movement, *Conference between C. M. Palmer and the Workmen of Jarrow,* 22 February 1866, which shows how the demand in the shipyards emanated from the joiners.
53 *Fortnightly Returns,* 20 February 1845, p. 3, 2 October 1845, p. 3, 15 April 1858, pp. 6–7, 10 March 1864, p. 7.
54 *Bee-Hive,* 16 April 1864, p. 5, 2 July 1864, p. 5, 13 August 1864, p. 5, 7 January 1865, p. 5. In Nottingham there were thirty to forty union men; in Birmingham and the Midlands of 1500–1800 men on strike only 600 were unionists.
55 *North British Daily Mail,* 11 July 1866, p. 2.
56 Howell, *Autobiography,* Vol. 1, n.p.
57 Boraston, Clegg, etc., *Workplace and Union,* pp. 177, 182, 183; Lupton, pp. 150–1.
58 *Webb Collection,* E, Section A, Vol. VI, f. 45.
59 Such a custom could, of course, make sense for the employer because the longest serving labourer was also likely to be a reliable and good worker. But in this case the gang leader would have had strong ties of loyalty to the group; a stranger would have no such ties and his line of responsibility would flow only to the employer.
60 *Royal Commission on Trade Unions,* Third Report, ques. 4326–32. The joiners did not re-open the job until April 1868 see ASC&J, Manchester 1st Branch, *Minute Book,* 22 April 1868.
61 British Association for the Advancement of Science, *Report of the 43rd. Meeting* (Bradford, 1873), p. 196.
62 V. L. Allen, 'The Origins of Industrial Conciliation and Arbitration,' *International Review of Social History,* Vol. IX (1964), Part 2, p. 238. This same implication of the dependence of strike action upon organisation is also to be found in Shorter and Tilly, *Strikes in France.* But I suspect that they have got it the wrong way around and that it is strike action that stimulates organisation. We may note the examples of Dewsbury and Plymouth, neither of which were cities of union strength but both managed in 1864 to secure advantageous codes of rules. See *Fortnightly Returns,* 25 August 1864, p. 5.
63 Associated Carpenters' and Joiners' of Scotland, Edinburgh Joiners' Union, *Letter Book,* 6 May 1872. It is a significant comment on the union as an agent of industrial relations that the longest letter in this collection is concerned with a claim for superannuation and death benefit – the largest single item in carpenters' branches concerned tool and other friendly society benefits.
64 General Union of Carpenters and Joiners, Ashton-u-Lyne Branch, *Minute Book,* 7 October 1859, 2 April 1860.
65 ASC&J, Manchester Branch, *Minute Book,* 10 December 1863.
66 GUC&J, Ashton Branch, *Minute Book,* 15 February 1862, 16 May 1864.
67 W. Hamish Fraser, *Trade Unions and Society. The Struggle for Acceptance 1850–1880* (London, 1974), p. 100.
68 Clyde Shipwrights, *Arbitration Between Clyde Shipbuilders' and Engineers' Associa-*

tion and the Clyde Associated Shipwrights (Glasgow, 1878), pp. 6–7 for the destructive role of the 1866 strike and the weakness of the men in the early seventies.

69 Fred Bower, *Rolling Stonemason* (London, 1935), pp. 45–6.

70 *Bee-Hive*, 4 October 1862, p. 5.

71 *Royal Commission on Trade Unions*, Fourth Report, ques. 8085, 8094.

72 Postgate, p. 456.

73 S. & B. Webb, *History of Trade Unionism*, p. 492; USB, *Annual Report*, 1879 p. vi; J. E. Mortimer, *History of the Boilermakers' Society* (London, 1973), pp. 67–8. Note also the *Select Committee on Manufactures*, ques. 4772–4 where, for London in 1833 it was reported that the men 'have gone into unions during the last fortnight.'

74 *Webb Collection*, E, A, Vol. 13, ff. 474–6.

75 J. D. M. Bell, 'Stability of Membership in Trade Unions,' *Scottish Journal of Political Economy*, Vol. 1, No. 1 (March 1954). Union membership as an expression of solidarity is a pattern which extends beyond this period. In correlating trade union membership increases with strike activity for the period 1896–1913, Cronin found it to be much closer in the same year than when lagged by one year. See Cronin, p. 145. For the work group as a reference group to understand union attachment see John Child, Ray Loveridge and Malcolm Warner, 'Towards an Organisational Study of Trade Unions,' *Sociology*, Vol. 7, No. 1 (January 1973), p. 75.

76 S. & B. Webb, *Industrial Democracy*, pp. 183–4; Allan Flanders, *Industrial Relations* (London, 1965), p. 11.

77 For a succinct characterisation of this feature of British industrial relations see O. Kahn-Freund as quoted in Flanders, *Industrial Relations*, p. 27: ' "A very firm procedural framework for a very flexible corpus of substantive rules, rather than a code laid down for a fixed time – such is the institutional aspect of much collective bargaining in this country." '

78 *Ibid.*

79 *Ibid.*, p. 29 for how national procedures for settling disputes always preceded national agreements on wages in Britain. Building is a particularly good example of this.

80 The importance of autonomous regulation has been widely recognised, especially by industrial sociologists but it has never been systematically examined as a category in its own right. See Clegg, pp. 4–5; Turner, p. 204: 'Craft unions preferred autonomous regulation to collective bargaining,' is typical of the common assumption that autonomous regulation was characteristic only of skilled, craft workers. See also, V. L. Allen, 'The Origins of Industrial Conciliation and Arbitration'; Clegg, Fox, Thompson, *A History of British Trade Unions Since 1889*, pp. 4–14.

81 Thus, the refusal to meet with any but their own men was quite rational given the prevailing conceptions of what constituted legitimate authority relationships. C. M. Palmer's habit of meeting with his whole workforce when general demands were made is a particularly good example of this. See also Place Collection, *Newspaper Cuttings*, Vol. 58, Part 1, p. 24 for the deputation of Birkenhead masons in 1846 who waited uninvited on the masters, handed a letter to them and requested an answer. In reply, the masters gave the letter to the waiter of the hotel, 'sending word that they had no answer to give.'

82 See *Manchester Examiner and Times*, 26 October 1857, p. 4, 4 November 1857, p. 4; *Manchester Guardian*, 6 November 1857, p. 4, 12 November 1857, p. 4, 9 December 1857, p. 3. For Bristol: *Western Daily Press*, 27 July 1860, p. 4, 2 August 1860, p. 4, 31 July 1860, p. 3, 16 October 1860, p. 1. In this case

there had been some informal contact with Harnott (Bristol was the HQ of the Society that year) before the strike began. But the negotiations that followed the strike were all conducted by letter or public meeting. The following year a code was drawn up by the men and submitted to the masters – most of whom worked to it, see 27 March 1861, p. 1. For Leeds: *Bee-Hive*, 28 May 1864, p. 5; *Leeds Mercury*, 24 May 1864, p. 3, 25 May 1864, p. 3, 27 May 1864, p. 3, 28 May 1864, p. 5, 30 May 1864, p. 3 for eventual meeting and negotiation. For Barrow: *Bee-Hive*, 6 May 1865, p. 4. For Liverpool: *Bee-Hive*, 19 September 1868, p. 5.

83 *Bee-Hive*, 10 February 1866, p. 5; ASC&J, Maidstone Branch, *Minute Book*, 8 November 1866, 21 June 1875. For a similar example from Doncaster see *Fortnightly Returns*, 29 June 1865, p. 7.

84 E.g. *Bee-Hive*, 30 April 1864, p. 5, 7 May 1864, p. 5, 16 May 1865, p. 5 for Huddersfield masons contemplating mediation by Chamber of Commerce.

85 Nat. Ass. Prom Soc. Sc., *Trades Societies*, p. 285. Even those like J. C. Proudfoot who were in favour of conciliation boards only envisioned them as temporarily being called into being as the need arose: 'Suppose, for example, that twenty workmen were in dispute with their employer, the twenty workmen could elect two representatives, and the employer could elect two representatives, and the people elected thus form the Board,' *Select Committee on Masters and Operatives*, 1856, ques. 2878. The arbitration rule forced on the Manchester masons in 1862 was dropped on their insistence in 1865 because 'you know how obnoxious the same rule was always to us,' *Bee-Hive*, 1 April 1865, p. 6.

86 *Fortnightly Returns*, 19 July 1849, p. 6, 31 May 1855, p. 4, 29 October 1865, p. 8. The Glasgow bricklayers had a well-established system of each side drawing up their separate rules and only meeting if they had serious differences. *Royal Commission on Trade Unions*, Fourth Report, 1867, Vol. xxxii, (3952), ques. 6779.

87 *Fortnightly Returns*, 26 December 1857, p. 5, 30 January 1862, p. 9.

88 See *Bee-Hive*, 29 November 1862, p. 5, 17 May 1873, p. 13 for examples from the masters.

89 See *Royal Commission on Trade Unions*, First Report, ques. 3068 for Mault: 'Until the establishment of our association [i.e. GBA] . . . the masters were so thoroughly disunited, that they never dreamt about taking any action as to trade rules . . . and . . . the initiative was taken in every case by the trades unions . . . they prepared a code of rules and the masters were content with either doing nothing against the obnoxious clauses . . . or accepting them per force at the hands of the union.' Permanent masters' associations begin to appear in the late fifties, not becoming common until the mid sixties. The difficulties in the way of united action was a consequence of the contract system and the large tail of small builders at the bottom end of the trade. Note also Atherton Lodge of the OSM in 1869 on their new rules: 'We do not think we shall have much difficulty in getting them: we are not troubled by a masters' association here,' *Fortnightly Returns*, 15 April 1869, p. 7. The Liverpool Architects' Presidential address in 1861 pointed out that the men were better able to withstand strikes than the employers who were only partially in support of their local association, see *The Builder*, 19 October 1861, p. 717.

90 *Fortnightly Returns*, 11 July 1844, p. 3, 10 March 1853, p. 4.

91 *Ibid.*, 11 September 1851, p. 3, 29 July 1852, p. 4, 25 July 1857, p. 6, 7 January 1859, p. 5, 24 November 1859, p. 4, 10 April 1860, p. 7, 16 August 1860, p. 7.

92 *Ibid.*, 18 May 1865, p. 9, 21 September 1865, p. 8.

93 *Bee-Hive*, 9 May 1863, p. 5, 24 December 1864, p. 5, 7 April 1866, p. 6, 11 January 1868, p. 5, 9 June 1866, p. 5.

94 Hyman, *Workers' Union*, p. 200, n. 66.
95 P. Graham, *Lecture on the Tendency of Trades Unionism* (London, 1875), pp. 11–12.
96 *Bee-Hive*, 30 March 1867, p. 7.
97 *Royal Commission on Trade Unions*, First Report, ques. 1491; S. & B. Webb, *Industrial Democracy*, pp. 304–8.
98 *Manchester Times*, 27 July 1833; *Reports from Civil and Military Authorities from Distressed Areas in the North*, PRO, HO 40/31 f. 60.
99 *Capital and Labour*, 15 April 1874, p. 156, 29 April 1874, p. 203.
100 *Royal Commission on Trade Unions*, First Report, ques. 3120.
101 W. T. Thornton, *On Labour* (2nd ed.; London, 1870), p. 328.
102 Graham, p. 10.
103 *Jarrow Guardian*, 24 January 1879, p. 3, 7 February 1879, p. 3.
104 James Hopkinson, *Memoirs of a Victorian Cabinet Maker* (London, 1968), p. 31; Thornton, p. 328.
105 *Statement of Facts*, p. 24; *Royal Commission on Trade Unions*, First Report, ques. 3123, 3125; Thornton, p. 329. At Birmingham Thornton claimed 'by agreement between masters and men, the number of bricks that may be carried varies with the height to which they are carried' and some labourers refused to wheel bricks across a canal and threatened to strike unless they were stacked on one side and hod-carried to the other side. For labourers' restriction of production in 1830s see Anon. [Charles Knight], *Trades Unions and Strikes* (London, 1834), p. 73.
106 *Bee-Hive*, 5 September 1868, p. 6.
107 *Ibid.*, 20 March 1869, p. 5.
108 *Select Committee on Manufactures*, ques. 1674, 1676.
109 *Ibid.*, 4771.
110 Charity Organisation Society, *Special Committee on Unskilled Labour* (London, 1908), pp. 104–5.
111 *Royal Commission on Trade Unions*, First Report, ques. 1748.
112 *Ibid.*, ques. 3373a.
113 *Western Daily Press*, 17 August 1860, p. 4.
114 Alan Fox, and Allan Flanders, 'The Reform of Collective Bargaining: From Donovan to Durkheim,' *British Journal of Industrial Relations*, Vol. 7 (1969); Clegg, p. 39.
115 In what follows the notion of work group control over certain aspects of the productive process is not seen as limited solely to the particular power relations at specific work sites but is regarded as a general phenomenon extending over a town or district. This is analogous to the situation in large factories of the present day where different work groups, operating with varying degrees of autonomy and coordination, may experience a common expansion of their work control power. The links between the various work groups is a complex matter which is not much illuminated by the historical sources but the walking delegates that seem to have been a feature of building trade unionism were presumably important in this respect. We do need to know much more about the workings of the labour market and the local contacts and relationships between the men but later in our period the COS Report on Unskilled Labour in London revealed the informal channels of communication and exchange of knowledge within the community of the trade. Contemporary experience as illustrated by the Cameron Commission report establishes that control by work groups can extend beyond the confines of a particular job to encompass a wider working and geographical area and our argument that

this was the case in the 1860s is both reasonable and coherent with the facts even if the mechanics of the process remain unclear.

116 Lupton, pp. 87, 91, 194–5. In the women's garment factory 'many of the objective conditions for control were present, and some control could have been exercised had the "will to control" been there.'

117 Leonard Sayles, *The Behaviour of Industrial Work Groups* (New York, 1958), pp. 101–2. For the brickmakers see Richard Price, 'The Other Face of Respectability: Violence in Manchester Brickmaking 1850–1870,' *Past and Present*, No. 75, 1975. In the case of brickmaking there were other factors such as the restrictions on family labour under the Workshop Acts of 1866 and 1876. These were important in destroying the family basis of the traditional work group in brickmaking.

118 Goodrich, *The Frontier of Control*, p. 175.

119 Sayles, p. 59.

120 The same applies generally to overtime which also threatens cohesion except where it can be controlled – as it was at Fawley. It is this, of course, which explains the constant efforts in nineteenth-century building to prohibit its working. See Clegg, p. 33.

121 G. D. H. Cole, *Workshop Organisation* (Oxford, 1923), p. 180; S. & B. Webb, *Industrial Democracy*, pp. 293–6 for the interesting letter from William Denny on the men's opposition to lump piecework which the Webbs seemed not to grasp was based upon the inability of the men to control the pace and amount of work under this system: 'It is imperative in such kinds of piecework as by their nature cannot be reduced to regular rates that either the employer should take the responsibility of safeguarding his workmen's interests, or that the workmen themselves should . . . obtain an effective control over them.'

122 Cole, *Workshop Organisation*, p. 65.

123 Mortimer, pp. 42, 70.

124 *Select Committee on Masters and Operatives*, 1860, ques. 873.

125 *Building News*, 4 April 1862, p. 243.

126 The only possible exception to this general rule seems to have been the painters who were reputed to welcome hourly payment because it 'causes more employment during the winter months in our trade.' *Webb Collection*, E, A, Vol. 12, f. 42. But there were many strikes against the introduction of the system, see William MacDonald, *The True Story of Trades' Unions* (Manchester, 1867), p. 22; *The Builder*, 25 May 1861, p. 361; *Birmingham Daily Post*, 10 May 1866, p. 7.

127 Harrison, *Before the Socialists*, pp. 30–1. But note that Brassey claimed in 1873 that for London 'the most important advances have been obtained by the unskilled workman.' See 'On the Rise of Wages . . . ,' p. 147. From Liverpool in 1864, a typical comment: 'For the last twenty years the trade has never been so brisk,' *The Builder*, 2 July 1864, p. 498.

128 M. A. Bienefeld, *Working Hours in British Industry: An Economic History* p. 95.

129 *The Builder*, 9 February 1861, p. 100, 9 March 1861, p. 159, 15 June 1861, p. 413.

130 *Ibid.*, 14 May 1864, p. 356, 4 June 1864, p. 423, 25 June 1864, p. 472.

131 Clapham, II, p. 453; Postgate, p. 455.

132 See Appendix B for a complete breakdown of Bowley's tables into percentage increases.

133 On the genesis of the Royal Commission see Webb, *History of Trade Unionism*, pp. 242–8; Fraser, pp. 62, 90.

134 E.g., walking time was 'twisted . . . very much to the injury of the masters,'

Royal Commission on Trade Unions, First Report, ques. 3364, 3369; Thornton, p. 330.

135 Some typical examples. *The Builder,* 16 February 1861, p. 16 on the Manchester bricklayers: 'One innovation after another [has] crept in so as to leave the masters completely at the mercy of their men.' *The Builder,* 31 December 1861, p. 955: 'Unions have become so powerful that they attempt to usurp the rights of capital, and not only to dictate to the masters the terms of labour, but endeavour to deprive them from having a voice in their portion of the agreement, and frequently dictate what men should be employed, and the amount of labour executed. See *Fortnightly Returns,* 5 September 1867, pp. 11–12, 19 September 1867, p. 11 for a strike against a foreman in Liverpool as an example of the 'dictation' the masters complained about. The foreman demanded that the men 'point in the manner laid down.' The men resented this 'tyrannical' behaviour, demanded his dismissal, ordered him 'shelved' and expelled him from the union. They refused to cooperate with a union investigating committee, or accept a compromise worked out by that committee, ignored the union's condemnation of the strike as 'illegal' and won their point.

136 Indeed, this was the largest single issue for the whole series, comprising 12.9% of all strikes. The specific issues included in this category with their total numbers are as follows: Enforcement of union membership, 358; Enforcement of union membership on foremen, 6; Enforcement of union fine, 44; Enforcement of union arrears, 29; Enforcement of union rules on men, 3; Against Foremen, 26; Against employment of blacklegs, 45; Dismissal of union men, 10; Against obnoxious men, 7; Others, 13.

137 It will be seen that craft enforcement strikes also increase during those years, of which those over worked stone were the most important composing 33% of such strikes in 1860s and 47% in the 1870s. This was a manifestation of the men's increased sphere of control. Worked stone strikes become important again in the 1890s.

138 These strikes were concentrated in the north and northwest – some 60% occurring in these regions. It was here that worker power had advanced furthest. Their basic pattern remained the same over the whole period, with some exaggeration of their characteristics in these years.

139 Hopkinson, p. 23.

140 *Webb Collection,* E, C, Vol. 50, 1865 Rules, p. 31; *Royal Commission on Trade Unions,* Fourth Report, ques. 8181.

141 *Royal Commission on Trade Unions,* Third Report, ques. 3369, Fourth Report, ques. 7664–6.

142 S. & B. Webb, *Industrial Democracy,* p. 175; Burgess, p. 105.

143 E.g., in York in 1856 and Lymm in 1857, codes of rules were drawn up which restricted worked stone, piecework, sub-contracting, gaslight working, demanded walking time, and sheds. Most of these rules 'have been considered established for the past three years.' *Fortnightly Returns,* 24 January 1856, pp. 4–5, 14 May 1857, p. 5. The working rules of the sixties contained no new demands and were merely the formalisation of old ones that were previously unattainable or only transiently achieved. For examples of rules achieved through mutual negotiation see *ibid.,* 12 November 1857, p. 7, 15 August 1860, p. 5, 6 April 1865, p. 8, 5 September 1867, p. 8.

144 There is an interesting quote from John Prior in 1867 which illustrates the potentialities of working rules for organisation and collective bargaining but whose ambivalent tone also illustrates the point being made here. The benefits of working rules, Prior argued, lay in 'the recognition on the part of the

employers of the right of the workmen to unite, in order to secure a voice in the settlement of the hours they are to work, and the rate of wages they are to receive. Although many of them will admit that labour is the property of the workman, and that to him belongs the right of naming the terms on which he will dispose of it, yet they tell us that they have nothing to do with our societies . . . The adoption of a code of rules puts an end to this objection, for the employers in accepting the regulations proposed by the operatives, it matters not whether they are modified or not, tacitly admit the right of the working-men to combine for the protection of their own interests,' ASC&J, *Monthly Reports*, January 1867. Prior, it should be noted, had been active in the West Country strike of 1865 which was a classic instance of the imposition of a code of rules upon the masters by the men.

145 *Bee-Hive*, 21 October 1865, p. 7. For this strike see *Fortnightly Returns*, 1 December 1864, p. 4, 18 May 1865, p. 9; *Western Morning News*, 13 May 1865, 15 May 1865, 16 May 1865, 25 May 1865, 6 September 1865, 12 September 1865.

146 For other examples from carpenters and bricklayers see *Bee-Hive*, 30 April 1864, p. 5, 7 May 1864, p. 5, 24 December 1865, p. 5, 3 February 1866, p. 5.

147 *Birmingham Daily Post*, 21 May 1868, p. 6; *Fortnightly Returns*, 11 October 1849, p. 4, 10 February 1853, p. 4, 11 August 1853, p. 4, 31 May 1855, p. 4.

148 *Ibid.*, 16 August 1860, p. 7, 27 September 1860, p. 8, 20 December 1860, p. 8. In this case a conciliation committee – which was an unusual demand for the men to make at this period – represented a defensive necessity and a symbol of their strength; the masters fiercely resisted a committee because autonomous regulation was working in their favour. This was an exact reversal of the situation that had evolved by the late 60s – Leeds being one of those towns where the masters launched their offensive against the dictation of the men. But, in 1860, the Leeds masters objected to 'binding themselves by signing any code of rules,' *Leeds Mercury*, 5 July 1860, p. 3; *The Builder*, 25 August 1860, p. 549.

149 *Fotnightly Returns*, 29 June 1865, p. 7. Other examples with the same pattern include Barrow; *Ibid.*, 19 May 1864, p. 6; Atherton, 15 April 1869, p. 7; Shrewsbury, 6 February 1868, p. 8: 'We have decided that the submitted code will come into operation on April 1st 1868.'

150 *Ibid.*, Volume for 1839 (in the back of which there is a list of the working rules agreed between masters and masons of Manchester), 18 February 1869, pp. 7–9.

151 *Ibid.*, 28 January 1864, p. 5, 11 February 1864, p. 5, 22 September 1853, p. 5, 22 May 1862, p. 6, 23 July 1867, pp. 7–8.

152 *Ibid.*, 24 March 1864, p. 8. See also the evidence of John Bristow that piece-work rules had become more intense since the 1850s. *Royal Commission on Trade Unions*, Third Report, ques. 4944, 4950. Apprenticeship regulation was reported for the first time in Glasgow bricklaying in 1863, see First Report, ques. 3468.

153 S. & B. Webb, *Industrial Democracy*, p. 77; *The Builder*, 15 May 1869, p. 391; *Birmingham Daily Post*, 21 May 1868, p. 6.

154 *Bee-Hive*, 22 February 1868, p. 5 for a trade union deputation to Gladstone on this speech. It is interesting that the delegation dissociated itself from such rules; Potter rightly pointed out that it was not a trade union rule. But even more interesting is the fact that Gladstone made this speech at the time he was emerging as the 'People's William' and the staunchest advocate of working-class political enfranchisement. It suggests the extent to which trade unionism

was beleaguered during these years and the political necessity for the 'respectable' leadership to assert itself and present the kind of image of trade union function that it succeeded in doing.

155 *Fortnightly Returns*, 27 January 1853, p. 3.
156 Nat. Ass. Prom. Soc. Sc. *Trade Societies and Strikes*, p. 207; *Bee-Hive*, 20 March 1869, p. 7, for a lower estimate of 15–20% addition to quarry cost of the stone.
157 *Royal Commission on Trade Unions*, First Report, ques. 3227. Not until the 1890s did the issue spread beyond the north and Midlands as a strike prone question. In the 1860s 65% of worked stone strikes were in the northwest and Yorkshire; in the 1890s, only 46% of these strikes were in those areas. Between 1850–75 there was a 76% success rate for strikes on this issue which was about average.
158 *Fortnightly Returns*, 22 May 1862, pp. 6, 10, 11 September 1862, p. 7, 11 February 1864, p. 5.
159 *Manchester Examiner and Times*, 27 February 1869, p. 7; Thornton, p. 323 for some Bradford men refusing to work factory window sills and heads that had been partially prepared on dressing machines.
160 *The Builder*, 19 October 1861, p. 717.
161 This is not a very important qualification because it was in the north that the critical changes in the structures of industrial relations were to occur.

NOTES TO CHAPTER 3

1 Burn, *Age of Equipoise*, p. 331.
2 P. J. Keating (ed.), *Matthew Arnold: Selected Prose* (London, 1970), pp. 15, 18.
3 For the importance of the 1870s in this respect see D. J. Coppock, 'The Climacteric of the 1890s: A Critical Note,' *The Manchester School of Economic and Social Studies*, Vol. xxiv, No. 1 (Jan. 1956). R. A. Church, *The Great Victorian Boom, 1850–1873* (London, 1975).
4 Which process was not complete until the 1880s: T. J. Nossiter, *Influence, Opinion and Political Idiom in Reformed England. Case Studies from the North East 1832–1874* (Hassocks, 1975).
5 See E. P. Hennock, *Fit and Proper Persons* (London, 1973), pp. 34–5, 49–50, 56, Pt. II, Chs. 3 and 5. It is interesting to note the prominence of builders in municipal affairs. Chamberlain and his big business cohorts gain control of the Birmingham Town Council from the 'pub-oriented' small businessmen in the early seventies. They immediately set about improving the environment. Hennock does not explain the economic and social structural underpinnings of this shift, but it clearly must be seen in the context of the need for a more 'efficient' population. Chamberlain's later career as a social imperialist can be seen as an enlarged version of the 'collectivist' reforms in Birmingham.
6 Burn, p. 331. The reason why an industrial relations crisis could occur at this time without being part of a wider, general crisis of capitalism was because of Britain's unilateral supremacy in the world. But this was the last time such a crisis was to occur in such isolation.
7 For masonry, joinery, and plastering the labour cost amounted to 60% of the total, for painting 50%. Carpentry and bricklaying were much lower at 25%. See T. Brassey, 'On the Rise of Wages . . .' p. 149; G. T. Jones, *Increasing Return* (Cambridge, 1933), pp. 67–9.
8 John Summerson, *The London Building World of the Eighteen-Sixties* (London, 1973), p. 12.

9 J. Parry Lewis, pp. 135–6.
10 *The Builder*, 31 December 1853, p. 778.
11 'Bankruptcies,' Royal Statistical Society, *Journal*, Vol. XLIV (1881), p. 591.
12 A. K. Cairncross, 'The Glasgow Building Industry, 1870–1914,' *Review of Economic Studies*, Vol. 2 (1934–35), p. 11.
13 Cairncross, 'Fluctuations in the Glasgow Building Industry 1856–1914,' in *Home and Foreign Investment 1870–1913* (Cambridge, 1953); S. B. Saul, 'House Building in England 1890–1914,' *Economic History Review*, 2nd series, Vol. XV, No. 1 (1962), pp. 132–6.
14 Cairncross, 'Fluctuations . . .' p. 34; 'The Glasgow Building Industry 1870–1914,' p. 11.
15 Cairncross, 'Fluctuations . . .' p. 16; *Royal Commission on Labour*, Group C, Vol. II, 1892, (c. 6795–III), Vol. XXXVI, Pt. III, ques. 17835, 17859–63, 17892, 18628–30; *Labour News and Employment Advertiser*, 23 August 1884, p. 3, 6 September 1884, p. 1, 20 September 1884, p. 1, 4 October 1884, pp. 1–2.
16 G. T. Jones, p. 89.
17 K. Maiwald, 'An Index of Building Costs in the United Kingdom, 1845–1938,' *Economic History Review*, 2nd Series, Vol. VII, No. 2 (1954), pp. 187–203.
18 *Ibid.*, p. 187.
19 Jones, p. 90.
20 Maiwald, pp. 192–3.
21 E. W. Cooney, 'Capital Exports and Investment in Building in Britain and the U.S.A., 1856–1914,' *Economica*, NS, Vol. XVI (Nov. 1949); 'Long Waves in Building in the British Economy of the Nineteenth Century,' *Economic History Review*, 2nd Series, Vol. XIII (1960–61).
22 J. Parry Lewis, pp. 115, 119, 129, 66.
23 *Manchester Examiner and Times*, 5 May 1869, p. 6.
24 Summerson, p. 14.
25 Karl Marx, *Capital* (Moscow, 1971), Vol. II, p. 415.
26 For a critique of Marx's tendency to see the relationship between productivity, surplus value and the rate of profit as ironclad, see T. Erdös, 'Surplus Value and its Rate in Contemporary Capitalism,' *Acta Oeconomica*, Vol. 5, No. 4 (1970).
27 Marx, *Capital* (Moscow, n.d. Reprint of English edition of 1887), I, p. 493.
28 *Ibid.*, p. 489: 'Every change in the magnitude of surplus value arises from an inverse change in the value of labour power.'
29 *Ibid.*, pp. 209, 488, 561.
30 Karl Marx, *Grundrisse* (Vintage Books Edition; New York, 1973), pp. 746–7; *Capital* (Moscow, 1966), III, Ch. 2.
31 Marx, *Capital*, III, p. 232.
32 *Ibid.*, p. 246.
33 Benjamin C. Browne, *Selected Papers on Economic and Social Questions* (Cambridge, 1918), p. 55.
34 Bienefeld, p. 127. For machinery see: *Builders' Weekly Reporter*, 22 February 1877, p. 204; M. P. Bale, *Woodworking Machinery* (London, 1880); *The Clerks' Journal*, 2 July 1888, p. 11.
35 Marx, *Capital*, III, p. 241. It has been argued that this was the background to the crisis of the late 1960s. See Andrew Glyn & Bob Sutcliffe, *British Capitalism, Workers and the Profits Squeeze* (London, 1972), p. 231.
36 There were 47 masons' strikes against sub-contracting between 1851–75 of which 32 were reported successes and 8 reported failures. Against pieceworking there were 70 strikes with 37 reported successes and 14 reported failures.

37 'Efficiency' in carpentry increased by 60% between 1850 and 1910, 80% of which came from the impact of machinery in the 1870s and 1880s. See G. T. Jones, p. 94.

38 For which see Marx, *Capital*, III, Ch. 14.

39 *Fortnightly Returns*, 6 August 1857, p. 6 for its formation.

40 *Ibid.*, 10 December 1857, p. 6; 29 April 1858, p. 7.

41 *Building News*, 9 December 1864, p. 903; *The Builder*, 2 July 1864, p. 498; Parliamentary Papers, *Select Committee on Master and Servant*, 1866, Vol. XIII, (499), ques. 2538–9.

42 *The Builder*, 10 December 1864, p. 899; *Bee-Hive*, 24 December 1864, p. 5.

43 *Royal Commission on Trade Unions*, Ninth Report, Vol. XXXIV, (3980–v), ques. 17293, 17487.

44 *Bee-Hive*, 10 December 1864, p. 5.

45 *Birmingham Daily Post*, 10 January 1865, p. 4, 9 January 1865, p. 5, 7 January 1865, p. 4. It was pointed out that 'the contest presents itself simply in the light of a struggle for unconditional supremacy on the part of the masters and unconditional submission on the part of the men.'

46 *Ibid.*; *The Builder*, 31 December 1864, p. 955 for the same theme.

47 *Birmingham Daily Post*, *ibid.*, 21 January 1865, p. 3; *Bee-Hive*, 4 March 1865, p. 4 for the agreed rules; ASC&J, *Monthly Reports*, February 1865, pp. 50–1. The masters first proposed the arbitration clause. There was also a clause prohibiting interference with non-union men.

48 'No doubt, the masters have been instigated by the doings of the men . . . but although, in some cases, the men, in their endeavours to make themselves as independent as possible of the masters, have . . . shown a disposition to be masters themselves, by resorting to such a measure . . . [the masters] are only giving countenance to the idea that *they* are inclined to tyrannise over the men,' *The Builder*, 17 December 1864, p. 920. From the bricklayers: ' "It was an infringement of their liberties – such an infringement as had not been proposed to the trade for centuries." ' *Birmingham Daily Post*, 29 December 1864, p. 5.

49 *Select Committee on Master and Servant*, ques. 2539.

50 *Fortnightly Returns*, 21 February 1867, p. 10, 16 May 1867, p. 13. There may have been a split in the Birmingham lodge. There was a strange and rapid turnover of lodge officers in 1867 and again in 1868. It is also possible that the reduction of hours being offered was a factor which induced the men to accept. For these events see *Fortnightly Returns*, 30 May 1867, p. 10, 28 May 1868, p. 12.

51 This from Sheffield who were already threatened with the same rules. Moves were made to disenfranchise the Birmingham Lodge. *Ibid.*, 30 May 1867, p. 9, 25 July 1867, p. 10.

52 *Ibid.*, 1 October 1868, p. 8. These proposed rules included restrictions on worked stone and piecework. *Birmingham Daily Post*, 21 May 1868, p. 6.

53 *Builders' Trade Circular*, 18 November 1869, p. 13.

54 *Ibid.*, 30 December 1869, p. 5; *Fortnightly Returns*, 12 November 1868, p. 7; Bienefeld, p. 105.

55 *Fortnightly Returns*, 1 April 1869, p. 8, 16 September 1869, p. 8.

56 See General Builders' Association, *Minute Book*, 11 May 1869, 1 July 1869, for Wigan carpenters, joiners and painters, Mansfield and Bradford carpenters whose rank and file refused to ratify an acceptance negotiated by their leaderships, and Bolton and St Helens whose carpenters and joiners accepted it. See *Bee-Hive*, 1 May 1869, p. 6, 8 May 1869, p. 6, 15 May 1869, pp. 4–6

for the resistance of Leeds and Manchester plasterers, Sheffield and Warrington carpenters, St Helens bricklayers and acceptance by Nottingham bricklayers, Derby carpenters and joiners.

57 It is not clear why there were these divisions. In the case of Manchester bricklaying, the Markeley dispute had been over this very issue. The London Order – for whom Markeley had founded a branch – were willing to accept hourly pay perhaps because they had experienced it in London and found it not as fraught with evil consequences as was believed. The carpenters are an interesting case on which more research would be worthwhile. Until the 1846 dispute the carpenters had been as militant as any of the other trades, but since that date those in Manchester, if not elsewhere, had been divided between those willing to pursue conciliatory policies and those who wished to behave more on the model of the masons. This division – which was reflected in 1869 in the confusion reported at a mass meeting to discuss the hourly payment issue – probably mirrored the division between the indoor–outdoor men with the latter leading the opposition to hourly pay because of the effects it would have upon the security of hours and wages. See *Manchester Examiner and Times*, 13 April 1869, p. 5.

58 *Bee-Hive*, 23 October 1869, p. 6 where it was reported that only ten employers were still holding out against the men – but these were those with the largest works. See also *Manchester Examiner and Times*, 13 April 1869, p. 5, 20 April 1869, p. 7.

59 The masters refused the masons' offers in April and September to accept a wage reduction. In April the men's deputation accepted the hourly system on a trial basis but a mass meeting repudiated this. See *Manchester Examiner and Times*, 12 April 1869, p. 3, 16 September 1869, p. 6. Similarly, the bricklayers offered to return to work on the masters' terms if they would drop the arbitration rule. See *Builders' Trade Circular*, 7 October 1869, p. 7.

60 *Builders' Trade Circular*, 9 December 1869, p. 8.

61 *Fortnightly Returns*, 5 August 1869, p. 11; General Builders' Association, *Minute Book*, 2 November 1869; 'Your committee confess that they are greatly disappointed at the manner in which so many branch Associations failed to carry out the undertaking.' But they added that those who were successful 'have incurred such a settlement as must materially affect the building trade of the whole country.' They reported that about half the carpenters and joiners were on the hour system as were the masons of Manchester, Salford, Wolverhampton, Bath, York, Wigan, Coventry, Sheffield, Birmingham, Liverpool and Lymm. This conflicts with other evidence and it may mean that some of the masons in those towns were so paid.

62 *Builders' Trade Circular*, 30 December 1869, p. 5; *Fortnightly Returns*, 16 September 1869, p. 8.

63 *Builders' Trade Circular*, 7 October 1869, p. 7. The strike cost the OSM £12,000.

64 *Ibid.*, 29 December 1870, p. 8; *Bee-Hive*, 31 December 1870, p. 721.

65 *Leeds Mercury*, 13 May 1864, p. 3, 24 May 1864, p. 3, 25 May 1864, p. 3, 27 May 1864, p. 3, 28 May 1864, p. 5, 30 May 1864, p. 3.

66 *Royal Commission on Trade Unions*, First Report, ques. 3332a.

67 *Royal Commission on Labour*, Group C, Vol. II, Appendices 30, 33. Table from ASC&J, *Annual Reports* for 1864, 1865, 1870, 1875, 1879. The GUC&J reported in 1864 that only 9 out of 61 towns were on the hourly system; by 1880, 130 out of 158 lodges were on the system. From the OSM, *Audit Reports*, a similar pattern is revealed with the greatest expansion coming in 1873 so that by 1883 only 28 of 291 lodges were working under the day system.

68 General Builders' Association. *Minute Book*, 13 January 1869. See also *Bee-Hive*, 17 April 1869, p. 6; *Sheffield Daily Telegraph*, 1 May 1869, p. 8.

69 General Builders' Association, *ibid.*

70 *Manchester Examiner and Times*, 5 May 1869, p. 6.

71 *The Builder*, 10 August 1861, p. 547; Marx, *Capital*, I, pp. 510–11.

72 Even amongst the carpenters, who were the most ready to accept the system, the pattern is one of reluctant acceptance. Thus, the Manchester carpenters 'had the greatest possible objection' to the system. And even when they were not clear why they disliked it, they recognised that 'our masters have some ulterior object in view which we are at present unable to see through, or they would not lock us out in order to pay us 4d. per week more.' And 'there was a general impression amongst the men that, as the employers were so anxious to enforce the hour system, there must be something behind it.' See *Manchester Guardian*, 5 May 1869, p. 6; *Manchester Examiner and Times*, 11 June 1869, p. 4.

73 *Builders' Trade Circular*, 12 August 1869, p. 13; *Sheffield Daily Telegraph*, 8 May 1869, p. 8; *Manchester Guardian, ibid.; Building News*, 18 October 1861, p. 846.

74 *Builders' Trade Circular, ibid.*

75 *Building News*, 22 March 1861, p. 243.

76 *Manchester Guardian, ibid.* The exchanges between Kettle and the men at Manchester in 1869 makes interesting reading and clearly reveal how Kettle as arbitrator was nothing more than a 'neutral' friend of the masters. He hectored the men on their communism, their laziness, their opposition to machinery.

77 *Leeds Mercury*, 25 May 1864, p. 3; Marx, *Capital*, I, pp. 510–11; *The Builder*, 10 August 1861, p. 547.

78 *Bee-Hive*, 26 December 1869, p. 7.

79 *Ibid.*, 18 November 1865, pp. 4–5, 17 November 1866, p. 4.

80 *Fortnightly Returns*, 3 October 1867, p. 8.

81 *Birmingham Daily Post*, 12 April 1866, p. 5; Frederic Harrison, 'The Strike of Stonemasons . . .' p. 713.

82 *Bee-Hive*, 22 May 1869, p. 6, 31 December 1870, p. 721.

83 *Ibid.*, 1 December 1866, p. 5; Frederic Harrison, 'The Strike of Stonemasons . . .' p. 718.

84 *Birmingham Journal*, 4 March 1865, p. 7; *Fortnightly Returns*, 10 April 1873, p. 11, 7 May 1874, pp. 10–11; *Bee-Hive*, 21 April 1866, p. 5.

85 *Bee-Hive*, 1 May 1875, p. 5, 29 May 1869, p. 6; Postgate, p. 210.

86 OBS, *Trade Circular*, April 1875, p. 1433.

87 General Builders' Association, *Minute Book*, 9 October 1867.

88 *Bee-Hive*, 5 June 1869, p. 6; *The Builder*, 24 April 1869, p. 329.

89 *Leeds Mercury*, 25 May 1864, p. 3.

90 See Chapter 4 for other influences that encouraged the system. It is interesting to note that Maiwald's figures show a plateau of wage costs in 1870–73 which it is tempting to attribute to the success of the hourly system.

91 *Fortnightly Returns*, 22 July 1869, p. 10.

92 *Manchester Guardian, ibid.; Bee-Hive*, 22 May 1869, p. 5; Joseph D. Weekes, *Report on the Practical Operation of Arbitration and Conciliation in the Settlement of Differences Between Employers and Employed in England* (Harrisburg, Pa, 1879), p. 35.

93 *Building News*, 12 May 1865, p. 342.

94 *Bee-Hive*, 20 March 1869, p. 7.

95 One of the reasons why rules which expressed masters' power could be accepted – sometimes with equanimity – was that they were not viewed as

permanent. The expectation was that the frontier of control would shift again. Thus Coulson, on some rules imposed after a defeated strike, claimed: 'It therefore depends on the men to what extent they can, by their unity, counteract the bad that is in the rules and make the good serviceable.' See OBS, *Trade Circular*, March 1867, p. 656. Courts of Conciliation by themselves were far less objectionable to the men. But at this period they are always linked with an arbitration rule and it was against that which the men reacted. Not until the middle-seventies and then the nineties do pure conciliation boards emerge. The linkage with arbitration in the sixties was a manifestation of the disciplinary purpose of the boards. It, therefore, seems to me quite wrong to argue as the Webbs and others have done that the difference between these terms was unclear. Of course they were used as co-terminous with collective bargaining which was implicit in both. But in the case of building, conciliation and arbitration were two distinct parts of the same process. If conciliation failed then arbitration was resorted to. See S. & B. Webb, *Industrial Democracy*, p. 224; Fraser, p. 106.

96 *Royal Commission on Trade Unions*, First Report, ques. 1367, 1425; Fraser, pp. 106–7 for the enthusiasm of the leaderships for conciliation and arbitration. The Webbs were quite wrong to argue that 'the Trade Unions from 1850–1876 so persistently strove for arbitration and so eagerly welcomed the gradual conversion of the governing classes to a belief in its benefits.' They went on to suggest that by the 1890s this attitude had been replaced by a 'growing antipathy.' The Webbs could only arrive at these conclusions by focussing solely upon what the leadership thought about the question: arbitration was never liked by the rank and file. It was the attitude of the leadership that changed for reasons which had to do more with their own power and responsibility than it did with the rank and file. See S. & B. Webb, *Industrial Democracy*, p. 228.

97 Henry Crompton, *Industrial Conciliation* (London, 1876), p. 113; *Webb Collection*, E, A, Vol. 13, f. 31.

98 *Bee-Hive*, 25 February 1865, p. 7.

99 *Builders' Trade Circular*, 4 November 1869, p. 9, 19 January 1871, p. 7, 6 July 1871, p. 8, 23 May 1872, p. 9.

100 *Birmingham Daily Post*, 14 May 1866, p. 8.

101 *Bee-Hive*, 28 August 1869, p. 6.

102 V. L. Allen, 'The Origins of Industrial Conciliation and Arbitration,' p. 240. See also, S. & B. Webb, *History of Trade Unionism*, p. 322; J. H. Porter 'Wage Bargaining Under Conciliation Agreements, 1860–1914,' *Economic History Review*, 2nd Series, Vol. xxiv, No. 3, (1970); J. R. Hicks, 'The Early History of Industrial Conciliation in England,' *Economica*, Vol. x, (1930).

103 Rupert Kettle, *Strikes and Arbitrations* (London, 1866); A. J. Mundella, *Arbitration as a means of Preventing Strikes* (Bradford, 1868); Nat. Ass. Prom. Soc. Sc., *Arbitration and Conciliation* (London, 1868); Parliamentary Papers, *Royal Commission on the Master and Servant Act 1867 and the Criminal Law Amendment Act 1871*, Second Report, 1875, Vol. xxx, (C. 1157), ques. 755; *Birmingham Daily Post*, 21 May 1868, p. 6.

104 Crises of industrial discipline, sometimes in conjunction with crises of competition and the need to cut labour costs, were the backdrop for the emergence of boards in other industries. The north of England iron trades board, Mundella's famous hosiery board, the Nottingham lace-makers' board, the pottery board of 1836, the sliding scales in South Wales and Northumberland, the boot and shoe board of 1895 all came out of bitter conflicts which arose from

the growing power of the men, were frequently imposed upon their defeat, and were all pragmatic answers to the problems of industrial discipline. See N. P. Howard, 'The Strikes And Lockouts in the Iron Industry and the Formation of the Ironworkers' Unions, 1862–1869,' *International Review of Social History*, Vol. xviii, (1973), Part 3; Wells, *The British Hosiery Trade*, Ch. ix; Norman Cuthbert, *The Lace Makers' Society* (Nottingham, 1960), p. 43 – in this case the need to secure discipline and order was directly related to the threat of foreign competition; Weekes, pp. 3, 15; J. H. Morris and L. J. Williams, 'The South Wales Sliding Scale, 1876–1879,' *The Manchester School*, Vol. xxviii (1960), pp. 162–4. For boot and shoe see Alan Fox, *A History of the National Union of Boot and Shoe Operatives 1874–1957* (Oxford, 1958), Section iv; S. & B. Webb, *Industrial Democracy*, pp. 185–92. The boot and shoe industry is an interesting case: the 1892 national conference was the imposition of the men, that of 1895 the result of a decisive defeat.

105 J. H. Porter, 'Wage Bargaining Under Conciliation Agreements' p. 461.

106 S. & B. Webb, *History of Trade Unionism*, pp. 323–4: 'The men gained their point at the cost of adopting the intellectual position of their opponents.' V. L. Allen, 'The Origins of Industrial Conciliation and Arbitration,' p. 254; Porter, 'Wage Bargaining Under Conciliation Agreements,' p. 474 where the argument is made that the use of conciliation boards 'imposed an effective limit upon the trade unions' power to gain advances.'

107 *Royal Commission on Trade Unions*, Fourth Report, ques. 7068 et al. See Appendix C on the changes in strike patterns that date from this period. Fraser, p. 111 for trade union delegates as ' "the greatest barrier we have and between the ignorant workmen and ourselves." '

108 *Royal Commission on Trade Unions*, Third Report, ques. 4253.

109 *Fortnightly Returns*, 30 January 1873, p. 8, 9 April 1874, pp. 11–12.

110 *Ibid.*, 10 April 1873, p. 11, 24 April 1873, p. 10.

111 *Ibid.*, 25 March 1875, pp. 12–13, 3 June 1875, p. 12, 12 August 1875, p. 12.

112 Weekes, p. 7.

113 *Fortnightly Returns*, 13 May 1858, p. 5, 22 July 1869, p. 11.

114 Thus, in 1867, the masons' trade meeting rejected the policy of trying to enforce the nine hours universally. See *Bee-Hive*, 26 October, 1867, p. 5.

115 *Ibid.*, 20 May 1865, p. 5, 22 September 1866, p. 6. The pattern of masons' strike activity in London 1860–72 is somewhat mixed – similar to that of the 1850s. In the 28 recorded strikes the men tended to be successful on issues such as meal hours (the largest single issue) and control over labour force, but less successful in resisting reductions or securing advances. There is a higher percentage of strikes over two weeks than the average (35% compared to 20%) which suggests a similarly 'stalemated' situation to the fifties.

116 See pp. 144–6 for grinding money disputes.

117 *Fortnightly Returns*, 11 April 1872, p. 12.

118 *Ibid.*, 26 May 1870, p. 8.

119 *Ibid.*, 28 March 1872, p. 12, 25 April 1873, p. 9; *Builders' Trade Circular*, 11 July 1872, p. 7.

120 *Fortnightly Returns*, 20 June 1872, p. 10, 9 April 1874, pp. 11–12.

121 *Ibid.*, 27 July 1876, p. 11; *Bee-Hive*, 30 December 1876, p. 6.

122 E.g. *Ibid.*, 4 January 1872, p. 7 (Barnard Castle), 6 June 1872, p. 9 (Kendall), 15 September 1872, pp. 9–10 (Doncaster, Altrincham, Halifax, Kirkby Lonsdale). For some examples from the carpenters see *Bee-Hive*, 10 July 1875, p. 5, 17 July 1875, p. 6, 31 July 1875, p. 5, 3 June 1876, p. 7.

123 *Royal Commission on . . . Criminal Law Amendment Act*, Second Report, ques. 394.
124 *Builders' Trade Circular*, 8 February 1872, p. 5. Complaints about 'tyranny' continue to appear – as, for example, against the Manchester masons who in 1871 were reported to be resuming their 'old habits of dictation,' *ibid.*, 3 August 1871, pp. 5–6. But these are isolated, episodic reflections of the continuum of work group activity and are no longer developed into an indictment of labour activity.
125 *Royal Commission on Trade Unions*, Fourth Report, ques. 7209.
126 Weekes, p. 26, quoting the President of the 1877 TUC: ' "Boards for settling disputes would not do away with unions, they would still be needed, and under increased necessity to enforce the decisions of the board when given in favour of the workmen." ' Weekes goes on to point out: 'In the practical workings of arbitration, trade unions have been found essential to its success. They have formed to centre around which the entire body of labour, non-unionists as well as unionist, has gathered and by which the workmen members of the boards have been elected.'
127 *Fortnightly Returns*, 6 January 1870, p. 10, 20 January 1870, p. 7, 3 February 1870, p. 17. The reasons for the favourable reception this suggestion received are interesting. Tamworth pointed out that because the masters were now organised into the GBA it was impossible for the men to impose their will. Autonomous regulation was, thus, finished and the society 'will be ineffective for much good in the future under its present organisation.'
128 *Webb Collection*, E, C, Vol. 50, 1871 Rules, pp. 33, 35; *Fortnightly Returns*, 26 October 1871, p. 8.
129 Thus, the General Alliance of Operative House Painters had a law binding all branches to arbitration on pain of denial of benefits. See *Bee-Hive*, 29 January 1876, p. 2.
130 Fraser, pp. 175–80.
131 It was enough at this first stage of the process of institutional incorporation that the Trade Union Act of 1871 should stop 'short at either positive encouragement of unions . . . or detached interference.' In the context of the previous legal situation and of the times, such ambiguity amounted to encouragement. Roy Lewis, 'The Historical Development of Labour Law,' *British Journal of Industrial Relations*, Vol. xiv, No. 1 (March 1976), p. 3.
132 P. H. J. H. Gosden, *Self-Help. Voluntary Associations in Nineteenth Century Britain* (London, 1973), pp. 98, 104, 163.
133 The parallels with the industrial relations legislation of the 1960s and 1970s are obvious and fascinating. See Glynn and Sutcliffe, pp. 182–8; Michael Moran, *The Politics of Industrial Relations* (London, 1977).
134 *Bee-Hive*, 16 November 1867, p. 6. So much for the idea that it is 'un-British' to bring the law into industrial relations.
135 *Royal Commission on Trade Unions*, Eleventh Report, Vol. xxxi (4123), p. xxiv; S. & B. Webb, *History of Trade Unionism*, p. 253.
136 *Royal Commission on Trade Unions, ibid.*, p. xxxvi; Fraser, p. 190; W. S. Jevons, *The State in Relation to Labour* (London, 1882), p. 114 for the influence of labour laws in stabilising and encouraging the growth of unions.
137 S. & B. Webb, *History of Trade Unionism*, p. 260.
138 Royden Harrison, *Before the Socialists*, pp. 289, 292–6, 298–9.
139 James Edward Davis, *The Labour Laws* (London, 1875), p. 41.
140 S. & B. Webb, *History of Trade Unionism*, p. 268; Harrison, *Before the Socialists*, p. 298.
141 Davis, p. 77; *Bee-Hive*, 20 January 1872, pp. 5–6. The Bolton case was quashed

on appeal but it illustrated the value of the Act as an agent of harassment and the uncertainty it threw over any collective action.

142 Davis, p. 43; *Capital and Labour*, 29 April 1874, p. 195, claimed that the Act 'has virtually put an end to the old abominable practice of picketing [as] is manifest from the fact that only eight convictions occurred' for that offence. This may explain the findings of Alan Anderson, 'Political Symbolism of the Labour Laws,' *Bulletin of the Society for the Study of Labour History*, No. 23 (Autumn 1971), pp. 13–15 that most cases involved unskilled labour. But his figures are derived from Returns published by the government which may be inaccurate.

143 *Royal Commission on . . . Criminal Law Amendment Act*, ques. 88, 127, 350, 615, 346.

144 *Ibid.*, ques. 652, 655–6, 660, 671, 677. Johnson also pointed out that whereas ten years ago the men 'had entirely taken the management of the business out of the hands of the employer . . . now it is very much improved.'

145 Davis, p. 96.

146 Henry F. A. Davis, *The Law and Practice of Friendly Societies and Trade Unions* (London, 1876), pp. 214–15. The major difference was that it was no longer illegal to watch or beset a house of work to obtain or communicate information.

147 *Capital and Labour*, 19 July 1876, p. 459. There were similar cases involving masons and bootmakers. On the use made of the picketing section of the Act see Anderson, 'Political Symbolism of the Labour Laws.'

148 *Capital and Labour*, 27 March 1878, p. 202; see 11 August 1875, pp. 437–9 for their opposition and 15 March 1876, p. 184 for the claim that 'the law has stripped employers virtually of every defence.'

NOTES TO CHAPTER 4

1 Frederic Smith, *Workshop Management* (London, n.d., 1884?), pp. 17–19.

2 *Builders' Trade Circular*, 8 February 1872, p. 5. Significantly, this was in a long article on the nature and function of working rules.

3 Eric Hobsbawm, 'Custom, Wages, and Work-Load in Nineteenth-Century Industry,' in *Labouring Men*, p. 345.

4 *Ibid.*, pp. 345–51; S. & B. Webb, *Industrial Democracy*, pp. 562–99.

5 Hobsbawm, p. 358; S. & B. Webb, *Industrial Democracy*, pp. 586–7.

6 Jones, pp. 93–6. By the mid-seventies there are suggestions that there was some dissatisfaction with the hour system; it is compared unfavourably to piecework in Frederic Hill, *Piece Work as Compared with Time Work* (London, 1876), pp. 5–6. But just how far the hourly system was successful in increasing the rate of exploitation is unclear. There are many factors that would have to be included in an accurate measurement of the rate of exploitation such as the amount, conditions, and speed of work, and the relation of all these to remuneration. But several things do suggest an increase over the period 1870–90 of which the decline in restrictive practices is one and, in London, the increase of subcontracting in the eighties is another.

7 *Builders' Trade Circular*, 5 September 1872, p. 5.

8 Smith, p. 33.

9 There may also have been continuing pressure on the rate of profit from materials costs. See Parry Lewis, pp. 149, 201; and Coppock, p. 14, for declining productivity – but how this compares to the 1860s is unclear.

10 Smith, pp. 2–3; 'In these days of excessive competition, it is more than ever

necessary that the employer should obtain the full equivalent of what he spends in wages.'

11 *Ibid.*, p. 5. The earliest demarcation dispute of this kind being the strike of bricklayers at Doultons. See *The Strike of the Bricklayers at Messrs. Doulton's Buildings at Lambeth in September, 1876* (London, 1877?).

12 Thomas Brassey, *On Work and Wages* (London, 1872), p. 26 and Ch. III for his arguments for the productivity advantages of high wages. But note that Brassey objected to the 'vain attempts to force up the rate of wages by regulations which tend to destroy the free liberty of the labourer.' See *Papers and Addresses*, Vol. 3: *Work and Wages* (London, 1894), p. 30.

13 Brassey, *On Work and Wages*, p. 257.

14 *Capital and Labour*, 26 July 1876, p. 475, 2 August 1876, p. 488, 8 January 1879, p. 15.

15 See pp. 187–8.

16 Richard Hyman, *Strikes*, p. 124: 'The basic necessity that every strike be settled means . . . that workers are obliged to specify grievances in a form which permits resolution *in negotiation with employers.*'

17 *Builders' Trade Circular*, 8 February 1872, p. 5.

18 Hyman, *Strikes*, p. 125.

19 Hyman, *Industrial Relations. A Marxist Introduction* (London, 1975), p. 27 where it is pointed out that the strong social pressures and institutional procedures 'encourage workers to express grievances and aspirations in economic terms rather than as demands for control and creativity in work.' A process whose origins lie in this very period.

20 *Manchester Examiner and Times*, 9 August 1869, p. 3.

21 *Manchester Guardian*, 5 May 1869, p. 6.

22 *Bee-Hive*, 4 October 1873, p. 4.

23 *Ibid.*, 21 October 1876, p. 5, 28 October 1876, p. 6.

24 *Royal Commission on Labour*, Group C, Vol. III, 1893–94 (C. 6894–XII), Vol. XXXIV, Appendix CLV; S. Higenbottam, *Our Society's History* (Manchester, 1939), pp. 112–13.

25 OBS, *Trade Circular*, April 1875, p. 1433, February 1876, p. 1525.

26 *Workman's Times*, 28 November 1891, pp. 4, 7.

27 Thus, the almost universal tendency of the literature to argue that trade unions could never succeed in pushing wages up beyond their 'natural' level and that strikes always resulted in a greater loss of wealth to workmen and the community than was gained by their success. The uniformly unimaginative answer to this infuriating dilemma was to 'educate' workers, to teach them the rules of the political economy game. These general views may be found in the following commentaries. S. Laing, *Letter to the Working Men . . . On the Present Contest between the Amalgamated Society of Engineers and their Employers* (London, 1852); Henry Booth, *Masters and Men* (London, 1853); George Price, *Combinations and Strikes* (London, 1854); A Preston Manufacturer, *Strikes Prevented* (London, 1854); Samuel Smiles, *Workmen's Earnings, Strikes and Savings* (London, 1861); Henry Fawcett, *The Economic Position of the British Labourer* (London, 1865); J. Ward, *Workmen and Wages* (London, 1868); Samuel Fothergill, *The Political Principles of Political Economy* (Manchester, 1871). For more perceptive and interesting attempts to grapple with this problem, we should note A Manufacturer, *Friendly Letters on the Recent Strikes* (London, 1854); and Godfrey Lushington's essay in Nat. Ass. Prom. Soc. Sc., *Trades' Societies and Strikes* (London, 1860) which together with Charles Neate's *Two Lectures on Trade Unions* (London, 1862) were the first examples

of attempts by members of the intelligentsia to rationalise acceptance of trade unions in society.

28 A Manufacturer, *Friendly Letters on Recent Strikes*, pp. 8, 19. This pamphlet is a very interesting attempt to draw a line between legitimate and illegitimate bargaining issues. Much of it is a condemnation of the unions' attempts to shackle the employers' freedom of action. Thus, it was claimed that in 1853 the men showed a 'great spirit of insubordination, and a tendency to encroach upon the authority of their employers.' In its advocacy of the men's right to a determination of wage levels, however, it is an early statement of the economic function of relationships and bargaining. It is not without significance, of course, that this sentiment – presumably by a textile manufacturer – should be expressed at the moment when industrial relations were formalised in spinning as a consequence of the 1853 strike.

29 *The Builder*, 13 August 1859, p. 529.

30 *Builders' Weekly Reporter*, 2 November 1877, p. 1175. See also, *Builders' Trade Circular*, 5 February 1872, p. 5, 30 May 1872, p. 5 for this same tendency in 1872.

31 *The Building World*, 14 December 1877, p. 414; *Capital and Labour*, 13 March, p. 165, 21 November 1877, p. 613; Central Association of Master Builders, *Minute Books*, 16 February 1878; Brassey, '*On the Rise of Wages . . .*' p. 157.

32 Jacob Waley, 'On Strikes and Combinations, with Reference to Wages and the Condition of Labour,' Royal Statistical Society, *Journal*, Vol. xxx (March 1867), p. 20. For the similarities of this to the so-called 'modern' doctrine of managerial rights see Alan Aldridge, *Power, Authority and Restrictive Practices. A Sociological Essay on Industrial Relations* (Oxford, 1977), pp. 31–2.

33 As they are in modern industrial relations, see Aldridge, pp. 38–42.

34 For which see examples in *Fortnightly Returns*, 30 January 1873, p. 11, 13 February 1873, pp. 7, 9, 31 July 1873, pp. 9, 10, 11 September 1873, p. 10, 23 October 1873, p. 11.

35 Between 1871 and 1875 wages' strikes composed 22% of all masons' strikes compared to an average (1836–96) of 31%.

36 See Appendix B.

37 *Fortnightly Returns*, 28 January 1875, pp. 10–11.

38 ASC&J, *Monthly Reports*, February 1868, p. 51. For other examples where this strategy was applied see *Bee-Hive*, 1 May 1869, p. 6; *Sheffield Daily Telegraph*, 1 May 1869, p. 8.

39 *Capital and Labour*, 27 December 1876, p. 758.

40 *Bee-Hive*, 1 December 1866, p. 5. The plasterers rejected this as 'being an encroachment upon an ancient and valuable right of our trade,' 6 April 1867, p. 5, 7 June 1873, p. 4.

41 *Builders' Trade Circular*, 11 July 1872, p. 10; *Capital and Labour*, 15 April 1874, p. 156, 31 May 1867, p. 367.

42 *Fortnightly Returns*, 25 March 1875, pp. 12–13, 3 June 1875, p. 12, 12 August 1875, p. 12.

43 For examples see *ibid.*, 4 January 1872, p. 1 – Barnard Castle no restrictions save on overtime; 28 March 1872, p. 12 – Sheffield only restriction on sub-contracting; 11 April 1872, p. 7 – Carlisle no restrictions; 20 June 1872, p. 10 – Newcastle no restrictions; 7 November 1872, p. 8 – Cardiff only restriction on apprentices; 15 September 1872, pp. 8–9 – Doncaster no restrictions; 31 July 1873, p. 10 – Hull only restriction on piecework.

44 For examples see *ibid.*, 12 October 1871, p. 8 – Mossley restrictions on worked stone and sub-contracting; 15 September 1872, pp. 8–9 – Altrincham, Halifax

and Kirkby Lonsdale restrictions on piecework, overtime, apprenticeship; 27 March 1873, p. 11 – Barrow restrictions on piecework and worked stone; 23 September 1875, pp. 12–13 – Preston restrictions on worked stone, overtime, apprenticeship.

45 For examples see *ibid.*, 6 March 1879, p. 11 for Ashton, Staleybridge, Hyde; 20 March 1879, p. 11 for Derby and Doncaster; 21 August 1879, p. 10 for Kidderminster. In 1880 there were no applications for working rules approval or ratification and only a very few between 1881 and 1884.

46 Michael Poole, *Workers' Participation in Industry* (London, 1975), p. 82.

47 For modern examples see Flanders, *The Fawley Productivity Agreements;* Charles Killingsworth, 'The Modernization of West Coast Longshore Work Rules,' *Industrial and Labor Relations Review,* Vol. 15 (Jan.–July 1962). See also Colin Crouch, *Class Conflict and the Industrial Relations Crisis* (London, 1977), pp. 60–1, and Ch. 6 for a brilliant exposition of the complex implications of productivity bargaining as a strategy of managerial authority. It is important to note Crouch's explanation of the way productivity bargaining increases the need for joint regulation between management and unions to undercut informal work group power and how it, thus, serves to enhance the power of the union as well as management. Obviously these forms were only loosely present in the 1870s but there is a significant parallel in the way that unions were, for the first time, given a regulatory role. But productivity bargaining during this period did not involve management inviting unions to discuss the mutual advantage of improvements that could be made in work organisation. It was a more unilateral form of productivity bargaining.

48 *Newcastle Guardian,* 1 February 1851, p. 8. The extent and means of work control amongst shipwrights would be a very fruitful topic of investigation. The passage quoted above fails to reveal the extent to which the Tyne shipwrights controlled their work: men could not be moved from one job to another, they could not be discharged until a job was finished, they prohibited piecework, maintained strict apprenticeship ratios, foremen were dismissed on their demand. Amongst others, the London shipwrights had wielded a similar power in the 1820s as the evidence before *Select Committee on the Combination Laws* revealed.

49 *Bee-Hive,* 15 September 1866, p. 6.

50 For the old quarter-day standard see ASC&J, Maidstone Branch, *Minute Books,* 2 November 1867, 3 April 1869. The Leeds carpenters demanded $3\frac{1}{2}$ hours in 1864, see *Bee-Hive,* 7 May 1864, p. 5.

51 CAMB, *Minute Books,* 9 July 1875, letter from Matkin. See also *Bee-Hive,* 25 February 1865, p. 7, for the suggestion that $2\frac{1}{4}$ hours was still given in London.

52 CAMB, *Minute Books,* 15 March 1875.

53 *Bee-Hive,* 23 April 1864, p. 5; GUC&J, *Monthly Trade Reports,* October 1867, p. 9.

54 *Bee-Hive,* 14 December 1872, p. 14.

55 CAMB, *Minute Books,* 15 March 1875; *Bee-Hive,* 26 June 1875, p. 7; *Building News,* 30 April 1875, p. ix.

56 CAMB, *Minute Books,* 24 May 1887.

57 Ass.C&J, Edinburgh (United) Branch, *Minute Books,* 12 October 1888.

58 *Fortnightly Returns,* 18 July 1850, p. 4; Henry Mayhew, *London Labour and the London Poor* (Dover Edition; New York, 1968), iii, p. 227 where the logic is well expressed: 'If there be work enough to employ the whole of the operatives for sixty hours a week, and if two-thirds of the hands are supplied with sufficient to occupy them ninety hours a week in the same space of time, then one-

third of the trade must be thrown fully out of employment.' Nor is it a theme that has died away: note the recent desire of the TUC to ban overtime as a means of combating unemployment.

59 *Edinburgh News*, 2 October 1852, p. 8; *Royal Commission on Trade Unions*, First Report, ques. 3363.

60 *Webb Collection*, E, C, Vol. 50, Masons Rules 1859, p. 19; *Fortnightly Returns*, 5 September 1867, p. 8 for Accrington rules.

61 GUC&J, Ashton-u-Lyne Branch, *Minute Books*, 4 February 1861.

62 *Birmingham Daily Post*, 11 May 1874, p. 5. Winter unemployment amongst Glasgow painters was 60–70%, see J. H. Treble, 'The seasonal demand for adult labour in Glasgow, 1890–1914,' *Social History*, Vol. 3, No. 1 (January 1978), p. 50. This may account for the low reputation in which painters were generally held. *Fortnightly Returns*, 26 January 1840, 27 February 1840.

63 *Bee-Hive*, 7 April 1866, p. 6, 24 December 1864, p. 5 for Bradford carpenters' and joiners' prohibition of overtime save in cases of emergency; *Fortnightly Returns*, 20 February 1868, p. 7, 23 July 1868, p. 7.

64 *Bee-Hive*, 19 November 1870, p. 624, 29 January 1876, p. 6; *Fortnightly Returns*, 6 May 1875, p. 12.

65 *Bee-Hive*, 18 March 1865, p. 6; GUC&J, Ashton-u-Lyne Branch, *Minute Books*, 15 February 1862.

66 *Fortnightly Returns*, 16 May 1867, p. 13, 7 November 1872, p. 8, 7 May 1874, pp. 10–11; *Builders' Trade Circular*, 5 January 1871, p. 6. For the similar situation in northeast shipbuilding where, following the 1871 strike, hourly pay had been introduced for the skilled men see *Jarrow Guardian*, 1 February 1873, p. 8 where a joiner was dismissed for refusing to work overtime and in a subsequent court case the issue was defined as 'whether the complainant [i.e. joiner] had to be master, or whether he had to be dictated to by the foreman . . . in a large works it was important to maintain proper discipline.'

67 *Fortnightly Returns*, 31 July 1873, pp. 9–10, 30 July 1874, p. 11.

68 *Ibid.*, 3 June 1875, p. 12.

69 *Bee-Hive*, 27 August 1864, p. 5 for a mass meeting to oppose overtime, which expressed their sentiment for its abolition and agreed to work it only when necessary. *Birmingham Daily Post*, 16 May 1864, p. 6.

70 *Bee-Hive*, 4 March 1865, p. 4, 21 April 1866, p. 5.

71 *Ibid.*, 16 July 1864, p. 5, 6 August 1864, p. 5, 20 May 1865, p. 5, 27 July 1872, p. 13; *Fortnightly Returns*, 14 July 1864, p. 6.

72 *Builders' Trade Circular*, 5 September 1872, p. 5; *Bee-Hive*, 31 August 1872, p. 3.

73 *Fortnightly Returns*, 27 August 1896, p. 10, 29 May 1902, p. 12 for the loss of this rule and the imposition of one which required it be worked at employers' request; OSM, *Journal* [Formerly *Fortnightly Returns*], 16 October, 1912, pp. 690–4.

74 London Master Builders' Association, *Minute Books*, 13 May 1902, 29 June 1911, 20 September 1911, 10 October 1911, 6 November 1911, 12 February 1912, 14 March 1912; OSM, *Journal*, 6 September 1911, p. 678.

75 Robert Q. Gray, *The Labour Aristocracy in Victorian Edinburgh* (Oxford, 1976), p. 47; *Royal Commission on Labour*, Group A, Third Report, 1893, Vol. XXXII (C. 6894), ques. 22103, 22117–122.

76 *Fortnightly Returns*, 26 May 1892, p. 12. For similar examples from the carpenters see working rules of Southport, Manchester, Accrington, Bristol, Cardiff, Birkenhead, et al. in GUC&J, *Monthly Reports*, April 1890, pp. 12–15, May 1890, p. 7, September 1890, pp. 10–11, November 1890, pp. 8–9.

77 LMBA, *Minute Books*, 13 May 1902; Parliamentary Papers, *Report on Collective*

Agreements Between Employers and Workpeople in the United Kingdom, 1910, Vol. xx (Cd. 5366), p. 6; Sylvia Grossman, 'The Radicalization of London Building Workers' (unpublished PhD Dissertation, Department of History, University of Toronto), p. 80.

78 See *Fortnightly Returns*, 26 May 1892, p. 10, 4 August 1892, p. 10, 23 November 1894, p. 11 for examples of the rule's revival. Worked stone strikes were the largest single issue of masons' strikes 1890–96, composing over 21% of the total. Of all worked stone strikes 35.8% occur during these years. The other period when these strikes were prominent was, significantly, the seventies – between 1870 and 1876 they composed 7.8% of all issues and 27.2% of all worked stone strikes occurred during these years.

79 A Working Man, *Reminiscences of a Stonemason* (London, 1908), p. 255. For the general development of machines see M. P. Bale, *Stone-working Machinery* (London, 1884).

80 *Master Builders' Associations' Journal*, March 1898, p. 7.

81 Thus, Manchester in 1875 proposed to introduce this version, see *Fortnightly Returns*, 25 March 1875, p. 13. See also *Manchester Examiner and Times*, 13 April 1869, p. 4 for a suggestion that the economist rule was present in Manchester at that date. In the light of the other evidence this would seem unlikely as the masters had singled this issue out as one of the main reasons for the counter-offensive of that year. It is more likely that a re-formulation of the rule was being discussed under the pressure of the masters' offensive, the general public disapproval of such rules and the support that it received from the London branches of the union.

82 *Fortnightly Returns*, 1 April 1869, p. 8.

83 *Ibid.*, 5 July 1894, p. 10.

84 *Ibid.*, 3 June 1897, p. 13. The case that supporters of the economist rule were making bore a close resemblance to the Webbs' argument that the sole purpose of the rule was to uphold the standard rate.

85 *Ibid.*, 17 June 1897, p. 10, 10 February 1898, p. 11. This argument was, in fact, confirmed by events. By 1911 it was obvious that the wages of the quarry districts had not been raised to the level of the higher paid areas. Precisely when Manchester reverted to the old rule is not clear; it will be recalled that the economist formulation had been accepted in 1875. What this reversion illustrates, however, is the transitional nature of 1870–90, and the long struggle that accompanied the new system before its full implications were realised. Equally, the 1898 struggle was to reveal the ultimate strength of these new structures in forcing a change in the custom.

86 *Ibid.*, 24 February 1898, p. 13 for the towns with the new rule. Those where the old was enforced included Manchester, Ashton, Blackburn, Preston, Oldham, Staleybridge, Ratcliffe and Hyde.

87 Parliamentary Papers, *Reports on Strikes and Lock-Outs of 1898*, 1899, Vol. xcii (C. 9437), p. xxiv; *Master Builders' Associations' Journal*, June 1898, pp. 17–21, July 1898, p. 13.

88 *Fortnightly Returns*, 30 June 1898, pp. 13–15. In response to this Manchester tried to reassert the principle of local autonomy – that each locality make its own rules on the question.

89 *Fortnightly Returns*, 28 July 1898, pp. 13–17 for the report from the Executive Council delegation.

90 OSM, *Journal*, 13 November 1912, p. 771, 27 November 1912, p. 815.

91 *Ibid.*, 27 December 1911, pp. 845–6, 21 January 1912, p. 39, 17 April 1912, p. 260, 1 May 1912, p. 273.

92 Hobsbawm, 'Custom, Wages . . .' pp. 350, 358, 361.
93 Aldridge, pp. 6–7.
94 S. & B. Webb, *Industrial Democracy*, p. 342.
95 *Ibid.*, p. 586.
96 *Liverpool Mercury*, 29 November 1833, p. 387.
97 Hobsbawm, 'Custom, Wages . . .' p. 349.
98 *Ibid.*, pp. 346–7. For a contemporary illustration see the recent (1978) difficulties at Swan Hunter over this very issue where an order for building some Polish ships was lost through inability to resolve 'leapfrogging' wage claims to maintain differentials. See *Manchester Guardian Weekly*, 5 February 1978, pp. 1, 3.
99 See Appendix C.
100 *Bee-Hive*, 7 May 1864, p. 5.
101 Higenbottam, p. 141.
102 OSM, *Journal*, 1 May 1912, p. 273 where 'it [i.e. the old rule] is second only in principle to trade-unionism and should be Rule 1 in every local code, or else the rules lose half their value.'
103 Hinton, p. 87.
104 Hobsbawm, 'Custom, Wages . . .' p. 351; Clegg, Fox and Thompson, pp. 114–15.
105 See Michael Moran, *The Politics of Industrial Relations* (London, 1977), Ch. 9 for a discussion of this same kind of division as it affects the difficulties of industrial relations policy at the present day. As 'citizens' workers are prepared to accept stronger restraints on wages, unions etc. than they are prepared to accept as proletarians.
106 *The N-F-Record*, Vol. III, No. IX (June 1914), p. 3.
107 See *Fortnightly Returns*, 15 October 1846, p. 4 for an example of union advice on when to strike.

NOTES TO CHAPTER 5

1 *Report on Collective Agreements* . . . , p. iii; Clegg, Fox and Thompson, p. 154˙
2 Sharp, *Industrial Conciliation and Arbitration in Great Britain*, pp. 192–6 who dates it wrongly as 1904. There was one board for the masons, bricklayers and carpenters, a board for plumbers had been formed in 1897, and a similar structure created for plasterers in 1899 which was integrated into the national system in 1909. London had its own system from 1896 and did not enter the national system until 1914–15.
3 Clegg, Fox and Thompson, p. 471: 'In 1889 only cotton weaving had a national agreement.' These systems did not all perform identical functions but they all had similar disputes procedures.
4 ASC&J, *Monthly Reports*, June 1906, pp. 331–3 for the creation of district boards in York and Barnsley.
5 As is suggested by Clegg, Fox and Thompson, p. 471.
6 National Association of Master Builders, *Minute Books*, 18 December 1877.
7 *Master Builders' Associations' Journal*, February 1899, p. 19 for NAMB actively encouraging member associations to federate into district associations.
8 See G. R. Searle, *The Quest for National Efficiency* (Oxford, 1971), which in common with most investigations of this topic has concentrated upon the ideas of the search rather than the practice, and upon its failures rather than upon the actual impact that it did have.

9 Quoted in A. L. Levine, *Industrial Retardation in Britain 1880–1914* (New York, 1967), p. 14.
10 Saul, pp. 130–1; Parry Lewis, p. 107; A. G. Kenwood, 'Residential Building Activity in North Eastern England, 1853–1913,' *The Manchester School*, Vol. 31 (1963), p. 127. By this time there was far less local variation in the cycle.
11 Grossman, pp. 71–3, 83.
12 See Appendix B for Manchester figures. In these cases I have averaged the difference between the winter and summer wage to form the base figure. NAMB, *Minute Books*, 26 January 1897; GUC&J, *Annual Report 1893*, p. 5; CAMB, *Minute Books*, 13 February 1893.
13 Parliamentary Papers, *Reports on Strikes and Lock-Outs of 1895*, 1896, Vol. LXXX, Pt. I [C. 8231], p. 16; *Report . . . of 1896*, 1897, Vol. LXXXIV, [C. 8643], p. xvii; *Report . . . of 1898*, 1899, Vol. XCII [C. 9437], p. xxiv.
14 The comparable figures of results from 1893 (when the Reports first become usable) to 1900 for the building trades have been given to me by James Cronin who has kindly allowed me to examine his important dissertation. These figures are as follows:

	Victory %	Failure %	Compromise %
1893	48.5	31.5	20.0
1894	45.4	34.5	20.3
1895	47.0	37.0	16.0
1896	53.2	26.8	20.0
1897	65.3	22.3	12.4
1898	42.0	36.0	22.0
1899	36.0	21.0	43.0
1900	35.0	32.0	33.0

The masons' strike statistics may, however, be a more accurate guide for our concerns because, as in the 1860s, it was their kind of trade which could most easily achieve an expansion of work control. The other trade to which this applied with especial force in the nineties was the plasterers.

15 *Fortnightly Returns*, 14 September 1893, p. 11; see also 24 April 1892 for Bolton working rules where the men were to have a voice in the matter of when and where sheds were to be erected.
16 E.g., *ibid.*, 26 May 1892, p. 10, 26 April 1894, p. 10, 24 May 1894, p. 10, 27 August 1896, p. 10.
17 *Ibid.*, 15 August 1892, p. 10 and 11 May 1893, p. 11 for a similar attempt in Manchester. The Birmingham masons were successful only in removing arbitration.
18 Grossman, pp. 196, 201; NAMB, *Minute Books*, 26 January 1897; *Master Builders' Associations' Journal*, February 1897, pp. 12–14.
19 NAMB, *Minute Books*, 27 July 1897; *Master Builders' Associations' Journal*, July 1897, p. 21, February 1897, p. 14.
20 *Master Builders' Associations' Journal*, November 1896, p. 17, February 1897, p. 27, May 1897, p. 23, August 1901, p. 15.
21 Cf. Clegg, Fox and Thompson, pp. 351–2, 475 who are quite wrong when they claim that employers 'felt no need to continue the battle against craft restrictions' after 1900. The reason the masters generally failed in the nineties was because of the power of the men but post-1900 was precisely the period when they did destroy restrictive rules. See also Levine, pp. 79–84, who unsurprisingly finds that trade unions were no drag on industrial growth – a fact

recognised by large employers at the time – but who does note the widespread efforts of the rank and file to practice ca' canny.

22 Edwin Pratt, *Trade Unionism and British Industry* (London, 1904), p. 24.
23 G. T. Jones, p. 90.
24 Parliamentary Papers, *The Industrial Council. Report of an Enquiry into Industrial Agreements*, 1913, Vol. xxviii [Cd. 6952], ques. 5294; *Master Builders' Associations' Journal*, March 1901, p. 18; Pratt, p. 32. Note that the employers had also downgraded their expectations from the 1830s when their ideal figure was 2000.
25 CAMB, *Minute Books*, 3 July 1893; *Industrial Council*, ques. 5378; *Master Builders' Associations' Journal*, February 1897, p. 13.
26 One indication of this defensive context is the larger role played by masons' strikes in the organisation of work category throughout the 1880s and 1890s. These strikes against piecework, sub-contracting, and overtime tended to be more important when employers were able to make efforts to circumvent work control and increase the pace of work. In the late 1830s they had composed 20% of all issues, in the 1840s 18%, in the 1850s, 1860s, and 1870s, they composed 8.9%, 7.8%, and 6.8% respectively; in the 1880s, 13.6% and in the 1890s, 9% of total strikes.
27 Grossman, pp. 15, 97; Maiwald, p. 195; *Royal Commission on Labour*, 1893–94, Vol. xxxiv, ques. 32196–216. There is a marked coincidence between the sharp rise in total costs (mainly due to a rise in materials) at the end of the nineties and the efforts to confront the men on their restrictive practices.
28 For the expansion of sub-contracting in the 1880s in London see OBS, *Trade Circular*, April 1883, pp. 2366–7, May 1883, p. 2378; *Webb Collection*, E, A, Vol. 12, f. 158–9; *Royal Commission on Labour*, 1892, Vol. xxxvi, Pt. iii, ques. 17385. It was less of a problem elsewhere partly because genuine sub-contracting had always played a larger role in the northern provinces, but for examples of its recurrence outside London see *Building Trades News*, January 1895, p. 11, July 1897, p. 7.
29 London Building Trades Committee, *Reports*, 1890, 1891; OBS, *Trade Circular*, July 1890, p. 8, August 1890, pp. 8–9.
30 *Webb Collection*, E, A, Vol. 12, f. 154, Vol. 6, f. 73; London Building Trades Federation, *Monthly Circular*, May 1894, p. 2, June 1894, p. 9; Grossman, p. 86. The 'lump system' of the 1960s signified the reappearance of this same kind of sub-contracting. See Robert Taylor, *The Fifth Estate* (London, 1978), pp. 292–7.
31 *Royal Commission on Labour*, 1892, Vol. xxxvi, Pt. iii, ques. 17385, 17350.
32 ASC&J, *Monthly Reports*, June 1877, pp. 88–92, September 1877, p. 137; Higenbottam, p. 137; *Webb Collection*, E, A, Vol. 11, f. 63.
33 *Royal Commission on Labour*, 1892, Vol. xxxvi, Pt. iii, ques. 17380.
34 OBS, *Trade Circular*, July 1890, p. 8; Grossman, p. 215.
35 ASC&J, *Monthly Reports*, December 1881, p. 186.
36 Charity Organisation Society, *Special Committee on Unskilled Labour*, pp. 106, 231. See also Dearle, p. 89.
37 See, for example, a successful strike of plasterers at the Imperial Institute in 1891 for the replacement of a sweating foreman who doubled the pace of the work, adulterated materials and paid below the standard rate. *Royal Commission on Labour*, 1892, Vol. xxxvi, Pt. iii, ques. 17339; 1893–94, Vol. xxiv, ques. 31979. For a similar strike on a Colls' job see CAMB, *Minute Books*, 10 June 1892, Minutes of Proceedings at a Conference Between Master Builders and Trades Delegates, p. 108.

38 *Building Trades News,* May 1895, p. 11. The general foreman had made his first appearance in London bricklaying as early as the 1860s: see OBS, *Trade Circular,* 1 June 1862, p. 84.

39 The changes in masonry work – which included machines and materials – forced a similar trend amongst the masons because they began to confuse and destroy the distinction between those who did 'rough' work and those who did the more skilled jobs. The former had before been 'looked down upon' and were not in the union but now became a target of organising efforts. See OSM, *Journal,* 3 May 1911, pp. 257–8.

40 *Building Trades News,* April 1895, pp. 8–9, June 1895, p. 8; Dearle, p. 152.

41 CAMB, *Minute Books,* 18 May 1896.

42 OBS, *Trade Circular,* November 1898, p. 13. And see LMBA, *Minute Books,* 22 November 1901 for a case of an ex-union man becoming a labour sub-contractor. The notorious Sam Wright was another example.

43 National Association of Operative Plasterers, *Transcripts of Shorthand Notes of Conference Between NAMB and NAOP,* 30 May 1899, pp. 42–51.

44 *Ibid.,* July 1899, p. 16.

45 See *Webb Collection,* E, B, Vol. 34, No. 18, pp. 2–9 for an interesting example from Newcastle of a man dismissed by the foreman because he refused to pay a union fine and his failure to find work until he had cleared the debt.

46 NAOP, *Transcripts of . . . Conference . . . ,* 18 April 1904, pp. 9–11, 12.

47 LBTF, *Monthly Circular,* January 1894, p. 3; ASC&J, London District Management Committee, *Report for June–November 1894.*

48 *Bee-Hive,* 13 May 1876, p. 4; Clegg, Fox and Thompson, p. 457 for the same phenomenon in coal mining; H. A. Turner, pp. 122, 300; see Cuthbert, p. 49 for similar developments in lace-making; ASC&J, *Annual Report for 1892,* p. 12.

49 Between 1889 and 1898, the OBS gained 25,000 members, the OSM 8000, and ASC&J 30,000. See Parliamentary Papers, *Sixth Annual Abstract of Labour Statistics for 1898–99,* 1900, Vol. LXXIII [Cd. 119].

50 Hyman, *The Workers' Union,* pp. 182–95 for one of the few penetrating attempts to address the roots of union expansion. There is a considerable US literature on this question, most of it not historically oriented and more concerned with the relationship with economic factors such as the trade cycle. See A. A. Blum, 'Why Labor Unions Grow,' *Labor History,* Vol. 9, No. 1 (Winter 1968). For an econometric analysis of modern fluctuations in union membership see George Sayers Bain and Farouk Elsheikh, *Union Growth and the Business Cycle* (Oxford, 1976).

51 See Parliamentary Papers, *Seventeenth Annual Abstract of Labour Statistics,* 1914–16, Vol. LXI (Cd. 7733).

52 CAMB, *Minute Books,* 19 December 1892.

53 *Ibid.,* 31 August 1893. This resolution was made by Trollope who was currently engaged in a struggle with the men at his Claridge's site over non-union labour!

54 *Building Trades News,* May 1895, p. 7. Although written in 1895, it is clear that this reflected the situation since 1893. The letter is an interesting reflection of the new significance of the union–non-union division.

55 CAMB, *Minute Books,* 27 April 1893. Cronin's statistics show the category of strikes over 'Employment of Particular Class of Person' first appearing in 1895. From these statistics, which are for the whole country, these strikes composed the following percentage of total strikes: 1895 – 10.9%, 1896 – 11.2%, 1897 – 17.6%, 1898 – 11.5%, 1899 – 10.7%, 1900 – 18.1%. Their success rate of 47.9% tended to be about average. There are only six strikes recorded in

the masons' strike data for London 1890–96, two of which were against non-unionists.

56 CAMB, *Minute Books*, 18 October 1894, 13 November 1894. This rule also appeared in the Birmingham and Wolverhampton carpenters' and bricklayers' rules that came out of the discharge note strike. See OBS, *Trade Circular*, July 1865, p. 387; *Bee-Hive*, 4 March 1865, p. 4. The engineering employers also demanded a similar rule in 1898: see Federated Engineering and Shipbuilding Employers, *Series of Examples of Interference and Restriction* (London, 1897).

57 CAMB, *Minute Books*, 18 October 1894, 7 December 1894; *Building Trades News*, November 1894, p. 3; *Report on Strikes and Lock-Outs of 1896*, p. xxii.

58 CAMB, *Minute Books*, 19 March 1895.

59 *Ibid.*, 15 July 1895.

60 *Ibid.*, OBS, Metropolitan Central Committee, *Report 1892*, p. 3.

61 CAMB, *Minute Books*, 19 February 1896, 27 April 1896; *Report on Strikes and Lock-Outs of 1896*, p. xxii.

62 CAMB, *Minute Books*, 8 May 1896, 12 May 1896, 22 May 1896, 21 September 1896, 28 September 1896; *Daily News*, 23 May 1896, p. 7. The carpenters' no-disability clause allowed them a maximum flexibility to appeal against a man whether he was obnoxious or non-unionist and since no hard and fast line could be drawn between the two, their rule was more advantageous than the others.

63 *Master Builders' Associations' Journal*, February 1898, p. 7; CAMB, *Minute Books*, 19 September 1898, 21 November 1898, 30 November 1898; NAMB, *Minute Books*, 22 November 1898.

64 *Report on Strikes and Lock-Outs of 1899*, 1900, Vol. LXXIII [Cd. 316], p. xlvi.

65 *Ibid.;* LMBA, *Minute Books*, 1 June 1899 for NAOP, *Notes on the Lock-Out*.

66 LMBA, *Minute Books*, 14 March 1899.

67 *Report on Strikes and Lock-Outs of 1899*, p. xlviii; NAOP, *Transcript of . . . Conference . . .*, 30 May 1899, pp. 64–5.

68 *Master Builders' Associations' Journal*, August 1899, p. 17; see also, June 1899, p. 13: 'The grievances of the master plasterers are the grievances of all the employers in the building trade.' The complaints listed by the employers to the trades were: compelling foremen to join a union, refusal to work with non-unionists, dictating the work boundaries of the trades, strikes on all these issues, refusal to fix material worked in any other district, limitation of apprentices, and refusal to submit all disputes to conciliation.

69 *Ibid.*, p. 13; *Report on Strikes and Lock-Outs of 1899*, p. xlix.

70 *Master Builders' Associations' Journal*, November 1899, p. 33.

71 R. Brown, 'The Temperton v. Russell Case (1893): The Beginning of the Legal Offensive Against the Unions,' *Bulletin of Economic Research*, Vol. 23, No. 1 (May 1971), p. 55.

72 *Master Builders' Associations' Journal*, November 1899, pp. 11, 33, August 1900, p. 17.

73 *Ibid.*, August 1899, p. 35, September 1899, p. 19.

74 Saul, pp. 130–1; Grossman, p. 83. The average success rate 1901–10 was 29% compared to 46%, 1893–1900. It should be noted that there was a considerable increase in strikes compromised – 1893–1900, 24%; 1901–10, 32% – which reflects the increasing impact of the conciliation systems.

75 LMBA, *Minute Books*, 5 August 1904, 28 February 1905, 10 April 1905; *Fortnightly Returns*, 10 November 1904, pp. 9–13, 19 January 1905, p. 8, 2 February 1905, p. 8; Clegg, Fox and Thompson, p. 352.

76 *Master Builders' Associations' Journal,* August 1901, p. 23, April 1902, p. 36, May 1902, p. 45.
77 *Master Builder and Associations Journal* [Formerly *Master Builders' Associations' Journal*], 2 December 1908, p. 39.
78 *Master Builders' Associations' Journal,* 4 December 1907, p. 23.
79 National Federation of Building Trades Employers, *Minute Books,* 24 January 1905; LMBA, *Minute Books,* 20 October 1904; Postgate, p. 371; *Fortnightly Returns,* 26 December 1901, p. 8, 13 November 1902, p. 8, 19 January 1905, p. 8, 2 March 1905, p. 11, 16 March 1905, p. 9.
80 *Master Builders' Associations' Journal,* May 1905, p. 26, September 1905, p. 27, January 1906, p. 23; *Fortnightly Returns,* 8 January 1903, pp. 9–10, 26 May 1904, p. 8, 23 June 1904, p. 6, 10 November 1904, pp. 9–13.
81 *Master Builders' Associations' Journal,* February 1902, p. 62; *Fortnightly Returns,* 9 January 1902, pp. 9–10, 13 November 1902, p. 8, 21 January 1904, p. 8, 18 February 1904, p. 9, 19 January 1905, p. 8, et al.
82 *Master Builders' Associations' Journal,* January 1905, p. 71.
83 For the negotiations leading up to the formation of the Board see *ibid.,* February 1905, p. 19, August 1905, p. 23; *Fortnightly Returns,* 12 May 1904, p. 8, NFBTE, *Minute Books,* 8 March 1904.
84 LMBA, *Minute Books,* 13 May 1902. But see 11 January 1904 for it working the other way. The carpenters and joiners in a Wandsworth shop worked overtime at their own request at regular pay and the Board urged the employer not to allow it. But the sanctions that the employers could exercise over their peers were far weaker than those at the disposal of the unions.
85 *Ibid.,* 21 April 1903, 28 April 1903.
86 *Ibid.,* 22 November 1901, 27 January 1902. The managing director wrote that 'We cannot readily, if at all, find efficient shop hands among non-society ranks.' The company had dismissed the man in 1899 from his position as foreman because this would have meant him being forced into the union and they then re-hired him as a sub-contractor for labour only. This incident illustrates the way in which the system worked and how the vague definition of obnoxious men in the 1899 agreement served to protect sub-contractors. He was claimed to be a genuine non-unionist!
87 CAMB, *Minute Books,* 27 April 1896.
88 LMBA, *Minute Books,* 27 September 1900.
89 *Ibid.,* 24 August 1905.
90 *Fortnightly Returns,* 12 October 1905, pp. 10–11. For similar arguments from carpenters' officials see ASC&J, *Monthly Reports,* July 1905, pp. 336–8.
91 ASC&J, *Monthly Reports,* August 1905, pp. 384, 398.
92 Especially as in 1896, 1899 and 1905 the employers threatened to make life very uncomfortable for the unions. In 1896 the London employers had threatened the bricklayers with a lockout: see CAMB, *Minute Books,* 18 December 1895. And, in 1905, it was later claimed that 'it was the apprehension of a big trouble coming . . . that brought this onto the carpet,' *Industrial Council,* ques. 5001.
93 Deller in NAOP, Circular in LMBA, *Minute Books,* 1 June 1899.
94 LBTF, *Monthly Circular,* September 1894, p. 3, December 1894, p. 3.
95 *Webb Collection,* E, A, Vol. 10, f. 151.
96 LBTF, *Monthly Circular,* September 1895, p. 7.
97 CAMB, *Minute Books,* 18 December 1895; NAOP, *Transcripts of . . . Conference . . . ,* 30 May 1899, p. 62.
98 NAOP, Circular in LMBA, *Minute Books,* 1 June 1899; *Master Builders' Associations' Journal,* August 1899, p. 18.

99 NAOP, *Transcripts of . . . Conference . . .*, 26 July 1899, p. 29.
100 *Ibid.*, pp. 49–53, 59–69.
101 NAOP, Circular in LMBA, *Minute Books*, 1 June 1899. The men claimed that the agreement had not obligated them to work with blacklegs which these men were. And, although the union officials could afford to coyly treat this and similar cases as the right of the men 'to make terms . . . just as an Employer can, if he chooses, decline to engage [them] upon those terms,' the fact was that this was a rank and file revolt against the clause negotiated by the union.
102 NAOP, *Transcripts of . . . Conference . . .*, 18 April 1904, pp. 32–42.
103 *Master Builders' Associations' Journal*, August 1899, p. 13.

NOTES TO CHAPTER 6

1 In mining, for example, the highly structured governmental hierarchy of the Durham Miners' Association continually competed for authority with the staunchly independent lodges who seldom managed to reverse leadership policies or agreements but who continually made their implementation more difficult. See Douglass, 'The Durham Pitman,' pp. 255–71.
2 D. C. Cummings, *A Historical Survey of the Boiler Makers' and Iron and Steel Ship Builders' Society* (Newcastle, 1905), p. 34.
3 S. & B. Webb, *Industrial Democracy*, p. 158.
4 Thus, the continuing weakness of unionism in the iron trades was an essential irrelevance to the successful operation of the north of England iron trades board after 1869. See N. I. Howard, 'The Strikes and Lockouts in the Iron Industry . . .'
5 As this history of the Durham miners' sliding scale illustrated. See Douglass, pp. 255, 259.
6 *Bee-Hive*, 9 May 1874, pp. 2–3. For the present-day tensions that result from efforts to impose a corporate role upon the unions see Crouch, *Class Conflict and the Industrial Relations Crisis*, esp. Part IV.
7 *Bee-Hive*, 17 July 1875, p. 12.
8 CAMB, *Minute Books*, 10 June 1892, Minutes of Proceedings at Conference between Master Builders and Trades Delegates, pp. 4–6.
9 NAOP, *Transcripts of . . . Conference . . .*, 30 May 1899, p. 40.
10 *Ibid.*, p. 58; CAMB, *Minute Books*, 16 December 1896, 29 March 1900.
11 NFBTE, *Minute Books*, 26 July 1899, 12 October 1910.
12 R. Bean, 'Employers' Associations in the Port of Liverpool, 1890–1914,' *International Review of Social History*, Vol. XXI, Pt. 3 (1976); Bob Holton, *British Syndicalism 1900–1914. Myths and Realities* (London, 1976), pp. 127–9.
13 Lord Askwith, *Industrial Problems and Disputes* (Harvester Press ed.; Brighton, 1974), p. 141; *Report on Strikes and Lock-Outs . . . in 1910*, 1911, Vol. XLI [Cd. 5850], p. 24. From the time of the STA in March 1909 to June 1910 there had been 35 illegal stoppages in the northeast – 27 of which had been by the boilermakers. See *Webb Collection*, E, B, Vol. 88, No. 28, p. 3, No. 35, p. 1.
14 *Master Builder*, 25 March 1914, p. 10; Higenbottam, p. 188.
15 Mortimer, p. 104.
16 *Newcastle Daily Chronicle*, 12 February 1886, p. 4, 23 February 1886, p. 5, 12 January 1886, p. 5. See also, L. L. F. R. Price, *Industrial Peace* (London 1887), pp. 9–11; *Jarrow Guardian*, 26 February 1886, p. 8.

17 Cummings, p. 128.
18 *Ibid.*, p. 126; United Society of Boilermakers' and Iron and Steel Shipbuilders,' *Monthly Reports*, March 1889, p. 7.
19 USB, *Monthly Reports*, December 1888, p. 8, April 1889, p. 10.
20 *Ibid.*, October 1899, p. 12, September 1899, pp. 15–16. For other examples of condemnations of absenteeism see August 1900, pp. 26–7, October 1900, pp. 7–9, June 1901, p. 32. In 1898, negotiations with the Clyde employers led the district committee to publish a schedule of fines for those absent for more than one day: see July 1898, p. 8, December 1898, p. 23.
21 Cummings, p. 133: 'For some years the General Secretary and the Executive had preached against illegal disputes, [and] advocated their suppression . . . Despite the fact that summary punishment was threatened very little improvement was accomplished.' On changes in the composition of capital see Sidney Pollard, 'The Economic History of British Shipbuilding 1870–1914' (PhD dissertation, University of London, 1950), pp. 71–3. On the need for greater labour control because of these changes see the very illuminating address by the manager of Palmers, John Price, 'The Use of Machinery in Construction,' North East Coast Engineers and Shipbuilders, *Transactions*, Vol. 5 (1888–89), pp. 43–9.
22 *Webb Collection*, E, B, Vol. 86, Agreement Between the Employers' Association and Boilermakers' and Iron and Steel Shipbuilders' Society (Newcastle, 1894).
23 USB, *Monthly Reports*, July 1894, p. 4. 15,950 voted in favour and 11,840 against but in the northeast 2,166 voted in favour and 7,347 against. See J. F. Clarke, 'Labour Relations in Engineering and Shipbuilding in the North East Coast in the Second Half of the Nineteenth Century' (MA Thesis, University of Newcastle, 1966), p. 453. Opposition to the agreement was not allowed to appear in the Reports.
24 *Industrial Council*, ques. 3539–40.
25 *Webb Collection*, E, B, Vol. 88, No. 4, pp. 4–6.
26 *Industrial Council*, ques. 3551.
27 *Ibid.*, ques. 3743–4.
28 *Ibid.*, ques. 3655. The union appears to have taken this upon themselves, the agreement provided for yard discussions between employers and men as the first stage of disputes resolution and it is, of course, likely that many matters were settled in this informal way.
29 *Report on Collective Agreements*, p. 95; USB, *Monthly Reports*, July 1909, pp. 29–30; *Industrial Council*, ques. 3740.
30 Thus, at the discussions leading up to the STA, Wilkie of the Associated Society of Shipwrights felt that a declaration from the employers that the agreement would level up wages would 'assist us in getting these things accepted.' And shipbuilder Robert Hunter remarked that 'we recognise that you have a difficult set of men to deal with outside.' See *Webb Collection*, E, B, Vol. 88, No. 1, p. 6, No. 3, pp. 4, 32.
31 The STA was not announced in the Boilermakers' Reports until one month after it was drawn up: see USB, *Monthly Reports*, April 1909, p. 20. In the ASC&J both the STA and the Edinburgh Agreement were put to votes of the whole society with the excuse that the agreements were national (that is, as far as shipbuilding was concerned) and, therefore, must be put to a national vote; but this also maximised the chances of acceptance. See ASC&J, *Monthly Reports*, May 1908, pp. 260–1, 272, March 1909, p. 159.
32 Amulree, p. 107; Parliamentary Papers, *Royal Commission on Trades Disputes and Trade Combinations*, 1906, Vol. LVI [Cd. 2826], ques. 2842–55. Webb also

saw Taff Vale 'as a step towards full corporate status [for trade unions], legally enforceable agreements, and compulsory arbitration.' See Clegg, Fox and Thompson, p. 318.

33 It is worth noting that both Samuel Stennett of the ASC&J and George Dew of LBIF were in favour of legal enforceability. See *Industrial Council*, ques. 2432, 2767–8, 3662, 5046, 5229, 10448, 11684, 12125, 14891.

34 LMBA *Minute Books*, 20 January 1900; OSM *Journal*, 21 January 1914, p. 53; *The N-F-Record*, Vol. III, No. IX (June 1914), p. 4. The idea of a monetary guarantee was first raised at the July 1899 conference, again at the London working rules negotiations of 1900 and in 1914 when it was linked with an arbitration board with power to award penalties. This latter proposal was particularly obnoxious to unions because it would have handed a disciplinary power to third parties outside of the industrial relations structure.

35 Clegg, Fox and Thompson, pp. 318–19, 323.

36 V. L. Allen, *Power in Trade Unions* (London, 1954), pp. 67, 172.

37 Clegg, Fox and Thompson, pp. 476–8 who note also: 'Useful as the changes [in union government such as representative executives] were in improving communications between leaders and the rank and file, they do not seem generally to have diminished the authority of the full-time officers.'

38 Turner, pp. 225–8; Hinton, pp. 81–3.

39 The 1859 strike of masons at Trollope's was illegal; the union had consistently refused to support the expense of meetings held to propagate the nine hours demand. The 1865 carpenters' movement was neither approved nor supported by the Amalgamated Society but the men went ahead 'at disorderly meetings called by no recognised body' claimed Beesly who was currently engaged in selling the ASC&J. In 1869 the masons' Central Committee had wanted to confine the struggle to Manchester and had tried to persuade the other towns to refrain from striking. See *Fortnightly Returns*, 13 October 1859, p. 6, 1 September 1859, p. 5; E. S. Beesly, 'The Amalgamated Society of Carpenters,' *Fortnightly Review*, NS, Vol. 1 (1867), p. 331. Beesly's impression is not confirmed by the *Bee-Hive*, 17 June 1865, p. 6, and see 8 May 1869, p. 6, for the OSM attempts to limit the 1869 conflict.

40 For a good example of how these movements started see *Bee-Hive*, 24 June 1866, p. 5, 30 June 1866, p. 5 where the London painters' strike of 1866 originated in three shops in the King's Road who first memorialised their employers and then sent delegates out to the other shops to join in.

41 *Reynolds's News*, 15 May 1853, p. 9, 5 June 1853, p. 9, 18 September 1853, p. 12, 26 June 1853, p. 1.

42 *Bee-Hive*, 7 October 1865, p. 5.

43 *Ibid.*, 17 June 1865, p. 5, 8 July 1865, p. 5, 15 July 1865, p. 5, 22 July 1865, p. 5, 29 July 1865, p. 5.

44 Howell, *Autobiography*, Vol. 2, p. 53; within a year of joining the union, however, Howell had been elected to a rules revision committee. For 1872 see Postgate, p. 295; *Bee-Hive*, 21 June 1872, p. 4. The one union official was Thomas Sadler of the General Union of Carpenters.

45 Thus, John D. Prior, General Secretary of ASC&J 1871–81 had been secretary to the Plymouth Strike Committee in the big strike in the southwest in 1865. *Bee-Hive*, 3 February 1866, p. 5.

46 *Webb Collection*, E, B, Vol. 34, No. 7.

47 An interesting reflection of this upside down conception of leadership was to be found in the Manchester Unity Bricklayers whose rules forbade the General Secretary from membership in any deputation to employers, see

Manchester Union of Operative Bricklayers, *Monthly Reports,* November 1871.
48 *Liverpool Mercury,* 12 June 1846, p. 282.
49 See ASC&J, Maidstone Branch, *Minute Books,* 19 November 1866, 21 June 1875; OSM, Constantine Lodge, *Minute Books,* 24 May 1876, 6 December 1876.
50 *The Builder,* 13 June 1846, p. 284; *Fortnightly Returns,* 11 June 1846, p. 4; *Liverpool Mercury,* 12 June 1846, p. 282.
51 *Manchester Guardian,* 12 November 1857, p. 4.
52 Building Trades Conference, *Minute Book 1858–1859,* 24 June 1859.
53 *Ibid.,* 13 December 1858.
54 *Ibid.,* 13 January 1859.
55 *Birmingham Daily Post,* 25 April 1864, p. 3, 26 April 1864, p. 4, 12 May 1864, p. 5; *Bee-Hive,* 7 May 1864, p. 5, 14 May 1864, p. 5.
56 *Bee-Hive,* 28 May 1864, p. 5.
57 *Ibid.,* 17 June 1865, p. 5, 8 July 1865, p. 5, 15 July 1865, p. 5, 29 July 1865, p. 5.
58 *Ibid.,* 2 June 1866, p. 5.
59 Parliamentary Papers, *Select Committee on the Combination Laws,* 1825, Vol. IV [437], ques. 306–7; *Sunderland Herald,* 11 February 1853, p. 5: 'If the proceedings were conducted with closed doors the shipwrights might imagine that some underhand work was being carried on.'
60 I have emphasised in this book the centralised aspects of the union but the strong persistence of work group activity is not in doubt and its relation to the centralised decision making would make an interesting study.
61 *Jarrow Guardian,* 6 February 1875, p. 3, 13 March 1875, p. 2.
62 *Royal Commission on Trade Unions,* Fourth Report, ques. 7148.
63 *Bee-Hive,* 14 January 1865, p. 5; *Birmingham Daily Post,* 21 May 1865, p. 6.
64 Ass.C&J, Edinburgh Branch, *Minute Books,* 20 February 1884, 26 April 1884, 30 April 1884, 11 July 1887, 8 August 1887, 20 September 1887; ASC&J, Edinburgh Branch, *Minute Books,* 3 May 1892, 11 November 1892.
65 Ass.C&J, Edinburgh Branch, *Minute Books,* 27 February 1890, 11 April 1890, 20 November 1890, 25 September 1891, 15 January 1892, 22 February 1892.
66 OBS, *Trade Circular,* September 1872, p. 1184; ASC&J, Manchester Branch *Minute Books,* 3 August 1869, 6 September 1870, 6 January 1872, 8 June 1872. These committees may have reflected the greater organisational needs consequent upon the introduction of hourly pay. In the case of the bricklayers their establishment was associated with the internecine warfare between the London and Manchester societies that had exploded with the Markley affair. The peace agreement between the two unions had provided for the establishment of joint committees in towns where they both had branches.
67 *Builders' Trade Circular,* 30 May 1872, p. 9; Carpenters and Joiners, *The Balance Sheet of the Carpenters and Joiners Short-Time Movement of 1872* (London, 1872), p. 15.
68 CAMB, *Minute Books,* 11 June 1872.
69 *Ibid.,* 14 June 1872; Carpenters and Joiners, *Balance Sheet . . . ,* p. 20; *Builders' Trade Circular,* 20 June 1872, p. 5.
70 Carpenters and Joiners, *Balance Sheet . . . ,* pp. 26–9; *Bee-Hive,* 3 August 1872, pp. 3–4, 17 August 1872, p. 5.
71 Carpenters and Joiners, *Balance Sheet . . . ,* p. 30; *Builders' Trade Circular,* 22 August 1872, p. 8; *Bee-Hive,* 24 August 1872, p. 5, 7 September 1872, p. 5.
72 *Bee-Hive,* 31 August 1872, p. 14, 14 September 1872, p. 14; OBS, *Trade Circular,* September 1872, pp. 1183–4.

73 E.g. Ass.C&J, Glasgow Branch, *Minute Books*, 28 November 1882.

74 ASC&J, *Monthly Reports*, April 1883, p. 58; GUC&J, *London District Committee Report for 1894*, p. 5. The decline of aggregate meetings must also have contributed to the increasing division between union and non-union men.

75 For the engineers Richard Croucher writes: 'Somewhere between 1871, when the Nine Hours Strike had been run by shop delegates, and 1908 District Committees had brought shop organisation to heel.' See Richard Croucher, 'The North East Engineers' Strike of 1908,' North East Coast Group for the Study of Labour History, *Bulletin*, No. 9 (October 1975), p. 52; *Webb Collection*, E, A, Vol. 33, f. 129; Mortimer, p. 104.

76 *Bee-Hive*, 5 October 1872, p. 4, 21 June 1873, p. 4, 19 July 1873, p. 4; Higenbottam, p. 332. In the 1875 and 1876 movements there was no debate about deputations possessing the power to settle, it was assumed that they had the right. See CAMB, *Minute Books*, 19 July 1875.

77 CAMB, *Minute Books*, 24 April 1893.

78 Higenbottam, p. 73; Postgate, pp. 186–7.

79 Postgate, p. 185; *Birmingham Daily Post*, 26 January 1865, p. 8; ASC&J, *Monthly Reports*, January 1865, n.p., February 1865, n.p., March 1865, p. 6. Neither the 1860 nor 1866 rules said anything about the conduct of strikes or about Executive powers in the event of disputes. Applegarth had no authority, therefore, for claiming that the dispute was illegal nor for his attempts to close the strike. For the Rules see *Webb Collection*, E, C, Vol. 12, No. 11.

80 ASC&J, Manchester 1st Branch, *Minute Books*, 21 January 1865. See also *Monthly Reports*, May 1867, p. 94 for the same branch protesting against the constant publication by the Executive Council of the rule giving them control over strikes which suggests that although they did not use the rule until 1872, they were very anxious to let the branches know they possessed it.

81 OBS, *Trade Circular*, November 1865, pp. 421–2, December 1865, p. 430, March 1867, pp. 651–2; *Webb Collection*, E, C, Vol. 5, Rules of 1871, pp. 36, 38.

82 *Webb Collection*, E, C, Vol. 50, Masons Rules, 1849, p. 15, 1862 Rules, p. 46. The Central Committee in 1859 had the power to close strikes but only if the whole Society voted to do so.

83 *Ibid.*, Rules of 1881, n.p.; see also, Vol. 12 for the GUC&J Rules of 1889 which gave their Executive the right to appoint delegations and Vol. 18 for 1882 Plasterers' Rules which gave their executives the right to close strikes.

84 *Ibid.*, Vol. 50; *Fortnightly Returns*, 4 August 1881, p. 9, 18 August 1881, p. 7.

85 S. & B. Webb, *Industrial Democracy*, pp. 28–9.

86 *Royal Commission on Trade Unions*, Ninth Report, ques. 17582–7; Mortimer, p. 61.

87 See *Newcastle Daily Chronicle*, 5 September 1864, p. 2, 14 September 1864, p. 2; *Jarrow Guardian*, 2 March 1872, p. 8, for speeches which illustrate this changing emphasis. By 1901, Palmers enforced a closed shop for the National Amalgamated Union of Labour.

88 Mortimer, p. 96.

89 *Ibid.*, p. 174; *Webb Collection*, E, C, Vol. 35, 1880 Rules. In the rules of 1874 – and this, presumably, reflects the traditional situation – the Executive had only the right to sanction strike pay.

90 *Webb Collection*, E, C, Vol. 35, 1890 and 1895 Rules.

91 ASC&J, *Monthly Reports*, September 1869, p. 185.

92 *Ibid.*, October 1874, p. 155, January 1875, p. 9 and see August 1877, p. 122 for another dispute at Newcastle which was closed by the Executive and was accompanied with a condemnation of the Newcastle men conducting policy

by trade meetings and allowing themselves to be 'overruled by the non-society men.'

93 *Ibid.*, September 1896, p. 224, October 1896, pp. 257–8.

94 For examples see *Fortnightly Returns*, 20 May 1897, p. 12, 27 April 1905, p. 9.

95 *South Wales Daily News*, 14 April 1892, p. 4, 23 May 1892, p. 5, 13 June 1892, p. 5.

96 *Ibid.*, 6 May 1892, p. 5, 3 June 1892, p. 5, 9 June 1892, p. 5, 15 June 1892, p. 5.

97 *Fortnightly Returns*, 27 April 1893, p. 13.

98 For this see: GUC&J, *Monthly Trade Reports*, April 1877, pp. 7, 9–11, June 1877, p. 33, July 1877, p. 15, October 1877, pp. 11–14, 72, December 1877, pp. 17–20; Postgate, p. 308; Higenbottam, p. 113. Neither Postgate nor Higenbottam seem to realise that Last was suspended from office by a delegate meeting because of his handling of the strike – Postgate says that Last either died or resigned. In December the Society voted 3198 to 1811 to discharge him.

99 *Workman's Times*, 24 April 1891, p. 4, 26 June 1891, p. 7, 3 July 1891, p. 7, 21 August 1891, pp. 4, 7; Grossman, p. 138.

100 *Workman's Times*, 25 August 1891, p. 7; Parliamentary Papers, *Report on the Strikes and Lock-Outs of 1891*, 1893–94, Vol. LXXXIII, Pt. 1 [C. 9890], p. 267. The masters' demand for non-union representation can be looked at as an attempt to ensure accountability; this is the only time that the demand is forcefully pressed. Furthermore, and paradoxically, it was the aggregate meeting's proposal that was the traditional one because it asserted the clear authority of the aggregate meeting to choose whom they pleased to be on the delegation. The United Trade Committee felt that this was not conciliatory enough to the employers and – accepting the distinction between unionist and non-unionist – caused the other course to be taken.

101 *Report on the Strikes . . . of 1891*, pp. 270, 273; *Workman's Times*, 23 October 1891, p. 7, 28 November 1891, pp. 4–5.

102 *Workman's Times*, 28 November 1891, p. 7; Grossman, pp. 142, 143–4 for dissatisfaction over the award.

103 *Daily News*, 19 May 1896, p. 4, 23 May 1896, p. 7, 30 May 1896, p. 3; Grossman, p. 182.

104 S. & B. Webb, *Industrial Democracy*, pp. 90–103.

105 *Ibid.*, p. 90.

106 Allen, *Power in Trade Unions*, p. 247; ASC&J, *Annual Report for 1893*, p. 511.

107 For examples see OSM *Journal*, 5 March 1913, p. 170: 'Bro. Freeman received instructions from the Executive Council as to the course he was to follow,' 9 July 1913, pp. 560–1.

108 ASC&J, *Monthly Reports*, June 1895, p. 115.

109 *Webb Collection*, E, A, Vol. 33, f. 21. The Webbs noted how the complicated method of their election resulted in their complete subordination to the Executive Council. See also, S. & B. Webb, *Industrial Democracy*, pp. 30–1.

110 *Webb Collection*, E, A, Vol. 33, f. 119. The length of time that delegates had to be union members increased from 5 to 10 years between 1880 and 1890. For a remarkable attack upon a candidate for the Clyde District Delegate job in 1887 see USB, *Monthly Reports*, February 1887, pp. 14–15: it was claimed that he harboured 'sedition and revolt against all rules and authority, coupled with such an amount of bitterness against all in this office [i.e. the Executive], that they show . . . his unfitness to fulfil the duties of a District Delegate . . . he has attempted to stir up feelings of disobedience.' It takes little imagination to visualise this man's opinion of the autocracy that Knight ran!

111 *Webb Collection*, E, A, Vol. 33, ff. 21, 128.
112 USB, *Monthly Reports*, July 1900, p. 21, May 1905, p. 28.
113 *Royal Commission on Labour*, Group A, Vol. III, 1893, Vol. XXXII [C. 6894], ques. 25562, 26396.
114 *Webb Collection*, E, A, Vol. 33, ff. 119, 128, 189; *Report on Collective Agreements*, p. 106.
115 ASC&J, *Monthly Reports*, August 1878, p. 122. It was noted after the 1873 movement that it was felt advisable to keep the Committee in existence to prevent disorganisation in the trade and 'it was resolved that a permanent committee should be appointed, consisting of the different societies of carpenters and joiners in London.' But, as Manchester illustrated, United Trade Committees were not unknown before this date.
116 *Ibid.*, March 1878, p. 42; *Labour News and Employment Advertiser*, 19 January 1878, p. 1, 16 February 1878, p. 3, for the clearly traditional nature of this movement.
117 ASC&J, *Monthly Reports*, November 1875, p. 172.
118 *Ibid.*, June 1877, pp. 88–92, July 1877, p. 108.
119 As, for example, over allowable exceptions to the working rules. *Ibid.*, November 1874, p. 177, September 1882, p. 141.
120 *Ibid.*, August 1878, p. 121, March 1882, p. 42, April 1882, p. 58.
121 Some small societies were still represented. *Ibid.*, August 1878, p. 122, December 1887, p. 219.
122 *Ibid.*, January 1893, p. 14; *Carpenters' and Joiners' Amalgamated Review*, April 1904, p. 5.
123 OBS, Metropolitan Central Strike Committee, *Report*, April–November 1892, pp. 1, 3, 6, 13, 18.
124 This is especially true of the LBIF: see Postgate, p. 417: 'The LBIF, though often unceremoniously thrust aside by the Executive Councils, did represent far more nearly the London rank and file.' This, also, is the implication in Grossman, Chapter 6.
125 *Webb Collection*, E, D, Vol. 16 for London Building Trades Committee, *Report for 1892*, pp. 4–5; Vol. 10, ff. 144–5, 153; *Workman's Times*, 4 September 1891, p. 7. Those who created the Federation included Weighill, Secretary of the London Lodges Committee, OSM; Herrick, President of OBS; Matkin, General Secretary of General Union of Carpenters; and Deller General Secretary of NAOP. For the LBIF see OSM, *Journal*, 10 February 1914, p. 107.
126 LBTF, *Quarterly Report for 30 June 1893; Monthly Circular*, April 1894, p. 8; *Industrial Council*, ques. 10525.
127 OSM, *Journal*, 4 March 1914, p. 148, 29 April 1914, p. 299.
128 *Daily Herald*, 12 June 1914, p. 6, 17 June 1914, p. 6, 18 June 1914, p. 6, 25 June 1914, p. 6.
129 *Ibid.*, 3 March 1914, p. 5, 11 May 1914, p. 4, 15 May 1914, p. 6, 7 July 1914, p. 7; Holton, p. 160.
130 *Solidarity*, March 1914, p. 3.

NOTES TO CHAPTER 7

1 George Dangerfield, *The Strange Death of Liberal England 1910–1914* (New York, 1935).
2 Henry Pelling, 'The Labour Unrest, 1911–1914,' in *Popular Politics and Society in Late Victorian Britain* (London, 1968), p. 164; Standish Meacham, ' "The

Sense of an Impending Clash": English Working-Class Unrest before the First World War,' *American Historical Review,* Vol. 77, No. 5 (December 1972).

3 The forms taken by this authority crisis assumed different shapes in each of its separate aspects. The Tariff Reform issue, for example, did not threaten to lead to civil war – as did the Irish crisis – but it must be seen as a struggle between certain sections of the industrial and financial capitalist class as to what kind of economic policies should predominate. The lines of demarcation in this struggle would probably not be found to correspond exactly to the industrial and financial sectors, but that would do nothing to alter the essentials of the case.

4 I am thinking here, for example, of the technological changes that re-defined the boundaries of craft skill and the social structural changes that may have changed the boundaries of the working and middle classes.

5 Gareth Stedman Jones, 'Working-Class Culture and Working-Class Politics in London, 1870–1900; Notes on the Remaking of a Working Class,' p. 462.

6 E. H. Phelps Brown, *The Growth of British Industrial Relations* (London, 1965), pp. 319–20, 332, 336; Pelling, p. 156. See also, Ronald V. Sires, 'Labor Unrest in England, 1910–1914,' *Jou nal of Economic History,* Vol. xv (1955) for a useful account of the unrest with no real interpretation.

7 Pelling, pp. 151, 157–60.

8 Standish Meacham, *A Life Apart. The English Wวrking Class 1890–1914* (Cambridge, Mass., 1974), p. 219. Meacham's book deals, of coursc, with wider issues than the labour unrest alone and what he has to say about the nature of working-class life and society in the period 1890–1914 is valuable and interesting.

9 *Ibid.;* see also his article ' "The Sense of an Impending Clash" . . . ,' pp. 1362–4, where it is argued that the unrest emerged from a combination of economic grievance and class consciousness which 'was almost certainly heightened by their [i.e. working class] understandable confusion at the rapid disappearance of Victorian institutions they had taken for granted . . . Was it not uncertainty, even fear perhaps, that as much as anything drove the English worker to act as he did in those years . . . ?'

10 Unofficial Reform Committee, South Wales Miners, *The Miners' Next Step* (Pluto Press, Reprints in Labour History No. 4; London, 1973).

11 For my use of this term see Appendix D.

12 Holton, pp. 29–35. On Liberal social reform policies see Roy Hay, 'Employers and Social Policy in Britain: the evolution of the welfare legislation, 1905–1914,' *Social History,* No. 4 (January 1977).

13 G. D. H. Cole, *The World of Labour* (Harvester Press reprint of 1919 edition; Brighton, 1973), p. 54; Goodrich, *The Frontier of Control.*

14 Goodrich, pp. 257–65. The distinction Goodrich drew between positive and negative control is useful in the sense that it points up the wider, more threatening intent explicit in this latest manifestation of the struggle. He recognised that negative control very easily shaded into a positive form but he viewed the former as primarily a defensive resistance to employer encroachments and, in my view, paid insufficient attention to the positive feature that negative control possessed of constantly challenging managerial prerogatives. Furthermore, he did not seem to recognise that traditional control was wider than purely craft control and that it provided the material basis for the later development of positive control. It is the transformation of negative to positive control aspirations that is the crucial historical problem of this period; a transformation that cannot be explained solely by the properties of industrial

unionism but also needs to be seen as a product of changes in the needs and pressures of the industrial structure, the need for cooperation in wartime which helped legitimise its demands, and the political temper of the time. Cole, in *Workshop Organisation* (Oxford, 1923), pp. 14–17 paid some attention to the pre-war developments of the workshop movement but generally regarded it of little significance until the war and he did not deal with the phenomenon until it became organised.

15 Cole, *The World of Labour*, p. 382.

16 Richard Hyman, 'Workers' Control and Revolutionary Theory,' *The Socialist Register 1974* (London, 1974), p. 260.

17 Richard Herding, *Job Control and Union Structure* (Rotterdam, 1972), especially pp. 117, 121–2, 125–6, 140–1, 178, 220–3. The United Auto Workers treatment of the speed-up question at Ford provides an example of these themes when, since the first contract in 1942, the union has successively bargained away an efficient enforcement of grievance procedures in return for an increased release time per day. None of this should be taken to argue that unionism will at no time present issues that challenge managerial prerogatives nor that the union does not represent an implicit and potential challenge to the concept of managerial authority. But historically it is true that only when the unions seem to be in danger of losing their own internal authority over their members will they embrace the ideas and vocabulary of work control and then, as at present, part of this is with a view to 'officialising' it. See Hyman, 'Workers' Control and Revolutionary Theory,' p. 257. To argue as Flanders does in 'Collective Bargaining: A Theoretical Analysis,' *British Journal of Industrial Relations*, Vol. 6, No. 3 (November 1968), that unions attain their significance as job regulators and guarantors of 'dignity' is perhaps true as a partial explanation of why men join unions. But as a description of how modern unions explicitly act, it is inadequate because it fails to address the question of whose concepts of 'regulation' predominate. Furthermore, most British unions are inordinately proud of their sole focus on bread and butter issues.

18 USB, *Monthly Reports*, July 1901, pp. 27–8, September 1901, p. 8, November 1901, p. 21, December 1901, p. 11.

19 Herding, pp. 221, 346. Hyman noted exactly the same phenomenon in the Workers' Union where as the increase in Executive authority grew so did unofficial workshop organisation; see *The Workers' Union*, p. 117.

20 Alan Fox and Allen Flanders, 'The Reform of Collective Bargaining: From Donovan to Durkheim,' *British Journal of Industrial Relations*, Vol. 7, No. 2 (July 1969), where it is argued – with reference to the pre-1914 situation – that it was the growth of such informal structures in the 1950s and 1960s that led to the consequent industrial relations crisis of the late sixties. The collective bargaining systems, they claim, were unable to cope with the 'transformation of power relations in the factories' which led work groups to develop their own systems and impose them unilaterally. Thus, the need for 'reforms' to bring the collective bargaining systems more into line with these realities – i.e. to control the informal systems. This thesis works less well for our period where the informal systems grew immediately and parallel with the imposition of formal systems. Its labour management focus ignores, therefore, the fact that these informal systems are not just a result of the dysfunctioning of the wider structures but endemic to their existence because they represent attempts to countervail the results of the official bargaining systems.

21 In engineering, stewards emerged as rank and file leaders as the industrial

relations system of the 1890s was imposed. See Hinton, pp. 79–80; J. B. Jeffreys, *The Story of the Engineers, 1806–1945* (London, 1945), p. 165.

22 Higenbottam, p. 8 for stewards in GUC&J rule books in 1866; GUC&J, Ashton-under-Lyne Branch, *Minute Books,* 15 February 1862 for a mention of their existence; *Webb Collection,* E, C, Vol. 50, *Masons' Rule Book,* 1849, p. 15 for their dues collecting function. Holton, pp. 14, 41, 52, 155; Postgate, p. 405; OSM, *Journal,* 29 November 1911, p. 748.

23 Hilton, *Industrial Relations in Constructions,* p. 6, for the recent recognition of stewards in building. They now have to be formally recognised by the union and will not be accredited by the employer until he has been so notified by the union. It is interesting to note the enduring nature of the issues associated with stewards. Thus, they are not permitted to leave work without permission of management, there are to be no shop meetings or ticket inspections in working hours unless management agrees. Precisely the same kinds of issues were current in London during 1890–1914. It was one of the central demands of the rank and file in 1914 that stewards be allowed to hold card inspections whenever they pleased; the final proposals presented to the men stipulated that no inspections were to take place during working hours. The 1960s were, of course, a time when the same problems of divergence between a collaborationist union leadership and militant rank and file also posed a tangible threat to the structures of industrial relations.

24 USB, *Annual Report for 1882,* p. xiii, *Monthly Reports,* November 1907, p. 28, September 1908, p. 15; Mortimer, p. 104; Cummings, p. 113.

25 Douglass, pp. 265–71. See also Holton, Ch. 7 for a similar pattern over the Minimum Wage Act of 1911 which the miners voted against but whose vote was overturned by the national leadership.

26 Cole, *The World of Labour,* p. 33.

27 Askwith, pp. 347–50.

28 Unofficial Reform Committee, *The Miners' Next Step,* esp. Ch. 2.

29 Peter N. Stearns, 'Measuring the Evolution of Strike Movements,' *International Review of Social History,* Vol. XIX, Pt. 1 (1974), p. 20; Meacham, *A Life Apart,* pp. 214–17; Pelling, p. 149.

30 LMBA, *Minute Books,* 12 February 1912, 14 March 1912. An example of the revival of work control aspirations was a Manchester strike in 1911 involving 200 plasterers, joiners and bricklayers in defiance of the conciliation rule over the refusal of the firm to allow walking delegates into the sites. See *Master Builder and Associations' Journal,* 7 June 1911, p. 28.

31 OSM, *Journal,* 22 May 1912, pp. 351–2, 10 July 1912, pp. 448–9, 2 October 1912, pp. 652–3, 16 October 1912, pp. 686–7. For bricklayers see OBS, *Trade Circular,* July 1914, p. 4.

32 *Master Builder and Associations' Journal,* 7 February 1912, p. 30.

33 Grossman, p. 185; CAMB, *Minute Books,* 24 August 1905, 29 August 1905, 30 August 1905, 31 August 1905; *Master Builders' Associations' Journal,* November 1905, p. 17.

34 CAMB, *Minute Books,* 14 March 1912, 30 May 1912, 8 May 1913, 19 May 1913, 21 May 1913, 22 May 1913, 26 May 1913, 6 February 1913; NFBTE, *Minute Books,* 11 November 1913.

35 ASC&J, *Monthly Reports,* December 1910, pp. 793–5, November 1911, p. 504.

36 OSM, *Journal,* 9 August 1911, pp. 504–5.

37 *Ibid.,* 11 December 1912, p. 864.

38 *Ibid.; Transport Worker,* December 1911, pp. 100–1. See OBS, *Trade Circular,* May 1912, pp. 19–20 for a nice illustration from the Southampton branch of

this process. At first they had supported Conciliation Boards but: 'Our experience has been a bitter one, and has convinced us that they are productive of much ill-feeling, and only act as a means for delaying or shelving altogether any attempts on the part of the operatives to improve their conditions.' The no-strike clause made it 'impossible for us to take that immediate action when necessary which alone is effective.'

39 This feature of the industrial relations system was very likely a major factor in creating the recognition of the need for amalgamation.

40 OSM, *Journal*, 9 August 1911, p. 504, 3 September 1913, p. 697, 1 October 1913, p. 713, 10 December 1913, pp. 1014, 1019.

41 Representatives to the Centre Boards were elected, those to the National Board were not. ASC&J, *Monthly Reports*, October 1911, p. 442. For resolutions hostile to participation in the National Board see November 1907, p. 631, January 1909, p. 26, December 1909, pp. 757–8, December 1910, pp. 793–5, February 1911, p. 58, May 1911, p. 199, June 1911, p. 243, July 1911, p. 289, August 1911, p. 355, September 1911, p. 403.

42 *Ibid.*, December 1912, p. 736, May 1913, p. 152; Postgate, p. 415.

43 OSM, *Journal*, 11 December 1912, p. 864.

44 Postgate, p. 412.

45 *Ibid.*, pp. 409–13 for the schemes for governmental re-organisation in building.

46 CAMB, *Minute Books*, 14 March 1912, 28 March 1912, 17 April 1912, 1 May 1912, 22 May 1912, 16 June 1912, 11 July 1912. The employers seem to have secured from the carpenters the stipulation – from which they had previously been exempt – that no distinction be recognised between union and non-union men.

47 *Ibid.*, 12 December 1912, 6 February 1913, 6 March 1913, 15 April 1913, 19 April 1913.

48 Grossman, p. 283.

49 CAMB, *Minute Books*, 27 May 1913, 2 June 1913; Grossman, p. 254. Shortening the time for appeals to the Boards was a common answer to the challenge to their existence and was one of the changes in the Supplement to the STA of 1910.

50 George Hicks was perhaps the most prominent official who supported amalgamation. He had been a founder-member and secretary to the Consolidation Committee and became an organiser for the OBS in 1912 but he opposed the formation of the Industrial Union in 1914. See Postgate, pp. 405, 414, 421.

51 OSM, *Journal*, 20 September 1911, p. 581, 18 October 1911, p. 656, 24 July 1912, pp. 472–3.

52 Postgate, pp. 407–8.

53 *Ibid.*, p. 410; Higenbottam, p. 124; Meacham, ' "The Sense of an Impending Clash" . . . ,' p. 1359.

54 Pelling, p. 159; Postgate, pp. 400–1.

55 On the difficulties of federation in Building see Cole, *The World of Labour*, pp. 266–70 where he concludes: 'It could only be made effective if the Unions sacrificed to it the whole of their power – if, that is, it became an amalgamation in everything but name. This, clearly, is not the kind of body proposed by those who advocate federation . . . they want a powerless body, whose sole use will be to scotch schemes of amalgamation.'

56 For this and for the way in which the war was used as the opportunity to implement an officials' federation scheme and for the revival of the old struggle between federation and amalgamation after the war see Higenbottam, pp. 116, 121, 125–6.

57 G. A. Phillips, 'The Triple Alliance in 1914,' *Economic History Review*, Vol. XXIV, No. 1 (1971), p. 63.

58 Higenbottam, pp. 122–4; Postgate, p. 413.

59 For protests against the way ASC&J pursued the question of amalgamation see ASC&J, *Monthly Reports*, January 1914, p. 53, February 1914, p. 87; see also, OBS, *Trade Circular*, November 1913, pp. 7–8; Higenbottam, pp. 124–5; OSM, *Journal*, 8 February 1914, pp. 129–34.

60 OSM, *Journal*, 6 March 1912, pp. 163–4.

61 Pelling, p. 152; see ASC&J, *Monthly Reports*, June 1911, p. 236, November 1911, p. 516 on the difficulties of recruiting: 'The great objection [especially from former members] was that the Society was no good to them. All they did was pay in: no action had been taken for years. Some said they were as good out as in as they never worked for less than the rate ... I gathered from our men that the non-union men not half gave them it, and said, "What is the use of the Society now?"'

Too much attention with too little close analysis has been given to the surge of union membership in 1911–14. In building, the increase of those years was a regaining of lost membership and in the case of the bricklayers, masons and labourers left them far below the levels they had attained in the late nineties. All building unions – save painters – lost members steadily from 1900–11. Furthermore, the great increase in membership was undeniably combined with a growing alienation – a paradox comprehensible only if we see that increased membership as conditioned by the necessities of increasingly complete collective bargaining systems. Thus, for those who equate trade union policy with working-class attitudes, the age was not one of revolt – the cooperation between trade unions, employers and government was closer than ever before. But that is just the point, this closeness was one of the causes of the alienation. The increase in union membership was a complex phenomenon, but it is important to realise that it did not necessarily mean an identification with official union behaviour or policy.

62 For the Clyde Vigilance Committee see USB, *Monthly Reports*, March 1907, p. 37, November 1907, p. 28, September 1908, p. 15. In 1905–6, the Tyne saw three delegates come and go within the space of 18 months. The reasons for this rapid turnover were unspecified but seemed to have been associated with ill-discipline on the part of the men see *Monthly Reports*, August 1906, p. 31.

63 This did not happen once during this period, but it is hard not to believe that the somewhat ungenerous treatment accorded Robert Knight on his retirement was associated with accumulated resentment at his autocracy. See USB, *Monthly Reports*, November 1900, p. 22, December 1900, p. 7, and January 1901, p. 12 for the large minority vote that he should obtain only £2.10s. per week superannuation instead of £3.10s.

64 See Douglass, pp. 281–2 for miners' distrust of all delegate representatives: 'When the lodge secretary goes to the gaffer, a deputation of marras will often go with him to see that he really does represent them.'

65 Holton, Ch. 9 for syndicalism's continued strength after 1912.

66 CAMB, *Minute Books*, 10 June 1892, Minutes of Proceedings at a Conference between Master Builders and Trade Delegates, pp. 210–11.

67 OSM, *Journal*, 21 January 1914, p. 53.

68 LMBA, *Minute Books*, 8 December 1913; *Daily Herald*, 27 January 1914, p. 3.

69 LMBA, *Minute Books*, 8 September 1913, 11 September 1913; Grossman, pp. 259–60; OSM, *Journal*, 18 March 1914, p. 203.

70 LMBA, *Minute Books*, 8 December 1913 for the recommendation that a lock-

out be declared unless a guarantee was given by the unions that all strikes would cease. See also, *The N-F-Record*, Vol. III, No. IX (June 1914), p. 4.
71 Postgate, p. 416.
72 LMBA, *Minute Books*, 6 April 1914, 10 March 1914; Postgate, p. 417.
73 Grossman, pp. 292, 295; *Daily Herald*, 5 June 1914, p. 4. One direct labour contract was signed with the Theosophical Society but it is interesting to note that both Dew and Stennett (Secretary and Chairman of LBIF) were reported to be unenthusiastic about the idea. This continuing hostility fed into the support for the Guilds system after the war which showed the revival in modern form of the same spirit that motivated the 'Owenite' builders of the 1830s. See Postgate, pp. 444–6.
74 *Daily Herald*, 4 August 1914, p. 7.
75 *Ibid.*, 10 January 1914, p. 4.
76 OBS, *Metropolitan District Committee Report for 1914*. The demand for the abolition of overtime was another link reminiscent of the past.
77 *Daily Herald*, 21 February 1914, p. 7, 2 March 1914, p. 4, 3 March 1914, p. 5.
78 *The N-F-Record*, June 1914, p. 4.
79 *Daily Herald*, 7 May 1914, p. 4, 9 May 1914, p. 6, 11 May 1914, pp. 4, 11.
80 *Ibid.*, 13 May 1914, p. 4, 15 May 1914, p. 6, 16 May 1914, p. 6, 23 May 1914, p. 6.
81 *Ibid.*, 12 June 1914, p. 6, 15 June 1914, p. 6, 17 June 1914, p. 6, 18 June 1914, p. 6.
82 *Ibid.*, 7 July 1914, p. 7; OSM, London Disputes Committee, *Minute Book*, 19 February 1914.
83 *Daily Herald*, 7 July 1914, p. 7, 10 July 1914, p. 7, 13 July 1914, p. 6, 5 August 1914, p. 7.
84 *The N-F-Record*, June 1914, pp. 4–5; Grossman, p. 300.
85 By 21,210 to 5824. *The N-F-Record*, June 1914, pp. 6–7. In what looked like a blatant attempt to influence the decision, the ASC&J announced that an increased levy on the men still at work would take effect the same day that the voting was to take place! See *Daily Herald*, 23 May 1914, p. 6.
86 *The N-F-Record*, June 1914, pp. 7–8. Previous to this the Conciliation Board mandate had been limited to acting on any *dispute* that arose between employers and workmen – and this had been expanded from its original 1896 function to monitor obnoxious men disputes.
87 *Daily Herald*, 10 June 1914, p. 6, 12 June 1914, p. 6, 22 June 1914, p. 6. The vote was 14,081 against to 4565 for. NFBTE, *Minute Books*, 9 June 1914.
88 See OSM, London Disputes Committee, *Minute Book*, 19 February 1914. The votes of the masons were:

April proposals	460 yes	449 no
May proposals	775 ,,	204 ,,
June proposals	795 ,,	99 ,,

89 *Daily Herald*, 10 July 1914, p. 6.
90 OSM, *Journal*, 24 June 1914, p. 499.
91 OSM, London Disputes Committee, *Minute Book*, 22 June 1914, 23 June 1914; Postgate, p. 419. There is no evidence in the London Disputes Committee Minute Book to support Postgate's claim that the General Council was called as a result of negotiations between Williams and the Committee. That may, in fact, have been so but subsequent events suggest that the Committee needed continual prodding from the general secretary to actually begin negotiations.
92 OSM, London Disputes Committee, *Minute Book*, 23 June 1914, 26 June 1914, 3 July 1914; *Daily Herald*, 6 July 1914, p. 6.

93 Thus, for example, in May (long after the LBIF had abandoned any assertion of its role as sole negotiating agent) rank and file meetings continued to demand that it be so recognised and in June, when the LBIF came out openly behind the National Executive's exhortations to accept the settlement, the Consolidation Committee continued to urge that the Federation put itself at the head of the rank and file by calling a delegate meeting to deal with the crisis. On 2 July a conference of rank and file representatives condemned LBIF support of sectional settlements but at the same time urged them to withdraw additional men from jobs. *Daily Herald*, 15 June 1914, p. 6, 3 July 1914, p. 6.

94 Grossman, pp. 290–1; ASC&J, *Monthly Reports*, May 1914, p. 250.

95 The LBIF did add the futile rider that no section was to return until all had settled. *Daily Herald*, 25 June 1914, p. 6; Grossman, pp. 295–6.

96 NFBTE, *Minute Books,* 27 July 1914.

97 *Ibid.,* 6 August 1914.

98 Higenbottam, p. 190; ASC&J, *Monthly Reports,* September 1914, p. 482.

99 See, *Report of a Court of Inquiry into trade disputes at the Barbican and Horseferry Road construction sites in London*, pp. 41, 45, 60, 62, 63 for loss of union control; pp. 46–7 for restriction of output controlled by the men; pp. 57–8 for unofficial organisation extending far beyond one site; p. 60 for union officials barred from addressing a mass meeting; pp. 65–7 for the need to formalise works committees in order to secure a better disciplinary control.

100 G. K. Chesterton, *All I Survey* (Freeport, NY, 1967), p. 126.

NOTES TO APPENDIX C

1 *Fortnightly Returns*, 26 January 1846, pp. 3–6; *Western Daily Press*, 11 August 1860, p. 3.

2 Strikes against reductions composed the following percentages of all winter wage strikes:

1836–40	1841–50	1851–60	1861–70	1871–80	1881–90	1891–96
100	96.0	94.4	92.8	93.7	100	50.0

3 *Fortnightly Returns*, 6 December 1838, 21 June 1849, p. 3.

4 Strikes over conditions of work in December composed the following percentages of total strikes in that month:

1836–40	1841–50	1851–60	1861–70	1871–80	1881–90	1891–96
3.0	19.6	21.5	30.8	18.9	16.5	30.8

5 Strikes over conditions of work continue as important during the winter months because they were seldom so specifically ruled upon by the agreements and were easier for individual employers to breach without arousing the ire of workers at other sites.

6 Thus, strikes over working rules as a percentage of all strikes in May:

1836–40	1841–50	1851–60	1861–70	1871–80	1881–90	1891–96
0.0	0.0	3.7	10.6	31.8	21.9	28.8

NOTES TO APPENDIX D

1 Crouch, *Class Conflict and the Industrial Relations Crisis.*

2 *Ibid.,* p. 40.

Bibliography

A. PRIMARY SOURCES

1. UNPUBLISHED

i. *British Library of Political and Economic Science*

Webb Trade Union Collection, Section A, Vols. VI, X, XI, XII, XIII, XXXII, XXXIII. Section B, Vols. XXXIV, XXXV, LXXXII, LXXXIII, LXXXVI, LXXXVIII, LXXXIX.

ii. *Greater London Council Record Office*

Central Association of Master Builders (after 1899 London Master Builders' Association). *Minute Books* 1872–1914.
London Master Builders' Association. Decisions of Conciliation Boards 1900–14.

iii. *Modern Records Centre, University of Warwick*

Amalgamated Society of Carpenters and Joiners. Maidstone Branch, *Minute Books* 1865–76.
– Manchester 1st Branch, *Minute Books* 1863–72.
General Union of Carpenters and Joiners. Ashton-u-Lyne Branch, *Minute Books* 1856–64.
National Association of Operative Plasterers. Transcripts of Shorthand Notes of Conferences Between the National Association of Master Builders and National Association of Operative Plasterers, 30 May 1899, 26 July 1899, 18 April 1904. (By permission TGWU.)
Operative Bricklayers' Society. Gosport Branch, *Minute Books* 1896–1901.
– Hull Branch, *Minute Books* 1891–92.
Operative Stonemasons' Society. Constantine Lodge, *Minute Books* 1867–85.
– London Disputes Committee 1914, *Minute Book.*

iv. *National Federation of Building Trades Employers*

General Builders' Association. *Minute Books* 1865–71.
National Federation of Building Trades Employers. *Minute Books* 1877–1914.

v. *National Library of Scotland*

Amalgamated Society of Carpenters and Joiners. Edinburgh Branch, *Minute Books* 1892–1906.

Associated Society of Carpenters and Joiners. Edinburgh Central Branch, *Letter Book* 1869–79.
– Edinburgh (United) Branch, *Minute Books* 1883–1907.
– Glasgow District Branches, *Minute Books*, 1876–87.

vi. Union of Construction and Allied Technicians Trades

Building Trades Conference. *Minute Book* 1858–59. (Now deposited in Modern Records Centre.)

2. PUBLISHED

i. Government documents

The Industrial Council. Report of an Enquiry into Industrial Agreements, 1913, Vol. xxviii [Cd. 6952].
Report of a Court of Inquiry into trade disputes at the Barbican and Horseferry Road construction sites in London, 1966–7, Vol. xxxvii [Cmnd. 3396].
Report on Collective Agreements Between Employers and Workpeople in the United Kingdom, 1910, Vol. xx [Cd. 5366].
Reports by the Chief Labour Correspondent of Strikes and Lock-Outs:
    1891, 1893–4, Vol. lxxxiii, Pt. i [C. 9890].
    1895, 1896, Vol. lxxx, Pt. i [C. 8231].
    1896, 1897, Vol. lxxxiv [C. 8643].
    1897, 1898, Vol. lxxxviii [C. 9012].
    1898, 1899, Vol. xcii [C. 9437].
    1899, 1900, Vol. lxxxiii [Cd. 316].
    1901, 1902, Vol. xcvii [Cd. 2236].
    1902, 1903, Vol. lxvi [Cd. 1632].
    1903, 1904, Vol. lxxxiv [Cd. 2112].
    1907, 1908, Vol. xcviii [Cd. 4254].
    1910, 1911, Vol. xli [Cd. 5850].
    1913, 1914–16, Vol. xxxvi [Cd. 7658].
Reports of the Commissioners Appointed to Inquire into Working of the Master and Servant Act of 1867 and the Criminal Law Amendment Act of 1871, First Report, 1874, Vol. xxiv [C. 1094]; Second Report, 1875, Vol. xxx [C. 1157].
Royal Commission on Labour, Group A, Vol. iii, 1892–93, Vol. xxxii [C. 6894]; Group C, Vol. ii, 1892, Vol. xxxvi, Pt. iii [C. 6795–iii].
Royal Commission on Trade Unions, First Report, 1867, Vol. xxxii [3873]; Second Report, 1867, Vol. xxxii [3893]; Third Report, 1867, Vol. xxxii [3910]; Fourth Report, 1867, Vol. xxxii [3952]; Ninth Report, 1867–68, Vol. xxxix [3980–v]; Eleventh Report, Vol. xxxi [4123].
Royal Commission on Trades Disputes and Trade Combinations, 1906, Vol. lvi [Cd. 2826].
Second Report on the Rules of Voluntary Conciliation and Arbitration Boards and Joint Committees, 1910, Vol. xx [Cd. 5346].
Select Committee on Artizans and Machinery, Fourth Report, 1824, Vol. v [51].
Select Committee on the Bank Acts, 1857, Vol. x [220].
Select Committee on the Combination Laws, 1825, Vol. iv [437].
Select Committee on Manufactures, Commerce and Shipping, 1833, Vol. vi [690].
Select Committee on Master and Servant, 1866, Vol. xiii [449].
Select Committee on Masters and Operatives, 1860, Vol. xxii [307].

Select Committee on Masters and Operatives (Equitable Councils of Conciliation), 1856, Vol. xiii [343].
Sixth Annual Abstract of Labour Statistics for 1898–99, 1900, Vol. lxxxiii [Cd. 119].
Seventeenth Annual Abstract of Labour Statistics, 1914–16, Vol. lxi [Cd. 7733].
Eighteenth Annual Abstract of Labour Statistics, 1926, Vol. xxix [Cmd. 2740].

ii. Periodicals and newspapers

Bee-Hive. 1862–76.
Birmingham Daily Mail. 1874.
Birmingham Daily Post. 1864–68.
Birmingham Journal. 1864–65.
British Queen and Statesman. 1841.
The Builder. 1846–70.
Builders' Trade Circular. 1869–73.
Builders' Weekly Reporter. 1869, 1877.
Building News. 1858–91.
Building Trades News. 1895.
The Building World. 1877.
Capital and Labour. 1874–82.
Carpenters' and Joiners' Amalgamated Review. 1904.
Clerks of the Works Association Journal. 1883–85.
Daily Herald. 1914.
Daily News. 1896.
Edinburgh News. 1852.
Evening News and Star (Glasgow). 1884.
Glasgow Evening Post. 1868.
Illustrated Carpenter and Builder. 1877.
Jarrow Guardian. 1872–80, 1886–91.
The Labour News and Employment Advertiser. 1878, 1884.
Leeds Mercury. 1860, 1864.
Liverpool Journal. 1846.
Liverpool Mercury. 1833, 1846.
Liverpool Standard. 1833.
Manchester Examiner and Times. 1857, 1869, 1875.
Manchester Guardian. 1843, 1846, 1857, 1869.
Manchester Times. 1833.
Master Builders' Associations' Journal (then Master Builder and Associations' Journal and Architectural Draughtsman, then Master Builder). 1896–1914.
The N-F-Record. 1912–14.
Newcastle Daily Chronicle. 1864, 1866, 1879, 1886.
Newcastle Guardian. 1851.
North British Daily Mail. 1866, 1871, 1877.
Nottingham Review. 1854.
Reynolds's Newspaper. 1852–53.
Sheffield Daily Telegraph. 1869.
Social Democrat. 1910.
Solidarity. 1914.
South Wales Daily Echo (Cardiff). 1893.
South Wales Daily News (Cardiff). 1892–93.
The Sun. 1841–42.
Sunderland Herald. 1851, 1853–54.

Sunderland Times. 1854.
The Times. 1859.
Transport Worker. 1911.
Weekly Chronicle. 1841.
Weekly Dispatch. 1841.
Western Daily News (Bristol). 1860–61.
Western Morning News (Plymouth). 1865.
Wolverhampton Chronicle. 1864.
Workman's Times. 1891.

iii. Reports

Amalgamated Society of Carpenters and Joiners. *Monthly and Annual Reports* 1860–1914. (Bishopsgate Institute.)
– *London District Management Committee June–November 1894.* (British Library.)
– *Rules 1860. (Webb Collection,* C, Vol. xii.)
Associated Shipwrights Society. *Rules 1882, 1885. (Webb Collection,* C, Vol. xci.)
Carpenters and Joiners (London). *Working Rules 1872, 1875, 1887.* (Greater London Council Record Office.)
General Union of Carpenters and Joiners. *Monthly and Annual Trade Reports.* 1865–93. (Modern Records Centre.)
– *Rules 1889. (Webb Collection,* C, Vol. xii.)
London Building Trades Committee. *Reports.* 1889–92. (*Webb Collection,* D, Vol. xvi.)
London Building Trades Federation. *Monthly Circular.* 1893–96. (*Webb Collection,* D, Vol. xviiib.)
– *Reports.* 1893. (*Webb Collection,* D, Vol. xviiia.)
Manchester Free Labour Society. *Report 1870.* (British Library.)
Manchester Union of Operative Bricklayers. *Monthly Reports.* 1869–74. (Modern Records Centre.)
National Association of Operative Plasterers. *Rules 1882. (Webb Collection,* C, Vol. xviii.)
Operative Bricklayers' Society. Metropolitan Central Strike Committee. *Reports.* 1892–96. (Modern Records Centre.)
– *Report and Balance Sheet November 1861.* (British Library.)
– *Rules 1871, 1875. (Webb Collection,* C, Vol. v.)
– *Trade Circular.* 1861–1914. (Modern Records Centre; British Library.)
Operative Stonemasons' Society. *Fortnightly Returns* (then OSM *Journal*). 1836–1914. (Modern Records Centre; British Library.)
– *London Dispute Committee 1914. Report and Financial Statement.* (Modern Records Centre.)
– *Rules 1849, 1852, 1855, 1859, 1862, 1865, 1868, 1871, 1881, 1891. (Webb Collection,* C, Vol. v.)
United Society of Boilermakers and Iron and Steel Shipbuilders. *Monthly and Annual Reports.* 1877–1910. (Bishopsgate Institute.)
– *Rules 1874, 1880, 1890, 1895, 1905. (Webb Collection,* C, Vol. xxxv.)

B. SECONDARY SOURCES

1. ARTICLES

Allen, V. L. 'The Origins of Industrial Conciliation and Arbitration,' *International Review of Social History,* Vol. ix, Pt. 2 (1964).

Anderson, Alan. 'Political Symbolism of the Labour Laws,' *Society for the Study of Labour History, Bulletin*, No. 23 (Autumn 1971).

Bean, R. 'Employers' Associations in the Port of Liverpool, 1890–1914,' *International Review of Social History*, Vol. xxi, Pt. 3 (1976).

Beesly, E. S. 'The Amalgamated Society of Carpenters,' *Fortnightly Review*, NS, Vol. i (1867).

– 'Trade Unions,' *Westminster Review*, Vol. 20 (October 1861).

Bell, J. D. M. 'The Stability of Membership in Trade Unions,' *Scottish Journal of Political Economy*, Vol. 1, No. 1 (March 1954).

Bevan, G. P. 'The Strikes of the Past Ten Years,' Royal Statistical Society, *Journal*, Vol. xliii (1880).

Bowley, A. L. 'The Statistics of Wages in the United Kingdom during the last Hundred Years. (Part VI.) Wages in the Building Trades – English Towns.' Royal Statistical Society, *Journal*, Vol. liii (June 1900).

Brassey, Thomas. 'On the Rise of Wages in the Building Trades of London,' Royal Institute of British Architects, *Sessional Papers* (1877–78).

Brown, E. H. Phelps and S. J. Handfield-Jones. 'The Climacteric of the 1890s: A Study in the Expanding Economy,' *Oxford Economic Papers*, NS, Vol. 4 (1952).

Brown, R. 'The Temperton v. Russell Case (1893): The Beginning of the Legal Offensive Against the Unions,' *Bulletin of Economic Research*, Vol. 23, No. 1 (May 1971).

Cairncross, A. K. 'The Glasgow Building Industry, 1870–1914,' *Review of Economic Studies*, Vol. 2 (1934–35).

Cairncross, A. K. and B. Weber. 'Fluctuations in the Building Industry in Great Britain, 1785–1849,' *Economic History Review*, 2nd. series, Vol. ix, No. 2 (1956–57).

Child, John, Ray Loveridge and Malcolm Warner. 'Towards an Organisational Study of Trade Unions,' *Sociology*, Vol. 7, No. 1 (January 1973).

Clarke, J. F. 'The Foreman – a neglected figure in the history of industrial relations?' North East Group for the Study of Labour History, *Bulletin*, No. 9 (October 1975).

– 'The Shipwrights,' North East Coast Group for the Study of Labour History, *Bulletin*, No. 1 (October 1967).

Cooney, E. W. 'Capital Exports and Investment in Building in Britain and the U.S.A., 1856–1914,' *Economica*, NS, Vol. xvi (November 1949).

– 'Long Waves in Building in the British Economy of the Nineteenth Century,' *Economic History Review*, 2nd series, Vol. xiii (1960–61).

Coppock, D. J. 'The Climacteric of the 1890s: A Critical Note,' *The Manchester School of Economic and Social Studies*, Vol. xxiv, No. 1 (January 1956).

Croucher, Richard. 'The North East Engineers' Strike of 1908,' North East Group for the Study of Labour History, *Bulletin*, No. 9 (October 1975).

Dyos, H. J. 'The Speculative Builders and Developers of Victorian London,' *Victorian Studies*, Vol. xi (Summer 1968).

Erdős, T. 'Surplus Value and its Rate in Contemporary Capitalism,' *Acta Oeconomica*, Vol. 5, No. 4 (1970).

Evans, Edward Owen, ' "Cheap at Twice the Price?" Shop Stewards and Workshop Relations in Engineering,' in Malcolm Warner (ed.). *The Sociology of the Workplace*. New York: Halsted Press, 1973.

Flanders, Allan. 'Collective Bargaining: A Theoretical Analysis,' *British Journal of Industrial Relations*, Vol. 6, No. 3 (1968).

Fox, Alan, 'Collective Bargaining, Flanders, and the Webbs,' *British Journal of Industrial Relations*, Vol. xiii, No. 2 (1975).

Fox, Alan and Allan Flanders. 'The Reform of Collective Bargaining: From Donovan to Durkheim,' *British Journal of Industrial Relations,* Vol. 7, No. 2 (1969).

Harrison, Frederic. 'The Strike of Stonemasons in London, 1861–1862,' National Association for the Promotion of Social Science, *Transactions* (1862).

Hicks, J. R. 'The Early History of Industrial Conciliation in England,' *Economica,* Vol. x (1930).

Howard, N. P. 'The Strikes and Lockouts in the Iron Industry and the Formation of the Ironworkers' Unions, 1862–1869,' *International Review of Social History,* Vol. xviii, Pt. 3 (1973).

Hyman, Richard, 'Workers' Control and Revolutionary Theory,' *The Socialist Register,* London: Merlin Press, 1974.

Jones, Gareth Stedman. 'Working-Class Culture and Working-Class Politics in London, 1870–1890; Notes on the Remaking of a Working Class,' *Journal of Social History,* Vol. vii, No. 4 (Summer 1974).

Kenwood, A. G. 'Residential Building Activity in North Eastern England, 1853–1913,' *The Manchester School,* Vol. xxxi (1963).

Killingsworth, Charles. 'The Modernization of West Coast Longshore Work Rules,' *Industrial and Labor Relations Review,* Vol. 15 (Jan.–July 1962).

Lewis, Roy. 'The Historical Development of Labour Law,' *British Journal of Industrial Relations,* Vol. xiv, No. 1 (March 1976).

Maiwald, K. 'An Index of Building Costs in the United Kingdom, 1845–1938,' *Economic History Review,* 2nd series, Vol. vii, No. 2 (1954).

Morris, J. H. and L. J. Williams. 'The South Wales Sliding Scale, 1876–1879,' *The Manchester School,* Vol. xxviii (1960).

Nairn, Tom. 'The English Working Class,' *New Left Review,* No. 24 (1964).

Neill, Archibald. 'Bradford Building Trades,' British Association for the Advancement of Science, *Report of the 43rd. Meeting* (Bradford, 1873). London: John Murray, 1874.

Phillips, G. A. 'The Triple Alliance in 1914,' *Economic History Review,* 2nd series, Vol. xxiv, No. 1 (1971).

Porter, J. H. 'Wage Bargaining under Conciliation Agreements, 1860–1914,' *Economic History Review,* 2nd series, Vol. xxvi, No. 3 (1970).

Price, John. 'The Use of Machinery in Construction,' North East Coast Engineers and Shipbuilders, *Transactions,* Vol. 5 (1888–89).

Price, L. L. F. R. 'On Sliding Scales and Other Methods of Wage Agreement in the North of England,' Royal Statistical Society, *Journal,* Vol. L (1887).

Saul, S. B. 'House Building in England 1890–1914,' *Economic History Review,* 2nd series, Vol. xv, No. 1 (1962).

Thompson, E. P. 'Eighteenth-century English Society: class struggle without class?' *Social History,* Vol. 3, No. 2 (May 1978).

Waley, Jacob. 'On Strikes and Combinations, with Reference to Wages and the Condition of Labour,' Royal Statistical Society, *Journal,* Vol. xxx (March 1867).

Weber, B. 'A New Index of Residential Construction and Long Cycles in House-Building in Great Britain, 1838–1950,' *Scottish Journal of Political Economy,* Vol. 2, No. 2 (June 1955).

Wilkinson, Frank. 'Collective Bargaining in the Steel Industry in the 1920s,' in Asa Briggs and John Saville (eds.). *Essays in Labour History, 1918–1939,* London: Croom Helm, 1977.

2. BOOKS

Aldridge, Alan. *Power, Authority and Restrictive Practices. A Sociological Essay on Industrial Relations*. Oxford: Basil Blackwell, 1977.

Allen, E., J. F. Clarke, N. McCord and J. F. Rowe. *The North-East Engineers' Strikes of 1871*. Newcastle: Frank Graham, 1971.

Allen, V. L. *Power in Trade Unions*. London: Longmans, 1954.

– *The Sociology of Industrial Relations*. London: Longmans, 1971.

Anderson, Perry and Robin Blackburn (eds.). *Towards Socialism*. Ithaca, New York: Cornell University Press, 1966.

Ashworth, Henry. *The Preston Strike*. Manchester: George Simms, 1854.

Askwith, Lord (George). *Industrial Problems and Disputes*. Brighton: The Harvester Press, 1974.

Aveling, S. T. *Carpentry and Joinery*. London: Fred. Warne, 1871.

Bain, George Sayers and Farouk Elsheikh. *Union Growth and the Business Cycle*. Oxford: Basil Blackwell, 1976.

Bale, M. P. *Stone-working Machinery*. London: Crosby, Lockwood, 1884.

– *Woodworking Machinery*. London: Crosby, Lockwood, 1880.

Bales, Thomas. *The Builders' Clerk*. London: Spon, 1877.

Bauman, Zygmunt. *Between Class and Elite*. Manchester: Manchester University Press, 1972.

Bendix, Reinhard. *Work and Authority in Industry*. New York: Wiley, 1956.

Beynon, Huw. *Working For Ford*. Harmondsworth: Penguin, 1973.

Bienefeld, M. A. *Working Hours in British Industry: An Economic History*. London: Weidenfeld & Nicolson, 1972.

Boraston, I., H. A. Clegg and M. Rimmer. *Workplace and Union*. London: Heinemann, 1975.

Bower, Fred. *Rolling Stonemason*. London: Cape, 1935.

Bowley, A. L. *Wages and Income in the United Kingdom Since 1860*. Cambridge: CUP, 1937.

Bowley, Marian. *The British Building Industry*. Cambridge: CUP, 1966.

Brassey, Thomas. *On Work and Wages*. London: Bell & Daldy, 1872.

– *Papers and Addresses*, Vol. 3. *Work and Wages*. London: Longmans & Co., 1894.

Broadhurst, Henry. *Henry Broadhurst, M.P. The Story of His Life*. London: Hutchinson, 1901.

Brown, E. H. Phelps. *The Growth of British Industrial Relations*. London: Macmillan, 1965.

Brown, Raymond. *Waterfront Organisation in Hull 1870–1890*. (University of Hull Occasional Papers in Economic and Social History No. 5.) Hull: University of Hull, 1972.

Browne, Sir Benjamin. *Selected Papers on Economic and Social Questions*. Cambridge: CUP, 1918.

Builders, *In Contracting With Builders and Others, Beware*. London: Longmans & Co., 1851.

Bulmer, Martin. *Working-Class Images of Society*. London: Routledge & Kegan Paul, 1975.

Burgess, Keith. *The Origins of British Industrial Relations*. London: Croom Helm, 1975.

Burnett, John. *A History of the Engineers' Strike in Newcastle and Gateshead*. Newcastle: John W. Swanston, 1872.

Cairncross, A. K. *Home and Foreign Investment 1870–1913*. Cambridge: CUP, 1953.

Carpenters and Joiners. *The Balance Sheet of the Carpenters and Joiners Short-Time Movement of 1872.* London: W. Austin, 1872.

Chalklin, C. W. *The Provincial Towns of Georgian England. A Study of the Building Process 1740–1820.* London: Edward Arnold, 1974.

Charity Organisation Society. *Special Committee on Unskilled Labour.* London: Charity Organisation Society, 1908.

Clapham, J. H. *An Economic History of Modern Britain.* Vol. II. 2nd edition revised. Cambridge: CUP, 1952.

Clegg, Hugh. *The System of Industrial Relations in Great Britain.* 2nd edition revised. Oxford: Oxford University Press, 1970.

Clegg, H. A., Alan Fox and A. F. Thompson. *A History of British Trade Unions Since 1889.* Vol. I. 1889–1910. Oxford: Clarendon Press, 1964.

Clerk of the Works. *The Builders' 'Lock-Out,' 1872.* London, 1872.

Clyde Shipwrights. *Arbitration Between Clyde Shipbuilders' and Engineers' Association and Clyde Associated Shipwrights.* Glasgow: Wm. Macrone, 1878.

Cole, G. D. H. *The Payment of Wages.* 2nd edition. London: Allen and Unwin, 1928.

– *Workshop Organisation.* Oxford: Clarendon Press, 1923.

– *The World of Labour.* 3rd edition revised. Brighton: The Harvester Press, 1973.

Connelly, T. J. *The Woodworkers 1860–1960.* London: Amalgamated Society of Woodworkers, 1960.

Cranbrook, J. *On Wages in Relation to Trades Unions and Strikes.* Edinburgh: A. Fullerton, 1868.

Crompton, Henry. *Industrial Conciliation.* London: Henry King, 1876.

Crouch, Colin. *Class Conflict and the Industrial Relations Crisis.* London: Heinemann, 1977.

Cummings, D. C. *A Historical Survey of the Boiler Makers' and Iron and Steel Ship Builders' Society.* Newcastle: R. Robinson & Co., 1905.

Cuthbet, Norman H. *The Lace Makers' Society.* Nottingham: Amalgamated Society of Lace Makers, 1960.

Daniel, Evan. *A Prize Essay on the Reduction of the Hours of Labour.* London: Sampson Law, 1859.

Davis, Henry F. A. *The Law and Practice of Friendly Societies and Trade Unions.* London: H. Sweet, 1876.

Davis, James Edward. *The Labour Laws.* London: Butterworths, 1875.

Dearle, N. B. *Problems of Unemployment in the London Building Trades.* London: Dent, 1908.

Doulton's. *The Strike of Bricklayers at Messrs. Doulton's Buildings at Lambeth, in September 1876.* London: E. & F. N. Spon, 1877.

Dunkerley, David. *The Foreman.* London: Routledge & Kegan Paul, 1975.

Dunning, T. J. *Trades' Unions and Strikes.* London: Published by the author, 1860.

Dyos, H. J. *Victorian Suburb.* Leicester: Leicester University Press, 1961.

Engels, Friedrich. *The Condition of the Working Class in England.* Stanford, California: Stanford University Press, 1968.

Federated Engineering and Shipbuilding Employers. *Series of Examples of Interference and Restriction.* London, 1897.

Flanders, Allen. *The Fawley Productivity Agreements.* London: Faber & Faber, 1964.

Flanders, Allen and H. A. Clegg (eds.). *The System of Industrial Relations in Great Britain.* 1st edition. Oxford: Basil Blackwell, 1954.

Foster, John. *Class Struggle and the Industrial Revolution.* London: Weidenfeld & Nicolson, 1974.

Fraser, W. Hamish. *Trade Unions and Society. The Struggle for Acceptance 1850–1880.* London: George Allen & Unwin, 1974.

French, J. O. *Plumbers in Unity 1865–1965.* London, 1965.

Friedman, Andrew L. *Industry and Labour. Class Struggle at Work and Monopoly Capitalism.* London: Macmillan, 1977.

Gillespie, F. C. *Labor and Politics in England 1850–1867.* London: Frank Cass, 1968.

Glyn, Andrew and Bob Sutcliffe. *British Capitalism, Workers and the Profits Squeeze.* Harmondsworth: Penguin, 1972.

Goodrich, Carter L. *The Frontier of Control.* London: Pluto Press, 1975.

Gouldner, Alvin. *Wildcat Strike.* Yellow Springs, Ohio: Antioch Press, 1954.

Graham, P. *Lecture on the Tendency of Trades Unionism.* London, 1875.

Gray, Robert Q. *The Labour Aristocracy in Victorian Edinburgh.* Oxford: Oxford University Press, 1976.

Harrison, Royden. *Before the Socialists.* London: Routledge & Kegan Paul, 1965.

Hennock, E. P. *Fit and Proper Persons.* London: Edward Arnold, 1973.

Henshaw, Richard S. *Notes on Labour in the Building Trade of London, 1800–1892.* Bromley, Kent: S. Bush & Son, 1892.

Herding, Richard. *Job Control and Union Structure.* Rotterdam: Rotterdam University Press, 1972.

Higenbottam, S. *Our Society's History.* Manchester: Amalgamated Society of Woodworkers, 1939.

Hill, Frederic. *Piecework as Compared with Time Work.* London: National Association for the Promotion of Social Science, 1876.

Hilton, W. S. *Foes to Tyranny.* London: Amalgamated Society of Building Trade Workers, 1963.

– *Industrial Relations in Construction.* London: Pergamon, 1968.

Hinton, James. *The First Shop Stewards' Movement.* London: George Allen & Unwin, 1973.

Hobhouse, Hermione. *Thomas Cubitt: Master Builder.* London: Macmillan, 1971.

Hobsbawm, E. J. *Labouring Men.* London: Weidenfeld & Nicolson, 1964.

Holton, Bob. *British Syndicalism 1900–1914. Myths and Realities.* London: Pluto Press, 1976.

Hopkinson, James. *Memoirs of a Victorian Cabinet Maker.* London: Routledge & Kegan Paul, 1968.

Hoskins, G. G. *The Clerk of the Works.* London, 1876.

Howell, George. *Autobiography.* Unpublished mss: Bishopsgate Institute.

– *The Conflicts of Capital and Labour.* London: Chatto & Windus, 1878.

Humphrey, A. W. *Robert Applegarth: Trade Unionist, Educationist, Reformer.* Manchester and London: National Labour Press, 1913.

Hyman, Richard. *Industrial Relations. A Marxist Introduction.* London: Macmillan, 1975.

– *The Workers' Union.* Oxford: Oxford University Press, 1971.

– *Strikes.* London: Fontana, 1972.

'Ithuriel.' *First Prize Essay on Trades Unions.* Glasgow, 1875.

Jeffreys, James B. *The Story of the Engineers 1800–1945.* London: Lawrence & Wishart, 1945.

Jevons, W. S. *The State in Relation to Labour.* London: Macmillan, 1882.

Jones, G. T. *Increasing Return.* Cambridge: CUP, 1933.

Kettle, Rupert. *Strikes and Arbitrations.* London: Simpkin and Marshall, 1866.

Knight, Charles. *Trades Unions and Strikes.* London: Charles Knight, 1834.

Knoop, Douglas and G. P. Jones. *The Medieval Mason.* 3rd edition. Manchester: Manchester University Press, 1967.

Knowles, K. G. J. C. *Strikes – A Study in Industrial Conflict.* Oxford: Basil Blackwell, 1952.

Lane, Tony and Kenneth Roberts. *Strike at Pilkingtons.* London: Collins, 1971.

Layton, W. T. *Capital and Labour.* London: Collins, n.d. 1914?

Levine, A. L. *Industrial Retardation in Britain 1880–1914.* New York: Basic Books, 1967.

Lewis, J. Parry. *Building Cycles and Britain's Growth.* London: Macmillan, 1965.

London Master Builders. *Statement of the Master Builders of the Metropolis In Explanation of the Differences Between them and the Workmen respecting the Trades Unions.* London: J. Moyes, 1834.

Lupton, T. *On the Shop Floor.* London: Pergamon, 1963.

MacDonald, William, *The True Story of Trades' Unions.* Manchester, 1867.

A Manufacturer. *Friendly Letters on the Recent Strikes.* London, 1854.

Marx, Karl. *Capital.* Vols. I, II, III. Moscow: Progress Publishers, 1966, 1971.

– *Grundrisse.* New York: Vintage Books, 1973.

Master Builders. *A Brief History of the Proceedings of the Operative Builders' Trades Unions in Manchester and the Consequent Turn-Out of the Journeymen Masons, Bricklayers, Joiners, Slaters and Other Trades.* Manchester: Taylor & Garnett, 1833.

Master Tradesmen of Liverpool. *An Impartial Statement of the Proceedings of the Members of the Trades Unions Societies and of the Steps taken in Consequence.* Liverpool: J. & J. Mawdsley, 1833.

Mathewson, Stanley. *Restriction of Output Among Unorganised Workers.* New York: The Viking Press, 1931.

Meacham, Standish. *A Life Apart. The English Working Class 1890–1914.* Cambridge, Mass: Harvard University Press, 1977.

Mortimer, J. E. *History of the Boilermakers' Society.* London: George Allen & Unwin, 1973.

Mundella, A. J. *Arbitration as a means of Preventing Strikes.* Bradford, 1868.

National Association for the Promotion of Social Science. *Trades' Societies and Strikes.* London: J. W. Parker & Son, 1860.

Newman, J. R. *The NAOP Heritage.* London: National Association of Operative Plasterers, 1960.

Nine Hours Movement. *Conference between C. M. Palmer and the Workmen of Jarrow.* 1866.

Onlooker [Mrs A. H. Telling]. *Hitherto.* London: National Association of Operative Plasterers, 1930.

Pelling, Henry. *Popular Politics and Society in Late Victorian Britain.* London: Macmillan, 1968.

Place Collection. (British Library.) *Newspaper Cuttings.* Vols. 55, 58.

Poole, Michael. *Workers' Participation in Industry.* London: Routledge & Kegan Paul, 1975.

Postgate, R. W. *The Builders' History.* London: Amalgamated Union of Building Trade Workers, 1923.

[Potter, George]. *The Labour Question.* London, 1861.

Pratt, Edwin A. *Trade Unionism and British Industry.* London: John Murray, 1904.

Price, L. L. F. R. *Industrial Peace.* London: Macmillan, 1887.

Robinson, Herbert W. *The Economics of Building.* London: P. S. King, 1939.

Rowe, J. W. F. *Wages in Theory and Practice.* London: George Routledge & Sons, 1928.

Royal Society of Arts. *Journal.* Vol. II. London, 1854.

Sayles, Leonard. *Behaviour of Industrial Work Groups.* New York: John Wiley, 1958.

Schloss, David F. *Methods of Industrial Remuneration.* 3rd edition. London: Williams & Norgate, 1898.

Scott, W. H., J. A. Banks, A. H. Halsey, T. Lupton. *Technical Change and Industrial Relations.* Liverpool: Liverpool University Press, 1956.

Sharp, Ian. *Industrial Conciliation and Arbitration in Great Britain.* London: George Allen & Unwin, 1950.

Shorter, Edward and Charles Tilly. *Strikes in France 1830–1968.* Cambridge: CUP, 1974.

Smiles, Samuel. *Workmen's Earnings, Strikes and Savings.* London: John Murray, 1861.

Smith, Frederic. *Workshop Management.* London: Wyman & Sons, n.d., 1884?

Statement of Facts Connected with the Turn Out in the Lancashire Building Trades. Manchester: Advertiser and Chronicle Office, 1833.

Stirling, James. *Unionism.* Glasgow, 1869.

Summerson, John. *The London Building World of the Eighteen-Sixties.* London: Thames and Hudson, 1973.

Taplin, E. L. *Liverpool Dockers and Seamen 1870–1890.* (University of Hull Occasional Papers in Economic and Social History No. 6.) Hull: University of Hull, 1974.

Tholfsen, Trygve R. *Working Class Radicalism in Mid-Victorian England.* London: Croom Helm, 1976.

Thornton, William Thomas. *On Labour.* 2nd edition. London: Macmillan, 1870.

Turner, H. A. *Trade Union Growth, Structure and Policy.* Toronto: University of Toronto, 1962.

Wainhouse, Abraham. *Trades' Unions Justified.* Manchester, 1861.

Webb, Sidney and Beatrice. *The History of Trade Unionism.* London: Printed by the Authors for the Trade Unionists of the United Kingdom, 1902.

– *Industrial Democracy.* London: Printed by the Authors for the Trade Unionists of the United Kingdom, 1913.

Weekes, Joseph D. *Report on the Practical Operation of Arbitration and Conciliation in the Settlement of Differences Between Employers and Employees in England.* Harrisburg, Pa, 1879.

Wells, F. A. *The British Hosiery Trade.* London: George Allen & Unwin, 1935.

Whitehead, Abraham. *The Builders' Dispute in London.* London, 1859.

A Working Man. *Reminiscences of a Stonemason.* London: John Murray, 1908.

3. THESES

Cronin, James. 'Times of Strife: Industrial Conflict in Britain, 1880–1914.' Unpublished PhD dissertation, Department of History, Brandeis University, 1976.

Grossman, Sylvia. 'The Radicalization of London Building Workers 1890–1914.' Unpublished PhD dissertation, Department of History, University of Toronto, 1977.

Index

349